Advance

THE **PRACTITIONER'S GUIDE** TO THE
SCIENCE OF **PSYCHOTHERAPY**

THE **PRACTITIONER'S GUIDE** TO THE

SCIENCE OF **PSYCHOTHERAPY**

RICHARD HILL AND MATTHEW DAHLITZ

FOREWORD BY JOHN ARDEN

W. W. NORTON & COMPANY
Independent Publishers Since 1923

Copyright © 2022 by Richard Hill and Matthew Dahlitz
Foreword by John Arden

All rights reserved
Printed in the United States of America
First Edition

For information about permission to reproduce selections from this book, write to Permissions, W. W. Norton & Company, Inc., 500 Fifth Avenue, New York, NY 10110

For information about special discounts for bulk purchases, please contact W. W. Norton Special Sales at specialsales@wwnorton.com or 800-233-4830

Manufacturing by Lake Book Manufacturing, Inc.
Production manager: Katelyn MacKenzie

Library of Congress Cataloging-in-Publication Data

Names: Hill, Richard, International lecturer, author. | Dahlitz, Matthew, author.
Title: The practitioner's guide to the science of psychotherapy / Richard Hill and
    Matthew Dahlitz.
Description: New York : W. W. Norton & Company, 2022. | Includes bibliographical
    references and index.
Identifiers: LCCN 2021031998 | ISBN 9781324016182 (paperback) |
    ISBN 9781324016199 (epub)
Subjects: LCSH: Psychotherapy. | Neurosciences. | Brain.
Classification: LCC RC480.5 .H53 2022 | DDC 616.89/14—dc23
LC record available at https://lccn.loc.gov/2021031998

W. W. Norton & Company, Inc., 500 Fifth Avenue, New York, N.Y. 10110
www.wwnorton.com

W. W. Norton & Company Ltd., 15 Carlisle Street, London W1D 3BS

1 2 3 4 5 6 7 8 9 0

To Ernest Rossi (1933–2020), who gave me
the joy and pleasure of mentorship
and transformed the rigors of study
into an adventure of possibility.
– Richard

To my beautiful wife Shera.
Your support and encouragement
make impossible days possible
and brilliant ones even brighter!
– Matthew

Contents

Acknowledgments

We are grateful to so many people who have poured into our professional lives, walked alongside, and given freely of their wisdom and knowledge. In many ways this book is the collaboration of a multitude. As with most authors who embark on writing a book, we could not have done this without the wonderful support of our families—with special mention of our extraordinary partners, Susan Davis and Shera Dahlitz, our children, and extended family. We love you all and thank you for the encouragement and sacrifices you have made as we've been hidden away with our laptops!

We would like to thank Deborah Malmud, vice president and editorial director at Norton Professional Books, for encouraging us to undertake this project, and for her guidance and the talented team of editors, especially the invaluable contribution of copy editor, Stephanie Hiebert, who have made this book a possibility.

To the many thousands of readers, listeners, and subscribers of *The Neuropsychotherapist*, which has developed into *The Science of Psychotherapy*, this book is for you! You have been our inspiration to write not only this book, but the many thousands of words that have gone into the magazine. Your enthusiasm and thirst to know more about the science of psychotherapy have kept us motivated to learn more so that we can share more. To be able to help you on the front lines of clinical practice is a gift. That we have helped you help others is simply wonderful. We believe this book is a continuation of that endearing relationship.

We have gained many friends over the years who have encouraged us and added to the vast pool of collective wisdom we now steward at

The Science of Psychotherapy. These wonderful people include Richard's friend, mentor, teacher, and colleague Ernest Rossi (1933–2020) who, over 15 years, became more like a father than just a teacher; as well as John Arden, Courtney Armstrong, Bonnie Badenoch, Eric Beeson, Ken Benau, Flavio Cannistra, Giovanna Celia, David Collins, Lou Cozolino, Mauro Cozzolino, Agostinho d'Almeida, Sherif Darwish, Bruce Ecker, Karen Ferry, Jose Carlos Victor Gomes, Michael Hoyt, Peter Janetzki, Carol Kershaw, Paul Leslie, Rebecca Mannis, Terry Marks-Tarlow, Raissa Miller, Scott Miller, Micaela Monteiro-Haig, Oliver Morgan, Robert Moss, Michael Munion, Bill O'Hanlon, Debra Pearce-McCall, Rita Princi-Hubbard, Venkat Pulla, Kathryn Rossi, Dan Siegel, Fabio Sinibaldi, Bill Wade, Reid Wilson, Garry Wiseman, Thedy Veliz, Michael Yapko, Jeff Zeig, the Board of GAINS, and many more.

Preface

Reading this book can be as straightforward as beginning at page 1 and working your way to the end. There are, however, several ways to navigate these pages. Imagine that the entire book is a whole human being and through the contents page you can find specific areas and aspects of that person. This differentiation of the whole person is not meant to imply that a person can be divided and treated as isolated parts. Quite the contrary: That the person must be looked at as a whole is the central argument of the book. Humans are collections of many elements that can be affected in many ways. Learning about the elements is meant to foster a better understanding of the whole.

Most sections contain a special Clinical Notes box. We appreciate that information without practical application can lose meaning and lose interest, so we hope that these boxes add clarity, as well as insight into what can be created with the information in the main body of the text. We also encourage you to make your own clinical notes that you can slide between the pages as you develop your own thoughts and ideas about the text.

Finally, we have written this book as a conduit that might connect us to you the reader both abstractly, through the words on the page, and also literally, by stimulating conversations at conferences, or associated with our online podcasts and other programs, or on social media. Even more valuable is the possibility that you might share what is in your mind with us through your own words. Please visit with us at *The Science of Psychotherapy* website, and let us see what we can create.

Foreword

Einstein noted that "science without religion is lame and religion without science is blind" (Knowles, 1999, p. 290). We can twist that analogy to "psychotherapy without science can be a presumptuous ritual with questionable benefit." Theory without sufficient backing of research to demonstrate its efficiency can be countertherapeutic. Yet despite these concerns, the 20th century saw the rise and fall of more than 100 types of different psychotherapies. Almost like mini-religions and cults with esoteric terminologies, they are often based entirely on concepts that make sense only within the context of the particular theory. They become walled-off silos with an infrastructure of presumed competency and proficiency, defined by the jargon of their theoretical schools. Many of these psychotherapies have achieved so much popularity that they are known simply by their initials. They have built economic franchises with their own publications, dues for membership, certifications, and conferences where devotees give esoteric lectures understood only by those with higher levels of acculturation within those schools. Many are led by a guru, a person with a branded name. A noted cognitive behavioral psychologist joked that one of the largest psychotherapy conferences in the world was not really about the evolution in the field, but "so that you can see them before they die."

The pop-psychotherapy marketplace even infiltrated the graduate schools. One applicant, during her interview for a postdoc position, informed me that, were she selected, her goal for the year would be to find her "theoretical home." In response, I suggested that the 21st century necessitates that we find common denominators between the different schools of psychotherapy based on science and discard the extraneous theoretical debris. This comprehensive book does an excellent job of just that. The common denominators explored throughout the following chapters illustrate research that is bio–psycho–social in nature. This integrative perspective subsumes the relevant contributions of the past and discards the purely theory-driven cul-de-sacs that are based only on the tight confines of a particular school.

Without a common language backed by research, clients of therapists are put at a disadvantage. Our societies have sanctioned us as experts in mental health, and we attempt to prove our expertise with framed diplomas decorating our offices and letters following our names. Even though therapists are generally well-meaning and compassionate, they are marinated in different theoretical schools. Clients are often confused to hear completely varying perspectives about their problems from two different therapists.

To resolve these problems, the authors of this book have for many years offered a website entitled *The Science of Psychotherapy*. There they have provided numerous articles, interviews, and seminars on cutting-edge research in the field. Fortunately, they have followed up those efforts with this book.

In bringing science to psychotherapy, we need to ensure that it is real science and not a mere veneer. Sure, conference attendance numbers and book sales go up when the latest brain terms are used. But we need to be careful to avoid reductionism when talking about specific brain regions, such as the currently in vogue vagus or the ever-popular right hemisphere. Yes, the right hemisphere is important, but only in balance with the left. For example, consistent research has shown that overactivity of the right hemisphere is associated with avoidance and withdrawal—accordingly, anxiety and depression.

The field of psychotherapy had been undergoing a sea change thanks to brain-imaging techniques, as well as advances in the study of immunology, metabolism, and epigenetics developed in the last 20–30 years. We can combine these advances with evidenced-based practices and outcome management tools to individually tailor the psychotherapeutic techniques that have been shown to engage particular systems throughout the body. We have learned a lot over the years about how we can calm overactivated areas while increasing activation in areas that need to be boosted. Essentially, we can teach our clients how to tune up their brains. By normalizing psychological disorders and their resolutions, we can explain and delineate road maps for recovery, guiding clients away from the pain that confuses and overwhelms them.

It has long been shown that from birth to death, the quality of our relationships profoundly affects not only how we view the world but also how our brains organize. Psychodynamic theorists were right all along that attachment styles are carried over into the therapy room. And so are the perspectives that reflect our embeddedness within particular socioeconomic and cultural contexts. It is therefore no wonder that psychotherapy research has for decades stressed the importance of the "alliance," "attunement," "transference"—whatever terminology was used. This book astutely reviews that research but goes beyond the wall of the well-established truisms detailed in a plethora of articles.

The sea change in psychotherapy was prophesied long ago. Before he embarked on theory without a brain-based perspective, Sigmund Freud said, "We must recollect that all of our provisional ideas in psychology will presumably one day be based on an organic substructure." The father of American psychology, William James, speculated that "the act of will activates neural circuits" (Arden, 2015, p. viii). Roughly a century later, we have the science to support these prophesies. Nobel laureate Roger Sperry argued that, "'Mental forces' could direct electrochemical traffic between neurons at the cellular level" (Schwartz & Begley, p. 42). And now we know that our mental activity can influence our immune system and gene expression, through the work of another Nobel laureate, Eric Kandel, who said, "Psychotherapy works by producing changes in gene expression that alter the strength of synaptic connections" (Kandel, 1998, p. 460). In other words, causation is multidirectional at all levels, even down to gene expression and metabolism.

The science of psychotherapy has now cross-pollinated with the fields of metabolism, psychoneuroimmunology, and epigenetics. Similarly, the critical importance of diet, exercise, and sleep for mental health has been demonstrated in the fields of nutritional neuroscience, exercise physiology, and sleep medicine. Genes can be either expressed or suppressed by many factors, such as diet, exercise, and sleep, and can lead to or away from depression. Psychosocial factors are of equal importance for mental health, including lack of social support, as well as traumatic interpersonal events such as intimate partner abuse, add to the risk of genetic vulnerability for anxiety and depression.

A few decades ago, the phrase "cells that fire together wire together" became part of our language. When helping people with anxiety and/or depression, we can also make relevant the phrase "cells that fire out of sync lose their link." With repeated firing, the brain rewires to develop a habit. This means that prior depressive episodes increase the potential of becoming depressed again, the severity of the depression, and the risk for more depression. Prior suicide attempts increase the risk of not only subsequent suicide attempts but also more episodes of severe depression.

When we reduce our focus to one factor of mental health, such as neurons firing, we lose focus on how it interacts with a wide range of other factors. For example, when we focus on one aspect, such as attachment, self-esteem, metabolic energy, genes, neurons, or some other important life-sustaining system, we miss the big picture: our overall health.

The science of psychotherapy in the 21st century accounts for how all these systems work *together* to maintain mental health. We need both the big picture and the small one to find the feedback loops between all the systems to potentiate health and well-being. Reductionism without the contextual big picture cannot explain how to help people psychotherapeutically, and without some reductionism we cannot identify the "parts." Furthermore, without the contextual consideration of the whole it would be difficult to understand how all the parts are connected. To account for how the parts contribute to the whole, we must address how complex systems, such as people, are organized and change.

Previous attempts to apply holistic perspectives to psychotherapy were limited by 20th century science. They failed to account for the interactions among the factors (parts) that work together to support the whole system. Initially, many "holistic" theories avoided the exploration of how genes, neurons, and the immune system are involved in the emergence of the self.

Fortunately, 21st century interdisciplinary science helps explain how all the factors in complex systems interact to create an individual self: you or me.

A variety of efforts have attempted to explain how the whole is greater than the sum of its parts. They represent the early precursors to the multidisciplinary field now referred to as the "science of complexity" (Mitchell, 2011). Despite the passing of more than a half century since Austrian biologist Ludwig von Bertalanffy's book *General System Theory* was published, the term "wholeness" remained associated with broad platitudes.

I am so pleased that Richard and Matt rely on the perspective of the interdisciplinary science of complexity, which is close to my heart, and the Santa Fe Institute, which functions as a center of activity in this field in the town where I live. The science of complexity explores how multiple systems work *together* to produce phenomena far greater than can be produced by any of them alone. This integrative perspective promotes common ground as we make sense of how the system self organizes and the systems from which the mind emerges, all made possible through energy.

The study of complex systems considers the collective, the system-wide behaviors, to be of fundamental importance. As an alternative to reductionism, complexity theory attempts to explain systems in terms of their constituent parts and the interactions between them. This approach investigates how the relationships between a system's parts give rise to its collective behaviors, which interact to form relationships with its environment. This book brings together the multidisciplinary sciences that account for how systems work together to produce more than each discipline can individually. No stone is left uncovered as it addresses the emerging research in metabolism, genomics, neuroscience, psychology, and psychoneuroimmunology.

Using the lens of the science of complexity, we can make sense of how the metabolic, immune, genomic, and nervous systems are interdependent parts of the "self." Harmonizing the patterns of activity among these life-sustaining systems contributes to our mental health. The systems that contribute to self-organization are hierarchical, in that they are embedded in one another. Our hierarchical systems range from genome, to organelles in cells, to cells, to organs, to body-wide systems. They all work together, interdependently, through feedback loops. The highest in the hierarchy emerges from the organization of the mental operating networks, which generate states of mind, which collectively we call the mind.

The concept of self-organization is central to the science of complex systems, so it is quite relevant to psychotherapy. *Self-organization* describes how order arises from local interactions between parts that were initially disordered. The process can be spontaneous, as occurs when sufficient energy is channeled by changes in self-care. The components of complex systems interact in such a way that the self-care activities cannot be summed up to help us understand how the entire system self-organizes. Given that we are constantly adapting to our respective environments, our self-organizing systems are constantly reorganizing through feedback loops.

As complex systems, we do not simply revert to a steady state as conceptualized by homeostasis. Yet for centuries, health was based solely on this concept, and during the last century psychotherapy followed along. However, homeostatic mechanisms provide only the primary means of stability, but complex systems such as humans are dynamic because they employ positive feedback processes. Indeed, given that we are living creatures and not machines, homeostatic mechanisms cannot offer the sole means of maintaining health and keeping us thriving. The degree to which homeostasis can regulate our health during changing demands is limited. Whereas homeostatic stability is regulated by a fixed set point and associated negative feedback loops, we need to explain how our physiological systems help adapt and change during changing conditions.

To address the limitations of homeostasis as the principal mechanism that maintains our health, a model referred to as *allostasis*, meaning in Greek "stability through change," emerged in the research on stress (Sterling, 2004). I am delighted to see this concept addressed prominently in this book (Chapter 4). Allostasis offers positive feedback adjustments of physiological mediators to deal with episodic and brief challenges to promote health. Our physiological resources mobilize when our brain anticipates needs, and then regulates the rest of our body to meet those needs.

Both homeostatic and allostatic parameters for each life-sustaining system widen as we move up the hierarchy. Yet at lower levels, homeostatic parameters are more prevalent. For example, the mitochondria maintain a much smaller operating parameter in terms of how energy is produced than does the immune system. The immune system contains mitochondria, without which it would not function. The brain, which operates at a higher hierarchical position, contains both immune cells and mitochondria in all brain cells. If the metabolic and immune cells chronically exceed their parameters, mood and neurocognitive disorders result.

Psychological disorders, ill health, and ultimately death result from disorganization of the interplay between the homeostatic and allostatic feedback loops within and between life-sustaining systems. The disorganization within a system cannot be isolated; it spreads to other systems. In response to trauma, disorganization can spread relatively quickly and can result in abrupt destabilizing shifts in self-organization. As neurons disconnect from neuronal networks, the immune system is overactivated or the metabolism becomes sluggish. The risk of widespread disorganization increases. When organ systems disorganize, the result is serious illness or, in the extreme, death. On the other hand, the greater the self-organizing connectivity, the greater the potential for health. The connectivity is driven by the basic biological energy underlying metabolism, and without a stable supply of energy that connectivity is lost. Our job as psychotherapists is not only to identify these systems but to help our clients orchestrate the harmonious self-organizing feedback loops. We are like the conductor of an orchestra, helping our clients make adjustments to all systems to support their overall health.

Given that the sea change occurring in the 21st century has offered amazing opportunities to understand the systems that were previously assumed independent, we must continue to learn how their complex interactions make us thinking and feeling beings. The science of psychotherapy necessitates that we keep casting the net wide, to explain not only what contributes to mental health support but also what helps our clients achieve overall health. We should abide by the lesson that Socrates learned from the Oracle of Delphi. Socrates was told that he was the wisest man in Athens. He responded, essentially, "No way!" To prove it, he interviewed those identified as wise men all over Athens. Many said, "Heck yeah, I am so wise that people pay me for my pearls of wisdom." Finally, Socrates realized that he was the only one to recognize his own ignorance. And that is wisdom.

The wisdom of the science of psychotherapy has demonstrated that we have so much more to learn. This book helps us build on what we have learned and reach for what we have yet to discover.

John Arden, Ph.D.
Santa Fe, New Mexico, 2021

THE **PRACTITIONER'S GUIDE** TO THE **SCIENCE** OF **PSYCHOTHERAPY**

What Is Mental Health?

When a client enters the therapy room for the first time, it is the beginning of a journey. At that moment the journey is both shrouded in mystery and flush with possibility. The first step is for a beneficially effective relationship to emerge between client and therapist. The client brings with them their problem(s), resistance, resilience, natural capacities, life experience, and a hope that the therapist will be able to help them recover. The therapist welcomes the client into a safe space, making available their knowledge, experience, intuition, informed assessments, and a desire to do what is necessary to help the client find what they need to create a beneficial outcome. This is not an easy task for either party. The challenge for the therapist is knowing what to do, when, and why.

Consider this case:

L. D. is a 56-year-old male who presents with symptoms that include lethargy, depression, partial memory difficulty, and temporal confusion. He does not report symptoms of depression, sleep disturbance, or appetite change, and he has normal blood pressure and no limb weakness. Previous medical records, however, show that he experienced several years of depressed mood during an extended breakdown of his marriage, which ended in divorce. After the divorce he went through a period of emotional and physical lethargy, as well as cognitive disorientation, and was unable to work. L. D. has returned to work in the family business, but for only 3 hours per day. His contribution to the workplace, however, has been limited, and his family has wondered why his motivation rises and falls across different tasks.

For instance, he appears to have enough motivation to call his friends to arrange to play golf but not to be interested in following through on work tasks. He has retrograde amnesia of the past 3 years. Earlier memories are intact. He has difficulty laying down and/or recalling new memories but seems to manage better with events that are more personally interesting; for example, he remembers watching sports the night before and, with a little prompting, who won. His family has noted some personality changes. Currently, his medications are clopidogrel, a preventative for vascular ischemic events; Lipitor, an atorvastatin, for reducing cholesterol; and ginkgo biloba, a traditional medicine used to enhance memory and cognition.

What might be the best therapeutic approach for L. D.? Which symptoms stand out? Which symptoms seem unusual or confusing? What more do you need to know, and what questions need to be explored? What are you thinking? And most important, why?

A number of things might draw your attention. L. D. suffered a difficult emotional stress for several years as his marriage collapsed, but after a distressing transition, he seems to have regulated his mood. At the same time, he is exhibiting deficits in memory and attention with a bias toward social and pleasurable activities. Given that memory issues are related to the function of the hippocampus, has there been some damage? Or was there enough trauma in the divorce to negatively affect his memory? L. D. does not report or appear to have movement dysfunction, so a stroke is less of a candidate, but he might have been affected by smaller transient ischemic attacks (TIAs). Perhaps he has early-onset Alzheimer's disease. A scan (MRI) of L. D.'s brain would be helpful, to see whether there is any neural damage or loss. Some psychometric testing might be useful, to check for cognitive capacities and/or deficits. We will return to L. D.'s case shortly.

Response-ability in Therapy

When a therapist sits with a client for the first time, and even as therapy progresses, there is a constant struggle between symptoms and resolution.

Sometimes the symptoms are specific issues that need immediate attention, but symptoms are also properties that rise to the surface to indicate something outside of the client's conscious awareness. The task is often difficult. There may be one central issue or a combination of effects and influences that trouble the client enough for them to seek therapy. Figuring out the problem is a powerful responsibility, but rather than an onerous burden on the therapist, it is a *response*-ability.

The therapist's capacity to respond improves through experience, continuous development of knowledge, and deliberate periods of reflection on practice between sessions (Chow et al., 2015). The explosion of information over the past few decades has produced bookshelves of excellent books, journals, and magazines that delve into the finer details of psychotherapy. It would take more than one lifetime to read them all. The purpose of this book is to provide a concise insight into a wide scope of topics related to the science of psychotherapy. We use the word "science" in its broader context: "the knowledge of." This book is neither an encyclopedia nor encyclopedic. It is both a learning resource and a single volume in which you can explore a knowledge base rapidly and effectively. We present the knowledge in the context of case studies and treatment applications as often as we can. Our intention is to enhance the therapeutic experience, but there is always more to learn. Each chapter is supported by resources listed in the References for your ongoing study and research. In addition, we urge you to embark on your own voyage of discovery with curiosity and fascination.

The essential framework of knowledge, cases, and application is oriented by three foundational principles: the client has natural capacities and resources, therapy is a cocreated experience, and therapy functions in a complex system.

1.1 Client Capacities and Resources

A number of factors contribute to the effectiveness of a therapeutic experience. Application of the medical model to psychotherapy and psychology resulted in the practice of diagnosis and implementation of an evidence-based therapeutic method or technique (Elkins, 2009). This was a very therapist-centered approach. More recently, the relationship between therapist and client—the *therapeutic alliance*—has been regarded as one of the most important factors in effective therapy (Flückiger et al., 2018). The method employed and the experience of the therapist are relevant but not major factors. The "Dodo bird verdict," first suggested by Saul Rosenzweig (1936), argued that, on the basis of efficacy studies, different psychotherapies produce similar results. Researchers began to look for common factors that are effective in all therapies. Kevin Duncan and colleagues (2010) concluded that the common factors necessary for therapeutic effectiveness were therapeutic alliance, complementarity with the therapist, secure environment, mirroring, and empathy. Asay and Lambert (1999) attribute 40% to client factors and only 15% to therapeutic method (Figure I.1).

Client factors are both within the client (personal characteristics, motivations, and resources) and external to the client (extratherapeutic factors: the environment, chance events, and placebo effects). Duncan et al. (2010) conclude that client factors account for 87% of the effectiveness of therapy (Figure I.2). Milton Erickson, a 20th century pioneer of psychotherapy, was one of the first to recognize the importance of the resources within the client. He would utilize the qualities of the client's environment—their compliance and their resistance; their symptoms; their verbal, bodily, and

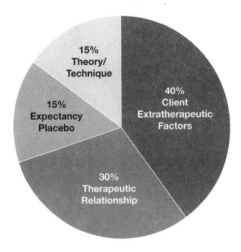

FIGURE I.1: Common Factors in Psychotherapy. *Adapted from Asay & Lambert (1999).*

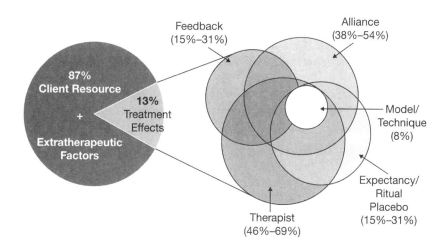

FIGURE I.2: Change Factors in Psychotherapy. *Adapted from Duncan et al. (2010).*

behavioral communications; their likes and dislikes; and their emotions—
all as tools for change. "Whatever the patient presents to you . . . you really
ought to use" (M. H. Erickson & Rossi, 1981, p. 16).

An invaluable resource is the client's natural intuitive capacity to know
whether they are OK or not OK (Buetow & Mintoft, 2011; Hill & Rossi,
2017). Fundamentally, this implicit, introspective awareness is one of the
main motivations to seek out therapy. Upon entering the therapy room, the
client may not have a clear idea of what is wrong, but they have a motivat-
ing feeling that *something* is wrong. Humans have biological, behavioral,
and emotional indicators that we are unwell. The symptoms of being physically unwell include pain, fever, nausea, tiredness, and an inclination to
isolate, rest, and eat simple foods. Equally, we have emotional, somatic, and
behavioral responses when we are psychologically unwell, some of which are
similar to physical illness, as well as affective symptoms of depression, anxiety, and distress. Pain, discomfort, and a feeling of dis-ease are among the
symptoms that provoke us to pay attention. The biological immune system
of humans literally creates a "sickness behavior" in response to inflammatory
activity (Dantzer, 2009). Our "mental-health" system produces symptoms of

ill health that range from straightforward mood changes to disruptive affective conditions and disturbing behaviors. The key to this intuitive capacity is that the human system *prefers* to feel OK and will try to move toward being OK when given the *opportunity and the appropriate circumstances*. Someone who seeks out therapy is responding to this natural need, tendency, inclination, and preference to feel OK. But the client is unable to appreciate the vast array of interactive elements and subsystems that underpin the state of their complex psychoneurobiological system.

To resolve this knowledge deficit, humans developed an invaluable extratherapeutic factor: a brain that can access knowledge and experience from external sources. It has become socially beneficial for individuals and groups to specialize in a particular study or trade. Early humans began specializing in toolmaking in the Upper Paleolithic period (Hayden & Gargett, 1988) and other crafts in the Neolithic period (de Laet et al., 1994), around 10,000–20,000 B.C.E. These behaviors evolved as a highly sophisticated social practice: when we do not know, we seek out someone who does. We are socially evolved to function successfully in cooperative, coregulating, and coinforming groups. We can follow another person's lead or learn from them to become more self-reliant (van Schaik & Burkart, 2011). Humans are interpersonal and social by nature (Cozolino, 2006).

This book, therefore, presents a wide-ranging scope of knowledge, information, and experience. Does such a wide-ranging scope defy the principle of specializing? Perhaps, but what does a psychotherapist specialize in? We suggest that a psychotherapist, in general practice, specializes in a single person, to enhance the psychotherapeutic experience, and to be a resource for the client as they seek to discover how to be OK.

1.2 Therapy Is a Cocreated Experience

Professional organizations around the world provide definitions of *psychology* and *psychotherapy*.

- The American Psychological Association's Presidential Task Force on Evidence-Based Practice published a formal definition in 2006:

"Evidence-based practice in psychology (EBPP) is the integration of the best available research with clinical expertise in the context of patient characteristics, culture, and preferences."

- The College of Psychotherapy and the Psychotherapy and Counselling Federation of Australia (n.d.) state, "Psychotherapy is the comprehensive and intentional engagement between therapist and client for the healing, growth or transformation of emotional, physical, relational, existential and behavioral issues, or of chronic suffering, through well-founded relational processes."

- The UK Council of Psychotherapy (n.d.) offers a general description of psychotherapy in practice: "Psychotherapy and psychotherapeutic counselling are talking therapies. They are used to treat emotional problems and mental health issues. As well as talking, the therapy could use a range of methods including art, music, drama and movement."

- The Network for Psychotherapeutic Care in Europe, representing more than 15 countries, presents a core definition that is used by most members (Bundespsychotherapeutenkammer, 2011): "Psychotherapy is defined as a form of treatment for mental and behavioral disorders classified by the International Classification of Diseases."

Research into the practice of psychotherapy is ongoing, but hardly new. Dr. Per Høglend observed in 1999 that "psychotherapy research has demonstrated, as experienced clinicians have believed for a long time, that the patients' personal characteristics are most important for the therapeutic alliance and for outcome" (p. 257). This observation indicates that the importance of client resources has been known for a number of years. Locher et al. (2019) conclude that the choice of therapy is most effective when it is collaborative: "For clients who accept the treatment rationale, psychotherapeutic success occurs more quickly and psychotherapy outcomes are significantly better than for those who do not agree with the treatment rationale" (p. 4). Clients are better able to access what they need for recovery in a cocreative environment. It is also necessary for the therapist to be flexible and sensitive to the client to enable cocreativity. Cooperative engagement in the therapeutic experience is achieved through collaborative relationship (Spencer et al., 2019); nonverbal attunement (Håvås et al., 2015); therapeutic relationship (M. J. Lambert & Barley, 2001); client responsiveness (Hill & Rossi, 2017); and mutual contribution (Tickle & Murphy, 2014).

A concerning issue for some is how to preserve the expert status of the therapist while still "creating a cooperative relationship . . . [where clients] meet a 'normal, friendly and knowledgeable therapist who is capable of admitting that he/she may be wrong'" (Neander & Skott, 2008, p. 289). This conundrum is resolved when the therapist positions the client as central to the therapeutic process (Rogers, 1951); when the qualities of experience and efficacy of the therapist, and the therapies they utilize, are taken into account (Ackerman & Hilsenroth, 2003); and when there is a comfortable, collaborative, and cocreative relationship between therapist and client (the therapeutic alliance; Ardito & Rabellino, 2011).

In a cocreative context, the therapist and client are more than just a dyad; they are a complex and dynamic system. Client factors, extratherapeutic factors, therapist skill and experience, the environment of the therapy room, and a host of other elements, known and unknown, are important and influential in the complex system of the therapeutic experience. Understanding complex systems—how they function and how they change the way therapists think—is the third foundational principle of this book.

1.3 Predictability and Unpredictability: Linear and Complex Systems

In the skies over Cornwall, England, tens of thousands of starlings regularly perform an aerial, almost balletic display, and in the cool waters of the Agulhas Bank off the southern cape of South Africa, millions of sardines school into a swirling sphere (Ballerini et al., 2008). The birds form a fluid display that ebbs and flows across the sky, and the fish swirl like Sufi dancers in a trance without a specific leader or organizer. These complex displays are a product of *self-organization*. A simple but special set of conditions and factors enables these extraordinary displays to spontaneously emerge. The shape and flow of these displays is the *emergent property* of an interaction between the individual birds or fish. It is impossible to predict the exact shape or flow for any given moment, other than that there will be a shape and flow. These displays are the product of self-organizing, complex, *nonlinear systems* (Wilkinson, 2011). In the same way, the symptoms that a therapist sees in their client are the emergent properties and qualities of the client's complex system (Hofmann et al., 2016). Understanding complex systems is fundamental for effective psychotherapy.

The opposite of a nonlinear system is, unsurprisingly, a *linear system*. Linear systems are more familiar and comfortable because they offer predictability. In the modern world, predictability is one of the foundations of the socioeconomic culture. Being able to design a process and predict the outcome is an essential part of business, education, and social cohesion. Humans need rules and regulations to maintain order. It is hard to imagine a community without laws or police to enforce those laws. It is only logical that psychotherapy would be framed around organized techniques with predictable outcomes. Experience soon proves that therapy can take twists and turns that require adjustment and even improvisation by both therapist and client. Some schools of practice may see this unpredictability as a problem. Others embrace it as the best way to produce effective therapy. Milton Erickson was clear about the importance of utilizing whatever manifested— or emerged—during therapy: "Too many therapists take you out to dinner and then tell you what to order" (M. H. Erickson, 1964/2008b, p. 2).

It is necessary to understand both linear and nonlinear systems. Linear processes occur within nonlinear systems. *Thinking-in-the-system* shifts the focus of learning from a predominantly linear to a nonlinear orientation. Therapists learn in order to have a larger set of resources to access when responding to the client's needs, as well as a larger set of resources for the best response to emerge spontaneously through self-organization and feedback.

Complex systems have another surprising quality. Despite being demonstrably unpredictable, a complex system will, predictably, seek to move toward order. Increasing order is achieved by the adoption and application of organizing principles, the utilization of feedback to amplify positive development of the system, and the continuous emergence of qualities and quantities that can both reflect the state of the system and also provide positive

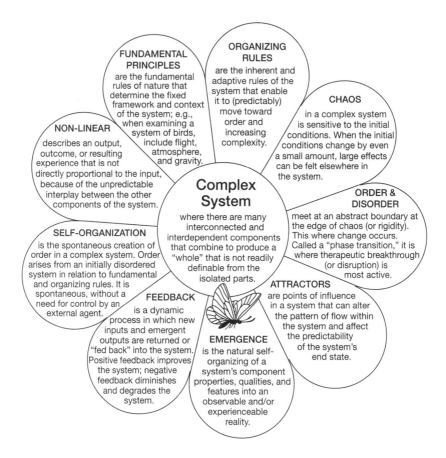

FIGURE I.3: Complex Systems Definitions. *Adapted from Hill & Rossi (2017).*

feedback, even when there is no additional external input (Wichers et al., 2019). It is necessary to understand these concepts and principles in order to orient thinking into a systems perspective. Consider the definitions in Figure I.3, but also consider how this construct might change your orientation to the therapeutic experience.

Self-organization and nonlinear dynamics are the natural stuff of life. In the frame of linear causation, the 13% contribution of the therapist (see Figure I.2) would indicate that the therapist has little effect in the therapeutic experience. In the frame of complex systems, that 13% can affect the experience in several ways.

For example,

- changing the initial conditions can produce surprising and potentially disproportionate effects,
- beneficial changes facilitated by the therapist can feed back into the system to produce ongoing benefits through self-organization, and
- introducing ways to reframe the problem can change the organizing rules or remove the fixed attractor that is keeping the client stuck in the problem.

This book will benefit the therapist in many ways. Each additional element of knowledge that the therapist gathers changes the therapist's *initial conditions*. It also stimulates positive feedback loops that can improve the therapist's quality and make them more effective at helping clients resolve problems. We encourage you to consider these possibilities as you continue working through this book.

Epilogue: The Outcome for Patient L. D.

L. D.'s symptoms were finally understood. A brain scan revealed bilateral damage in the thalamus, caused by thrombosis in a Galen vein. The clot caused partial damage to several of the nuclei within the thalamus and also damaged neurons connecting to the frontal lobes and neurons in the mammillothalamic tract connecting to the medial temporal lobe. This is why L. D. suffered loss of certain memories and poor self-regulation, even though the hippocampus was intact. Bilateral thalamic strokes are often fatal, but with the confirmation from the neural scan and additional psychometric testing, the symptoms make sense—assuming you know something about the functions related to thalamic nuclei. With this knowledge, it is possible to develop an effective treatment plan or seek out the appropriate experts (Hill, 2014).

Symptoms are not just indicators that a problem exists, but clues that help us find the problem and formulate the appropriate response. Sometimes the same symptoms are evident for different underlying reasons, as with L. D. What do we need to know, and what do we need to know about what is known? We posed this question to John Arden, author of *Mind–Brain–Gene* (2019). He replied, "How does a therapist keep abreast of all these different fields? Well, it's difficult! . . . If you are a therapist in the 21st century and you aren't making an effort to keep pace of all this, then you are way back in the mid-20th century." His challenge—and ours, "That's an invitation to do it!" (The Science of Psychotherapy, 2018b).

CHAPTER 1

The Brain

1.1 The Brain

Why is it important to know about the divisions of the brain? Many fabulous psychotherapists who do transformative work with their clients would not be able to tell you much about the neurobiology of the brain. So, what is the point?

Memory research over the last century is a good example. The work of Eric Kandel, Joseph LeDoux, and Bruce Ecker, to name just a few of the outstanding researchers in memory processes, has contributed to our understanding of the inner workings of memory—a knowledge that is not just academic but profoundly practical for psychotherapy. To grasp this knowledge requires knowing something about the brain as a system, specifically having an awareness of what is going on inside the nervous system of the client in your office. And many more invaluable discoveries about the brain over the past few decades have opened up new doors of possibility and effectiveness: brain plasticity, mirror neurons, neural networks, and so much more that this book will address. "Awareness is everything," we tell clients, and it is equally true, if not more so, for the therapist.

The therapist should be aware, for example, that a client's workaholic behavior is driven in part by an overactive executive network that is affected by a salience network interpreting their environment and circumstances as undesirable—unless they work harder and never stop. Much of the impetus for the client's behavior is implicit, beyond conscious awareness, founded on higher order neural architecture laid down in childhood. The client is being

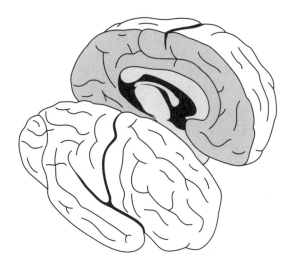

FIGURE 1.1

compelled by an invisible force to pedal ever faster on the treadmill of work. But that force is not invisible to the informed therapist who understands what is going on in the client's brain.

Knowing how the machinery of the nervous system works means having a better chance of conceiving a therapeutic process that can quickly get to the core of the issue. In this case, the process might be a combination of bringing into conscious awareness the underlying schema driving the client's salience network so that it can be modified, or helping the client activate other "modes" of mental activity. There are many modalities and creative ways to achieve these activities. An understanding of the science does not necessarily dictate a single intervention; far from it. It informs the therapeutic process, enabling the most impactful and effective therapy to emerge from a particular therapist's reservoir of techniques and methods, or even the cocreation of a process that is uniquely attuned to the client. Everything a therapist knows, and knows about, adds to an understanding of the client's issue and the effectiveness of the therapeutic experience.

A quick reminder that therapy is not just about the brain. We are looking at the brain now in the context we described in the Introduction: We are differentiating the elements to enrich your understanding of the whole person sitting in front of you.

The Big Picture

The brain, and the nervous system as a whole, can be considered in several different ways. We can discuss the brain in terms of electrical qualities: the brain waves of various amplitudes, frequencies, and locations and which behaviors, thoughts, and consciousness they correspond to. We can also discuss the chemical system: the neurochemicals and hormones that affect people's mental lives. Discussion can revolve around discrete areas of the brain: their functions, the neural networks that make up those areas, and the interplay and interconnections between these discrete areas in a fascinating discipline called "connectomics." Each of these ways of looking at the nervous system can be put into an even broader context: interactions with other parts of the body (such as the gut, the heart, and the immune system), as well as with other individuals (the way people modulate one another's nervous systems).

Because humans have such a complex nervous system, which is continually changing in a nonlinear way, it can be difficult to understand the problem and predict outcomes of therapy with certainty. The challenge for the psychotherapist, who is dealing with the most complex system known, is to have a good understanding of the system while being open and flexible when dealing with it. Therapy is likely to be beneficial when the conditions and the process are true to the client.

In the past, Paul MacLean's "triune brain" model occupied center stage, but new research reveals this model to be rather unsophisticated, overly simplified, and out-of-date in terms of what is really important about brain function. It can also give a false impression of discrete layers (based on evolutionary assumptions) acting separately, which is not really how the whole system works. So, we will not be using that model.

We have a much more sophisticated picture of the central nervous system than we did even a decade ago. The rapid advancements in imaging technology have made it possible to map the myriad connections across the brain like never before, to obtain a finer-grained picture of normal versus pathological brain activity, and to tinker much more with live brains to see what happens when a specific part is "poked."

In this section we will touch on two of these ways of conceptualizing the brain: the division of left and right hemispheres, and the activity patterns of several "modes" of mental activity. Later we will look at other important divisions of the brain, including the electrical and chemical processes that light up the brain, and at how all that works together to form memories, emotions, and interpersonal connections.

Let us begin with the left and right sides of the brain.

The Divided Brain

Iain McGilchrist, in his wonderfully detailed book *The Master and His Emissary: The Divided Brain and the Making of the Western World* (2009), describes the asymmetry of the brain and the very different natures of the left and right hemispheres. This horizontal understanding of the mental system, as opposed to the vertical triune perspective, gives us insight into the distinctly different yet complementary functions of the two hemispheres. In short, the right hemisphere handles broad attention (what we attend to comes first through the right hemisphere); is good at making connections so that we can appreciate the wholeness of dynamic structures and relationships that change over time; is attuned to emotion; and is empathic, intuitive, and moral. In contrast, the left hemisphere has narrow attention; is good at deconstructing things into parts; and has an appreciation for static, decontextualized, inanimate structures and abstractions. McGilchrist (2009) summarizes the "two worlds" of the hemispheres in this way:

> The brain has to attend to the world in two completely different ways, and in so doing to bring two different worlds into being. In the one [that of the right hemisphere], we experience—the live, complex, embodied world of individual, always unique beings, forever in flux, a net of interdependencies, forming and re-forming wholes, a world with which we are deeply connected. In the other [that of the left hemisphere] we "experience" our experience in a special way: a "re-presented" version of it, containing now static, separable, bounded, but essentially fragmented entities, grouped into classes, on which predictions can be based. This kind of attention isolates, fixes, and makes each thing explicit by bringing it under the spotlight of attention. In doing so it renders things inert,

mechanical, lifeless. But it also enables us for the first time to know, and consequently to learn and to make things. This gives us power. (p. 31)

Allan Schore explains that the early-maturing right hemisphere is the locus of attachment formation and essentially the gateway to affect regulation later in life—so much so that developing an expanded capacity for right-hemisphere processing (an emphasis on right-brained affective skills rather than a left–cognitive bias) is central to clinical expertise (Schore, 2012). In a similar vein, Bonnie Badenoch (2008) warns therapists to be grounded in right-brain engagement with clients or run the risk of being disengaged from the regulating and integrating influence of right-brain-to-right-brain connection with clients. She further encourages therapists to widen their window of tolerance, be conscious of implicit vulnerabilities, and develop mindfulness to be present with both the client and the self. There is a place for left-brain focus when thinking about specific interventions, but as McGilchrist admonishes, the left should remain servant to the right hemisphere as master.

Table 1.1 summarizes the characteristics of each hemisphere. As you read through the list, think about our human capacity to be biased toward one way of being over another, according to these hemispheric characteristics.

TABLE 1.1 CHARACTERISTICS OF THE BRAIN

LEFT HEMISPHERE	RIGHT HEMISPHERE
• Less white matter—prioritizing local information transfer within regions (reflected in an increased ability to localize attention) and enhancing its self-referring nature.	• More white matter—facilitating faster transfer of information across regions (reflected in an increased ability to hold global attention).
• More reliant on dopamine.	• More sensitive to testosterone.
• Superior in the expression of anger.	• More reliant on norepinephrine.
• Attention highly focused on detail; local, narrowly focused attention—sees parts.	• More intimately connected with the limbic system; identifies emotions faster and more accurately than the left and is more involved in emotional expression (except anger).
• Attends narrowly to the right field of view, the right side of the body, the right side of objects (demonstrated in what is known as "hemineglect" following a right-hemisphere stroke).	• Open to broad awareness; on the lookout in a broad and flexible way with vigilance and global sustained attention; sees the whole.

- More engaged with the known, the learned, the expected; prefers what it knows; "grasps" what is in focus and has been prioritized.

- Efficient when routine is predictable.

- Finds solutions perceived to fit best with current knowledge or schemata.

- Processes information in an increasingly focal way that suppresses information not immediately relevant.

- Suppresses the right-hemisphere ability to make distant associations among words or objects (and the broader scope of attention in general).

- Takes a local, short-term view.

- Identifies things by labels rather than context; does not deduce from context like the right hemisphere does; in conversation takes things more literally and has difficulty understanding implied meaning. Things are decontextualized and interpreted by an internal logic.

- Proficient at abstraction—storing and manipulating information in abstracted types, classes, categories, and representations that are impersonal, fixed, and equivalent. Recognizes objects in a category in a generic, nonspecific way, but not the uniqueness of individuals.

- Codes nonliving things and has an affinity for the mechanical.

- Better than the right at identifying simple shapes that are easily categorized.

- Interested in the utility of things—machines, tools, human-made things.

- Sees one's own body as an assemblage of parts from which it maintains a level of detachment.

- Processes information in a nonfocal manner.

- Attends to the peripheral field of vision and the entire left–right visual field.

- Alert and attentive to the new and the novel; awareness begins in the right hemisphere, grounding and integrating the experience, before being further processed in the left on a more detailed level.

- More engaged than the left in learning new information; explores.

- Outperforms the left when prediction is difficult; more capable of shifting the frame of reference (important for problem-solving).

- Can associate words or objects that are not closely related; can understand unfamiliar (nonclichéd) metaphor.

- Better able to integrate perceptual processes from different senses.

- Has a longer working memory.

- Recognizes broad or complex patterns.

- More involved in insight and deductive reasoning.

- Sees things in context and in terms of relationships; attentive to context in conversation—vital for a sense of humor.

- Can recognize the individual and uniqueness within a category, such as individual faces in the category of faces.

- Interested in the personal and living, rather than the impersonal and nonliving.

- Plays a primary role in empathy, the theory of "mind," identification with others, social interaction, and emotional understanding.

• More sophisticated in language and symbol manipulation, with greater vocabulary and more subtle and complex syntax than the right hemisphere has.	• Connected with the self as an embodied whole. • Specializes in nonverbal communication, the implicit, subtle unconscious perceptions, emotional shifts, subtle clues, and meanings. • Appreciates depth in time and space.

CLINICAL NOTES

The two hemispheres of the brain have very different ways of being in the world, and it is possible to discern a left-leaning or right-leaning bias in line with characteristics listed in Table 1.1. If you can see a hemispheric bias in your client, then you can implement exercises for the less dominant hemisphere to restore some balance. Also consider the extent of existential bias in the culture/society, or family, or workplace, or school. Influences from within and without can create an imbalance of the hemispheres. McGilchrist's hypothesis is that the entire Western world is leaning toward a left-hemisphere way of being, which is increasing population-wide stress, depression, and psychopathology. His book, *The Master and His Emissary,* provides valuable insights and a broad understanding of the current cultural milieu and offers proposals for what can be done to nurture a healthy balance.

Neural Networks

Another way to understand the brain's broad ways of operating is to consider collections of neural networks, spanning both hemispheres, that are often activated together, depending on our focus of attention. There are three commonly understood networks—the salience network, the central executive network, and the default mode network—collectively referred to as the "intrinsic connectivity networks" (Lanius et al., 2015). Another interesting neural network is the nuntius nuclei (Hill & Rossi, 2017; also refer to Section 6.5) which we will describe here, briefly.

SALIENCE NETWORK

Once again Susan finds herself in a swirl of strong and mixed emotions and that all-too-familiar sinking feeling that everything is her fault. No amount of "let's be rational" from her husband will quench the undeniable feeling that her boss hates her and is looking for any excuse, just like this one, to fire her. She can't sleep. She feels nauseated. Relational tension has always been at the forefront of Susan's experience of life, and no more strongly than at this moment. Her salience network is working overtime tonight.

As the name suggests, the *salience network* (SN) determines what is important and warrants attention in relations to emotions and the necessary actions to take. Emotions come from bodily sensations and also from higher cortical regions that interpret what those bodily sensations mean (LeDoux & Brown, 2017). The SN (which includes the dorsal anterior cingulate cortex, rostral anterior cingulate cortex, subgenual anterior cingulate, thalamus, amygdala, basal ganglia, and insula) provides guidance for making interpretations, choices, and actions on the basis of internal feelings (interoception) and external information, especially in social or emotional contexts. In this circumstance, Susan's SN is directing her attention to emotions and behaviors that are maladaptive. Reframing what is important can reorient the SN toward more productive and adaptive brain activity.

CENTRAL EXECUTIVE NETWORK

Brad's ability to comprehend the impossibly complex world of theoretical physics was second to none. That's probably why he found himself one of the youngest professors ever to gain tenure at his prestigious university. But his friends would too often joke that Brad could work out the theory of the universe but was hopelessly lost trying to work out a woman! And it was true. Brad was rather lost about his own feelings and those of others. But he was happy to be on his own. After all, there was way too much work to do and he didn't really have time for relationships. His central executive network was his primary mode of operation, almost to the complete exclusion of his salience network.

Focusing on a complex task that requires complete attention, problem-solving, and working memory engages the *central executive network* (CEN). The CEN engages for all self-directed activity that is decisive and/or consciously deliberate. This network uses primarily the dorsolateral prefrontal cortex (where working memory is used to plan, do abstract reasoning, and demonstrate self-control) and the posterior parietal cortex (important for spatial perception and attention). Most information workers engage their CEN most of the time at work, to write reports, do calculations, plan projects, strategize, and run campaigns. Equally, the CEN engages for decisions to respond to an inner sensation, such as feeling hungry. The SN focuses attention on the feeling, and the CEN enables movement to the kitchen and following a recipe to prepare a meal.

DEFAULT MODE NETWORK

"David, you're going to be late again!" The familiar and frustrated cry from David's mother rang out down the hall. David was always running late. He had a reputation as a "dreamer" and off in his "own little world," as his mother would say. His friends would call him "Walter," after the character Walter Mitty, who was always caught up in some imaginary fantasy. David didn't mind so much, because he thought of himself as a writer, and being in one's own little world is actually the fiction writer's job! Or so he convinced himself. But he did find it challenging to actually write anything, and even more challenging to work out why it mattered so much if he was late for anything. David lived in his default mode network. It was comfortable there, and he did not care much to move from that way of being.

The *default mode network* (DMN) is the mental space of daydreaming, ruminating, thinking about the future or the past, and wondering whether a particular relationship really is as solid as originally thought. It is a mode that is anything *but* paying attention to the present moment. It is called "default" because when the focus is no longer the immediate task or the environment or concentrating on information, the default is a state of reflection. It is a resting state from the hard work of focused attention to the here and now. The DMN includes the dorsomedial prefrontal cortex, ventromedial prefrontal cortex, subgenual anterior cingulate cortex, posterior cingulate cortex, and hippocampus.

These networks work together in a very dynamic way. For example, as a task becomes the focus, the CEN becomes more activated while the DMN and SN decrease in activity.

Here is an example of a creative task:

> I am moved by a story about a mother who lost a child in an unfortunate accident. My SN is in full gear as I have a gut reaction to the story and can empathize with the sadness the mother must be feeling. As a composer, I feel it is important to honor the moment, and I feel drawn to write a musical piece. My CEN activates as I start planning what I need to do to create such a piece of music, do what is needed to clear an hour in my schedule, make sure I remember to use that new library of string sounds, and take care of anything else needed to get myself organized. Once these tasks are done, there is a natural shift when my DMN starts to take center stage as I begin the abstract task of imagining the finished piece, the emotion of it, the general character, even an impression of the musicians playing the piece. My SN starts to work in tandem with the DMN as I move into an appropriate sense of pleasure and melancholy about the imagined finished piece. When I finally sit down at the piano and sketch out ideas, my brain is in a constant dynamic flow in and out and around all three networks as I focus on technical aspects of writing and playing, then acknowledge the emotional gut feelings about what I want to communicate and allow myself moments

of getting lost in the imagination of composing and the creative magic of the music seeming to appear out of nowhere into my fingers. Then I return to the CEN to write down the music and to the SN to enjoy the sight and sounds of my creation.

This example shows how the whole brain and all the networks work together, each one taking center stage at different times. Sometimes the activity is more toward the outside of the brain as cognitive tasks are being executed; sometimes it is more inward as feelings and impressions are used as resources to shape the composition.

CLINICAL NOTES

As with the two hemispheres, some people exhibit a bias when it comes to the networks. Psychotherapists hope that their clients will demonstrate a rich dynamic and balance of all the networks. Such a balance makes people flexible and adaptive—not too fixed on being cognitive, not too fixed on being led by emotions, and not too caught up in dreamland. Clients benefit a lot when they become aware of bias toward one particular mental mode. With a little psychoeducation and practical coaching, most people can learn how to use all their mental systems.

NUNTIUS NUCLEI

Another example of a network of brain regions that act together is a proposed network for curiosity called the *nuntius nuclei* (Hill & Rossi, 2017; refer also to Section 6.5).

The nuntius nuclei is a collection of brain regions that Richard Hill proposes act in concert when turning on a brain state of curiosity. These nuclei activate production of the neurotransmitters that stimulate other areas of the brain, especially the midbrain and cortex, to change mental states. Various combinations and concentrations of neurotransmitters become the neurobiochemical milieu that is dynamically linked to mental and affective states. Curiosity activates almost all of the major neurotransmitter-producing nuclei. The nuntius nuclei are active when the brain is stimulated into a curious state, producing a particular balance in the biochemical milieu.

A curious state of mind affects other mental and physiological systems. An orientation of curiosity produces qualities such as thinking outside the box (flexible, integrative, creative, efficient, open, approach oriented) and a broadening sense of possibilities. Positive attention and arousal increase in preparation to be physically active. The nuclei collectively produce and distribute dopamine, serotonin, acetylcholine, norepinephrine, oxytocin, and endorphins, which are the neurochemicals dynamically involved in the mental state of exploration and discovery, as well as trust, social engagement, creativity, and pleasure/reward for successful activity.

The nuntius nuclei share a number of elements with another system, the *reticular formation*, projections from the brainstem to the thalamus that act in the regulation of movement, arousal and sleep–wake transitions, and pain circuits (Faraguna et al., 2019). As we will show throughout the book, neurobiology uses specialized cells and structures in numerous ways and via numerous pathways. Recognition of all this variation highlights the fact that humans are complex organisms to manage and regulate. There are many other combinations of regions and systems, such as the hypothalamus–pituitary–adrenal axis and the stress response (S. M. Smith & Vale, 2006), as well as the thalamostriatal pathway and goal-directed learning (Bradfield et al., 2013), which we will discuss in the sections and chapters to come.

1.2 Important Neocortical and Subcortical Divisions

Brain research has sought to find discrete regions and make divisions in order to reduce the complexity of the brain into manageable elements. In the early 1900s, German neurologist Korbinian Brodmann gradually developed a system of numbered regions that he selected because of different neural structure or activity or connection (Zilles, 2018). The system provides a categorized map of the brain. As technology has enabled researchers to see the activity of the brain through MRI, fMRI, spectrometry, and EEG, these regions and divisions have been become more specific and functionally

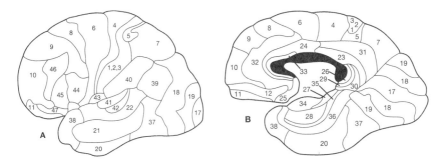

FIGURE 1.2: Panel A: Outer cortex. Panel B: Inner cortex. See Table 1.2 for a key to the part(s) of the brain specified by each number.

defined. We depict the Brodmann regions in Figure 1.2 and give the neural correlates in Table 1.2, to give you both a look into Brodmann's work and a map you can refer to as you work through the book (see J. Zhang, 2019, for a detailed description of brain anatomy and architecture).

Even this map, however, does not present every region in the brain. Some numbers are not visible, and some are not included, because they are for nonhuman primates. Most elements of the limbic region are not shown, including the basal ganglia, which include the caudate, striatum, putamen, and globus pallidus. The important limbic areas of the brain are described in the next section, the discussion of subcortical regions.

In dividing up the brain for analysis (something the left hemisphere is very adept at and even compelled to do), it is important to remember that these divisions are not acting in autonomous, disconnected, self-contained ways. Such discrete and separate functioning is simply not the nature of the brain, which, it is important to remember, is a neural *network*. The divisions are not as clear as is implied by some illustrations of the brain, especially those that differentiate regions by using different colors. There are very few colors in the brain! The brain might be analogous to a part of the city that has more universities and libraries, which could be called the "education district." But the education district is functional only when the roads, power lines, and communication networks, as well as the flow of people, are vitally linked to that area. The education precinct might be administered from the other side of the city, where the government buildings are located, and an

TABLE 1.2 BRODMANN AREAS CORRELATED TO BRAIN REGIONS

BRODMANN AREA	BRAIN REGION	BRODMANN AREA	BRAIN REGION
1, 2, 3	Primary somatosensory cortex	23, 31	Posterior cingulate cortex
4	Primary motor cortex	24, 32, 33	Anterior cingulate cortex
5	Superior parietal lobule	25	Subgenual area
6	Premotor cortex	27	Resubiculum
7	Visuomotor coordination	26, 29, 30	Retrosplenial cortex
8	Frontal eye fields	28, 34	Entorhinal cortex
9, 46	Dorsolateral prefrontal cortex	35, 36	Perirhinal cortex
10	Anterior prefrontal cortex	37	Fusiform gyrus
11, 12	Orbitofrontal area	38	Temporopolar area
13, 16	Insular cortex	39, 40	Wernicke's area
15	Temporal lobe	41, 42	Auditory cortex
17	Primary visual cortex	43	Primary gustatory cortex
18	Secondary visual cortex	44, 45	Broca's area
19	Associative visual cortex	47	Inferior frontal gyrus
20	Inferior temporal gyrus		
21	Middle temporal gyrus		
22	Superior temporal gyrus		

aerial view of the city might not reveal precisely where the education precinct starts and ends.

There is another danger, which is to assume that there is homogeny—consistency—between individual brains in the function and integration of each division. The main purpose for each discrete part of the brain can only be generalized. The neural networks are as individual as fingerprints and are deeply shaped by individual experiences and genetic dispositions, as we will describe in Chapter 3.

Important Subcortical Regions

THALAMUS

The thalamus (from the Greek word meaning "chamber") is centrally located between the cerebral cortex and the midbrain (Figure 1.3)—a two-lobed structure sitting on top of the brainstem (Patestas & Gartner, 2016). Each lobe has eight different nuclei, most of which project into the cortex. The thalamus plays a primary role in relaying sensory and motor signals to the cerebral cortex, and in regulating sleep, consciousness, and alertness—rather like a hub for the flow of information from the senses to the cortex,

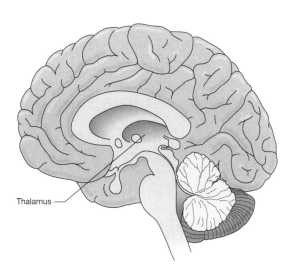

Thalamus

FIGURE 1.3

as well as for feedback from the cortex. It is believed that the thalamus not only is a gateway of information flow from the brainstem and lower brain structures but also processes information feedback from the cerebral cortex.

"If the brain works like an orchestra, our results suggest the thalamus may be its conductor," says Dr. Michael Halassa, a neuroscientist at MIT who studies these circuits in psychiatric disorders. "It helps ensembles play in-sync by boosting their functional connectivity" (National Institutes of Health [NIH], 2017).

The thalamus also plays a major role in the support of motor and language systems and, in concert with the hippocampus, spatial memory critical for establishing episodic memory. Sleep regulation—in particular, slow-wave sleep cycles—is also coordinated through the thalamus and parts of the cortex as sleep changes from state to state, again working with the activity of the hippocampus.

HYPOTHALAMUS

The hypothalamus (from the Greek words meaning "chamber underneath") is a structure with a variety of vital functions that links the nervous system to the endocrine system via the pituitary gland, for the regulation and

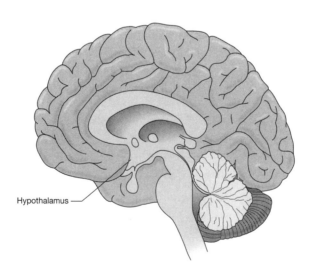

Hypothalamus

FIGURE 1.4

coordination of basic life functions (Patestas & Gartner, 2016). It is the body's homeostatic control center. As the name would suggest, the hypothalamus is located below the thalamus and above the brainstem (Figure 1.4). It receives inputs from sensory systems such as the smell, taste, visual, and somatosensory systems, and it monitors blood temperature, blood sugar, mineral levels, and a variety of hormones. It is closely connected to other limbic structures, such as the hippocampus, amygdala, and cingulate cortex, and it forms part of the continuum of emotional responsiveness.

To maintain bodily equilibrium, the hypothalamus acts as a control center for fluid and electrolyte balance, energy metabolism, circadian rhythms, sleep, fatigue, thirst, body temperature, hunger, and even sexual and reproductive behavior. This system synthesizes and secretes certain neurohormones that stimulate or inhibit the secretion of pituitary hormones and, importantly, initiates responses by the hypothalamic–pituitary–adrenal axis (HPA axis; Figure 1.5) to threats.

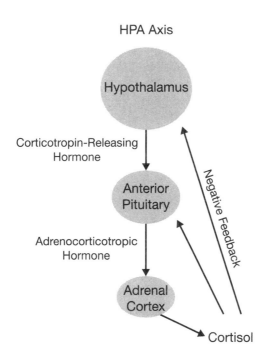

FIGURE 1.5: The HPA Axis, Showing the Flow of Hormones

When we are faced with a threat, the hypothalamus and anterior pituitary gland work together to mediate a physiological response. The neurohormone known as corticotropin-releasing hormone (CRH), which is manufactured in the paraventricular nucleus of the hypothalamus, triggers the anterior pituitary gland to release adrenocorticotropic hormone (ACTH) into the bloodstream. ACTH then triggers the release of glucocorticoids such as cortisol from the adrenal cortex above the kidneys, to enhance the ability to fight or flee from a threat. Feedback mechanisms in the hippocampus, hypothalamus, and pituitary gland monitor the rising levels of cortisol in the blood and modulate the HPA-axis stress-response cascade as the threat lessens (Kandel et al., 2012).

CLINICAL NOTES

When someone feels they are dealing with an extreme, uncontrollably stressful situation (such as the severe physical or sexual abuse of a child, or constant life-threatening situations as in war), the feedback mechanisms that dampen the HPA-axis stress response can be damaged, causing glucocorticoid levels to continue escalating. Excessive amounts of glucocorticoids can damage activated glutamate synapses and pyramidal cells in the hippocampus (where there are many glucocorticoid receptors), destabilizing previously formed neural connections and thus neural/mental function in the hippocampus. Researchers have found that these effects correlate with a reduction in volume of the hippocampi of individuals who have suffered extreme stress and have been diagnosed with PTSD. This destabilization of the hippocampus interrupts the ability to organize, encode, and recall memory. People often say, "I seem to have lost my mind!" and that description is close to the truth: They have lost the normal functioning of their brain. Being unable to access memory disconnects us from many of the resources that have been developed over previous life experiences. Many brains will become more responsive to memories in the amygdala, which are memories of intense events and also trigger activation of the HPA axis. Some degree of homeostasis—what might be colloquially described as "calm"—can be recovered in many ways, although attending to vagal tone is a good place to start (refer to Section 2.3).

AMYGDALA

The amygdala is located in both hemispheres of the brain (Figure 1.6) and is involved in a range of cognitive processes. The lateral amygdala receives input from visual, auditory, and somatosensory systems: The central nucleus is connected with the brainstem, which controls innate behavior and associated physiological responses, and the medial nucleus is connected with the olfactory system. Most of the pathways into the amygdala are excitatory, using glutamate as a transmitter. Information flow through the amygdala is modulated by a number of transmitters, including norepinephrine, serotonin, dopamine, and acetylcholine.

The amygdala has been most recognized as the emotion-processing center, which receives incoming sensory information and processes it for an emotional response. The response may be a defense to a perceived threat, a

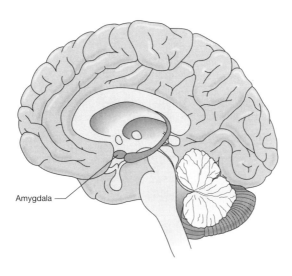

Amygdala

FIGURE 1.6

critical function of this early-warning system. The left and right amygdalae have separate memory systems, but they work together to evaluate incoming information and process an emotional response, encoding, storing, and retrieving memories associated with certain cues in the environment. The right amygdala is more strongly associated with negative emotions such as fear and sadness; the left amygdala has been associated with both positive and negative emotional responses.

CLINICAL NOTES

The amygdala is probably the most cited, and blamed, part of the brain for anxiety and touted the "emotional center" of the brain. But it is important to recognize that the amygdala is just a pattern-recognition system, and not the source of emotions like fear. Fear is a higher order construct of the cortex, and although the amygdala plays a key role in the nonconscious detection of possible threats, it is not the source of the consciousness of fear (refer to Section 1.7). Someone who feels afraid is interpreting the threat detection of the amygdala and other incoming internal and external information in such a way as to have the experience of fear. Skydiving for one person might evoke a thrilling joy, and for another, total fear and dread.

The amygdala has an attentional role, focusing attention on the most important stimuli in the environment; it is thus an important part of the salience network described earlier. The amygdala helps to define a stimulus and primes an immediate response, such as processing social cues (e.g., evaluating faces), before the information is more finely processed in higher cortical areas like the medial prefrontal cortex. Evaluating faces (e.g., the trustworthiness of a face) is an important social processing skill that is carried out very quickly in the salience network.

The amygdala also plays a part in processing reward learning and the resulting motivation, and modulating emotional states such as aggression, maternal instincts, and sexual and digestive behaviors, as well as attention, perception, and explicit memory—generally thought to be part of processing the emotional significance of something encountered. Such processing causes the amygdala to respond with the release of hormones, or neuro-modulators, that can alter the cognitive processing in cortical areas and also activate the body for an appropriate response via the hypothalamus.

In the case of depression, the amygdala is often found to be enlarged from continual hyperactivation, with studies showing increased metabolic activity in the amygdala of depressed subjects. The degree of amygdala activation is positively correlated with the severity of the depression. The depressive symptoms do not seem to dampen the anxiety-response readiness for negative events or the ability to recall negative memories to ruminate upon.

HIPPOCAMPUS

The hippocampus (Figure 1.7) is another very important structure in the limbic system. It is involved in the formation of declarative memories that are processed and transferred to neocortical areas through the process of memory consolidation and, notably, in the contextual anchoring of experience in time and space. The way the hippocampus transfers information to the neocortex to consolidate memory may be explained by what is called

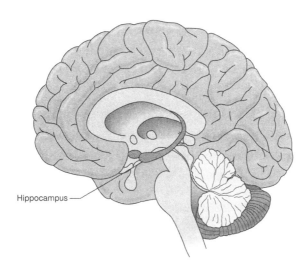

FIGURE 1.7

the "hippocampal–neocortical dialogue" (Buzsáki, 1996). Structured interactions between the hippocampus and neocortex happen during slow-wave sleep, when sharp wave patterns dominate the hippocampus and there are bursts of neuronal activity in synchrony with state changes in the cortex. This dialogue between hippocampus and neocortex may be part of the process of consolidating memory into a long-term state during sleep.

Some researchers conceptualize the hippocampus not as a storage location for memory but as a control center that connects areas of the neocortex to activate the effective recall of memory (refer to Section 1.4). This perspective might suggest thinking of the hippocampus as the brain's search engine, enabling fast and efficient searching of established memories in the neocortex to help assess and plan. A well-known function of the hippocampus is the capacity to learn and retrieve spatial memory—the what, when, and where qualities of an experience.

Researchers have found that *neurogenesis*—the creation of new neurons—happens in the hippocampus with new learning. There is an upsurge of new neurons and associated circuits when a new task is learned, particularly in the case of physical tasks and in enriched, stimulating environments. Damage to the hippocampus, however, can have significant effects on overall cognitive functioning, especially on spatial memory, and on explicit memory in general. Damage to the hippocampus can be caused by prolonged exposure to stress hormones such as glucocorticoids (to which the hippocampus is particularly sensitive), highlighting the seriousness of chronic stress and its physiological impact. Basic feedback mechanisms in the hippocampus that help modulate the release of glucocorticoids during stress may be compromised, compounding the effects of chronic stress by leading to chronically elevated cortisol levels. Some people suffering from PTSD have been observed to have a smaller hippocampal volume than the general population with one study finding that this volume did not necessarily increase after therapy and symptom reduction (Lindauer et al., 2005). A compromised hippocampus may not anchor emotional reactions to a traumatic event in a specific time and space, and such reactions can recur inappropriately, as is typical in PTSD.

CLINICAL NOTES

The hippocampus is implicated in major depression, with findings of hippocampal volume being reduced by as much as 8%–19% in people who have major depression. The reduction in volume is positively correlated with the duration of the depressive state. Similar correlations can be found in bipolar disorder and borderline personality disorder. Reduced hippocampal volume may be a risk factor rather than a consequence of chronic or excessive stress, in which case individuals with a smaller hippocampus will be more prone to fear responses when exposed to traumatic events and less able to regulate that fear response (i.e., to keep the HPA-axis stress-response cascade in check) and effectively integrate explicit and implicit memory of the trauma into long-term memory. This possible influence by hippocampal volume helps clarify that a client's capacity to manage stress might have a neural basis. The task of the therapist is to discover the individual capacities of the client, in light of which specific strategies can be created. Cocreated programs are often the most effective, enabling clients to find the most within themselves. Clients do not perform at various percentages of effectiveness in response to therapy. They perform at 100% effectiveness of their own capabilities, which are determined by their unique limitations.

Early interest in the functions of the hippocampus was sparked by the study of Henry Gustav Molaison, known as H. M., who in 1953, at the age of 27, had almost all of his hippocampi removed in an attempt to stop epileptic seizures. As a result of the procedure, H. M. lost his ability to hold on to new semantic and episodic memories. Without his hippocampi he was unable to consolidate new learning into long-term memory. He could, however, remember what had happened a long time previously, and the older the memory, the better he seemed to remember—just the opposite of what is normally observed. H. M.'s general knowledge of the world (his semantic memory) was intact, but everything that had happened after his surgery seemed new to him: He could remember new experiences for only a few seconds. Even his ability to recognize himself as he aged was lost, although he could recognize himself in old pictures. Interestingly, H. M. was able to learn complex motor skills and to retain these skills (what is known as procedural or implicit memory), but he was unable to remember learning them (declarative or explicit memory). Researchers Scoville and Milner (1957) realized that the hippocampus is critical to memory consolidation, storing memories temporarily until they are transferred to more stable cortical systems—a concept called "standard consolidation theory" (Pinel & Barnes, 2014). For a more contemporary view of the hippocampus, memory, and memory reconsolidation, refer to Section 1.4.

Important Neocortical Divisions

OCCIPITAL LOBE

Across the back of the brain is an area of the cerebrum—the occipital lobe (Figure 1.8)—that is dedicated to processing visual information into meaningful chunks of perceptual material. The region is divided into a number of subregions, known as the primary visual cortex, the ventral stream, and the dorsal stream. The primary visual cortex processes low-level descriptions

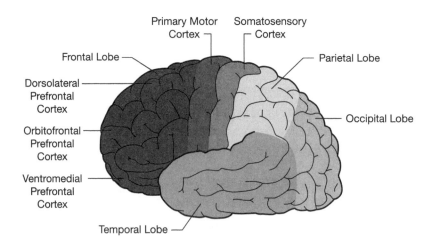

FIGURE 1.8: Important Neocortical Divisions

of orientation, spatial frequency, and color properties. The ventral stream, sometimes called the "what" pathway, provides important information for the identification of stimuli; and the dorsal stream, sometimes called the "where" or "how" pathway, helps guide movement in response to outside stimuli.

CLINICAL NOTES

It is worth noting that in borderline personality disorder there may be a deficit in the operation of the occipital lobe, leading to difficulties evaluating emotional facial expressions, as well as other difficulties in processing visual information, which could lead to body dysmorphic disorder. Humans have a high reliance on visual information. Some species rely more on senses other than vision; for example, dogs have an olfactory sensitivity, and bats, an aural sensitivity. For humans, closing the eyes is a simple way of reducing external stimuli and focusing mental attention. This technique is particularly relevant to engaging the imaginative focus of the DMN, which helps to calm the activity being created by the demands of the CEN or the more primal demands of the limbic area, especially the amygdala.

PARIETAL LOBES

The parietal lobes (located just above the occipital lobe; refer to Figure 1.8) play a major role in processing sensory input and integrating information such as spatial/navigational sense, touch, and language, as well as in the dorsal stream of the visual system. These lobes help people become oriented and understand where they are in space. The parietal lobes also assist in the comprehension of speech and of other sensory input.

TEMPORAL LOBES

Processing and integrating information about smells and sounds (such as recognizing the sounds of one's language), and how these relate to memory and emotions, is the domain of the temporal lobes, which are located at the lower front of the brain, just above the brainstem (refer to Figure 1.8).

Closely associated with the hippocampus, the temporal lobes play a part in the formation of explicit long-term memory. The primary auditory cortex is situated within the left temporal lobe and processes the semantics of speech and vision: speech comprehension, naming, and verbal memory.

FRONTAL LOBES

The frontal lobes are of particular interest to psychotherapy (refer to Figure 1.8) because they are home to the *prefrontal cortex* (PFC), an area vitally involved in executive functions such as concentration, organization, judgment, reasoning, decision-making, creativity, emotional regulation, social–relational abilities, and abstract thinking—in other words, all the functionality that humans rely on for healthy relationships. We will look at the PFC separately because of its special importance to psychotherapy. The frontal lobes, in general, regulate voluntary movement, the retention of non-task-based memories that are often associated with emotions, dopamine-driven attention, reward motivations, and planning, to name just a few.

PREFRONTAL CORTEX

The PFC is the part of the cerebrum that lies directly behind the eyes and the forehead. More than any other part of the brain, this area organizes and regulates personality, goals, and values. For example, someone who has a long-term goal and is pursuing that goal with value-congruent action maintains a neural representation of that goal so as not to be distracted or influenced by competing goals or alternate values (Grawe, 2007). Damage to the PFC affects personality (refer to Section 4.6) and the ability to orient behavior in line with values and goals. The PFC is vital to the sense of self and others that is necessary for healthy interpersonal relationships and decision-making.

As is the case with so many discoveries in neuroscience, damage to a brain area is often what leads to an understanding of what that area can do. Phineas Gage was a young, reflective, determined, and goal-oriented man who, despite his youth, had been promoted to foreman on an American railroad construction project. But in an unfortunate accident on September 13, 1848, an explosion drove a tamping rod up through the left side of his face and out the top of his head. The rod passed through and destroyed much of his left PFC. Amazingly, Gage survived and was even speaking within minutes of the accident. He was still conscious and talking to a physician about half an hour later, having introduced himself by saying, "Doctor, here is business enough for you." After Gage's recovery, Dr. John Harlow (1868) noted an early observation of a change in Gage's personality:

> The equilibrium or balance, so to speak, between his intellectual facul-
> ties and animal propensities, seems to have been destroyed. He is fitful,
> irreverent, indulging at times in the grossest profanity (which was not
> previously his custom), manifesting but little deference for his fellows,
> impatient of restraint or advice when it conflicts with his desires, at
> times pertinaciously obstinate, yet capricious and vacillating, devising
> many plans of future operations, which are no sooner arranged than
> they are abandoned in turn for others appearing more feasible. A child
> in his intellectual capacity and manifestations, he has the animal pas-
> sions of a strong man. Previous to his injury, although untrained in the
> schools, he possessed a well-balanced mind, and was looked upon by
> those who knew him as a shrewd, smart businessman, very energetic
> and persistent in executing all his plans of operation. In this regard his
> mind was radically changed, so decidedly that his friends and acquain-
> tances said he was "no longer Gage." (pp. 13–14)

Clearly, some important functions of Gage's personality had been altered by his injuries, although he did become more functional and socially adapt-able as the years went on. Given a structured environment in which clear sequencing of tasks was part of the rehabilitation, Gage managed to retrain his brain to regulate itself in reference to values and goals.

The left and right sides of the PFC have different biases, with the left side oriented more toward approach, positive goals, and positive emotions, and the right side specialized more in avoidance and negative emotions. It is also worth noting that the left side of the PFC hosts more dopamine receptors and, therefore, more dopamine activity (associated with motivation and reward), while the right has greater norepinephrine activity (associated with anxiety).

Individuals who appear to have a bias toward positive emotions may have a more activated left PFC, whereas right-PFC activation is correlated with more negative emotional experiences. Any suggestion of a clear binary division is an oversimplification, given that the experience of positive or negative emotions does not hinge purely on left-PFC or right-PFC activation, but there is nonetheless evidence of a strong correlation. Studies of the neural correlates of depression have revealed that left-PFC activity is underactive relative to right-PFC activity. It seems that less access to the positive bias of the left PFC may make it more difficult for the depressed individual to engage in positive goal-oriented thought and behavior. Similarly, the left PFC is more responsive to rewards than is the right PFC, which is more responsive to punishment.

Studies have found that the depressed individual is generally more sensitive to what may be perceived as punishment and does not respond as well to rewards. Moreover, the relative underactivation of the whole PFC in depressed individuals could account for their reduced motivation for planning, problem-solving, creativity, and so forth. In depression, not only is the PFC underactivated, but its volume has been found to be reduced as well. A depressed person with an underactive PFC of reduced volume will not demonstrate the rational problem-solving abilities of someone without such deficits; the neural integrity to support such resilience is simply not there. This is where the active, approach-oriented, and positively biased PFC of a therapist can be of great value to the depressed client. We will discuss the supportive right-brain-to-right-brain activity of therapy further when we address specific psychopathologies.

The PFC has been divided into several functionally distinct regions, as described in the paragraphs that follow.

Dorsolateral Prefrontal Cortex (dlPFC). The dlPFC is the topmost part of the PFC (see Figure 1.8) and is considered to have overall management of cognitive processes such as planning, cognitive flexibility, and working memory. This area of the PFC specializes in problem-solving and how to direct and maintain attention to a task. When the focus is on what is happening now, the dlPFC engages working memory and connects with the hippocampus for the retrieval and consolidation of long-term explicit memories.

A dysfunction in this area may lead to problems with working memory, processing in the hippocampus, and long-term memory, as well as with the integration of verbal expression with emotions. Such memory deficits have been associated with PTSD because of an underactive left dlPFC. Other dlPFC deficits can manifest as a lack of spontaneity and affect (flat rather than negative), and attention deficit (an inability to maintain sufficient attention to see a task through to completion). In obsessive–compulsive disorder (refer to Sections 4.3 and 5.1), the dlPFC plays an important role in strengthening attentional skills to momentarily break the compulsion circuit and give the orbitofrontal cortex a chance to inhibit the runaway activation of the amygdala. As with many brain regions, there are significant hemispheric differences within the dlPFC, the left side being associated with approach behaviors, and the right side, with more avoidant behaviors.

Orbitofrontal Cortex (OFC). The OFC (see Figure 1.8), like the dlPFC, is involved in the cognitive processing of decision-making, but because of its close connection with the limbic system, the OFC is particularly associated with the ability to make decisions on the basis of emotional information. The OFC also plays a major role in forming social attachments and regulating emotions. This region can be thought of as a convergence zone for sensory and emotional information, effectively integrating external and internal worlds. Social information is processed and used to guide perceptions and interactions, and the OFC plays an important role in the interpretation of complex social interactions, including, for example, the ability to understand a joke. The OFC may play a role in the ability to predict the reactions of others and may modulate behavior accordingly. When there is dysfunction in the OFC, the normal cortical–subcortical modulation is not optimal, as is likely the case in borderline personality disorder (Schore, 2012; also refer to Section 4.6.2). As with other areas of the PFC, the OFC has hemispheric differences. The left OFC is associated with positive emotions, while the right OFC is associated with more negative emotions.

Ventromedial Prefrontal Cortex (vmPFC). The vmPFC (Figures 1.8 and 1.9) assists in the making of decisions based on the bigger picture gathered

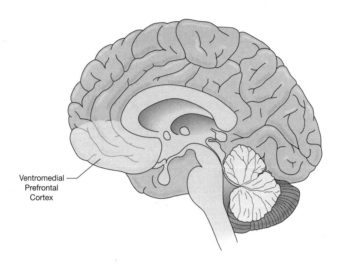

Ventromedial
Prefrontal
Cortex

FIGURE 1.9

from connections to the amygdala, temporal lobe, ventral tegmental area, olfactory system, and thalamus. The vmPFC is very well connected, receiving and sending a lot of information that influences many brain regions, including the amygdala. The vmPFC plays an important role with the OFC in regulating emotions, especially in social situations. It is also vital for personal and social decision-making and the ability to learn from mistakes. The human capacity to make judgments and allow emotions to assist in decision-making is mediated by this region of the brain. Activation of the vmPFC is also associated with courage, suppression of negative emotions, compassion, shame, and guilt.

CLINICAL NOTES

To understand the brain, researchers break it down (differentiate it) into all sorts of divisions. Psychotherapy, however, deals not with discrete sections of the brain but with a complex, whole person. It is important to understand both the divisions of the brain and the lack of boundaries at the same time. The insight to be gleaned from having an understanding of these "different" areas is the degree of integration in the brain. Ideally, the brain is operating in a connected, interactive way. Lack of integration is one of the reasons for mental health issues. In his book *The Developing Mind* (2020), Daniel Siegel talks about how to understand and improve integration among brain regions.

1.3 Neurons, Glia, and Neurochemicals

The human nervous system is a complex of neural tissue and chemicals that create a neural communication system which is itself a complex of synaptic connections relying on electrical and chemical signaling. This nervous system has two main divisions of cells: nerve cells (neurons) and glial cells (which form a tissue called "glia"). Glial cells have traditionally been recognized as a kind of support network for neurons, providing many essential functions to facilitate the neural network. However, they have more recently been acknowledged to form a communication network themselves, working in tandem with neurons (Verkhratsky & Butt, 2007).

The function of a neuron is determined by its location in the brain, its mode of connection with neighboring cells, and its individual functional character. For us humans, for example, our function in society is determined by where we are, to whom we are connected, and how we interact with others

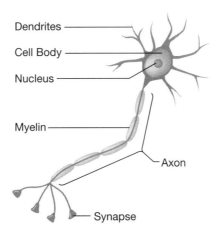

FIGURE 1.10: Main Components of a Neuron

in our environment (Cozolino, 2014). The anatomist János Szentágothai estimated that individual neurons are able to contact any other neuron via no more than six interneuronal connections (Drachman, 2005).

Although there are different types of nerve cells, performing a variety of functions, it is helpful to consider a generic model that represents the fundamentals of all neurons (Figure 1.10). Neurons communicate by means of two primary processes that have been comprehensively studied: an electrical signal within the neuron, and chemical signals between neurons. Using various chemicals known as *neurotransmitters*, neurons transmit signals across a very small gap between cells in an area known as the "synaptic cleft." Most neurons can send and receive signals by different types of neurotransmitters, and different neurotransmitters work at different speeds.

Figure 1.11 is a radically simplified representation of a *synapse*, the point of contact between two neurons. The upper part represents the presynaptic terminal of one cell's axon; the lower part, the postsynaptic dendrite of another cell. Communication flows from the presynaptic terminal to the dendrites of a neighboring cell. Dendrites are like the branches of a tree that

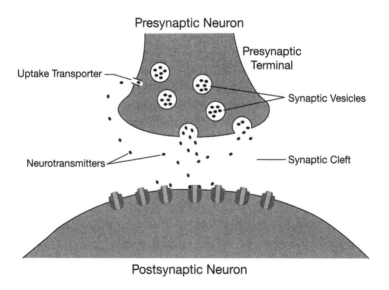

FIGURE 1.11: Activity of Neurotransmitters in the Synaptic Cleft

spread out to reach other cells and are the main areas for receiving incoming signals (Kandel et al., 2012).

Synaptic vesicles are packets of neurotransmitters that migrate to special release sites called "active zones." These packets come to the surface of the presynaptic terminal and release their contents, by a process known as "exocytosis," into the synaptic cleft. The released molecules diffuse across the gap, and some are received by receptors on the opposite-facing dendrite. The receptor sites on the dendrite bind to specific neurotransmitters, producing either an inhibiting or an excitatory effect on the receiving cell. Neurotransmitters bind to dendrites when ion channels in the membrane of the cell open, essentially producing a *membrane potential* in the dendrite (a positive or negative charge within the cell).

Neurons can contain many different types of ions, but the most common are sodium ions (Na^+) and potassium ions (K^+), and the balance of Na^+ and K^+ inside and outside the cell is what determines the overall charge, or potential, of the cell. This balance is regulated by sodium–potassium pumps that continually exchange Na^+ inside the cell for K^+ outside the cell. The more positively charged a neuron becomes, the more likely it will pass a certain threshold of potential (e.g., from −70 to −67 millivolts), in a process called *depolarization*, and "fire." Conversely, an increase in the membrane potential (e.g., from −70 to −72 millivolts), known as *hyperpolarization*, decreases the likelihood that the neuron will fire. Depolarizations are termed *excitatory postsynaptic potentials* (EPSPs) because they increase the likelihood of firing, and hyperpolarizations are termed *inhibitory postsynaptic potentials* (IPSPs) because they have the opposite effect. Neurons have a resting potential somewhere between −60 and −70 millivolts, whereas the resting potential of glial cells measures between −80 and −90 millivolts (R. Lewis et al., 2011).

Ionotropic receptors, such as AMPA (alpha-amino-3-hydroxy-5-methyl-4-isoxazole propionic acid), accept transmitters that directly alter the receiving cell's potential and are thus fast-acting. By contrast, NMDA (N-methyl-D-aspartate) receptors require prior activation of the postsynaptic neuron through another channel before their ion channels can be opened (Grawe, 2007, pp. 36–37). Some neurotransmitters will cause the receiving dendrite to become more positively charged; others will cause the dendrite to become more negatively charged. The receiving dendrite sums the incoming chemical signals to arrive at a resultant synaptic potential, which is then communicated to the main body of the cell. All these signals are summed at the beginning of the axon, the axon initial segment (Bender & Trussell, 2012). If the resulting charge rises above a resting potential, an electrical signal flows down the axon to the presynaptic terminals, causing the membrane of each terminal to open channels that allow calcium into the cell. In turn, the influx of calcium causes the synaptic vesicles to release their chemicals into the synaptic cleft. This (albeit simplified) description of the process illustrates the binary nature of neurotransmitters: Either they initiate an action potential or they do not.

Some neurotransmitters in the synaptic cleft are reabsorbed into the presynaptic terminal. This uptake (or reuptake—hence the name "selective serotonin reuptake inhibitors," or "SSRIs," for antidepressant medications), via plasma membrane transporters, serves two purposes: recapturing the chemicals for reuse, and terminating the synaptic action of the cell (Kandel et al., 2012). Drugs that are used to inhibit the reuptake of neurotransmitters will, in effect, keep the neurotransmitter in the vicinity of the postsynaptic dendrite, so that when receptors are available for that particular chemical, they will bind with it. Antidepressants are designed to inhibit the reuptake of serotonin, keeping it in the synaptic cleft and prolonging postsynaptic activation. Another process whereby neurotransmitters are removed from the synaptic cleft is degradation, in which enzymes chemically break down the neurotransmitter and the resulting molecules are taken up by the presynaptic terminal. Within the presynaptic terminal, the neurotransmitter is then reassembled and repackaged for release once again. Finally, glial cells also remove neurotransmitters from the synaptic space, to prevent further interaction with the postsynaptic cell.

A single neuron does not produce much information on its own through firing or not firing. Firing entails a certain rate, intensity, and resulting neurotransmitter output at the synapse. A single neuron simply responds to specific inputs from other neurons, or directly from the environment in the case of sensory cells. To make sense of the flow of information coming from our sensory organs, the neural system is orga-nized into a hierarchy of increasingly complex networks. Approximately 86 billion individual neurons, boasting an average of 7,000–10,000 synaptic connections each, together contribute to neural network profiles that rep-resent an aspect of brain function (such as perceiving a particular sound), and these profiles integrate with many others to carry out various functions of the nervous system, some of which are concentrated in different areas of the brain (Siegel, 2012).

The hierarchy of neural networks is organized from sensory input, to the perception of complex objects or complex understanding, to even more complex cognitive and affective processes. For example, the "raw" visual data streamed from the sensory input of the retina is recognized by neurons in a fragmented fashion, whereby individual parts of the scene are processed by neurons tuned to recognize small, specific elements. These fragments are then assembled by more complex neural networks involving higher order cells that recognize the assembly of the parts. At the top of the hierarchy are cells and networks in the cortex that recognize the picture as a whole. Realization of this broader perception makes possible additional cognitive or affective processes resulting from this input. The flow of information is not serial, but a complexity of parallel processing that uses feedback from various brain regions. No single neuron can recognize the complexities of an object like a chair. Only the summation of complex networks, along with experience, enables recognition of a chair for what it is. Nor does one area of the brain handle a specific mental function in isolation. Just as neurons do not perceive on their own, neural profiles activate and integrate with other regions across the nervous system (Siegel, 2012).

The brain is further organized into functional systems that, to some extent, can be identified by elements of the physical architecture of the cen-tral nervous system. From a single sensory-input neuron, the scale of oper-ations increases to complex hierarchies of neural networks that form maps representing input features in specific areas of the cortex. These complex signals are, in turn, processed within broad functional systems of organiza-tion according to the physical architecture of the brain.

CLINICAL NOTES

Healthy functioning of the synapse is fundamentally important to the "flow of energy and information" (Siegel, 2012, p. 3) within the brain both for specific neural pathways and for neural integration. In *Synaptic Self* (2003), Joseph LeDoux argued the importance of synaptic function in "that your 'self,' the essence of who you are, reflects patterns of interconnectivity between neurons in your brain" (p. 2). Blocks, resistance, and dis-integration will have some relationship to synaptic function, although it may be hard to establish, just from observing, whether the synapse is having a causal effect or is part of a more dynamic systemic process. Essentially, without flow across the synapse, no neural process can be completed. Medication is often used to try enhancing synaptic function (e.g., keeping serotonin or dopamine in the synaptic cleft for a longer period of time) or to try enhancing or inhibiting the activity of other synaptic molecules. If a client appears not to be completing mental processes or to be unable to make connections, it is reasonable to explore issues of synaptic function.

Glial Cells

The brain contains two major classes of cells: neurons and glial cells. (The latter form a tissue called "glia.") Although both are neural cells, the fundamental difference between the two classes has conventionally been understood to be that neurons are electrically excitable, whereas glial cells are nonexcitable. The number of glial cells compared to neurons is still controversial. For some time, glial cells were thought to outnumber neurons by 10:1. Later calculations argued that the proportion was 1:1, or any of various ratios in between (von Bartheld et al., 2016). The density of glial cells can vary dramatically at different times, so it may be difficult to know for sure. The answer is not really important, compared with the critical tasks that glial cells do in the brain. In the central nervous system, glial cells are referred to as "neuroglial cells," and they can be categorized into four types: astrocytes, oligodendrocytes, and ependymal cells (the macroglial cells), plus microglial cells (Jäkel & Dimou, 2017; Verkhratsky & Butt, 2007).

Glial cells have traditionally been regarded as passive supporting cells. (The Greek word *glia* means "glue.") Rudolf Ludwig Carl Virchow (1821–1902), who coined the term for neuroscience, thought of glia as a sort of "nerve putty"—a connective tissue void of any cellular elements (Verkhratsky & Butt, 2007). Today, however, the understanding of the way glial cells function in the nervous system is very different. Glial cells play a vital role in the growth and development of neurons, as well as their maintenance and death.

- Astrocytes provide the stem elements to birth neurons; they compartmentalize neurons, synapses, and capillaries into functional units and help modulate chemical signals between neurons.
- Oligodendrocytes myelinate the axons of neurons in the central nervous system (as Schwann cells do in the peripheral nervous system), creating faster communication pathways.
- Ependymal cells are found in the ventricles of the brain and the central canal of the spinal cord. They play a part in the production of cerebrospinal fluid, which is the liquid "cushion" for the brain. These cells move the fluid between the spinal cord and the brain and are a component of the choroid plexus.
- Microglial cells scavenge and degrade dead cells and protect the brain from invading microorganisms. Microglial cells are the immune system of the brain and react to inflammatory molecules that cross the blood–brain barrier. Their protective response can sometimes become destructive and damage neuronal tissue, and in doing so they are implicated in neurodegenerative diseases.

In 1984, researchers (Kettenmann, et al., 1984) discovered that astrocytes and oligodendrocytes possess GABA receptors. GABA (4-aminobutyric acid, formerly named "gamma-aminobutyric acid," which is where "GABA" comes from) is an inhibitory neurotransmitter whose role counters the role of glutamate: If glutamate is the accelerator of the brain,

GABA is the brake. A few years later, other studies revealed that astrocytes can communicate over long distances by propagating calcium waves. Since then, it has been demonstrated that glial cells can express practically every type of neurotransmitter and can detect the activity of neighboring neurons. In fact, far from being mere passive, nonexcitable glue for neurons, glial cells form a whole other communication circuit in tandem with the neuronal circuit, the two systems communicating with each other via chemical and electrical signaling.

CLINICAL NOTES

The communication network of glial cells could be considered the "slow brain"—a support system for a broad array of connections and cortical growth (Allen & Lyons, 2018; Kottmeier et al., 2020). This slower system is vitally connected to the voluntary muscular signaling from the body, which has a bidirectional effect on the brain, influencing body posture and other responses. Much is still being discovered about these cells that make up the greater part of the brain, but what is not in doubt is that there is much more to glial cells than was ever imagined before. Inflammation in the body because of infection or caused by prolonged release of cortisol from stress and anxiety can have a negative influence on the glial cells, especially the microglial cells (inflammation will come up repeatedly in Chapter 4 as we explore disorders). Overstimulation of microglial cells is an important element of numerous problems with brain health. Lifestyle practices such as good sleep, diet, and exercise habits are simple but immediate ways to reduce inflammation in the body.

Neurochemicals

The brain is a complex system of neural networks, and the pathways of these networks describe thinking patterns. But that is only half the story, since the networks themselves cannot work without the electrochemical action of neurotransmitters. A synergy exists between established neural pathways and the activation of these pathways, which is mediated by neurochemicals. Therapists want to know what they can do in practice to enhance positive (i.e., helpful) neurochemical activity and, likewise, what inhibits or dysregulates such activity, without reverting to pharmacology. Therefore, a basic understanding of the specific neurochemicals that modulate the nervous system—those listed in Table 1.3—is essential to understanding what drives certain pathologies, why certain interventions are effective, and why some are not.

In terms of their speed of action, neurotransmitters can be divided into

TABLE 1.3 CLASSES OF NEUROTRANSMITTERS

CLASS	SUBCLASS	NEUROTRANSMITTER
Small-molecule neurotransmitters		
Amino acids		Glutamate
		Aspartate
		Glycine
		4-Aminobutyric acid (GABA)
Monoamines	Catecholamines	Dopamine
		Epinephrine
		Norepinephrine
	Indolamines	Serotonin
		Melatonin
Acetylcholine		Acetylcholine
Unconventional neurotransmitters	Soluble gases	Nitric oxide
		Carbon monoxide
		Hydrogen sulfide
	Endocannabinoids	Anandamide
Large-molecule neurotransmitters		
Neuropeptides	Pituitary peptides	
	Hypothalamic peptides	
	Brain–gut peptides	
	Opioid peptides	
	Miscellaneous peptides	

two main groups: those that act slowly and bring about enduring changes, and those that act quickly and have a more temporary effect on brain activity. The fast-acting neurotransmitters are amino acids, the most prominent of which are glutamate, aspartate, glycine, and GABA. Glutamate, aspartate, and glycine come from the proteins we consume; GABA comes from a simple modification of glutamate. The slower-acting neurotransmitters are biogenic amines.

AMINO ACIDS

Glutamate. Glutamate act as excitatory neurotransmitters in the brain and are essential to normal functioning. Receptor sites are either the fast-acting ionotropic types such as AMPA, which primarily activate or inhibit, or the slower-acting NMDA types, which facilitate a strengthening of the synaptic connection known as "long-term potentiation." Glutamate binds with activating receptors (AMPA), resulting in fast activation of the postsynaptic neuron.

GABA. GABA is an inhibitory neurotransmitter that plays counterpart to glutamate: If glutamate is the accelerator of the brain, GABA is the brake. There is an obvious need in an active system of this kind to modulate and balance activation with a dampening or braking system, and this is where GABA comes into its own. It acts quickly, binding with GABA receptors to produce an inhibiting effect on the postsynaptic cell. GABA and AMPA interactions are seen across the brain and result in much of the fast action of our neural processes, including many of our thought processes and much of our sensory input and sensory processing.

MONOAMINES

The monoamines are slower acting and more localized in distribution than the amino acids, and they are known to be released from nonsynaptic sites. Monoamines are synthesized from a single amino acid (hence the prefix "mono-"). There are two broad groups of monoamines: catecholamines and indolamines. Among the catecholamines are dopamine, epinephrine, and norepinephrine, all synthesized from tyrosine, which is then converted to L-dopa and dopamine. Among the indolamines are serotonin (5-hydroxytryptamine, or 5-HT) and melatonin.

Catecholamines. Catecholamines trigger physiological changes to prepare the body for physical activity such as the fight-or-flight response.

Dopamine. Dopamine has many functions, including motivation, arousal, reinforcement, reward, motor control, and executive function. From a therapeutic point of view, dopamine can be equated with reward because it leads to something pleasurable or satisfying such as stimulating appetite or sexual arousal, or even complex social and cognitive pleasures (such as understanding what is going on in a client's brain). Most dopaminergic neurons are in the midbrain and hypothalamus.

Norepinephrine and Epinephrine. Norepinephrine and epinephrine have dual functions as hormones and neurotransmitters. They play a part in the fight-or-flight response. Norepinephrine is produced by certain neurons, as well as by the adrenal glands, but epinephrine is produced by only the adrenal glands. Norepinephrine is a psychoactive molecule in the brain, promoting blood circulation to the skeletal muscles. Epinephrine is not a psychoactive compound but increases energy production via glucose release in response to rising norepinephrine levels. It also relaxes muscles to dilate the bronchial tubes and allow increased oxygen intake. Epinephrine and norepinephrine were called "adrenaline" and "noradrenaline" until the brand name Adrenalin was registered by a drug company. Somewhat confusingly, neurons releasing norepinephrine are still referred to as "noradrenergic" and those releasing epinephrine are described as "adrenergic."

Indolamines. The indolamines are a family of neurotransmitters that includes serotonin and melatonin (derived from serotonin).

5-HT. 5-HT (serotonin) is involved in the regulation of mood, appetite, and sleep, as well as memory and learning. It is considered a major antidepressant in a theory of depression revolving around serotonin levels.

Melatonin. Melatonin helps regulate circadian rhythms (day–night cycles). Rising melatonin levels cause sleepiness. Interestingly, the nightly release of melatonin is typically delayed as children become teenagers, leading to later sleeping and waking times. Melatonin is also a powerful antioxidant.

CLINICAL NOTES

The monoamine hypothesis of depression postulates that a lack of serotonin flow in the brain leads to symptoms of depression (as well as anxiety, obsessions, and compulsions). One chemical approach that has been engineered to address this problem is serotonin reuptake inhibition. The serotonin that is released into the synaptic cleft (the space between a neuron's axon and a neighboring dendrite) is recaptured by the presynaptic cell through a reuptake mechanism that recycles serotonin in the cell. A selective serotonin reuptake inhibitor (SSRI) will block the reuptake mechanism to preserve more serotonin in the synaptic cleft, so that more of the chemical is available to connect to the neighboring dendrite. Research varies on the effectiveness of medications such as SSRIs, with some showing no benefit above placebo and some showing detrimental effects, including increased suicidal tendency in teens. The link between serotonin level and depression is a very broad area of knowledge but, we suggest, vital to know something about.

ACETYLCHOLINE

Acetylcholine (ACh) is another small-molecule neurotransmitter that is used by motor neurons of the nervous system (at the neuromuscular junction) to activate muscles. Neurons releasing ACh are described as "cholinergic." ACh also plays a role in the autonomic nervous system and in the central nervous system, where it modulates plasticity, arousal, reward, enhancement of sensory perceptions, and sustained attention. ACh is involved in memory and learning: Memory can be enhanced when drugs are used to increase the activity of ACh in the brain. Disruption of ACh neurotransmission can disrupt memory, as in the case of the neurodegenerative disease Alzheimer's.

UNCONVENTIONAL NEUROTRANSMITTERS

There are a few classes of what are known as "unconventional" neurotransmitters. We will consider two of these: soluble gases (or gasotransmitters) and endocannabinoids. Soluble gases such as nitric oxide and carbon monoxide pass through cell membranes and stimulate the production of second messengers before being deactivated when they are converted to other molecules. In some synapses, these soluble gases perform what is known as retrograde transmission, delivering a feedback signal from the postsynaptic neuron to the presynaptic neuron (seemingly, to regulate the presynaptic neuron). Anandamide (*N*-arachidonoylethanolamine, or AEA) belongs to the endocannabinoid class of neurotransmitters. AEA is a fatty acid neurotransmitter that has effects in both the central and the peripheral nervous systems. Much is still unknown about this neurotransmitter, but it has been shown to play a role in the regulation of feeding behavior, as well as in motivation, pleasure, and reward. Its name comes from the Sanskrit *ananda* ("joy, bliss, delight") and "amide" (an acid).

NEUROPEPTIDES

In addition to the small-molecule neurotransmitters already described, there is a large group (more than 100) of proteinlike, large-molecule neurotransmitters known as "neuropeptides," which can be grouped into the following categories: pituitary peptides (first identified as pituitary hormones), hypothalamic peptides (first identified as hypothalamus hormones), brain–gut peptides (first identified in the gut), opioid peptides (with a chemical structure similar to that of opium), and miscellaneous peptides (as a catchall for the rest). Peptides often coexist and act with other neurotransmitters, but they have much more diverse effects, such as gene expression, local blood flow, synaptogenesis, and changes in glial cells. These actions tend to be prolonged and can have significant effects on behavior.

1.4 Memory

"I have no idea why I married her in the first place, she's so infuriating!" Peter, in an agitated lament, had just recalled a string of painful memories about his ex-wife Lisa. It was a little over a year since the divorce, well over 2 years since they separated, and the disagreements about the children seemed to be more heated than ever.

"What do you remember about Lisa when you were first married?" I prompted, in an attempt to garner some civility from Peter toward the other parent of his three children.

"I don't know . . . ," he sighed. He didn't express much enthusiasm for the direction I was wanting to take and quickly went back to his rather critical character sketch of "Lisa the Infuriating."

I (M. D.) had known Peter and Lisa for about 4 years—2 years in couples therapy trying to save their marriage, and 2 years helping Peter through the fallout of separation and divorce. Initially, they seemed genuine and motivated to get their marriage back on track. They oscillated between affection and frustration toward each other while grappling with many unresolved issues from their pasts. Back then it was much easier for each of them to recall fond memories of their relationship and the reasons why they married in the first place. Four years later, any semblance of positivity about the other seemed to have evaporated. Their memories were completely biased toward the negative attributes of the other, the hurtful words spoken, the things missed, the things unsaid, the love not expressed; every memory recall of the relationship was embellished with negativity and reconsolidated in that way. Like a narrative continually reedited until it bore little resemblance to the original text, so, too, were these memories of former lovers.

Memory is not like a photo album, a roll of film, or an audio recording. It is the reconstruction of many fragments of associated neural pathways and the creative "filling in" of the missing pieces. Each time a memory is recalled, it's in danger of being remembered in a slightly different way. Eric Kandel (2006), Nobel Prize winner for his research on memory, puts it this way:

> Recall of memory is a creative process. What the brain stores is thought to be only a core memory. Upon recall, this core memory is then elaborated upon and reconstructed, with subtractions, additions, elaborations, and distortions. (p. 281)

Peter had literally changed his mind about Lisa. Each time he recalled aspects about her, in the context of working through a divorce, he would emphasize the negative aspects of her character and his own pain. In the search for reasons why he should have more custody of his children, Peter's recall of Lisa focused on her lack of ability as a mother—indeed on her not being a good person in general. It seemed that his fragmented memory traces of "Lisa" could be recalled into only a caricature of "the enemy." It had not always been like this, yet Peter's self-constructed reality was now firmly entrenched in a very different image of Lisa from the one he had held in the first years of their marriage.

The Nature of Memory

The brain is continually storing information, either consciously or unconsciously, and recalling that information to give an individual a sense of who they are in the world, and how to relate to the environment around them. A never-ending cycle of encoding, storage, and retrieval imparts the ability to talk, drive a car, and remember that, for example, Susan likes two sugars in her coffee. This process of encoding and storing experience as memory is everything. Imagine having no memory for speech, walking, or being moved in any meaningful way, or not remembering the past? You would have no concept of self or place—no concept of who you are, where you are, or what surrounds you. From the unconscious reflexes and motor control that allow you to walk with little conscious effort to the complexities of advanced cognition such as solving equations in theoretical physics, memory is the indispensable operant. Memory links a personal past with the present and enables projection into the future; it absolutely influences the next move a person makes. Individual lives and the memories they are built on are uniquely crafted by the complex interplay of each person's neural architecture and genetic expression immersed in the experience of their environment. Memory is divided into several broad categories, as outlined in Table 1.4.

Given that memory is essential and that it can change, as observed with Paul's memory of his ex-wife, then it is important for therapists to know the mechanisms of memory formation, storage, and retrieval. Eric Kandel and others have discovered that repetition is one mechanism whereby the information being received is converted from short-term to long-term memory through altered gene expression and the growth of new synaptic connections. These changes, which are termed *experience-dependent neuroplasticity*, require protein synthesis to create more permanent synaptic connections between neurons. When a neuron is activated repeatedly, the "second messenger system" within the cell causes changes in the cell nucleus, where the genes are located, to form neural networks of explicit and implicit memories. *Second messengers* are small intracellular molecules that are produced after the first neurotransmitter has activated the receptor. Second messengers activate intracellular signaling pathways that amplify the signal and activate or inhibit transcription factors, inducing a cellular response.

CLINICAL NOTES

Trauma can be multiple experiences (which can create a complex trauma condition) or a single event. A client may have had a "one-trial learning" experience (a single exposure to a stimulus) that involves a strong emotion embedded in memory as a traumatic event. Those who have been traumatized by a single transient event (such as being held up at gunpoint) can attest that one event can form a remarkably stable and enduring memory. However, experiences that occur after the event can become absorbed into the single trauma disturbance through reconsolidation of the traumatic memory, which can increase the intensity of the current PTSD experience.

TABLE 1.4 TYPES OF MEMORY

MEMORY TYPE	DESCRIPTION	KEY BRAIN AREAS
Sensory	Neural traces from sensory input lasting less than a second	All sensory input going to specific sensory areas of the brain
Short-term	The holding of a limited amount of information for less than about 18 seconds without manipulation or rehearsal (Revlin, 2012); may be limited to five to nine discrete bits of information at any one time (first proposed by G. A. Miller, 1956)	Hippocampus; subiculum
Working	A prefrontal cognitive capacity responsible for the transient holding, processing, and manipulation of information (Diamond, 2013)	Dorsolateral prefrontal cortex
Long-term explicit	The conscious memory of facts and events, also known as declarative memory; can also be divided into episodic memory (autobiographical events and experiences) and semantic memory (facts, concepts)	Medial temporal lobe: perirhinal, entorhinal, and parahippocampal cortices; hippocampus
Long-term implicit	The unconscious memory of skills and tasks, also known as procedural memory; can be further divided into priming, procedural, associative learning, and nonassociative learning	Neocortex (priming); striatum (procedural); amygdala (emotional responses in associative learning); cerebellum (skeletal musculature in associative learning); reflex pathways (nonassociative learning)

Hippocampus

Any discussion of memory, especially explicit memory, would be incomplete without consideration of the hippocampus. We introduced the hippocampus in Section 1.2 but will expand on this structure of the brain a little more here. Each hippocampi has slightly different functions: damage to the left hippocampi is associated with difficulties in forming new verbal memories; damage to the right hippocampi produces deficits in other forms of non-verbal memory (Moss, 2016). Memory works better when there is context, and the hippocampus (considered as a whole) puts things in context when encoding and reassembling memory. The hippocampus is active during the processes of navigating space or recollecting personal events, and it negotiates the large overlap of spatial/navigational and autobiographical information needed for orientation. There are even cells in the hippocampus, named "place cells" (O'Keefe & Dostrovsky, 1971), that respond to a certain spatial location to assist in orienting the individual.

Concerning its function in memory, Robert Moss (2016) describes the hippocampus not as a storage device but rather as an association device, because of its role in bringing together various elements stored in the cortex into a coherent and meaningful recollection. Moss conceives of discrete bits of information (learning) as stored in cortical columns: When various bits of information are needed to re-create a memory, cells in the hippocampus are activated and, through the thalamus, connect to various cortical columns to activate those bits of memory simultaneously. The hippocampus does not itself hold the bits that re-create the memory. Instead, it coordinates the synchronized activation of those bits held in the cortex. Moss (2016) offers the following example to illustrate:

> Quiroga et al. (2005) described a cell in a patient's hippocampus that consistently activated each time different pictures of Jennifer Aniston were shown, but the same cell did not show such activation to other pictures of objects or animals, or other famous faces. This gives the impression that the cell is the location of the memory. However, my belief is that the visual facial recognition of Jennifer Aniston and the associated word columns of her name occur in separate cortical

circuits. For those circuits to be consolidated as an association memory (i.e., her name with her face), the single hippocampal neuron is needed to reactivate the separate circuit columns and the common column in the perirhinal cortex. When shown her picture, the visual column tied to her face activated the common column that in turn activated the hippocampal cell. This explanation fits well with the finding that patients with anterograde amnesia caused by hippocampal damage retain long-term memories that occurred years before they developed the amnesia. Thus, if you know Jennifer Aniston by sight and have future damage resulting in the loss of the hippocampal cell that was involved, you will have no problem recognizing her face and giving her name provided the cortical columns in the circuits relating to her remain intact. (p. 18)

It may be possible for long-term memories capable of recall to be established without hippocampal intervention, through the association of circuits between the critical cortical bits—integrative connections of color, sound, emotion, spatial information, and other bits that are all stimulated at the same time upon recall.

The concept that consolidation of memories progresses from short-term memory to long-term memory has been challenged in a recent study in *Science* suggesting that short-term memory formation in the hippocampus and long-term consolidation in the cortex occur simultaneously (Kitamura et al., 2017). The researchers proposed that the simultaneously formed long-term memories remain "silent" initially but gradually mature, changing in anatomy and physiological activity, until the long-term cortical memory is fully recallable. Using mice and a technique called "optogenetics," whereby target cells can be turned on or off with light, the researchers mapped the development of a fear memory. After just 1 day, memory of the fear event was detected in the cortex. This finding is contrary to the standard theory of memory consolidation (that memories transfer gradually over time). According to this study, memories are formed rapidly and simultaneously in the prefrontal cortex and the hippocampus: "They're formed in parallel but then they go different ways from there. The prefrontal cortex becomes stronger and the hippocampus becomes weaker," said Mark Morrissey, a coauthor on the paper (Trafton, 2017, para. 18). If the finding is supported by future studies, it will add greatly to our understanding of the functioning of the brain and memory formation.

Recall and Trauma

The term "state-dependent recall" describes the phenomenon whereby a current internal state replicates the state that was encoded at the time of a significant event, setting in motion spontaneous recall of that memory. With an increase in heart rate, more rapid breathing, or a particular emotion that closely resembles the original response of a trauma, a traumatized individual might experience the memory of the trauma itself flooding back. In fact, just about anything that matches the original internal experience can trigger some aspect of what the individual went through emotionally and physiologically at the time. Even body posture may be a catalyst for state-dependent recall:

> Feedback from postural proprioceptive nerves could have the same memory power as the proprioceptive nerves of internal sensations that must be involved in state-dependent recall under the influence of drugs or alcohol. Asking a client to reconstruct his posture before and during a trauma will often bring details to awareness. However, such a technique must be used with caution, as it can easily stimulate more recall than the client is prepared to handle. Postural state-dependent recall can also be caused unwittingly, as, for example, when a physically abused child either freezes or screams when casually or inadvertently tossed over another's knee in play. (B. Rothschild, 2000)

In the case of childhood traumatic events, it has often been observed that explicit memories are difficult to recall, while implicit emotional memories flood the PTSD sufferer until a change of context in the individual's life, potentially years later, triggers an explicit recall of the event. As Dan Siegel (2012) has noted, however, delayed recall of explicit autobiographical memory is subject to (unintentional) creative license:

Although delayed recollection may be quite accurate, explicit memory is exquisitely sensitive to the conditions of recall. Recounting the elements of explicit autobiographical memory is a social experience that is profoundly influenced by social interaction. Thus, what is recounted is not the same as what is initially remembered, and it is not necessarily completely accurate in detail. Actual events can be forgotten, and non-experienced "recollections" can be deeply felt to be true memories. (p. 80)

CLINICAL NOTES

The mind can be extremely suggestible, and every act of retrieving a memory can be altered by social context and new information. People can be convinced a memory is totally accurate when in fact it may be quite different from its original consolidation (which itself may not have been a completely accurate representation of what really occurred). Psychotherapists must be careful to assume a neutral stance with respect to the accuracy of a client's memories. Excessive interest in the trauma over the person may generate unconscious pressure on the patient to keep the therapist engaged by elaborating the narrative of trauma (Siegel, 2012).

Memory Reconsolidation

Memory reconsolidation is the modification of a memory at the level of its neural encoding. It is a substantive change brought about by new learning. We will consider memory reconsolidation in more depth in Section 5.2; here we briefly introduce the science.

The concept of reconsolidation is based on the understanding that when a memory is retrieved from long-term storage, it is held in a labile (unstable) state in short-term memory while it is being used (Nader & Hardt, 2009). Reconsolidation may be a way in which new information is integrated into an existing memory trace—a kind of maintenance of consolidation intended to keep retrieved memory up to date. Most of the laboratory research on reconsolidation has focused on fear conditioning, which psychotherapists have been able to apply to emotional memory.

The work of Bruce Ecker and colleagues (Ecker et al., 2012) has demonstrated that emotional memories can be strengthened, weakened, altered in their details, or completely nullified and canceled through a reconsolidation process, thereby bringing about true unlearning of an emotional memory. Reconsolidation is a natural, neural process that can transform an acquired behavior or emotional response by fundamentally revising the memory associated with it (Ecker, 2015).

Implicit memory is the main type of memory involved here, in the form of emotional learning, such as how to avoid particular vulnerabilities and instances of suffering. Implicit memories, or "learnings," are often attained without awareness, entirely within the implicit learning system, in the presence of strong emotions. Accordingly, they can prove powerful and durable. All sorts of emotional and traumatic experiences form implicit emotional learnings whose purpose is essentially adaptive—to help individuals cope with life as they perceive it. But these implicit memories frequently become maladaptive later in life, when we no longer need to respond in the same self-protective patterns. Children who need to do outstanding work to attain their parents' love and approval may carry that learning into adult life and become workaholics, not realizing that their behavior is more a desperate attempt to meet a basic emotional need than a reflection of a passion for work. The very behavior that helped them adapt to circumstances as children now alienates the people from whom they most want love and affection. There is no conscious realization that this is the case; it is implicit, an automation. Such encoding happens mainly in the subcortical regions that store implicit, tacit, emotionally urgent, procedural knowledge, rather than the neocortical regions involved in explicit memory, which store conscious, episodic, autobiographical, declarative knowledge (Ecker, 2015).

For psychotherapists, an understanding of memory reconsolidation can be revolutionary in therapy, and in Section 5.2 we will take a closer look at the practical application.

1.5 Interpersonal Networks

Mirror Neurons and Empathy

Some people believe they suffer because they have become irrevocably isolated and disconnected from others, while others believe they are empowered by being an island unto themselves in a simplistic form of solipsism. The latter have had to alter their belief because of a surprising interaction one day between a macaque monkey in an experiment to map motor neurons in the brain and an Italian experimenter eating lunch. That fateful day revealed the existence of mirror neurons.

Neuroscientist V. S. Ramachandran (2000) predicted that

> mirror neurons will do for psychology what DNA did for biology: they will provide a unifying framework and help explain a host of mental abilities that have hitherto remained mysterious and inaccessible to experiments. (p. 1)

Marco Iacoboni, a mirror-neuron researcher from the University of California, Los Angeles, made a similar comment:

> It's going to make a big change. Psychological studies started with the idea that a solitary mind looks at the world in a detached way. Mirror neurons tell us we're literally in the minds of other people. (Jaffe, 2007)

These statements from two of the giants of modern neuroscience set the stage for this chapter. The discovery of mirror neurons was serendipitous and surprising, as often happens in scientific investigation. It was so surprising that at first the team did not immediately understand what they had discovered. Even after they confirmed the nature of their discovery, the journal *Nature* rejected their first paper for being of low public interest (Taylor, 2016).

The Serendipitous Discovery

Giacomo Rizzolatti's team—Giuseppe di Pelligrino (1992 team); Vittorio Gallese, Luciano Fadiga, and Leonardo Fogassi (1992 and 1996 teams)—was examining neurons in a macaque monkey's brain to try to isolate the specific neurons involved in controlling the muscles of the hand. They sought to learn which neuron(s) fired when the monkey performed particular actions, such as reaching for or grabbing food items and bringing the food up to the mouth. They succeeded in isolating those particular neurons.

The story goes that when they broke for lunch one day, the machinery was still connected and active while the macaque observed one of the experimenters eating. Unexpectedly, the macaque's motor neuron fired. At first, the researchers were not sure what had happened. Perhaps it was just an accident or an error in the machinery. They were eventually able to confirm that certain neurons fired when the monkey was making the action *and* when the monkey observed an experimenter performing the same action. It must have been challenging to realize that the monkey was not only able to see that food was being eaten but was also able to neurologically engage with that experience as if it were making that action itself (di Pelligrino et al., 1992; Gallese et al., 1996). This breakthrough fundamentally changed the understanding of how humans perceive and process the movement of others and how we are connected to others. We are simply not able to be isolated from others if we can see them and they can see us.

Mirror neurons can be defined by three fundamental functions:

1. They are particular neurons in the brain in particular locations.
2. They are neurons that achieve an action potential when an expressive act is both executed and observed/perceived (neurons that fire both when an action is executed and when it is observed being performed by an "other").
3. They are initiating elements in a system that leads to other outcomes—a mirror neuron system (MNS).

The classic MNS is initiated predominantly in motor areas. We won't delve deeply into the neurobiology, but the principal cortical areas involved

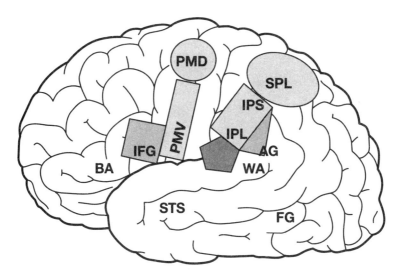

FIGURE 1.12: Brain areas, according to Rizzolatti and Craighero (2004), that respond to transitive distal movements (squares/rectangles), reaching movements (circles), tool use (pentagon), intransitive movements (triangle), and observation of upper-limb movements (teardrop portion of the STS). IFG = inferior frontal gyrus; IPL = inferior parietal lobule; IPS = intraparietal sulcus; PMD = dorsal premotor cortex; PMV = ventral premotor cortex; SPL, superior parietal lobule; STS = superior temporal sulcus. Other regions of the MNS include Broca's area (BA) and Wernicke's area (WA), as well as the angular gyrus (AG), fusiform gyrus (FG), and primary motor cortex (PMC; Acharya & Shukla, 2021).

and the corresponding types of motor acts are highlighted in Figure 1.12. These regions form the core of the MNS in humans.

Understanding Others

The MNS enables the creation of an automatic (i.e., before conscious reflection) understanding of the motor acts performed by others in several ways that are functionally beneficial to an individual's safety, motor-skill development, and social interactivity. The MNS enables an implicit understanding of the actions of others that compares the actions being observed to the observer's internally stored representations of action experiences, or what is described as a personal "motor repertoire," creating *motor resonance* (activation of an observer's motor system). An observer can thus have a nonconscious sense of familiarity with way the other moves, the intention of the action, and the future goal. This sense of familiarity imparts the ability to automatically sense whether someone is friend or foe without the delay of conscious consideration (Iacoboni et al., 2005). Daniel Siegel (2012) describes it experientially:

> If you are from New York City and I raise my hand in front of you, you may imagine that I am hailing a cab. If you are currently a student, you may imagine that I am intending to ask a question. If you have been abused, you may feel that I am going to hit you. Prior learning shapes the empathic interpretation and the internal simulation. (p. 166)

Motor resonance is very useful to survival, as a protective/defensive capacity and as a socializing capacity. Mirror neurons respond not only to direct actions but also to goal orientations and intention. Experiments show that when a known object is placed behind a screen, the mirror neurons still fire when the observer *assumes* that the action is taking place. Coming to understand that individuals can implicitly recognize the intention of the actor and the end goal of the action was an enormous breakthrough. Mirror neurons also enables us to learn how things are grasped, manipulated, and used (Freedberg & Gallese, 2007) which may be how the MNS assists in imitation and learning about the possibilities for goal-based orientation in personal and social behavior. The MNS in humans is directly involved in imitation of simple movements (Iacoboni et al., 1999), in imitation learning of complex skills, and in the perception of actions that communicate (Buccino et al., 2004). Mirror neurons have also been found to respond to the related sound of an event, so the MNS is not merely a vision-based system (Gazzola et al., 2006).

Research into mirror neurons in humans has been limited because it has not been possible to conduct testing at the single neuron level. The recording of neuronal activity on a regional basis, however, has made it possible to hypothesize functionality of the MNS (Hunter et al., 2013). Extrapolating the simple motor actions that were the subject of research to broader aspects of human behavior opens the door to consider motor activity such as facial expressions, gestures, and body positions as part of someone's personal emotional expression. These are all movement-based expressions that engage the MNS which introduces the possibility that the MNS contributes to social cognition and empathy in what Gallese (2001) describes as the "shared manifold" hypothesis.

Gallese (2003) proposed that "sensations and emotions displayed by others can also be empathized and therefore implicitly understood through a mirror matching mechanism" (p. 176). All humans exhibit a wide range of expressive activity that includes actions and the emotions and feelings they display. The MNS makes it possible to automatically establish a meaningful, embodied interpersonal link. Because the same neural substrates are activated when these expressive acts are both executed and perceived, the MNS can be included as part of the neurological basis that underpins a "we-centric" space. Mirror neurons produce an "embodied simulation" (Gallese, 2009) that is a felt sense of the "other." These natural mechanisms are the deep biological basis for that very human sense of identification and connectedness with others. "Social identification, empathy, and *we-ness* [emphasis added] are the basic grounds of our development and being" (p. 520).

Super Mirror Neurons

A curious thing about the activation of mirror neurons during observation is that the observer rarely imitates the action at the same time, although responsive actions and emotions may be triggered. Marco Iacoboni (2008) determined that a special set of mirror neurons, which he called "super mirror neurons," act to regulate the observer's motor activity. Super mirror neurons seem to act as a functional neuronal layer on top of the classic mirror neurons to control their activity. Super mirror neurons prevent the observer from repeating the action and thus may play a role in the capacity to distinguish between self and other (Iacoboni, 2008).

Navigating the world of others requires empathic understanding of the self as well as of the other. Gilligan (1982/1993) describes how a sense of the other creates a responsibility to the other. When responsibilities to others are accepted, the self is prepared to receive the other in relation to the world. In another view, when responsibilities to the self are placed above responsibilities to others, the self is defined in separation from others and tends to position the world in relation to self. According to Iacoboni, "mirror neurons put the self and other back together" (Iacoboni, 2008, p. 155), creating a "sense of us" and "some kind of magical connection between people" (Iacoboni, 2007). Gallese (2003) said that mirror neurons "instantiate a supra modal intentional shared space" that allows human beings "to appreciate experience and implicitly and pre-reflexively understand the emotions and sensations we take others to experience" (p. 177). Super mirror neurons "show that we are not alone but are biologically wired and evolutionarily designed to be deeply interconnected with one another" (Iacoboni, 2008, p. 267).

What Is Empathy?

"Empathy" emerged from the German word *Einfühlung*, which means literally "in feeling" or "feeling into." The term was coined by German philosopher Robert Vischer (1873/1994) to describe the transference of self or the capacity to transpose the self into the inner being of an object and explore its formal character from within. The concept was particularly relevant to the appreciation of works of art and inanimate objects. Theodore Lipps expanded the meaning to include visual illusions, claiming that observers at the circus could feel themselves inside the acrobat (Jeffers, 2009; Lipps, 1903). Iacoboni (2008) added, "As if we were inside that person" (p. 109). It may be equally pertinent to say that the movement of the observed person was inside the observer. Edward Titchener (1909), professor of psychology at Cornell University, translated *Einfühlung* into English, creating the word *empathy* as meaning a subjective "feeling as." This definition distinguished the term from "sympathy," which meant an objective "feeling *for*."

Empathy plays a major role in socially appropriate emotional responses and behaviors. Definitions for empathy are varied but include several important elements: a feeling of commonality that is typically based on socially shared emotional experiences (Szanto & Krueger, 2019); cognitive mechanisms such as perspective taking (Tusche et al., 2016); understanding the difference between self and others during interpersonal interactions (Woodruff, 2018); an automatic understanding of emotional facial expressions (Pfeifer et al., 2008); and the social emotional expression in body movement (Becchio et al., 2012).

Some researchers suggest that mirror neurons are a contributing element, but not a necessary one. According to Lamm and Majdandžić (2015), "empathy recruits similar neural networks as the direct experience of the emotion one is showing empathy for" (p. 16) and might be described separately as "affective resonance." Humans have the ability to understand and share the emotions of others by (partially) processing those emotions with their very own emotion system. Observing an emotional experience has been shown to elicit motor resonance, which then triggers an affective response, but it is not yet clear whether this is a linear process or cocreated. Observing others being touched engages the somatosensory system to code the affective qualities of vicariously perceived touch. The empirical evidence suggests that empathy neither requires the MNS nor can be exhaustively explained by it. That is not to say, however, that mirror neurons are not important elements in the process of eliciting empathy, by enabling the observer to tap into an automatic motor resonance in order to understand and experience an empathic, or affective, resonance.

Taking into account that there may be more than one type of mirroring system, the relevant message for therapeutic practice is that during a therapy session, the client's emotional responses and motor activity not only are something to observe and consciously consider but actually register within the psychotherapist's brain in ways that evoke implicit (nonconscious), automatic responses. The same thing happens within the client as they observe the therapist. This is the science behind the need for therapists to be sensitive and aware of both their clients and themselves for the implicit information being generated by mirroring systems within and between.

Clinical Implications

The effectiveness of the MNS is affected not only by damage to brain tissue but also by congenital dysfunctions. Deficits in the MNS are found in people with autism spectrum disorder (ASD). Poor socialization and limited sensitivity to the intentions and the emotions of others are features of ASD. Marco Iacoboni and colleagues studied the neurological activity of 20 child subjects, half of whom had autism (Dapretto et al., 2006). The subjects were shown pictures of faces expressing various emotions, such as fear, happiness, and sadness, as well as pictures of faces with a blank expression. The ASD children had no activity in the MNS when asked to imitate facial expressions, whereas the control group did. This study showed that there was a demonstrable MNS difference between ASD and non-ASD children. The more severe the condition, the less active the MNS seemed to be. During childhood the MNS can develop poorly or slowly as a result of adverse childhood experiences that might include traumas, insecure attachments, and unenriched environments, where restricted movement and observational learning can limit the development of a motor repertoire.

Neurocognitive diseases have been shown to include damage to the MNS. Elisabetta Farina et al. (2017) showed that normal aging has little effect on the MNS, but mild cognitive impairment and Alzheimer's disease produce deficits in MNS function. Parkinson's disease damages the motor-activity areas of the basal ganglia and has been shown to affect the MNS, contributing to the movement issues of Parkinson's (Alegre et al., 2011). The MNS is important in recovery and rehabilitation after a stroke. Diana Carvalho et al. (2013) concluded that "studies showed how the interaction among vision, proprioception and motor commands promotes the recruitment of mirror neurons, thus providing cortical reorganization and functional recovery of post-stroke patients." Watching a therapist perform the action can be helpful in stimulating motor activity within the brain of the stroke patient as if they were doing the action themselves. The discovery of mirror neurons enables the use of not only personal repetitive exercises but also observation as a way of rehabilitating damage to the brain. This therapeutic approach can also be useful after orthopedic surgery where the brain is intact but areas of the body need to rediscover how to move correctly.

CLINICAL NOTES

A psychotherapist may not feel directly involved in recovery and rehabilitation of these "medical" issues, but the road to recovery is always made harder by lack of confidence and negative impacts on self-worth. Therapists can reassure and encourage themselves with psychoeducation, but also participate by contributing their facial expressions, the tone of their voice, and the mirroring of a positive body sense. Jean Decety from the University of Chicago offers this reminder: "The best response to another's distress may not be distress, but efforts to soothe that distress" (Decety & Jackson, 2006, p. 55), which can be facilitated not only by the therapist's words but also by the activity of the therapist's presence.

1.6 Cortical Columns

As we have discussed, there are many ways to understand the brain, looking at it from the different perspectives of structure, connectivity, chemical milieu, and so on. We want to introduce a model of the brain by neuropsychologist Robert A. Moss, who, motivated by a need to understand the mechanisms of chronic pain, developed an elegant model of brain organization and function that is instructive beyond pain management. Moss's models are the dimensional systems model and the clinical biopsychological model. In Section 6.3 we will look more closely at the practical application of the clinical biopsychological model for chronic pain. All the details that follow come from Moss (2020a) and Moss (2020b), and we are very grateful for Moss's personal guidance as we wrote this section.

Chronic pain has long been recognized as linked to multiple factors: early-life trauma, PTSD, social support factors, attachment styles—all of which suggest the involvement of complex brain mechanisms (Moss, 2020b). Moss brings to the table a brain-based model that attempts to explain the involvement of the cortical perception of pain, and in doing so, presents a general model of brain organization that we think is worth knowing about.

Studies have shown that patients who experience chronic pain show decreases in gray matter in a number of brain regions that may be the consequence of frequent pain receptive input (Kregel et al., 2015; May, 2008; Moss, 2020b; Rodriguez-Raecke et al., 2013; Seminowicz & Moayedi, 2017). These changes are not the cause but the consequence of incoming pain signals (nociception). Nociceptors convey pain information from organs to the spinal cord to the brain. Areas such as the periaqueductal gray can activate pain control, while areas like the parabrachial nucleus send information to regions, such as the amygdala, that are involved in emotional responses to pain.

The complex pathways involved in the sensory–discriminative and cognitive–affective aspects of pain traverse brain regions that have many functions. Moss summarizes the areas involved in pain perception and control as the thalamus, somatosensory cortex, insula, middle temporal gyrus, precuneus, parahippocampal gyrus, dorsolateral prefrontal cortex, ventrolateral prefrontal cortex, ventromedial prefrontal cortex, orbitofrontal cortex, anterior cingulate cortex, middle singular cortex, nucleus accumbens, caudate, putamen, periaqueductal gray, parabrachial nucleus, amygdala, cerebellum, salience network (activated when focused on pain), and default mode network (activated when focused away from pain). The most common alterations associated with chronic pain affect the regions associated with emotion and motivation: prefrontal cortex, anterior cingulate cortex, hippocampus, amygdala, basal ganglia, and nucleus accumbens (Moss, 2020b pp. 201–202).

That's a lot of regions involved in pain! But just looking at the regions only goes so far. To tease out what's going on in these cortical regions requires delving down to the level of neural circuitry, and this is where Moss comes in with his understanding of *cortical columns.*

Think of the cerebral cortices as a massive collection of circuits made up of columns. Each column is a collection of several hundred minicolumns, each containing 100–200 neurons. Moss suggests thinking of a column as a binary digit (bit) in the highly complex and integrated circuitry of the cortex. All the columns, which represent discrete bits of information, relate to one another in various ways to create memory and processing systems. Subcortical areas of the brain help facilitate columnar circuitry; for example, the hippocampus allows the binding of parallel circuits of columns, the basal ganglia inhibit those circuits, the cingulate cortex facilitates volitional activation of them, and the cerebellum enables habitual activation without cortical attention. It is indeed a grand proposal.

At the core of this model is the idea that all memory is represented by circuits—cortical columns lit up together in association to recall a memory—whether a word, a sensation, an emotion, a picture, or something else. The stronger the synaptic connections within a circuit of cortical columns, the better the integrity of the memory.

> Forgetting is the result of weakened synaptic connections which means the downstream columns in the circuit fail to activate. In this case, the column's activation by one or more other columns fails to be maintained. However, with structural changes, such as axonal sprouting and increased dendritic spines between neurons of columns, then the likelihood of "forgetting" is greatly reduced because the connections are resistant to disruption and damage. (Moss, 2020b, p. 203)

Cortical columns in the left temporal cortex, for example, code for spoken language and are perceived as language when activated. Similarly, the parietal lobe, which specializes in bodily sensations, has columns that are experienced as bodily sensations when activated. Explicit memories come from the cortical column circuits that the left frontal cortex has verbal awareness of; with implicit memories, there is no such awareness.

Now let us consider the dimensions of the dimensional systems model—a way to conceptualize the organization of cortical columns (this is an extremely simplified adaptation of Moss, 2020a, pp. 45–46):

> **Dimension 1: Internal–external.** Medial cortical columns code for internal and self-referential information; lateral columns code for external stimuli (and there are transitional zones that code for both).
> **Dimension 2: Proximal–distal.** In relation to the body, different areas code for proximal stimuli (like somatosensory stimuli) and distal stimuli (like vision or audition).
> **Dimension 3: Simultaneous–sequential.** Some areas, such as the ventral cortex, process in a sequential manner; other areas, like the dorsal cortex, process in a simultaneous manner (and some areas do both at the same time).
> **Dimension 4: Reception–action.** The parietal, temporal, and

occipital lobes contain all receptive, or sensory, information; the frontal lobes code for all action-related information.

Dimension 5: Unorganized–organized. Columns progress from less organized (lower order) coding to more organized (higher order) coding as they move away from the primary sensory receiving areas (bottom-up processing); and reciprocally, columns from frontal areas progress from more organized decoding to less organized (lower order) decoding (top-down processing) as they move toward premotor and primary motor areas.

Dimension 6: Analytical–global. Here, Moss divides the hemispheres. The right hemisphere has fewer columns but is faster and more global in processing; the left hemisphere has more columns and more interconnections, allowing for slower, more detailed "analytical" processing. Each hemisphere processes the same incoming sensory information at the same time, but in a different and complementary manner. For example, the negative reaction of a spouse will register in the right hemisphere as facial expressions and vocal intonations while the left is busy processing the actual words being spoken, or maybe shouted.

As for the control of cortical columns within these dimensions, Moss outlines some important regions as playing critical roles. For inhibition there are the basal ganglia, well known for their role in motor and nonmotor loops of activity, one of which is the "OCD loop," wherein the basal ganglia play an important inhibitory role. When not functioning properly, the basal ganglia can allow looping thoughts or motor movements through a "broken gate" in the neural circuitry. For automatic cortical functions, the cerebellum assumes control of columns in overlearned behavioral responses so that we don't have to think about automatic behavior.

Relating the theory back to pain, Moss (2020b) explains the logic of this column arrangement:

The basis for the involvement of each pain-related cortical region is that a column forms in each region that reflects the summation of information coded by all columns that project to it in AND-gate fashion. In posterior cortical serial circuits, there is a direct progression from lower-order to higher-order receptive columns in serial fashion. Each serial circuit will end with its highest-order column that represents all the information of lower-order columns in that circuit. If there are other posterior cortical serial circuits associated with ongoing processing, the highest-order columns of all circuits project to a common column in other posterior areas (typically referred to as "hubs"). . . . The highest-order columns of parallel circuits are in the medial temporal cortex (i.e., parahippocampal, perirhinal, and entorhinal cortices) which in turn project to the hippocampus, allowing complex memory consolidation (e.g., explicit memory) involving the associated parallel circuits . . . each posterior receptive column has an associated frontal action column. Lateral cortical receptive columns have lateral cortical action columns. Medial temporal lobe receptive columns have medial frontal action columns. Thus, there is a logical pattern of connections. (p. 212)

The hemispheres of the brain are semi-independent, with connections between the hemispheres corresponding to the same cortical areas on either side. The closer the cortical columns are to the primary sensory areas, the more similar they are (thus, incoming sensory information is processed similarly in either hemisphere) and, as the columns move farther away from these primary areas, the processing differs in the hemispheres. As mentioned earlier, the left hemisphere has more columns, for more detailed processing, and the right hemisphere has fewer columns, for faster global processing. The right hemisphere is particularly attuned to nondetailed emotional and interpersonal memories, stored in the right, and quickly responds to voice intonations, facial expressions, and emotion, especially input associated with negative emotional memories (stored in the right posterior lobes). That is not to say that negative emotional reactions are solely the realm of the right hemisphere, nor is that all that the right hemisphere concerns itself with (refer to Section 1.1). Emotional memories activated in the cortex are paired on both sides and activated on both sides, and their corresponding subcortical structures activate the physiological and motivational response.

CLINICAL NOTES

According to Moss's model, whichever hemisphere can best respond to a situation assumes control of the response. For example, the controlling right frontal lobe can inhibit the corresponding left frontal lobe to avoid potentially incompatible responses. The left will continue to process in the background, and if the right hemisphere's response is not effective, then the left will exert inhibition on the right and take over the response. This coordination enables parallel processing of both hemispheres while deploying the most effective response from one. When neither hemisphere is able to address an emotionally overwhelming event—something beyond the control of either—then the two hemispheres can simultaneously inhibit each other, resulting in a sense of depersonalization and emotional numbing. In addition, during calm and rested states, frontal lobe activation (detailed and logical analysis) tends to dominate, inhibiting the right-frontal, emotional side. During tired or stressful times, however, left-side processing takes more effort, and the right-frontal responses are more likely to kick in. Note that the concept of congruence is important here. **Congruence** is the measure of agreement between the hemispheres and corresponding cortical columns in the higher order representations of the frontal lobes. When there is inconsistency (internal conflict between the behavioral responses of the hemispheres), the inhibitory action from one lobe to the other is greater and, as in the example of being emotionally overwhelmed, both frontal lobes may be attenuated.

Another important aspect of hemisphere difference concerns the formation of personality. Both hemispheres have their own memories, with the right side storing nondetailed sensory emotional content in the right posterior lobes and nondetailed action/response memories in the right frontal lobe. Memories form faster in the right hemisphere, so emotional memories form before left-sided verbal memories. These emotional memories become the native emotional language, and individuals use them to know how to feel and respond to others.

> Just as individuals learn a left hemisphere native verbal language that remains for life, they learn a right hemisphere native emotional language that remains for life. Thus, the sensory emotional memories leading to the activation of positive and negative reactions (i.e., what feels positive and what feels negative to each person) in response to the behavior of others are stored in the posterior right cortex. The behavioral expression (i.e., one's "personality") involves right PFC columnar circuits. Therefore, one's interpersonal relationship behavior patterns are largely a function of right hemisphere processing and memory. (Moss, 2020b, p. 234)

In Section 6.3 we will look at how this model is applied to chronic pain management in relation to columnar circuits and the connections with sub-cortical structures, focusing particularly on emotional memories and how to restructure them.

1.7 Emotions

"Emotion" is a word that everyone knows and uses regularly. It is often used interchangeably with "feeling," but what do these words really mean? Understanding emotion is, surely, fundamental to the practice of psychotherapy. Joseph LeDoux (2020), best known for his work with the emotion of fear and the brain region called the amygdala, states:

> In the end, our understanding of emotion in the brain is only as good as our conceptualization of what an emotion is. If we don't know what we are looking for, we will surely fail to find it, and will continue to mislead others in the process. (p. R4)

Is LeDoux suggesting that it is necessary to understand the *concept* of emotions before learning about a biology of emotions? Or is he suggesting that although the biology of emotions is important, it is only one of the factors that provides information about the concept? This question makes it difficult to decide where to discuss emotions. We discuss them in this chapter on the brain, but we might well have included them in the chapter on the body, because emotions/feelings are also the outcome of sensory and molecular stimuli throughout our biology. Emotions might best be discussed in a separate chapter that is not restricted to just one differentiated aspect of psychoneurobiology. So, having acknowledged that emotions are not simply to do with the brain, or simply to do with the body, we hope you might read this as a transitional section between this chapter (The Brain) and the next (The Body). We will explore some of the theories and ideas, as well as a case study, so that you might better know what you are looking for. No single area of the brain or the body *causes* an emotion. Emotions/ feelings emerge from system-wide reactivity to stimuli, sub-cortical neurological responses, and conscious cortical representations. We will explore what the terms "emotions" and "feelings" mean, how emotions and feelings function, and how this knowledge helps psychotherapists work better with the emotional states of clients.

Emotions Are Everywhere

"Emotion" is the core word in the title of a number of psychotherapeutic modalities and popular programs. Motivational programs reveal dozens of talks, presentations, and workshops that will teach emotional mastery, emotional intelligence, coping with your emotions, emotional leadership, emotional self-regulation, and the power of emotions.

In the therapeutic space, the word "emotion" features in the titles of numerous modalities: emotion-focused therapy, emotional processing therapy, emotion regulation therapy, emotional efficacy therapy, dynamic emotion focused therapy, and emotional freedom technique. Some other therapies strongly emphasize emotional regulation, such as dialectical behavioral therapy (DBT), eye movement desensitizing and reprocessing (EMDR), and cognitive behavioral therapy (CBT). Emotion is evident in the language of many, if not all, therapies.

Is there a difference between emotions and feelings? In an interview with *Scientific American Mind* (Lenzen, 2005), Antonio Damasio was asked that very question:

> MIND: You differentiate between feelings and emotions. How so?
> Damasio: In everyday language we often use the terms interchangeably. This shows how closely connected emotions are with feelings. But for neuroscience, emotions are, more or less, the complex reactions the body has to certain stimuli. When we are afraid of something, our hearts begin to race, our mouths become dry, our skin turns pale and our muscles contract. This emotional reaction occurs automatically and unconsciously. Feelings occur after we become aware in our brain of such physical changes; only then do we experience the feeling of fear.

According to Damasio, an emotion is something that happens physiologically, whereas a feeling is something in conscious awareness. To feel, we need a representation in the brain's cortical processes (conscious awareness) of what is happening in the body and subcortical brain. Emotions evolved as devices that would stimulate a behavioral response or reaction, but Damasio argues that the feeling of an emotion is distinct from *having* an emotion (Damasio, 2000). Emotions make life more survivable by stimulating response to a danger or an opportunity or any of the many things in between.

Ralph Adolphs, who is considered a leading authority in the study of emotions, sees emotion as a functional state (Adolphs & Andler, 2018). An understanding of emotion requires examination of its biological roots in humans and animals. Adolphs clarifies five distinct areas for investigation:

- the functional emotion state—the physiology;
- the conscious experience—the feelings;
- the behaviors caused by an emotion state—the actions and reactions;
- conceptual awareness of the experience—the ability to reflect/consider, talk about it, and encode/remember; and

- attribution—the ability to recognize emotion in others, which may lead to empathy, projection, and anthropomorphizing animals.

This subject of inquiry has become known as *affective neuroscience*, a term first coined by Jaak Panksepp (1998). Panksepp developed a theory of fundamental emotional systems (which we will expand on shortly) which distinguishes the difference between emotions and feelings in this way: "Subjectively experienced feelings arise, ultimately, from the interaction of various emotional systems with the fundamental brain substrates of 'the self'" (p. 14).

Different Theories

That there are a number of different theories about emotion might seem confusing, but such confusion is exacerbated by the difference between linear thinking and thinking in systems. Thinking in a linear, cause-and-effect fashion means looking for what *causes* emotions. Thinking in terms of complex systems means trying to understand how emotions emerge from the complex activity of the entire system: What are the interacting elements, and how are they interacting? The elements of a system do not necessarily look like or even indicate what the final emergent property will be or look like; the elements, on their own, do not necessarily predict the nature of the emergent property. A simple metaphor of the difference between linear and complex-system thinking is the poem by John Godfrey Saxe (1872) titled "The Blind Men and the Elephant." In this poem, each blind person draws linear conclusions about the animal they have encountered that are based on the part of the elephant they are touching. The person touching the tail deduces that it is a ropelike creature, the person touching the ears deduces it is a like a fan, and the trunk leads to the conclusion that the animal is a thick snake. When thinking in the system, however, these perspectives are simply *differentiations*, the different elements, that, when integrated, produce the emergent property of an elephant. In considering a client's emotional state, a therapist's perspective can affect their deductions, diagnosis, and therapeutic plan of action.

Consider this case:

*J.C. presented with concerns about the way she reacts to things emotionally. She said she didn't seem to have much reaction at all. It had troubled her most of her life. She seemed to know when something was exciting or scary or lovely or inspiring, but she just didn't feel it. She had been to many therapists, from standard psychologists to alternative practitioners, but still hadn't found resolution. She had even gone to a high-energy motivational seminar, but while everyone around her was jumping up and down, whooping with excitement, she found herself just wondering what all the fuss was about. She was swooped up by one of the many "helpers" and into a private room where a number of well-known, popular techniques were applied, but these only distressed her more. She knew she was behaving as if upset, distressed, somewhat ashamed, and confused, but she did not **feel** these things. She just knew that she thought they were the things happening to her because she had learned over time what these behaviors mean. What a perplexing dilemma. During therapy sessions, J.C. gradually revealed that her parents were alcoholics. From her earliest memories, she was never sure what mood they would be in. From about 6 years old, she taught herself to respond equally to their gushing kindness or angry criticism. Over time she found it easy not to respond at all. Her attachment style seemed to be ambivalent, with some elements of avoidant—but not disorganized. Was she suppressing her emotional reactions? Did she have some other form of discharge or projection of her emotions? What accounted for her dull and/or unresponsive affect? How could she exhibit behaviors indicating she should be feeling something but not actually feel it?*

To understand this case, it will be helpful to learn more about emotions. Ralph Adolphs provided a breakdown of the overall "emotional experience," but there are several other important and valuable voices in the discussion. Each one supplies a perspective or facet that helps to describe the complexity of the system. We have chosen to explore basic emotional systems developed by Jaak Panksepp (Montag & Panksepp, 2017); basic emotional sets (W. A. Mason & Capitanio, 2012) and categories described by Paul Ekman (1992); core emotions from Robert Plutchik (2001); and the positive emotional set from Barbara Fredrickson (2013a). We will conclude with Joseph Ledoux and Richard Brown's (2017) integrating concept of emotion and consciousness, which presents what we suggest is a description of the entire "emotion elephant." This review should be good preparation for helping the emotionally confused J. C.

Many Facets of the Same Gem

Over his lifetime of work, Jaak Panksepp presented a clear theory of emotional systems (Panksepp, 1998). He determined that seven emotional systems arise from subcortical brain regions and delineated a distinct brain anatomy, neuropharmacology, and physiology. In a presentation for TedX-Rainier (TEDx Talks, 2014), Panksepp reminds the audience that science tends to answer not "why" questions but "how" questions. Fundamentally, "we have feelings because they tell us what supports our survival and what detracts from our survival." *Emotions* stimulate actions and reactions that assist in our survival and are automatic (i.e., largely nonconscious).

Panksepp presents the seven primary drives in capital letters—SEEKING, PLAY, LUST, CARE, RAGE, FEAR, PANIC. Table 1.5 indicates some of the emotions and potential disorders that emerge out of the basic emotional systems. Like Antonio Damasio, Panksepp found that in humans, strong emotions decrease cortical activations. He also found that cortical damage, especially to the frontal area, leads to increased emotionality. The frontal cortex has often been described as the "executive brain" that controls the inhibition and/or regulation of emotions (Siegel, 2020).

Paul Ekman (1992) determined that there were six universal emotions, principally as a result of his investigations of facial expressions. The six universal emotions produced unique facial expressions: anger, disgust, fear,

TABLE 1.5 BASIC EMOTIONAL SYSTEMS

Basic emotion	"TOWARD" EMOTIONS			"AWAY" EMOTIONS		
	Seeking	Play	Lust	Care	Rage	Fear	Panic
Emergent emotions	Interest, frustration, craving	Joy, glee, happiness, playfulness	Sexual appetite, jealousy	Nurturance, love, attraction	Anger, irritability, hatred	Anxiety, worry, fright	Guilt/shame, sadness, distress
Disorders	OCD, addictions	Mania, ADHD	Fetishes, sexual addiction	Dependency, attachment disorders	Aggression, personality disorder	GAD, phobias, PTSD	Panic attacks, depression, agoraphobia

Note. Adapted from Panksepp (1998) and Montag & Panksepp (2017). GAD = generalized anxiety disorder.

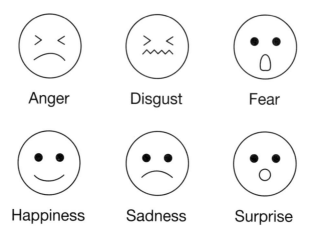

FIGURE 1.13: The Six Universal Emotions Described by Paul Ekman

happiness, sadness, and surprise (Figure 1.13; some references include a seventh expression, for contempt).

Ekman found that these expressions are recognized across gender, age, culture, and social environment. He noted a distinction between emotions that he saw as short-lived, in response to a stimulus/trigger (which relates to Damasio's framing of emotions as a response to biological stimulus), and longer-lasting emotions or feelings, which he called *moods*. Affective disorders are unresolved and persisting moods that become dysfunctional (Eckman, 2003). Persistent mood can also interfere with someone's threshold to an emotional response; for example, irritable mood may lower the threshold to the emotion of anger. This is not exactly the same as Damasio's concept of emotion and feelings, but it is similar in that feelings have an emotional basis and there is a feedback influence from emotions to feelings and from feelings to emotions. Panksepp has described the systems of emotion that generate the phenomenological experience, which include the facial expressions emerging from the activation of those systems.

Ekman considers emotions important as evolutionary developments; in survival, he says, "emotions are (an) . . . automatic appraisal influenced by our evolutionary and personal past, in which we sense that something important to our welfare is occurring, and a set of psychological changes and emotional behaviors begin to deal with the situation" (Ekman, n.d., para. 1) This idea is more thoroughly explored by Robert Plutchik, who endeavored to unify some of these theoretical perspectives by developing a *psychoevolutionary* theory of basic emotions. He also contends that emotions are important for survival: "Emotions are an essential part of who we are and how we survive" (Plutchik, 2001, p. 344). Plutchik suggests that emotions

- serve an adaptive role in dealing with survival issues;
- consist of prototype elements;
- can occur as combinations, mixtures, or compounds of the primary emotions; and
- can exist with varied intensity or degrees of arousal.

It is not hard to see areas of correlation, similarity, and complementarity. Ledoux and Damasio also see the connection to survival, and Ekman describes emotions as "important to our welfare." Plutchik describes a deeper interplay between emotional prototypes to explain the variety and nuance of emotional expression. His theory postulates eight primary emotional dimensions, arranged in four pairs of opposites, with each having opposite physiological reactions:

- Joy is the opposite of sadness. Physiology: Connect versus withdraw.
- Fear is the opposite of anger. Physiology: Get small and hide versus get big and loud.
- Anticipation is the opposite of surprise. Physiology: Examine closely versus jump back.
- Disgust is the opposite of trust. Physiology: Reject versus embrace.

Plutchik hypothesized that basic emotions can alter in relation to intensity (see Table 1.6) and could combine to produce mixed emotions, personality traits, and psychopathology. He identified a number of emotions that emerges when two basic emotions combine; for example, surprise and fear combine to be felt as awe, and joy and trust combine to be felt as love.

TABLE 1.6 PLUTCHIK'S EMOTIONAL INTENSITIES

More intense		Basic emotion		Less intense
Ecstasy	←	Joy	→	Serenity
Admiration	←	Trust	→	Acceptance
Terror	←	Fear	→	Apprehension
Amazement	←	Surprise	→	Distraction
Grief	←	Sadness	→	Pensiveness
Loathing	←	Disgust	→	Boredom
Rage	←	Anger	→	Annoyance
Vigilance	←	Anticipation	→	Interest
More intense		**Basic emotion**		**Less intense**
Ecstasy	←	Joy	→	Serenity
Grief	←	Sadness	→	Pensiveness
Terror	←	Fear	→	Apprehension
Rage	←	Anger	→	Annoyance
Vigilance	←	Anticipation	→	Interest
Amazement	←	Surprise	→	Distraction
Loathing	←	Disgust	→	Boredom
Admiration	←	Trust	→	Acceptance

Barbara Fredrickson made an important observation of the clinical research of emotions that opened up another avenue of investigation and a unique perspective of emotions. She found that most research was based on negative emotions such as fear, disgust, or anger. Positive emotions seemed to be more difficult to research because they are less distinct and have similar facial expressions, and recall of positive emotions is less distinct. The response of the autonomic nervous system to positive emotions is small or even non-existent, and research has a problem-focused orientation (Fredrickson, 2004). Negative emotions tend to contract focus and attention to the threat or discomfort that is "causing" the emotion which creates specific negative biological responses and limits the experience to defensive and protective behaviors.

Fredrickson (2013b) argues that positive emotions do more than just signal optimal functioning (i.e., make you feel good), actually producing optimal functioning that extends beyond the momentary pleasantness into the long term. She describes the experience of positive emotions as "broaden and build" (Figure 1.14), concluding that "people should cultivate positive emotions in themselves and in those around them, not just as an end-states in themselves, but also as a means to achieving psychological growth and improved psychological and physical well-being over time" (Fredrickson, 2004, p. 1367). If emotions are responses to opportunities and beneficial situations, then positive emotions broaden people's options, widening their array of thoughts and actions. Fredrickson shows that "joy . . . creates the urge to play . . . and to be creative. . . . Contentment . . . creates the urge to sit back and savor current circumstances and integrate these . . . into new views of self and the world" (p. 1369). She goes on to describe other positive emotions and their expansive nature, such as interest, compassion, and gratitude.

LeDoux and Brown (2017) present a theory of emotion showing that the different aspects of emotions presented by theorists, such as the ones we have been exploring, are all part of a connected process that functions at different levels of biological and neurobiological activity and in different levels of consciousness. Although their theory seems to challenge the

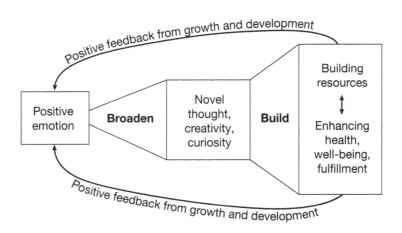

FIGURE 1.14: "Broaden and Build" Concept by Barbara Fredrickson.

Note. Adapted from Frederickson (2004, 2013b).

conventional ideas of emotions as largely products of subcortical activity, we find that this theory gives therapists an understanding of emotions that enhances what can be done during therapy. It incorporates the subcortical concepts and introduces the idea that a higher order representation of subcortical activity leads to emotional experience. They also argue that emotions are experienced in more than one way. As with Damasio, who distinguishes a difference between emotions and feelings, LeDoux and Brown explain how nonconscious experiences become conscious and how mental processes create the "self" that experiences an emotion. Fundamental to understanding a client's emotional states is realizing that to have a "felt sense," the feeling/emotion needs to be felt by "someone." They propose that

> although emotions, or feelings, are the most significant events in our lives, there has been relatively little contact between theories of emotion and emerging theories of consciousness in cognitive science. . . . What differs in emotional and non-emotional experiences . . . is not that one originates subcortically and the other cortically, but instead [it's] the kinds of inputs processed by the cortical network. (LeDoux & Brown, 2017, p. E2016)

In his presentation on the topic "Rethinking Emotion" (Picower Institute for Learning and Memory, 2012), LeDoux noted that although he had been describing the way threat activates the amygdala and produces a fear *response* for much of his career, he had not intended that to mean he was talking about the conscious *experience* of fear:

> I certainly don't think that the amygdala is creating and unleashing fear, at least not directly. The mistake I made over all this time is that I kept calling it fear responses and the fear system. So, it is more appropriate to think of these as *defense reactions* [emphasis added] . . . it is a threat defense system . . . [that] help us face challenges and take up opportunities.

LeDoux and Brown refer to the work of Adolphs and Panksepp, acknowledging their concepts as reasonable descriptions of the physiological response to stimuli. Ledoux and Brown call these *first-order representations* which is the inner, bottom-up activity that engages subcortical regions (e.g., the amygdala in the case of a threat) resulting in behavioral and biological responses that are largely nonconscious and certainly do not produce cognitive, self-directed actions. As Figure 1.15 shows, a series of stepped processes leads toward consciousness and emotion. A *higher order representation* (HOR) of a physiological process—stimulus to subcortical to first-order representation—enables a phenomenological experience (i.e., a subjective experience of the first-order response). A second, higher order representation of the first HOR enables objective, conscious awareness of the experience. This awareness is "felt" and "known" in the context of semantic memories (general world knowledge) and factual aspects of experiential knowledge (HOROR). In the final process, the HOROR is represented in conscious awareness in the context of episodic, or autobiographical, memories that produce the sense of "self." The result is a "felt sense" (HOROR) that is happening to "someone"—an emotion. In this representation it is possible to have a conscious awareness of emotion.

LeDoux and Brown propose that because emotions depend on the self, they can never be unconscious. When we "feel," we know we are feeling. Without the self, there is no emotion of fear or love or joy. An event needs

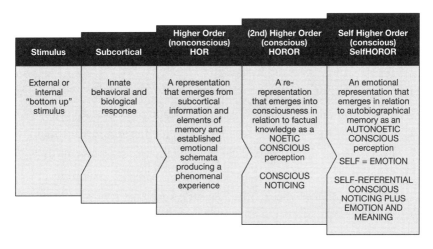

FIGURE 1.15: Summary of Emotional Representation

to affect *you* to produce an emotion. "You" are the product of memories, including both semantic (the "what" of life) and episodic/autobiographical (the "when" and "where"). The self is the awareness that what, where, and when happened to the person that is *me*. The memories of who you are, what has happened, when it happened, *and* how you think, feel, and act in that situation is what is commonly called a *schema*. The schema is a fundamental element of therapeutic practice, used specifically in treatment approaches such as *schema therapy* (J. E. Young et al., 2003).

This stepped process is readily understood when thinking-in-the-system (Section 1.3). The process is neither hierarchical nor linear. Because systems have feedback this model is both top-down and bottom-up. Emotions can exist as a cortical process in relation to self without having to directly affect subcortical and physiological functions, or vice versa. It is possible to have a fear emotion but register no activity in the amygdala. It is then possible for the cortical activity to activate the amygdala in a feedback response to thoughts—a mind-to-body, top-down process. This may be an imagined thought, or a thought taken from outside the individual brain (i.e., another person's thought). Such responses are broadly described as mind-to-body and ideodynamic responses (Hill & Rossi, 2017).

This idea can be applied to an understanding of pain. Pain is certainly a physiological experience, but it is also an emotional response. Pain can be very individual. The emotional aspect of pain may explain why pain exists sometimes when there is no physiological cause, or how a physiological cause is intensified by an emotional state. This model may be the key to understanding why pain can be relieved or even resolved with therapies that focus only on mentalizing. LeDoux and Brown (2017) summarize their intention in their conclusion:

> Fear can occur when the defensive survival circuit is damaged. Furthermore, existential fear/anxiety about the meaningless of life or the eventuality of death may not engage survival circuits at all. Our theory can thus potentially account for all forms of fear: those accompanied by brain arousal and bodily responses and those that are purely cognitive and even existential. Although we have focused on fear, we believe

that the basic principles involved can be leveraged to understand other emotions as well. (p. E2023)

Other theorists have presented concepts of basic, fundamental, and core emotions, as well as combinations of basic emotions. Cowen and Keltner (2017) from the University of California, Berkeley, used a self-reporting analysis to identify at least 27 distinct categories of emotion that have a continuous gradient between them. Thinking of emotions in the context of Ledoux and Brown's theory of higher order representations makes it easy to understand that there are fundamental responses, but once these initial responses begin to interact with semantic and autobiographical memory, there is a wide range of representations, and then representations of those representations, that become the complex array of an individual's emotional experience.

Case Conclusion

Does the preceding exploration of the theories and possibilities regarding emotions make it easier to resolve J. C.'s problem? J. C. was aware of her first-order representation, from which emerged some physical and behavioral responses, but she was unable to feel anything on a personal level. She seemed to lack the second higher order response. Does that mean that she was unable to connect her sense of self to the stimulus? After an exploration of the literature and inquiries of people with similar experiences, it seemed clear that in J. C.'s case, something at the neurobiological level could be interfering with her mental processing of emotional experiences. There is a condition that explains all her "symptoms": *alexithymia*, a developmental condition in which the neuronal connections between the limbic area and the prefrontal cortex are limited. J. C. was unable to have a second higher order response because she had not developed a relationship, either affectively and neurobiologically, with her sense of self. This realization helped J. C. understand why she suffered from the inability to feel her emotions. Equally, the therapist was able to think beyond the standard training for an affective disorder.

CLINICAL NOTES

Emotions are the most common issue that clients bring to the therapy room. The information here in Section 1.7 is not, in itself, a therapy, but is vital in helping you understand what the client is really dealing with, regardless of the particular technique or method you use. We hope this information will help you determine the most appropriate therapeutic approach. Understanding that emotions can be experienced on a number of levels is the key takeaway here. Appreciating the distinction between the sensations that a client knows are happening and those that the client actually feels is very useful, helping to direct the therapist's attention to which part or parts of the system are activated. Most clients experience higher order representations related to the self; in other words, emotions happen to *them*. Which part of their autobiographical memory is responding by creating the emotion they feel? Is it a past experience, a traumatic event, something that needs to be resolved, some aspect of development that needs attention, or some bias that has developed over time? In the case of J. C., there was a distinct dissociation from self. There were other possible avenues to explore: J. C. might have had a developmental emotional blockage, or she might have adopted a protective or suppressive persona in response to early-life adverse experiences. By paying attention to the information that her own system was providing, and assessing that information in the context of how emotions function, the therapist could go more directly to the core of the issue and avoid spending weeks on emotional-release protocols that would have had little or no positive effect.

CHAPTER 2

The Body

2.1 Brains in the Body

What Is a Brain, and Where Did It All Start?

When they hear "brain," most people think of the organ in the skull that has some 86 billion neurons and associated neural tissue. The skull-based brain (or head-brain) and spinal cord are referred to as the *central nervous system* (CNS). The *peripheral nervous system* (PNS) consists of the nerves that spread throughout the body from the spinal cord. The CNS and PNS create an information highway that sends messages *from* the head-brain (*efferent* messages) and *to* the head-brain (*afferent* messages). An unusual group of 12 (arguably 13) nerves emanates directly from the head-brain, but they are still classified as peripheral nerves.

The *cranial nerves* are a unique set of nerves that emerge from the brainstem (nerves III–XII) and the cerebrum (I and II). These peripheral nerves in the skull mostly convey information to the head and neck. The 10th cranial nerve (X), the vagus nerve, is unique in that it spreads throughout the body, transmitting information efferently (as part of the sympathetic nervous system) and afferently (as part of the parasympathetic nervous system) between most of the viscera (including the heart, lungs, and digestive system) and the head-brain (refer to Section 2.3). In addition, neural networks in the heart and the gut function autonomously, and the skin has a special relationship with the nerves that produces behaviors responsive to the inner and outer environment independent of the head-brain. How and when did these systems come to be?

Nerves

The Earth formed about 4.5 billion years ago. It is thought that RNA and DNA appeared some 4 billion years ago. The first cell (called the "last universal common ancestor," or LUCA; refer to Section 3.1) emerged when DNA became enclosed by a membrane, about 3.8 billion years ago (Xu et al., 2020). It was a long time before simple nerve nets first appeared, probably in the coelenterates, which included cnidarians and ctenophores, or what we now call "jellyfish." There is reasonable evidence that nerve nets came into being about 500–600 million years ago, and possibly as far back as 700 million years (Cartwright et al., 2007; Villegas et al., 2000). So, it took 700 million years for the first cell to emerge, and then another 3.5 billion years for multicelled organisms to reach a level of complexity that warranted the evolution of nerves as a survival advantage.

Nerves make it possible to transmit information rapidly, from one part of the organism to another, to trigger actions and reactions. Nerves also receive information from the outside environment that can be transmitted within the organism to enable necessary action, especially movement. Early movement was likely very basic, consisting of forms of movement either toward or away, which is still one of the fundamental parameters of our autonomic nervous system. The development and diversification of animals during the Cambrian explosion, which started some 540 million years ago, was a time of rapid evolution of the important organ systems, including the head-brain (Budd, 2015).

This timeline suggests that the head-brain is one of the most recent developments of evolving neural tissue in humans. Much of the evolutionary history of nerves and neurons is retained in human biology and continues to function in the body today. If you think of a brain as a collection of neuronlike nerves that can process information to control body functions such as motor functions, blood flow, mucosal transport, and secretions, and to modulate immune and endocrine functions, then the head-brain is not alone. Not only does the body contain several neural systems, but they are connected and communicate with one another for overall health and survival.

Gut-Brain (Second Brain): Enteric Nervous System

The *enteric nervous system* (*ENS*) is sometimes referred to as the "second brain." It regulates a variety of gastrointestinal functions and communicates bidirectionally with the CNS and PNS. The ENS is able to regulate gastrointestinal functions independently from the CNS. It determines the movements in the gastrointestinal tract and regulates processes that include gastric acid secretion, changes in blood flow, and hormone release. The immune system interacts directly with the ENS as a functioning component of gut health (Rao & Gershon, 2016).

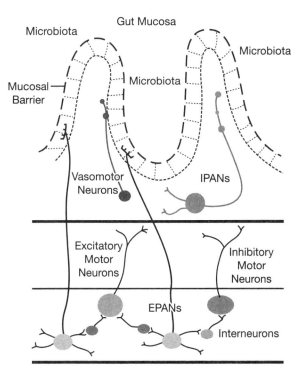

FIGURE 2.1: **Principle Neurons of the ENSn.** *Note.* EPANs = extrinsic primary afferent neurons; IPANs = intrinsic primary afferent neurons. *Adapted from Costa et al. (2000).*

The ENS contains between 200 and 600 million neurons (Figure 2.1), with 100 million neurons in the small intestine alone. Most of the neurotransmitters present in the CNS are also present in the ENS (Furness, 2006). Nearly 90% of the body's serotonin is produced in the digestive tract. In the body, serotonin stimulates muscle activity and is important for bowel activity and bladder control (Berger et al., 2009). The production of serotonin is stimulated by trillions of symbiotic bacteria (the microbiota) that are vital for a successfully functioning gut (De Vadder, 2018). Damage to the gut microbiota caused by bad diet, infections, and medications, including antibiotics, can result in an irritable bowel and other gut malfunctions. These gut malfunctions can lead directly to feelings of depression or anxiety (Clapp et al., 2017). Probiotics and bacteria-rich foods such as activated yogurt are intended to help restore a healthy gut "flora" (Liang et al., 2018).

The condition of the gut microbiota and the efficiency of the ENS are essential to a sense of well-being and are a part of the collection of body functions that help people feel OK or not OK (refer to Section 2.2 for discussion of the gut–brain axis). Damage to the ENS can be life-threatening, but low-level, chronic problems in the ENS affect digestive functions in a way that can cause a feeling of unwellness and create discomfort and pain that are difficult to diagnose. Many people experience depression because of chronic gut issues. Some suffer from a feeling of being unsafe, which can trigger anxiety and PTSD.

HOW DOES THE ENS "THINK"?

Conceptualizing the ENS as a brain that thinks in the same way as the head-brain is a misunderstanding of the nature of neural processes. The ENS cannot do calculus or decide which movie to see, although it can contribute an awareness of a person's biological "opinion" about such decisions. The main role of the ENS is to control digestion, from swallowing to the release of enzymes that break down food to the control of blood flow that helps with nutrient absorption and, finally, to elimination.

Jay Pasricha, MD, director of the Johns Hopkins Center for Neurogastroenterology, suggests that "for decades, researchers and doctors thought that anxiety and depression contributed to these problems. But our studies and others show that it may also be the other way around" (Johns Hopkins Medicine, n.d.). There is good evidence that irritation in the gastrointestinal system sends signals to the CNS that trigger mood changes (Valles-Colomer et al., 2019). Pasricha goes on to say, "The enteric nervous system doesn't seem capable of thought as we know it, but it communicates back and forth with our big brain—with profound results."

Heart-Brain (Little Brain): Intracardiac Nervous System

Heat functions, or cardiac functions, are responsive to the autonomic nervous system: Up-regulation triggered by the sympathetic nervous system and down-regulation triggered by the parasympathetic nervous system lead, respectively, to quickening and slowing of the heart in response to conditions at the time. The body up-regulates in response to threats, excitement, and anticipation; for example, the heart speeds up in response to something frightening, but also to a loved one. The heartbeat slows down during states of relaxation and calm—for example, while being mindful of something beautiful like a sunset, or when in the safe arms of a loved one. Heart rate is closely related to what is happening to a person or what emotion the person is feeling. It is not surprising that the heart is thought of synonymously with emotions. The heart is definitely more than just a beating pump.

Numerous functions within the heart are regulated by a local nervous system, the intracardiac nervous system (INS). This complex system consists of ganglionic plexuses and interconnecting ganglia. (A *nerve ganglion* is a group of nerve cells in the periphery, and a *plexus* is a branching network.) The INS regulates and modulates the information from the autonomic nervous system (Durães Campos et al., 2018). Pioneering neurocardiologist Dr. J. Andrew Armour (1991) was the first to describe this complex and intrinsic nervous system as a "heart-brain."

The heart-brain (Figure 2.2) is composed of approximately 40,000 neurons that are much like neurons in the brain. Dr. Armour (2008) describes it in more detail: "This 'little brain' on the heart is comprised of spatially distributed sensory (afferent), interconnecting (local circuit) and motor (adrenergic and cholinergic efferent) neurons that communicate with [other ganglionic nerves]" (p. 165). The vagus nerve carries information from the

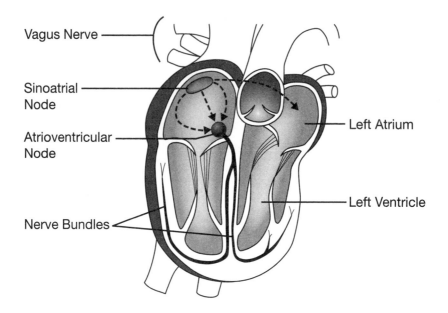

FIGURE 2.2: The Thinking Heart

heart to the brain. Signals from the heart-brain redirect to the medulla, hypo-thalamus, thalamus, amygdala, and cerebral cortex. There are more afferent signals from the heart to the brain than efferent from the brain to the heart, so it is reasonable to assume that these signals affect our mental processes. Ali Alshami (2019) suggests that afferent messages from the heart via the vagus nerve are involved in the cognitive and emotional regulation of pain. As with the ENS, the INS does not think in the same way as the head-brain. Some researchers allude to the heart's "wisdom" and refer to it as a source of emotion, but this is an overattribution. The heart certainly con-tributes considerable and influential input into cortical thinking processes, however, so it is appropriate to say that the state of the heart is important to a person's emotional state and mental well-being.

An example in which emotions affect the heart is *takotsubo cardiomyop-athy*, or "broken-heart syndrome" (Akashi et al., 2008). This temporary heart condition is a response to intense emotional or physical experiences; the heart's main pumping chamber changes shape, affecting the heart's ability

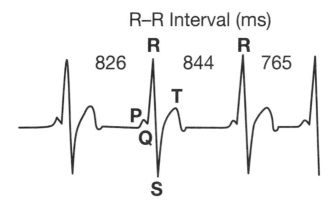

FIGURE 2.3: An ECG Trace Showing Differing R–R Intervals. The heartbeat cycle includes depolarization at P, main contraction and release of the large ventricular muscles at the QRS complex, and repolarization at T.

to pump blood effectively. Intense emotions overstimulate the sympathetic nervous system, which can lead to cardiac myofibrillar degeneration—heart muscle injury. Intense, or high-valence, heart stresses cause stronger behavioral, pain, and/or emotional responses, but low-impact events are less obvious. Heart attack victims have been shown to experience emotional changes several days *before* an attack (Lane & Godfrey, 2010).

An obvious message from the heart is an increase or decrease in heartbeat when there is no physical activity. A change of heart rate is important, but those beats convey a deeper message, beyond just faster or slower. Subtle differences in the amount of time between beats require a measurement tool such as an ECG. The variation between beats is called *heart rate variability* (*HRV*). HRV represents the change in the time interval between successive heartbeats, the R–R interval (refer to Figure 2.3; Laborde et al., 2017). The length of time between heartbeats varies. More variation indicates a healthier state. The subtle differences between pulses might be described as the heart's "thoughts," but HRV is a response to the state of health, not a "decision" that the heart makes.

It is not essential for a psychotherapist to know how to read an ECG, but it is interesting to note that the letters in Figure 2.3 refer to important events in the heartbeat cycle. The QRS complex represents the main contraction and release of the large ventricular muscles. There is a period of change in preparation for contraction at P, which is technically referred to as "depolarization," and then the period of "repolarization" around T, where the heart returns to relaxation before the next beat. The amplitudes and distances between these letters indicate a variety of potential heart problems. Learning how to regulate HRV can be very helpful as a therapy.

CLINICAL NOTES

One of the best-known organizations that not only conducts research but also develops practical programs to improve health through HRV regulation is HeartMath (McCraty, 2017). HeartMath's programs are designed to teach people how to self-regulate emotional states and levels of stress by regulating heart function through biofeedback. Positive emotions help to balance the autonomic nervous system and return the heart to harmonious and healthy rhythms (Shaffer et al., 2014). Vagal tone (which we explore in Section 2.3) is also very important in regulating HRV.

Brain in the Skin (Peripheral Nerves): Touch

The skin is the body's largest organ and the first and last contact between the internal and external environment. The skin shifts and changes in response to changes without and within, protecting the body, and reflecting activity within the body. The skin is involved in thermoregulation and participates in the defense against microorganisms (Slominski et al., 2007). It is not surprising that the skin reacts with observable changes to external insults such as burns, cuts and lacerations, toxic chemicals, and insect, animal, snake, or spider bites. The skin exhibits responses to internal change. When someone is ill or experiencing visceral dysfunction (e.g., liver or kidney maladies) or an allergic reaction (i.e., increase of histamines) or shock, or is emotionally charged, the skin can change color and tone and may break out into rashes or blisters. The skin can respond quickly to inner and outer environmental changes and emotional states, despite any willful desire to hide it (i.e., it is independent of cognitive control).

THE SKIN AS A MESSENGER

Facial blushing/flushing can indicate alcohol consumption, intake of spicy foods, gastric stimulation, dehydration, increased blood pressure, overexercise, social anxiety, self-consciousness, embarrassment, shyness, shame, anger, and romantic stimulation, as well as some serious diseases and neuroendocrine dysfunction (Drummond & Lance, 1997; Hannah-Shmouni et al., 2016). Goosebumps or hair standing on end (piloerection) can indicate cold, threat, preparation to attack, intense anxiety, fear, excitement, passion, awe (especially of music or beauty), opioid withdrawal, and ingestion of a variety of drugs (Benedek & Kaernbach, 2011; Keltner & Anderson, 2000). Reactions in the skin offer an abundance of information for a psychotherapist, but the many causes make it difficult to be sure of the specific message. Skin reactions are important not just because they indicate that something is affecting the client but also because they show how the client is managing the situation. Are they comfortable with what is causing the skin response? Are they resistant or deflective or in denial? Without any words being spoken, the skin assists the therapist to see beyond the cognitive talk.

Psychological distress can cause or aggravate multiple skin disorders. Psoriasis and atopic dermatitis are inflammatory skin diseases that are known to worsen with psychosocial stress. The presence or an outbreak of psoriasis is not to be ignored, because it is a strong indicator of life stress and emotional disruption (Sathyanarayana Rao et al., 2013). The brain and skin communicate via the peripheral nerves and the circulation of hormones and other products of the endocrine and immune systems in the blood (Figure 2.4; Chen & Lyga, 2014). The skin has a system that produces a chemistry similar to that of the HPA axis in the brain (refer to Section 1.2). Corticotropin-releasing hormone (CRH) is produced in the hypothalamus and transported to the pituitary gland, triggering the production of pro-opiomelanocortin (POMC) and then adrenocorticotropic hormone (ACTH), which is transported by blood to the adrenal cortex, on top of the kidneys, to stimulate the production of cortisol and epinephrine as a part of the sympathetic nervous system response to a stressful demand. The skin has also been found to be able to produce these hormones in response to stressful demand—similar to the HPA process (E. Lee et al., 2020). Andrzej Slominski (Slominski et al., 2012) showed that skin is able to independently regulate the peripheral response to stress and, in some acute conditions, activate adrenal and HPA activity (Nejati et al., 2013; Slominski et al., 2013).

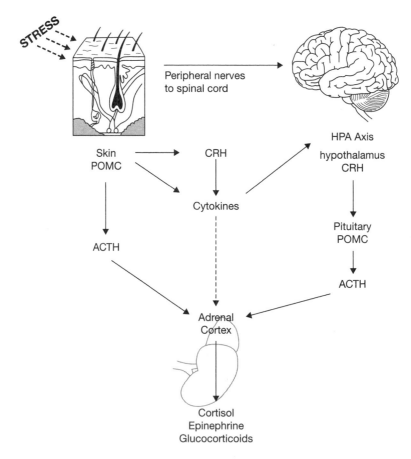

FIGURE 2.4: Mechanisms of the Skin-Brain. ACTH = adrenocorticotropic hormone; CRH = corticotropin-releasing hormone; HPA = hypothalamic–pituitary–adrenal; POMC = pro-opiomelanocortin.

Although what we just presented is a lot of technical information, it demonstrates that systems of the body, such as the HPA axis, are not contained or restricted to one area. The skin is able to respond without and/or before communication with the head-brain to independently regulate local systems and even influence nonlocal systemic functions. The skin is able to sense and respond to environmental factors including temperature, injuries, pH, UVB radiation, and humidity. The HPA analog is just one of the direct relationships that the skin has with other systems in the body that can be reflected in emotional shifts. More activities in the skin that are relevant to emotion and behavior include the following:

- The skin has genes that produce receptors for thyroid hormones (e.g., thyroid-stimulating hormone receptor). Thyroid dysfunction is marked by affective disorders, including anxiety and depression, and even psychosis in some people. The skin can indicate thyroid issues. Hyperthyroidism can cause warm and moist skin in response to increased temperature, diffuse nonscarring alopecia, and facial flushing. Hypothyroidism can cause coarse, rough, dry skin with a sickly pallor; nail damage; and some hair loss (Puri, 2012).
- Serotonin and melatonin are produced in the skin from L-tryptophan via enzymatic action of tryptophan hydroxylase, which is present in the skin. Seasonal affective disorder (SAD) is caused by reduced exposure to sunlight. The retina was thought to be the only light detection mechanism, but circulating serotonin and melatonin can be increased by exposing the skin to bright light (Sansone & Sansone, 2013).
- Vitamin D is a key factor in a host of vital biochemical processes, from calcium and bone metabolism to gene expression in brain function and development, and the regulation of SAD. The synthesis of vitamin D begins in the skin, with the interaction of ultraviolet rays and cutaneous chemicals, including cholesterol, to produce the first stage of vitamin D: vitamin D_3, or cholecalciferol. Healthy levels of vitamin D are essential for mental health (Sotodeh-Asl et al., 2014).

The skin can reveal much to assist in providing good therapy for a client (Dattola et al., 2020; Park, 2015). Attention to the health or ill health of the skin can be invaluable assistance in understanding clients. As with so many issues of mental and physical health, exercise, diet, and sleep are fundamental factors in skin health.

Skin–Gut–Heart–Brain Axis

Is it reasonable to suggest that there is an axis between each of the "brains" described in this chapter? It is clear that the types of activity that each brain is able to do, and needs to do, vary. To be considered a brain there must be a neural network that autonomously regulates local and nonlocal processes. The body is a complex and integrated system, so it is unsurprising that research has explored its connections and interactions: the gut–skin axis (Salem et al., 2018), the brain–skin connection (Paus et al., 2006), the gut–brain axis (Carabotti et al., 2015), the heart–brain axis (Tahsili-Fahadan & Geocadin, 2017), and the gut–brain–heart axis (Singh et al., 2018). Almost all of the potential combinations have been explored. One aspect that is common to all of the systems is that they affect psychological, emotional, and behavioral activity. How someone feels and behaves can indicate much more than what is happening in the head-brain. There is still so much to discover. That is what makes the field of psychotherapy so exciting.

CLINICAL NOTES

The existence of these "brains" within the body shows that the conversation between brain and body is more than just raw information from the various communicators, such as hormones, peptides, and neural impulses—that information coming from these body-brains exhibits some degree of discernment, albeit not the cognitive discernment that the head-brain is capable of. The messages of low HRV from the heart through the vagus nerve to the brain convey the heart's expression of not being well. The heart has already interpreted the information from the body as messages that there are problems and clarified that information into a simple message of low HRV. The brain is informed of the heart's "opinion" and can enhance it with other information coming from other sources in the blood and from spinal signaling. Equally, the enteric system sends the brain information that is an interpretation of the complex of activities in the gut. Tuning in to these conversations that manifest as emotion/feelings, behavior, and other responses requires sensitive observation from the therapist that is informed by knowledge, experience, and, where necessary, input from other brains (colleagues) through consultation and referral.

2.2 Gut–Brain Axis

Sarah was tired; that was obvious. She was also depressed, anxious, and overweight. A self-confessed "comfort eater," Sarah had been on a downward spiral for months now, living on junk food and Netflix, after losing her job 6 months earlier. She missed not only her work but her network of social connections in the office. Life was miserable, except for those moments of enjoying a burger and Coke or some scene on a Netflix series that momentarily pulled her out of her depressed stupor. She seemed to be battling viral infections continually and had been taking back-to-back courses of antibiotics. Clearly, a lot of work was needed for Sarah to climb out of this dark place.

Someone who is continually fatigued, overweight, anxious, depressed, and afflicted by irritable bowel is likely to be systemically inflamed. The immediate concerns in Sarah's case were her diet and the state of her gut, particularly the millions of resident bacteria that play a vital role in her health. The gut–brain axis is a two-way line of communication between neural, hormonal, and immune systems that rely on healthy gut bacteria. One of the paths of least resistance, at least in this very early stage of therapy, would be for a naturopath to run tests on the state of Sarah's gut. If her gut could be cleaned up so that happy, "good" bacteria could flourish again in her intestinal tract, then one important aspect of her depressed and anxious state would be taken care of, making it easier to deal with some other vital elements.

The Guest That Lives Within

No human is alone. The human body is itself an extremely diverse ecosystem of trillions of bacteria and other microorganisms that live on and in each individual, especially in the intestines (Montiel-Castro et al., 2013). It is a two-way, symbiotic relationship that keeps people healthy, both physically and mentally.

Sarah's case is a classic example of the psychotherapist dealing with an important element in a complex system that was probably not covered in the coursework for a psychology or counseling degree. It is not that therapists need to be naturopaths or bacteria experts, but gut health is another "attractor" or possibly "disruptor" or point of influence in the wider complex system (refer to the Introduction), that can have both linear and nonlinear effects on a client's mental well-being. We have had clients for whom treating the gut had transformative effects on their mental well-being, and others for whom the effects were nominal at best. At the very least, therapists need to be aware that gut health is a significant variable and that clients can be educated and referred to specialists to explore just how much this variable is affecting their mental well-being.

The *microbiome–gut–brain axis* is a bidirectional communication pathway between the gut and the CNS that is significantly influenced by the microorganisms that symbiotically live in the gut. The body is host to an enormous population of these microorganisms, collectively called "microbiota" or "microflora," with the genomes in the microbiota termed the *microbiome*. These gut microbes outnumber the cells in the body by a factor of 10, contain 150 times more genes than the body's own cells have (S. R. Gill et al., 2006; Qin et al., 2010; Theoharides, 2015), and comprise more than 1,000 species (Qin et al., 2010; Relman, 2012) and over 7,000 strains (Ley et al., 2006). A growing body of research implicates the gut microbiome in the regulation of the CNS and behavior in general, while the CNS affects microbiota development and composition; it is a bidirectional communication network (Mawe & Hoffman, 2013; Mayer, 2011; Rhee et al., 2009).

The gut's own nervous system—the ENS, or "second brain" (Gershon, 1998; refer to Section 2.1)—is an extensive neural network containing more neurons than are found in either the spinal cord or the PNS (Furness, 2012). The ENS does not act alone; rather it acts in concert with the microbes inhabiting the gut. The microbiota has only recently been genetically catalogued (Human Microbiome Project Consortium, 2012) and shown to have a major influence on the nervous system.

The microbiota colonizes the large intestine shortly after birth and plays a significant role in the development of the endocrine and immune systems, which in turn influence the CNS (Clarke et al., 2013; Cryan & O'Mahony, 2011). There is also a more direct influence on brain development, via messaging through the vagus nerve by gut microbes affecting brain-derived neurotrophic factor (Bercik et al., 2011), GABA receptors (Bravo et al., 2011), and basic neurogenerative processes (Sharon et al., 2016).

How Does the Microbiome Influence the CNS?

The gut microbiome influences the CNS in several ways: through hormones via the circulatory system, through the vagus nerve via the nervous system (Bravo et al., 2011; Cryan & O'Mahony, 2011), and through neurotransmitter modulation such as elevating plasma tryptophan, a precursor to serotonin (Desbonnet et al., 2008). The lymphatic system may also be a channel for gut–brain communication (Monteiro-Haig, 2017a).

Just as gut microbes can influence the CNS, the CNS can change gastrointestinal motility, secretion, and intestinal permeability—actions that alter the gut environment for resident bacteria (Rhee et al., 2009). Stress can induce permeability of the gut, allowing bacteria to cross the epithelial barrier, which, in turn, trigger a mucosal immune response that changes the composition of the microbiome and exacerbates the immune system's inflammatory processes (Kiliaan et al., 1998). Stress-induced circulating cortisol directly affects the microbiome. It is very much a complex dance.

Figure 2.5 shows the direct and indirect pathways of communication from the gut microbiota to the CNS:

1. The immune system pathway shows immune cells monitoring the gut lumen and releasing cytokines in response to microbe activity. The cytokines travel via the bloodstream to the brain (the CNS), where they trigger activity in the brain's immune system, the microglial cells.

2. Vagus nerve sensory terminals at the gut are stimulated by microbe-activated neurotransmitters such as serotonin. This stimulation may alter activity in the hypothalamus and the HPA axis. As increased stress generates more cortisol, protective bacteria are challenged, and invasive bacteria exacerbate symptoms like anxiety (Dinan & Cryan, 2012). Taking probiotics has been shown to reverse anxiety-like symptoms in animal research (Stilling et al., 2014).

3. Neuroactive compounds and precursors to neurotransmitters, initiated by the microbiome (such as neuropeptides released from the gut epithelium) and entering the bloodstream, may directly influence the CNS.

The microbial content of the gut is critical to normal development of the HPA axis, brain-derived neurotrophic factor (a key neurotrophin involved in neuronal growth), and the expression of NMDA receptors in the cortex and hippocampus (Sudo et al., 2004). A number of studies have investigated changes in gene expression in the brains of "germ-free" mice—mice raised in a particular way that significantly reduced their gut microbiota. Researchers found decreased hippocampal expression of brain-derived neurotrophic factor, which is important for brain plasticity, and alterations in normal neurotransmitter signaling (Mayer et al., 2014). In other words, the "bugs" in our gut matter—a lot!

Apart from defending the body from infection, the immune system can have a big impact on mental well-being when it comes to inflammation. Eighty percent of the immune system is in the gut (gut-associated lymphoid tissue) alongside the body's symbiotic friends the microbiome (Lazar et al., 2018). Figure 2.5 shows how gut microbes can stimulate the immune system to produce cytokines that can travel to the brain via the circulatory system, cross the blood–brain barrier, and activate the brain's immune cells and

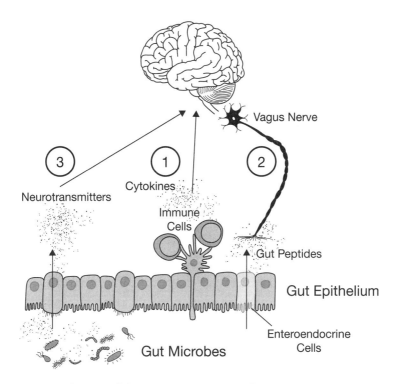

FIGURE 2.5: Pathways of Communication From Gut to Brain. *Adapted from Montiel-Castro et al. (2013).*

glial cells. The result is a negative effect on mental and emotional state, as well as problematic implications for autoimmune disorders. In addition, lipopolysaccharides on the surface of microbes can cause inflammation and a condition known as *leaky gut*, in which increased permeability of the gut allows lipopolysaccharides into the bloodstream, causing systemic inflammation. It is a negative feedback loop that generates symptoms that send some clients to a medical practitioner and others to a psychotherapist. The client is probably in need of help from both.

CLINICAL NOTES

Different foods have a big impact on the gut microbiome, but it would be an error to look at these things in isolation. For example, cheese increases bifidobacteria (Sabikhi et al., 2014), which can have positive effects for the host through their metabolic activity, but it can decrease *Bacteroides* and *Clostridium* species of bacteria, which are protective against intestinal infections (Lopetuso et al., 2013). Being a dairy product, however, cheese is also commonly inflammatory for many people, and the negative effects of an inflammatory response by the immune system can typically outweigh the positive effects of microbiome population changes. A nutritional expert could be useful for some clients.

Psychopathology and the Microbiome

AUTISM AND THE GUT–BRAIN AXIS

The constitution of the newborn's gut microbiota contributes to early brain development and behavior. In individuals with autism, studies have found much higher counts of microbes that produce neurotoxins than in healthy controls (El-Ansary et al., 2013). Microbes, such as *Clostridium*, that produce neurotoxins could be implicated in the development of autistic behavior. There has also been a growing interest in dietary factors that may improve or worsen autistic symptoms, with particular focus on clostridial species of bacteria, given that they are elevated in patients with autism (Finegold, 2011). Also common with ASD are gastrointestinal disorders such as leaky gut, alterations in gut motility, digestion and absorption problems (White, 2003), and the onset of ASD symptoms following long-term antibiotic use and hospitalization (Atladóttir, Thorsen, Østergaard, Schendel, et al., 2010; Atladóttir, Thorsen, Schendel, Østergaard, et al., 2010). These observations suggest that alteration of the gut microbiome by diet or antibiotics may affect brain function in autism.

Propionic acid has been shown to induce autistic features in animals (El-Ansary et al., 2012), and it is produced by many intestinal bacteria as they break down carbohydrates and amino acids (Haskå et al., 2011). Some parents report that their children's autistic symptoms increase with a diet high in carbohydrates or foods containing propionic acid as a preservative

(Horvath et al., 1999). Researchers have been exploring the benefits of diet modification on behavior and affect. Ryan Lee et al. (2018) found that a low-carbohydrate, moderate-protein, high-fat diet was helpful in reducing imitation behaviors, as well as fear and nervousness. Repetitive behaviors showed very little change, and some of the children had only minor improvements, but these studies open a positive door to the use of diet and being mindful of the health of the gut to improve the lives of ASD patients and their families. In another very different approach to modifying the gut microbiome in ASD patients, researchers used fecal transplantation. They found a statistically significant change in ASD symptoms that persisted through to an 8-week follow-up (D. Kang et al., 2017).

CLINICAL NOTES

We are not suggesting that psychotherapists dabble in microbiome modification of ASD clients. It is possible, however, for a psychotherapist to be the only practitioner involved, because the symptoms are largely emotional or behavioral. Knowing about the science of these body-to-brain communications and interactions can only help to support reasonable concerns and enable informed recommendations and referrals.

DEPRESSION AND ANXIETY

A number of studies have found microbiota differences between depressed patients and healthy controls (Groen et al., 2018). Essentially, the families of microbiota that promote wellness are underrepresented, and microbes that can produce negative effects are overrepresented. There is a significant association between the presence and balance of various microbes in the gut and depressive symptoms, but that is not the full story. Given that humans are complex systems and the gut–brain axis is a two-way street, both depression and anxiety disorders involve a multitude of mental and physiological variables. Studies tracking the makeup of the microbiome in patients with depressive disorder and their symptoms come up with rather inconsistent results. There are microbiome changes that correlate with changing symptoms, but individual variability and differences in the studies probably account for the lack of clarity. Diet is a feature of major depression (increased appetite/weight for atypical depression, and decreased appetite/weight for melancholic depression) and may play a role in modification of the gut microbiome (Groen et al., 2018), and feedback can perpetuate the depression.

Changes in the motility of the colon are also a feature of depression and anxiety, and these changes can alter the composition and stability of gut microbiota with ripple effects through the microbiome–gut–brain axis (Lach et al., 2018). Anxiety symptoms such as stomach cramps and diarrhea affect the gut's microbiome in such a way that they are likely to have a nonlinear influence on the CNS.

Antidepressants such as SSRIs can also have an impact on gut microbiota, demonstrating an antimicrobial activity and even increasing the activity of some antibiotics (Munoz-Bellido et al., 2000). While we are on the topic of antidepressants, note that tryptophan (the precursor to serotonin) is not only obtained by diet, but also synthesized by gut microbes: Gut microbiota have been shown to influence the serotonergic system via their effect on tryptophan metabolism and serotonin production, with implications for both CNS and ENS function (O'Mahony et al., 2015). Certain strains of microbiota (e.g., *Bifidobacterium infantis* 35624) have been demonstrated to positively affect tryptophan metabolism and availability via inhibition of inflammatory pathways that trigger the enzymes involved in the kynurenine pathway (Desbonnet et al., 2010). Subsequent positive impacts include improved availability and modulation of serotonin in the prefrontal cortex, which is associated with positive influences on mood (Albert et al., 2014; Desbonnet et al., 2008).

There is still a long way to go in understanding the very complex interactions between antidepressant drugs and the microbiome, as well as the resulting impact on the CNS and, ultimately, mental wellness. The deeper we dive into the nonlinear complex system that humans are, and add a trillion other little living things into the mix, the more daunting the task to understand cause and effect becomes.

Sarah did go to a naturopath as her therapist suggested, and she got feedback before the next therapy session. As had been suspected, she was chronically and systemically inflamed. The naturopath explained how Sarah's leaky gut was allowing inflammatory elements into her bloodstream that were affecting her brain and the rest of her body. The broad-spectrum antibiotics she had been taking had likely damaged a significant amount of her microbiota, and she was now on a schedule of pre- and probiotics to bring back a state of *eubiosis* (microbial balance). Sarah was put on a program to heal her gut and nurture the healthy microbiome that is able to decrease inflammation. In addition, the standard lifestyle changes of diet, exercise, meditation, relaxation, and sleep hygiene—all of which play a vital role in the health of symbiotic "gut bugs"—were recommended.

Sarah was in therapy for only a few months, but long enough for her therapist to see that she was motivated to improve her health, was less depressed and anxious, was losing weight, and was actively looking for another job. She was not back to 100%, but she was on the right trajectory and felt that her engagement with the local gym, and an occasional visit to the naturopath, were priorities for her. She would be OK.

CLINICAL NOTES

Gut health and the microbiota can play a significant role not only in general well-being but in mental health. As a clinician, the therapist should consider the client's gut health and refer the client to a specialist (a naturopath, functional medicine doctor, or nutritionist) if the health of a client's gut–brain axis is in question. This case is another reminder of the value of immediately "prescribing" changes in the lifestyle activities of sleep, diet, and exercise. More work than just lifestyle adjustments is often needed, but they can facilitate beneficial change and can be recommended immediately.

2.3 Vagus Nerve

One of the fundamental principles in the self-organizing process of human biology is the need for safety. Human biology is fiercely devoted to avoiding, minimizing, and repairing any harm that might be encountered. Although it is beyond the scope of this chapter, there is an argument that, despite the general rejection of Cartesian duality and reductionism, there is still an academic and cultural remnant that separates biology from psychology. The brain continues to be discussed as if it were something distinct from the body, and vice versa. It is helpful to differentiate elements of a system to explore details, as we are doing in this book, but in life, everything is inextricably connected and dynamically relevant.

Having reaffirmed the connectivity and relevance of everything, let us explore the vagus nerve, which provides clear evidence that the body and the brain are connected and communicate. We will explore how an understanding of the vagus nerve can improve the effectiveness of the psychotherapist's professional practice. Stephen Porges is one of the leading lights in seeking to understand the finer details of the functions of the vagus nerve. His polyvagal theory (Porges, 1995) has changed people's understanding and appreciation of the "wandering" nerve. We will explore those ideas and discoveries in the latter half of this chapter, but first let us look at the vagus nerve as if polyvagal theory were not yet created.

The vagus nerve is the 10th (X) and longest of the cranial nerves. It plays a significant role in the activity of the parasympathetic nervous system and is integral to both maintaining and retuning the body to a state of safety and social engagement (Berthoud & Neuhuber, 2000). To understand the vagus nerve requires a clear understanding of the autonomic nervous system. Many readers will already be familiar with this complex system, but we want to be sure the picture is clear.

Autonomic Nervous System

The body's rapid-response survival system is the autonomic nervous system (ANS), which is divided into two branches: the sympathetic nervous system and the parasympathetic nervous system (Waxenbaum et al., 2020). The sympathetic branch mobilizes the body to defend against danger, aggravations, and irritants, whether real or imagined (as experienced in PTSD). It is elemental in the fight-or-flight response. The choice of fight or flight is conditioned on which option gives the greatest chance of survival or a future advantage. In most animal groups, the alpha male may need to fight to maintain order, superior position, and access to females for reproduction. Human culture is more complicated, but the fundamentals are similar. The efferent sympathetic nerves convey information from the head-brain through the spinal column, where connections to peripheral sympathetic nerves are made at spinal ganglia (clusters of nerve cells along the spinal

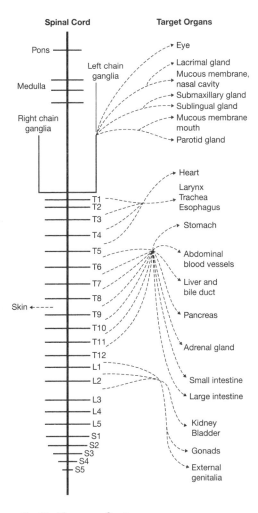

FIGURE 2.6: Sympathetic Nervous System

column). The long postsynaptic, or postganglionic, nerves reach out to the relevant organs of the viscera to innervate a sympathetic response. The sympathetic nervous system is referred to as the *thoracolumbar outflow*. The primary neurotransmitter at sympathetic nerve endings is norepinephrine (noradrenaline).

Sympathetic impulses speed up the heart, activate the production of epinephrine (adrenaline), shut down digestive processes, up-regulate activity in the immune system to prepare for injury, turn off the production of insulin so that glucose is available to energize muscles, and turn down activity in the salivary glands. That is why the prospect of making a public presentation often causes a dry mouth, shaky legs, a flushed face, and the urge to throw up. There is more, but that is a snapshot. As Figure 2.6 shows, the sympathetic nervous system transmits stimuli from the eyes to the genitals in a rapid distribution from the spinal column.

The parasympathetic nervous system is often thought of as a simple system that helps return the body to calm, although it is more than just that. The parasympathetic nervous system is referred to as the *craniosacral outflow* because it is composed largely of cranial nerves III, VII, IX, and X, plus the sacral, pelvic splanchnic nerves at S2–S4 at the base of the spinal column. As Figure 2.7 shows, the cranial nerves extend out, creating a synaptic connection with the specific target organ.

The parasympathetic cranial nerves are the oculomotor nerve (III), which innervates the eyes; the facial nerve (VII), which innervates the lacrimal gland, the salivary glands, and the mucous membranes of the nasal cavity; the glossopharyngeal nerve (IX), which innervates the parotid (salivary) gland; and the vagus nerve (X), which innervates the viscera of the thorax and the abdomen, including the heart, lungs, stomach, pancreas, small intestine, upper half of the large intestine, and liver. The sacral nerves innervate the kidney, bladder, lower bowel, and penis. The vagus nerve stands out among the group. It is the longest of the cranial nerves; has the widest distribution throughout the throat, neck, and abdomen; and links the gut-brain, heart-brain, and head-brain. These unique qualities warrant special investigation.

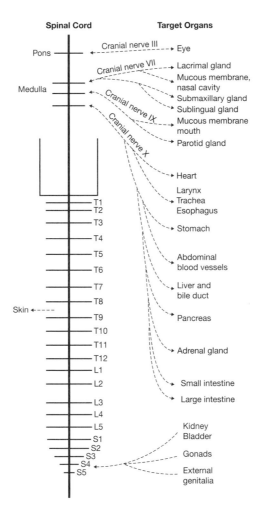

FIGURE 2.7: Parasympathetic Nervous System

Vagus Nerve Structure and Function

The vagus nerve emerges from the lower part of the brainstem (medulla oblongata) and leaves at the base of the skull (jugular foramen), passing close to the jugular, and then extends throughout the abdomen (Monkhouse, 2006). Efferent information (*from* the brain) is conveyed through the vagus nerve more extensively than through any other single nerve. Afferent information (*to* the brain) is also conducted via the vagus nerve (Berthoud

& Neuhuber, 2000). It is an important two-way street that, according to Julian Thayer (2007),

- affects the movement of muscles in the pharynx, soft palate, and larynx, as well as in the tongue, playing a critical role in the control of speaking and swallowing;
- carries sensory information about pain, touch, and temperature from the throat parts of the inner and outer ear and the meninges near the back of the head;
- receives sensory information from internal organs in the neck, chest, and abdomen such as the esophagus, heart, and digestive tract;
- carries sensory information from both baroreceptors in the aorta, which detect changes in blood pressure, and chemoreceptors in the aorta, which sense oxygen levels in the blood;
- prevents inflammation by detecting the presence of inflammatory cytokines, alerting the head-brain to release anti-inflammatory responses;
- helps make memories by stimulating the transfer of the neurotransmitter norepinephrine to the amygdala, which improves the consolidation of memories;
- assists breathing by releasing the neurotransmitter acetylcholine (equally, breathing practices can stimulate and improve vagus nerve function);
- controls heart rate via electrical impulses to the heart's natural pacemaker in the right atrium; and
- initiates the body's relaxation response by releasing acetylcholine to calm muscle activity and stimulating the release of enzymes and proteins such as prolactin, vasopressin, and oxytocin, to reestablish social engagement.

Vagus Damage

The vagus nerve can be damaged by some diseases, including diabetes and alcoholism. Abdominal surgery can result in unintentional damage, as can tumor growths and their subsequent removal. Temporary dysfunction can be caused by pressure on the neck from something like a tight shirt collar or jewelry, and sometimes just by the head turning rapidly, which can cause compression of the vagus nerve. Damage to the vagus nerve can be experienced in the throat as hoarseness of the voice, difficulty swallowing, and a deficient gag reflex; and it can produce gastrointestinal symptoms such as nausea, bloating, diarrhea, and gastroparesis (in which the stomach empties too slowly; Erman et al., 2009).

Vasovagal Syncope

Overstimulation of the vagus nerve is a common cause of fainting. Trembling or getting queasy at the sight of blood or while getting a flu shot can be a *vasovagal syncope* (Fenton et al., 2000). Other common triggers include standing for long periods of time; heat exposure; fear of bodily injury; and straining, such as to have a bowel movement or to lift a heavy weight. Early signs or symptoms of vasovagal syncope include light-headedness; nausea; the feeling of being extremely hot or cold (accompanied by sweating); ringing in the ears; an uncomfortable feeling in the heart; fuzzy thoughts; confusion; a slight inability to speak or form words (sometimes combined with mild stuttering); fuzzy or tunnel vision; black, cloudlike spots in vision; and a feeling of nervousness. The symptoms may become more intense over several seconds to several minutes before loss of consciousness (if that happens).

The problem is a stress-based *over*stimulation of the vagus nerve. The normal parasympathetic response lowers blood pressure and slows the heart rate, but when the parasympathetic response is overactive and sympathetic activity is reduced or inactive, the syncope will escalate. During extreme syncope, consciousness can be lost as blood flow is restricted to the brain. The first-aid response is to lay the person down with feet above the head to increase blood flow to the head.

Fainting, or syncope, has other causes that are worth noting because it is not unknown for someone to experience syncope during a therapy session. *Postural orthostatic hypotension* (Fedorowski, 2019) is a sudden loss of blood pressure when standing up quickly, especially after sitting for long periods in a bent-over position compressing the abdomen. *Postprandial hypotension*

(Trahair et al., 2014) is light-headedness after a meal, especially if it is a large meal with a lot of carbohydrates.

Polyvagal Theory

Stephen Porges developed the polyvagal theory (Porges, 1995) as he tried to understand and explain what struck him as a *vagal paradox*: that parasympathetic activity of the vagus nerve can create a healthy cardiac vagal tone (Junichiro & Fumihiko, 2003) *and* a bradycardia (an abnormal slowing of the heart rate to less than 60 beats per minute). Bradycardia can lead to vasovagal syncope (Porges, 2009). The question of how vagal mechanisms could mediate both healthy vagal tone and bradycardia was important because one is protective and the other is potentially lethal. Porges published a paper in 1992

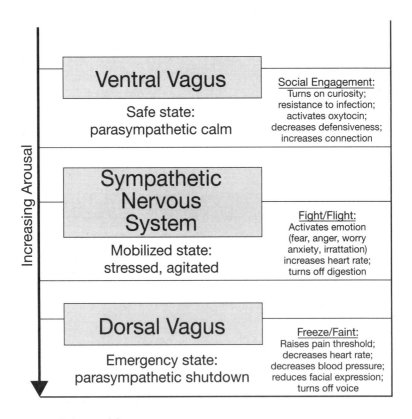

FIGURE 2.8: Polyvagal System

that looked at vagal tone as a biomarker of stress vulnerability. He continued to research and determined that the answer was in the evolutionary history of the development of the ANS. He concluded that the vagus nerve has two branches (Figure 2.8). The phylogenetically younger branch (the ventral vagus) emerges from the nucleus ambiguus and is myelinated; the older branch (the dorsal vagus) emerges in the dorsal motor nucleus and is unmyelinated. This distinction implicates a three-tiered system in the ANS that operates in a phylogenetic hierarchy—the lower tier activating only when the higher tier ceases to be active—in response to the presence or absence of danger.

Alternative Arguments

Before we describe the concepts and application of the polyvagal theory in greater detail, it is important to note that the theory is not without criticism or argument. There is some consensus that the ANS response has three tiers and that the vagus is a key element in the mechanisms that produce those states. Some researchers disagree, however, with the theory's position that the ventral vagus is solely a mammalian evolutionary development (Grossman & Taylor, 2007; Monteiro et al., 2018). Strong evidence suggests that the myelinated ventral preganglionic nerve fibers can be found in some reptiles, birds, and fish (Farmer et al., 2016; Hayano & Yuda, 2019; Junichiro & Fumihiko, 2003), and there are doubts about the size of the connection between vagal tone and emotional states, or vagal tone and psychopathology (Beauchaine et al., 2019).

We encourage you to explore arguments related to any theory or supposition. It can be confusing to consider lots of opposing arguments, but it is to the benefit of anyone seeking knowledge to look for disagreements, because they offer the possibility that a resolving idea is lurking somewhere between the opposing viewpoints.

Scanning the Environment for Threats and Safety—Neuroception

Stephen Porges coined the term "neuroception" (Porges, 2004) to describe the nonconscious neural processes that assess the environment for safety, danger, and especially anything life-threatening. It is well established that there is a 400- to 600-millisecond time lapse between neural activity and conscious response (Lamy et al., 2009). This preconscious reactive period, called a *reflexive response*, is evolutionarily advantageous because it stimulates instant activity *before* there is conscious thought about the situation. A number of important neurological processes are component elements of neuroception.

One example is mirror neurons, which react automatically to the movements of others, triggering reflexive behavioral and emotional responses. Most people have experienced feeling uneasy about someone or a situation without really knowing why. The colloquial phrase "gut feeling" is from stimulation by the vagus nerve (Bonaz et al., 2018). Another example is the ability to nonconsciously determine that a face is familiar. The fusiform face area, which is located in the inferior temporal cortex (the underside of the brain) close to the visual cortex and connects to the limbic area, produces an emotional reaction to facial familiarity. Memories in the amygdala of past traumatic events can trigger a strong defensive reaction to an unfamiliar face or to a face that has characteristics of a face in fearful memory (Fenker et al., 2005). PTSD is a neuroceptive response to the environment in relation to implicit memories encoded in various neural areas, including the amygdala and basal ganglia (Fenster et al., 2018). Another influence on neuroception is attachment, which can produce strong reactions to social situations, relational situations, and family situations (Brumariu & Kerns, 2008; Cummings et al., 2015). Social anxieties, fear of speaking in public, and distrust of authority figures are just a few examples of involuntary reactions that are the result of stimulation of the ANS in response to neuroceptive mechanisms (Bertsou, 2019; Brook & Schmidt, 2008; C. D. Smith et al., 2005).

Neuroception triggers the sympathetic nervous system when there is danger, and the parasympathetic nervous system when the danger has passed. As examples, Porges describes the behavior of a baby who coos at a caregiver but cries at a stranger, and of a toddler who enjoys a parent's embrace but views a hug from a stranger as an assault (Porges, 2011). A frightened person prepares for danger with defensive behaviors. When the environment is safe and people in the environment are trustworthy, these mechanisms of defense are deactivated, and behaviors that encourage social engagement and positive attachment are possible. These responses are activated through changes in vagal tone.

Vagal Tone

The quantity and quality of activity in the vagus nerve are termed *vagal tone*. Increased (higher) vagal tone is better for health and well-being. Vagal tone is marked by a lower heart rate and a improving the ability of the heart to respond to availability of oxygen. Two measures of the heart indicate higher vagal tone: heart rate variability (HRV) and respiratory sinus arrhythmia. We discussed HRV in Section 2.1 in relation to the heart-brain—the variation in the R–R interval as seen in an ECG (refer to Figure 2.3).

Another variation is the difference between heartbeats during an inward breath versus during an outward breath. This difference is called a *respiratory sinus arrhythmia* (RSA), and it is also visible in an ECG. The RSA (Figure 2.9) is an efficiency mechanism that speeds up the heart a little when there is increased oxygen (inward breath) and slows it when there is less oxygen (outward breath). "Arrhythmia" is a general term for an alteration of the rate and regularity of heartbeat. When the heart is beating too fast (more than 100 beats per minute), the condition is described as *tachycardia*; when it is slow (less than 60 beats per minute), *bradycardia*. An arrhythmia can be dangerous when associated with a serious heart condition, but the term "RSA" means simply an irregular heartbeat in relation to respiration. The "S" (for "sinus") comes from the name for the small bundle of cells at the top of the right atrium, called the *sinoatrial node* (refer to Figure 2.2), that initiates the

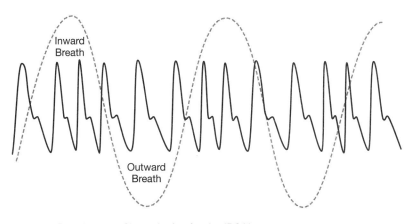

FIGURE 2.9: Respiratory Sinus Arrhythmia (RSA)

electrical impulse to stimulate a heart contraction (Kashou et al., 2019). The vagus nerve directly affects heart rate by stimulating or calming the sinoatrial node. That is one of the reasons why vagal tone is so important.

A positive HRV and RSA indicate not only vagal tone and good heart health but also positive emotional states, social engagement (Fredrickson, 2013a), and improved cognitive performance (Alba et al., 2019). Barbara Fredrickson (2013b) showed that the quality of vagal tone improved during a 6-week program of warmth and kindness experiences between participants and toward the self. This experiment showed two important things: first, that vagal tone is not fixed and, like brain plasticity, can alter in relation to experience; second, that vagal tone can be increased through caring social experience.

Restoring Vagal Tone: The Vagal Brake

Activating the ventral vagus is like controlling a "vagal brake" that can be applied or released to restore positive vagal tone and return to the social-engagement tier of the polyvagal complex. It is possible to voluntarily improve HRV and return the psychobiological state to the social-engagement tier (Laborde et al., 2017). The vagal brake can be activated in a number of ways. The following simple activities help restore vagal tone, reducing the extent to which an individual becomes or remains anxious or overwhelmed.

- **breathing techniques:**

    - **coherent rhythm:** Breathe slowly and regularly with a breath pattern of 5 seconds inward and 5 seconds outward. This technique helps generate a coherent heart rhythm and a shift from stressful emotional states.
    - **deep, slow diaphragmatic breathing:** Inhale deeply, paying attention to fully expanding the abdomen 360 degrees. Take a slow breath in and then a slower breath out. It may feel more comfortable to start with a tempo of 3 seconds in and 3 seconds out, then begin to lengthen both the exhalation and the inhalation. The slower the exhale, the more the vagus nerve is stimulated toward a relaxation response.

- **chanting, singing, humming:** The vagus nerve is connected to the vocal cords and the muscles at the back of the throat. Singing, humming, chanting, and even gargling can activate these muscles to stimulate the vagus nerve. Music produces positive mood, and singing requires a long outward breath. There are many opportunities to strengthen vagal tone through music, vocalization, and breath (Vickhoff et al., 2013).
- **exercise:** Moderate physical exercise avoids overstimulation of heart rate while innervating the lungs, throat, and diaphragm. Natural parasympathetic activity slows the heart and turns on the ventral vagal complex. Doing moderate exercise with others can also activate social engagement (Nagai et al., 2004).
- **socializing and laughter:** States of anxiety or a flat affect turn off the desire to socialize or laugh, but that is exactly when it is needed most. Activities can be as simple as dining with trusted people and, ideally, telling stories; or watching a comedian or something funny that stimulates the muscles of the face, the pharynx, and breathing (Kok et al., 2013).
- **ear massage:** The auricular branch of the vagus nerve extends to the lobes of the ear and the scalp just behind the ear. Using the fingers for massage creates a mild vagal response. Use of a TENS (transcutaneous electrical nerve stimulation) machine can amplify the response, showing benefits for blood pressure, mood, and sleep (Bretherton et al., 2019).

CLINICAL NOTES

The vagus nerve is an important connector and communicator between body and brain. More than that, it is a way of consciously and voluntarily altering the workings of vital organs, including the heart, lungs, and gut. The vagus creates an interplay with almost all of the viscera and even the skin. If this chapter conveys only one thing, then we hope it is the realization that all people are connected and seek connection in so many ways. The vagus is the "wandering" nerve for everyone's benefit. Make the most of it!

2.4 Biofeedback

In a complex system such as a human being, the process of feedback is fundamental to operation of the system. In *feedback*, the output of a system (or subsystems) is sent back as input. For example, singers can hear if they are slightly out of tune and can subtly correct their pitch. Feedback is everywhere, from adjusting hormones in the circulation, to balancing on two feet, to quickly modifying a business presentation after noticing the worried look on the boss's face. A therapist is tasked with monitoring a multitude of cues from clients as feedback about the effectiveness of the session. Feedback is not only useful; it is an imperative. It can be done consciously, but it also occurs nonconsciously in the many systems that operate simultaneously in day-to-day life.

In this section we will consider some deliberate uses of feedback to capitalize on the natural tendency for the body to shift from a rigid or chaotic state to a more regulated and flexible state, if given the right feedback. Feedback from one's own body is called *biofeedback*.

From ancient Hindu practices to modern uses of EEG, humans have been on a quest to control or heal the body through biofeedback for a long time. Broadly speaking, the idea is to consciously try to change the signals that the body produces (heart rate variability, brain wave activity, muscle tone, etc.) and alter the output of the system—for example, eliciting more brain waves at a certain frequency in certain areas of the brain to bring about greater regulation and flexibility.

There are mixed conclusions about the efficacy of biofeedback in general. A recent systematic review on biofeedback and neurofeedback for anxiety concluded that it was not superior to other treatment conditions and could not be distinguished from other nonspecific effects of treatment (Tolin et al., 2020). Another systematic review specifically looking at "biofeedback interventions for addressing anxiety and depression in children and adolescents with long-term physical conditions" did conclude that bio-feedback methods were effective (Thabrew et al., 2018). Researchers have found biofeedback to be effective in treating back pain (Sielski et al., 2017), as well as depression and PTSD (Blasé et al., 2016), and OCD (Ferreira et al., 2019), but many of these reviews warn that the high heterogeneity and inconsistencies of methodologies, sample sizes, and data capture across studies make it very difficult to measure the overall efficacy of biofeedback as a therapy. For those working in the field, like Sebern Fisher, whom we will talk about in our discussion of neurofeedback, the proof is in the pudding, and efficacy for some individuals can be compelling and life-changing.

There is a wide range of both research and practice in the field of bio-feedback. We will look at two of the most familiar areas of biofeedback that relate to psychotherapy: neurofeedback (using EEG), and heart rate variability (using ECG). For now, note simply that many other tools and processes provide feedback, including muscle action potentials, skin temperature, skin electrical activity, blood flow, respiration, and CO_2 levels.

Brain Waves

In Chapter 1 we looked at brain structure and the elements of networks and neurochemicals to understand the way the nervous system works. Another element apart from the network of neurons, glia, and neurochemicals is the electrical activity of the brain—not only the discrete electrical pulses of individual neurons but the continual waves of activity that pulse through the entire nervous system. These brain waves occur at different frequencies and different amplitudes and correlate with different states of the brain (refer to Table 2.1). Along with cortical blood flow (which correlates with activity in different regions of the brain), then, at a very basic level the nervous system has the following elements to take into consideration:

- neural/glial networks,
- neurochemicals,
- blood flow, and
- brain waves.

TABLE 2.1 BRAIN WAVE FREQUENCIES

WAVE NAME	FREQUENCY (HZ)	ASSOCIATED BRAIN STATE
Infra low (also "slow cortical potential")	0.0001–0.1 (some say <0.5)	Related to glial and astrocyte electrical properties; possibly basic cortical (ultradian) rhythms
Delta	0.1–3	Sleep or deep meditation
Theta	4–7	Drowsiness, creativity, deep meditation
Alpha	8–12	Relaxation
Low beta	12–15	Calm alertness, musing
Beta	15–22	Doing demanding cognitive tasks
High beta	22–36	Increased muscle tension, high anxiety, or excitement
Gamma	36–45	Deep insight, universal love, altruism

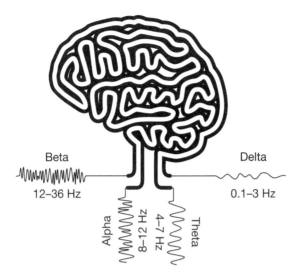

Neurofeedback

In neurofeedback, electrical activity of the brain is fed back in some way to the same brain. The means of neurofeedback might be audible tones, visual images on a screen, or typically a simple video game whereby certain frequencies from certain parts of the brain change something in the game. I (M. D.) remember an early neurofeedback training game in which you had to "drive" a car down virtual streets just by thinking about it—imagining the car going forward or to the left or to the right. It was rather clunky, but fun once my brain got the hang of it. It required a strange state of not trying too hard but relaxing and letting my imagination do the work—a counterintuitive state for someone trained to exert effort to achieve an outcome!

Today there are many such video games, with advanced graphics and all sorts of scenarios for various clinical goals and different neurofeedback systems. The ultimate goal for these games and the clinical protocols is to train the brain to self-regulate at the neural-network level for stability and resilience.

This fascinating way of training the brain is wholly based on the brain observing itself and shifting brain wave activity to achieve a goal (like moving the car forward in the video game). The training is typically either inhibit training or reward training (or both at the same time). *Inhibit training* aims to lower overarousal to create stability and return the brain to a resting state. For example, with autism, high anxiety, or trauma, there is often a need to reduce the activity of the right hemisphere. *Reward training* is about challenging the brain to be active at certain frequencies in certain areas. Reward training can improve local networks and even the functioning at astrocyte/glial level. Children with ADHD often have increased theta activity and decreased beta activity compared with other children of the same age. Beta activity is associated with more focused attention; theta activity is evident during cognitive inactivity or cognitive wandering. In ADHD cases, neurofeedback training aims to increase beta activity and decrease theta—improving overall ability to focus and pay attention.

The protocols for neurofeedback either are created for the individual by a skilled clinician who recognizes exactly what sort of training needs to take place, or are based on quantitative EEG (QEEG), a set of EEG norms that are matched against the client's EEG. Other models or approaches used by neurofeedback practitioners include the coherence model (informed by quantitative EEG), the arousal regulation model, and infra-low frequency training. We do not have the space to dive into all these neurofeedback protocols, but for those interested in the clinical application for developmental trauma, Sebern Fisher (2014) has a wonderfully accessible book on the topic, *Neurofeedback in the Treatment of Developmental Trauma: Calming the Fear-Driven Brain*. We highly recommend this book for anyone working with trauma because it gives a clear introduction into the brain wave perspective on trauma.

According to Fisher, early trauma may be encoded in the lower frequencies (theta and delta) not easily accessible to a conscious mind operating at higher frequencies. Babies' brains cycle in the lower frequencies of delta until about 2 years, and from 2 to 5 years of age they are primarily in theta, so it is plausible that trauma in these early years is related to these frequencies. A return to these frequencies may bring to life the trauma of the past. For Fisher and her work with developmental trauma, much of the trauma goes back to a lack of self-regulation established in the important mother–infant relationship. A person who is not mothered well will not have secure affect regulation. In an interview with Dr. David Van Nuys, Fisher offers the following:

> One of the things that happens when you train for affect regulation in neurofeedback is that affect regulation comes on board—people start to feel mothered. Even though they wouldn't say this, this is what is in fact happening, over time. Truly the gift of a good mother is affect regulation—that's what gets us through the full catastrophe of life; that we have affect regulation. If our mothers can't give it to us, then we rely on therapists or institutions to provide that, and what is new on the horizon is that we can teach the brain to regulate itself and be given the gift of mothering in that process. (Van Nuys, 2015)

In an interview with us, Fisher recounted the story of a 4-year-old boy who was in an emergency placement by the Department of Social Services because he had attempted to burn down his foster home. He was completely dysregulated, had made attempts on his sibling's life, had no language apart from swear words, was not toilet trained, and made sexual gestures. In his new foster home, he would crawl around on the floor saying "No, no, no, no" until about midnight, when he would fall asleep. He had been starved and would stuff himself with food under the dinner table. Fisher described him as a "feral" and terrified child. After about 5 or 6 days, the clinicians started doing neurofeedback with him—a challenging task, given that he was so dysregulated. It was very difficult to keep him still, and he would constantly pull off the electrodes. After the first session he slept through the night, for 12 hours. It was a remarkable shift. He went from having night terrors that disrupted the night for everyone in the house to sleeping soundly after that point. After this treatment, when Fisher visited, the boy would offer to share his food with her, rather than jealously guarding it under the dining room table.

CLINICAL NOTES

Practitioners like Fisher can cite many cases in which such positive outcomes prove the effectiveness of neurofeedback for dealing with

PTSD and complex trauma. A 2020 systematic review, indeed, found that neurofeedback demonstrated positive results in at least one outcome measure for the majority of participants across all studies covered in the review (Panisch & Hai, 2020). However, the authors of this review said that there need to be more randomized controlled trials with larger samples, along with longitudinal follow-up studies. The existing studies vary widely in size, design, measures, and reporting of results. Nevertheless, for the clinicians working with this technology and seeing some remarkably positive results, the proof is indeed in the pudding.

Heart Rate Variability

Another popular form of biofeedback is used to regulate heart rate variability (HRV; refer to Section 2.1). The coordination between sympathetic and parasympathetic arousal can be measured by HRV, which is a measure of the subtle differences in timing between heartbeats (as opposed to heart rate, which is a measure of beats per minute). A high HRV mediated through the vagus nerve and stellate ganglia (a collection of nerves found at the level of the sixth and seventh cervical vertebrae—the last vertebrae of the neck) indicates a healthy flexibility of attention to current situations. Healthy feedback that positively regulates HRV helps to maintain an appropriate balance between the two branches of the ANS and thus a balanced response to various stimuli. This balance is maintained when there is flexibility between activation of the sympathetic nervous system that activates the body with chemicals like epinephrine for action to meet a threat to basic homeostasis, and the deactivation or calmative effect of the parasympathetic nervous system, which puts the breaks on the sympathetic nervous system and uses acetylcholine to focus the body on activities such as rest, repair, and digestion.

Biofeedback using HRV as the feedback measure or indicator usually involves a monitor on the finger or earlobe that measures pulse, and the data are displayed visually as a moving graphic on a screen and/or as a sound.

Progress toward more adaptive HRV, often referred to as *coherence*, is fed back to the user so that they can respond with more of what is increasing the coherence. A 2017 meta-analysis of HRV to treat stress and anxiety found that this form of biofeedback led to a large reduction in self-reported stress and anxiety (Goessl et al., 2017), but again the authors caution that there need to be more well-controlled studies.

The heart has a lot more influence on the CNS besides simply through HRV. The heart's own complex neural architecture (the so-called heart-brain, or intrinsic cardiac nervous system; refer to Section 2.1) can act independently of the cranial brain and inform the CNS, thus giving credence to the wisdom of "listening to your heart." The heart also communicates to the brain and the rest of the body not only though the nervous system but biochemically, biophysically, and electromagnetically.

The complexity of neural networks that maintain such regulation has been variously labeled the central autonomic network, the anterior executive region, and the rostral limbic system. These descriptions attempt to capture the interplay between structures such as the anterior cingulate cortex (ACC), insula, orbitofrontal cortex, amygdala, central gray, ventral striatum, brainstem, and ventral/dorsal vagal system, which perform a balancing act within the ANS. Some research has found that individuals with generalized anxiety disorder (GAD) have a reduced HRV because of a breakdown in the regulatory feedback mechanisms in the central autonomic network that results in chronic hyperarousal.

The popularity of HRV as a measure of physiological and psychological flexibility is apparent from the tens of thousands of recent research articles that use this easily applied measurement. You can even get a relatively cheap monitor (that clips onto your finger or earlobe) with accompanying software that will measure your HRV and offer training to help you increase your HRV and thus your overall autonomic flexibility. For a long time, I (M. D.) have used such a device (manufactured by HeartMath) with clients and on myself, initially out of curiosity, but then as a mindful exercise. These easy-to-use biofeedback devices can both pique the curiosity of clients and help them nurture states of greater self-regulation.

Dr. Rollin McCraty, director of research at the HeartMath Institute has spoken extensively about the heart–brain connection and what he calls *physiological coherence*, a measurable state characterized by increased harmony between mind, emotions, and body. HRV is a critical marker of this state of coherence. In his article "Heart-Brain Neurodynamics: The Making of Emotions" (2014), McCraty explains that "both the brain and the entire body are involved in the full experience and expression of emotions" (p. 86). He conceives of emotion as emerging from a whole-body complex system, with the heart being a significant influence, given its "unique degree of afferent input and its consistent generation of dynamic rhythmic patterns that are closely coupled with changes in emotional state" (p. 86).

McCraty capitalizes on the heart's influence on the overall coherence of the body by producing positive, emotion-driven shifts in HRV that, in turn, alter the patterns of cardiac afferent input to the brain. The net effect is a physiological shift toward increased coherence and the experience of positive emotions. Using HRV as feedback, people are able to practice techniques that enhance greater HRV and ultimately reinforce neural pathways critical to better self-regulation. Like neurofeedback, this form of biofeedback aims for flexibility and affect regulation—but from the head to the heart and back again.

CLINICAL NOTES

HRV is a very easy measure for any clinician to employ for therapeutic effect, with relatively inexpensive hardware and software. Using HRV monitoring and the many meditation and gaming software applications, you can readily set up a biofeedback program for clients that can help increase their overall nervous system coherence. Getting advice from those who specialize is always recommended, but a lot can be done with a good general knowledge of what is being achieved and how the achievements can be measured.

2.5 Trauma and the Body

J.D., a woman in her early 40s, presented with anxiety and persistent migraines. Rapport developed quickly, and she was very open and engaged, but it soon became clear that the roots of the problem were deeper than just cognitive. She and I (R. H.) began in a conversational narrative style to see what talking might reveal. After a couple of sessions, I shifted her attention to what her body was doing when she was anxious. We paid particular attention to how her body felt as a migraine developed. Among the disparate stories and various triggers for her migraines, we could see that the body reacted in a similar way. She would start to develop tension between her shoulder blades. The tension would pull at her back and spine, working its way toward the head. At the same time, muscles in her shoulders became tense, raising her shoulders, and tightening her neck, which pulled at her head. The migraine would begin, and before long it would be full-blown. She would be unable to keep her eyes open, and she would have to lie down and seek relief with pain medications.

We needed to reduce the intensity of her reactions, so we first learned to recognize the tension as it began and used a variety of relaxing techniques and movement to interrupt the progression into migraine. This approach helped but did not resolve what was driving the reaction. We continued with recollections. What emerged were several near-fatal events during her teenage years. Her body told us which event to focus on because she felt a sudden tension pulling her shoulder blades. J. D. recalled riding her horse at a show-jumping event. Something went wrong on one of the jumps, and the horse began to fall. She had to grasp the reins and desperately pull tight to hold on. She and the horse took a terrible tumble. Had she landed under the horse, she would surely have been killed or very seriously injured. This was what her body was holding. This was the memory her body used to develop protective mechanisms for future danger. In adulthood, anything that seemed risky in any way—not only to her but also to her loved ones—triggered her muscles to tighten and feel unsafe. The best escape was to shut down, for fear that she, her husband, or her children would be trapped, unable to escape the danger. This is the reaction that her traumatic experience had embodied and "embrained." It was necessary for survival.

J. D. had become stuck, locked, in the most traumatic moment of the experience. That is what her body remembered, but the truth is that she had survived. Could we find a way to complete the experience beyond the trauma? She was very good at visualizing, so we decided to focus her attention on visualizing the experience. This time, she would try to remember what she had done that helped her survive. I helped her to relax, and when she felt safe, she visualized her way through the jump. We got to the point where she tightly gripped the reins, and I encouraged her to move forward to what happened next. To her surprise, she remembered how she could feel the horse faltering, so she pulled on the reins but knew she had to get away from the horse. She pushed with her legs, let go of the reins, and threw her arms out, away from the horse, like she was diving. This action propelled her away from the horse, even though she landed hard on the ground. J. D. opened her eyes in astonishment. She had not nearly died; she had saved herself. She had not lost control; she had done what was necessary to save herself. For the first time she could feel her back relaxing instead of tensing as she recalled the event.

Over time, we worked through other traumatic events of her past and discovered that each time, she had made decisions and taken actions that saved her from danger. Then she thought about more recent events that would cripple her with anxiety and migraine, only to discover that something had always happened to help her or protect her. As we finished our sessions, J. D. declared that instead of being under constant threat, the truth was that she was "a little blessed." Her body had based a lifetime of development on an incomplete memory. By completing the experience, her body was able to reorganize her protective systems—her autonomic nervous system, HPA axis, immune system, endocrine system, and all the other systems in her body—on the basis of her new memories, to now reflect a person who was blessed, not cursed.

After decades of research and discovery, it seems broadly accepted that psychological trauma has an "embodied" reality and is not solely a "problem in your head" (Iani, 2019). Many voices have labored over this point; Peter Levine, Pat Ogden, Bessel van der Kolk, Alan Fogel, Babette Rothschild, John Arden, Robert Scaer, Antonio Damasio, Allan Schore, and Daniel Siegel are just a few of the names that come to mind, and there are many others. We know that "the body keeps the score," to quote van der Kolk (2014), and we will show you some of the ways the body is involved in trauma and how the body can be used as a resource for trauma recovery.

CLINICAL NOTES

Because it is a complex issue, we examine trauma also in Chapter 4, where we look at specific trauma disorders, and in Chapter 3, where we look at the role of genetics and epigenetics in trauma. These discussions, collectively, provide a framework on which you can build your own in-depth study. We encourage you to read and study authors who have lifetimes of specialized knowledge and experience, but first we will present an overview of trauma in the body. Therapies that you can utilize in your practice are described in Section 5.4, and pertinent elements in somatic therapies are covered in Section 5.3. A broad theoretical insight into the way barriers and limitations are formed in the brain and in the function of the neurons are described in Chapters 1 and 2. The clear message here is that trauma is an important issue in mental health that affects a lot of people, and there are many avenues that therapists can use to help their clients.

Body Systems and Traumatic Memory

She went into a full-blown anxiety attack. She appeared paralyzed and unable to breathe. Her heart was pounding wildly, and then seemed to almost stop. . . . Surrendering to my own intense fear, yet somehow managing to remain present, I had a fleeting vision of a tiger jumping toward us. Swept along with the experience, I exclaimed loudly, "You are being attacked by a large tiger. See the tiger as it comes at you. Run toward that tree; climb it and escape!" To my surprise, her legs started trembling in running movements. She let out a bloodcurdling scream. . . . She began to tremble, shake, and sob in full-bodied convulsive waves. (Levine, 1997, p. 29)

The now classic *Walking the Tiger: Healing Trauma*, by Peter Levine (1997), introduced the powerful somatic aspect of psychological trauma. Levine drew the parallel between the cathartic release experienced by the woman described in the quote and the way that prey animals such as impalas "shake off" the freeze response after a near-death encounter with a predator. He reasoned that humans do not shake off the residual energy of a traumatic event as naturally as an impala on the African plains does. Humans are able to hold on to that energy and miss the opportunity to discharge the nervous system.

What Levine described as the "mystery of trauma" is no longer a mystery: Trauma is embodied, so the resolution of trauma involves the body. Cortical reasoning and *psychological* factors need to be considered together with *physiological* factors to enable the most effective therapy. Humans encode and remember trauma explicitly and implicitly. Memories are explicitly encoded in the brain as episodic, or autobiographical, memories that can be retrieved and remembered. However, memories are encoded implicitly in the amygdala, and subsequently as automatic behaviors and thoughts in the basal ganglia. These memories are not recalled as events but are expressed as behaviors and emotions. The body establishes sensitivities to emotive, somatic, and environmental triggers. Sensitivity is encoded in the epigenome (Pizzimenti & Lattal, 2015), in the heightened reactivity of the immune and endocrine systems to biochemical insults such as chronically expressed cortisol and subsequent inflammatory cytokines from persistent stress (M. B. Young et al., 2018), as well as in the brains within the body: the "gut-brain" and the "heart-brain" (refer to Section 2.1). In the years following a trauma, the body systemically self-organizes its development in the context of trauma (i.e., needing to protect itself from future danger). The body and brain lock into structural developments organized around defensiveness and protectiveness. Trauma is described by Bessel van der Kolk as "blocking" or "freezing" future development (van der Kolk, 2014). The result is a psychoneurobiological system that is unable to mentally integrate, manage, or resolve the hypo- and hypersensitive reactions from the body to the brain and vice versa. As van der Kolk says, "We cannot reason ourselves out of being frightened or upset" (Bullard, 2014).

These systems, however, can be flexible and "plastic," as is possible in the brain. Therapy can use the same systems that are overprotecting to help disentangle the trauma history. When the environment is changed, as in the case of J. D.'s remembering her fall with her horse, changes can occur throughout various systems, bringing both the body and the brain back into a state of *flexibility* and *regulation*—two of the principal foundations of health that are disrupted by trauma (Hayes & Andrews, 2020).

Preparatory Sets

Trauma is experienced as a single event or as generalized events over time, creating a complex trauma. Single events are one-off events such as devastating weather, a violent attack, assault, or a traffic accident. Generalized events are repeated or cumulative. Many of the latter occur in the home—neglect, physical and sexual abuse, constant criticism, and oppressive discipline. Generalized events can also be experienced in the local community, schools, and work environments, where persistent bullying, disciplinary control, undervaluing through low wages or punishments, and constant undervaluing and/or devaluing of self-worth cause trauma that is embodied within.

Payne and Crane-Godreau (2015) proposed the concept of *preparatory sets* to describe the collection of mechanisms that the individual brings into play to deal with the various demands of life. When these sets are functioning productively, a demand triggers arousal that promotes an action response. The action is preceded by a preparation for the action response—a preparatory set. In the brain this preparation is largely subcortical and automatic, meaning distinct from conscious, slower, self-directed decision-making. This preparation activates brain-to-body information through peripheral nerves, especially the vagus nerve. Depending on the type of demand—whether from mentalization or received through the body's senses—certain bio-physical responses activate immediately. It is a system-wide readying to take action and involves simultaneous physical and neural activation.

The resulting actions—whether behaviors, emotions, thoughts, move-ments, body system responses such as activation of the immune system, endo-crine system, or even activity-dependent gene expression (refer to Section 3.1)—are both elements of and the *performance* of the preparation set. Once activity begins, an ongoing natural process of feedback produces further cas-cades of activity that continue to create effects and produce emergent proper-ties. If the preparatory set and the systems within the individual are healthy (i.e., flexible and adaptive), then there is a successful and beneficial experience—a positive feedback dynamic. If, however, the preparatory set is maladaptive, as happens when the systems within the individual are framed around trauma (i.e., the systems are rigid or easily triggered into chaotic functions), then the ongoing experience is unhealthy—a negative feedback dynamic.

Payne and Crane-Godreau (2015) define four kinds of maladaptive pre-paratory sets:

- **well organized:** Despite good organization, the preparatory set is not well matched to handling this particular situation.
- **disorganized:** The preparatory set lacks organization.
- **persistent:** The preparatory set arose in response to an earlier situ-ation but has continued beyond its utility.
- **situational:** The preparatory set arose in response to the present situation but is not well adapted to handling that situation.

"By definition, a PS [preparatory set] is organized to enable effective action. Once the action is successfully completed, the PS subsides. We sug-gest that one cause for a PS not subsiding (persisting) is the failure to com-plete the action pattern" (p. 7).

Trauma Is an Incomplete Experience

Payne, Levine, and Crane-Godreau (2015), explore Levine's somatic-experiencing form of trauma therapy, which aims to resolve symptoms using "bottom-up processing by directing the client's attention to internal sensations, both visceral (interoception) and musculoskeletal (proprioception and kinesthesis) rather than primarily cognitive or emotional experiences." By engaging in the internal senses and sensations of the body (interoception) and in the movement, posture, balance, and sense of body positioning in the environmental space (interoception and kinesthesis), the client is given the opportunity and appropriate circumstances to resolve the "symptoms resulting from chronic and traumatic stress. This is accomplished through the completion of thwarted biologically based, self-protective and defensive responses, and the discharge and regulation of excess autonomic arousal" (Payne et al., 2015).

J. D. was able to complete her experience and change the nature of her preparatory set. The way to solve her problem was to get her neurobiology "unstuck" from the traumatic moment of her near-fatal experiences so that she could move forward into the part of the experience that proved she was "a little blessed."

Window of Tolerance

The *window of tolerance* is the space between activation of the sympathetic nervous system and deactivation of the parasympathetic nervous system. Humans normally fluctuate between sympathetic and parasympathetic during the day. The process of arousal and returning to normal (normalization) is a measure of how well someone manages the demands of daily life. In hyperarousal (sympathetic), the arousal is out of proportion with the event and can result in anxiety or a panic attack. In hypoarousal (parasympathetic), the calmative effects do not stop and may lead to fainting (syncope) and an inability to reactivate the social engagement system, which can lead to depression. Stephen Porges's (2009) neuroception, in which the nervous system scans the environment to unconsciously distinguish between safety and threat, is overly sensitive when the window of tolerance is slim.

Daniel Siegel refined the definition to incorporate systems theory, suggesting that "the original notion of a window of tolerance as indicating that span of harmonious functioning that rests between chaos and rigidity may be more accurate and useful than a different version of the notion of the window, which is a span between low versus high degrees of arousal or activation" (Siegel, 2020, p. 342). We also argue that there is an edge of chaos and an edge of rigidity within which a harmonious flow of activity can be experienced (refer to Section 3.1). Traumatic "stuckness" is both rigid because of the lack of flexibility and chaotic when the maladaptive preparatory sets react rapidly and inappropriately to stimuli and triggers.

Perception and neuroception by traumatized people may be overly sensitive or conditioned to amplify things that would cause the ANS to be either hyperaroused or hypoaroused, taking them outside their window of tolerance (which is typically narrow). When someone is outside their window of tolerance, the emotional distress can shut down the prefrontal cortex because they are dysregulated by the out-of-balance activation of one branch of the ANS.

Restoring Balance

Systems theory offers the reassurance that just a small change can result in large and unpredictable results. Somatic-experiencing therapy encourages engaging the body's natural systems to shift toward balance with the possibility of generating a cascade of positive feedback.

Levine describes these natural systems as "brain-mind therapeutic and educational systems" (Payne & Crane-Godreau, 2015). It has been shown that preparatory sets can be altered through engaging in voluntary practices that promote biophysical balance in the body:

- proprioceptive or interoceptive imagery
- affective imagery
- adopting a specific posture
- performing specific movements
- breathing in certain patterns
- paying attention in certain ways
- modulating expectation/appraisal

Other movement practices for balance and awareness have been developed by many cultures over time and can also be very useful: Qigong, tai chi (Jahnke et al., 2010), and yoga (van der Kolk et al., 2014) involve similar processes. Social dancing can have beneficial effects, as can singing, especially in a choir that promotes breathing and social engagement. These practices encourage attention to posture, breathing, movement, and proprioceptive and interoceptive sensation, as well as tactile and spatial awareness. Bodily attention, voluntary movement, and imagery are effective ways to accomplish therapeutic goals, as with J. D. (Read & Stoll, 2009). A breakthrough for the client may generate a spontaneous parasympathetic discharge such as trembling, flushing, or crying (Payne et al., 2015). These are healthy actions that are the body's way of normalizing—not unlike the impala's response.

> *S.B. was witness to the 9/11 attacks in New York City on September 11, 2001. She was walking to work in Lower Manhattan, close to the north tower of the World Trade Center, when it was hit at 8:46 a.m. She, along with many other onlookers, watched the unfolding of the attack on the second tower and subsequent collapse of the towers just before 10:00 a.m. She was not injured at all during the ordeal, but she saw many injured people in the streets as she evacuated the area along with a sea of other people. A year later, S.B. was living in Brisbane, Australia, and attempting to start a new life with a new career. The trauma of 9/11, however, held her in a hyperaroused state. She was edgy, experiencing palpitations and sometimes panic attacks, especially when in the city. She was "neurocepting" danger when there was no real danger. Her window of tolerance had been narrowed; her ANS was less flexible and highly attuned to potential danger.*

S. B. used the concept of a window of tolerance to help her identify hyperarousal triggers in her environment: being in the city, feeling closed in by buildings, hearing and seeing planes overhead coming in to land at Brisbane airport. She increased her awareness of the sensations in her body, writing them down and seeing them within the framework of her window of tolerance. With that awareness, S. B. tracked a week of her life which she recorded on a chart that was adapted from Ogden & Fisher, (2015, p. 239, not included here), detailing the arousal levels of her nervous system from early morning to late evening.

CLINICAL NOTES

The window of tolerance can be an excellent tool, not only for the clinician to conceptualize hypo- and hyperarousal triggers but for the client to define and track such triggers, while learning to manage arousal levels. Psychotherapists are always cautious not to give the impression that any particular thing is the "magic bullet" therapy that works for everyone and does everything. Equally, in the context of complex systems, small changes can result in large outcomes. Natural self-organizing processes can produce results that are astounding, given how minor or simple the process or breakthrough leading to those results might seem. The therapist needs to be alert to the changes that occur for the client, because they are often unable to be predicted precisely. Every tool has the potential to be an element that will be the start of a cascade of "healing."

Conclusion

Each section of this chapter explored aspects of the body, and their profound effects on people's mental lives. Our message is clear: Psychotherapists are better prepared when they have a broad education in the biopsychosocial milieu in which all people exist. It is more than metaphorical to have a "gut-wrenching" experience that "takes your breath away" and ultimately leaves you with "heartache"; physiological realities are at play in the body as much as in the mind. The integrated bidirectional communication flow between body and brain demands that the entire nervous system, and indeed every cell in the body, be considered as integral elements of a nonlinear continuum. In other words, it is not possible to point to one part of the brain, or body, and say, "That is where the trauma resides" or "This part is the source of the PTSD symptoms," but it is possible to look at the body and say, "We know more *about* you now," and that knowledge is fertile ground for facilitating effective psychotherapy.

CHAPTER 3

The Molecules of Mental Health

3.1 Gene Expression

Healthy Genes and How They Function

In Chapter 1 we looked at the brain with its 86 billion neurons and quadrillion synaptic connections, plus a similar number of glial cells (Azevedo et al., 2009) connecting through neurotransmitters, neuropeptides, hormones, and a host of other biochemical elements (Uddin et al., 2018). Then, in Chapter 2, we looked at the body with its 37.2 trillion cells (Bianconi et al., 2013), specialized organs, peripheral nerves, and nervous systems, all engaged in a collaboration of complexity that make it possible to sustain life and reproduce (Bartsch et al., 2015). The complexity involved in the 3.2 billion base pairs in the double helix of DNA, and the associated biochemical milieu, makes the rest of human biology look simple.

On one hand DNA is a blueprint; on the other it is the heart of 37 trillion factories differentially producing the proteins that create humans and then re-create them every moment of the day. Every cell in the body and brain has a nucleus that contains roughly the same DNA, yet each cell uses DNA uniquely. The study of DNA, genetics, and genomics is an incredibly exciting, continually evolving, deep, biomolecular insight into how things happen inside each individual, between individuals, and in concert with the environment they inhabit. Let us begin with the basics and then explore some of the things that will clarify more about human beings, human behaviors, and human emotions.

BACKGROUND

DNA is constructed from four base chemicals that bind in pairs called *nucleotides*—adenine, thymine, guanine, and cytosine (always an A–T and G–C pairing)—which reside on the inner surface of two parallel, twisting, sugar and phosphate rails. Linus Pauling came close to working out the three-dimensional shape of DNA, but the double-helix form (Figure 3.1) was confirmed by James Watson and Francis Crick in 1953—their invaluable breakthrough made possible by X-ray crystallography images created by Rosalind Franklin (Pray, 2008).

The Human Genome Project completed coding the human genome in 2003, revealing approximately 20,000 protein-coding genes stored in 46 chromosomes (chromosomes 1–22 in pairs, plus an X–X or X–Y pair) in every cell. Protein-coding genes are estimated to account for only about 1.2% of the DNA code (Piovesan et al., 2019). To add some perspective, the single-celled amoeba named *Amoeba dubia* has 670 billion base pairs (Parfrey et al., 2008); the California poplar (*Populus trichocarpa*) has only 485 million base pairs, but 45,555 genes (Tuskan et al., 2006); and there is only a tiny difference between the genomes of primates and humans, especially the bonobo chimpanzee which is the closest relative of humans, with about 98.7% commonality (Prüfer et al., 2012).

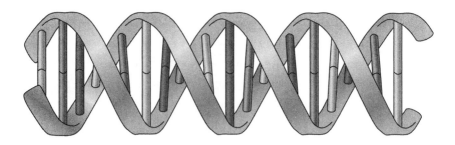

FIGURE 3.1: Segment of a DNA Strand

DNA in a reproducing cell is believed to have come into existence about 3.7–4 billion years ago (the Earth formed about 4.5 billion years ago). The first imagined cell was named the *last universal common ancestor*, or *LUCA*. LUCA was the beginning of all life that has followed (Xu et al., 2020). There is no definitive story about the biochemical "early life experiments" (Gleiser, 2012, p.347) that led to DNA, although there are a number of theories. Walter Gilbert (1986) argued for an "RNA world" as the first phase of self-replicating molecules. Regardless of which theory proves to be correct, the outcome of the emergence of DNA was single-celled microorganisms, called *prokaryotes*, which include bacteria and archaea and, eventually, complex, multicelled organisms, called *eukaryotes*, include fungi, plants, and animals such as human beings.

In his book *The Deep History of Ourselves* (2019), Joseph LeDoux defines an organism and highlights what is a necessary organizing principle of organic life:

> An organism is a living thing, an entity that functions as a physiological unit, the component parts of which operate with a high degree of cooperation and a low degree of conflict to help ensure wellbeing and sustain the life of the overall entity and to reproduce itself so that its kind can continue. (p. 24)

If "*a high degree of cooperation and a low degree of conflict*" is a general organizing principle for successful, sustaining systems in nature, then that principle can be applied to mental health and therapeutic practice as confidently as it is to molecular activity in the DNA. Daniel Siegel (2015) observed that the "DSM-IV-TR (Diagnostic Statistics Manual of Mental Disorders) can be viewed as a collection of syndromes in which the various symptoms represent examples of chaos or rigidity" (p. 198). Chaos and rigidity—these are the two destructive extremes of conflicted systems. Everyone has felt the chaos of anxiety or the rigidity of depression. Systems seek to produce outcomes in the cooperative spectrum between rigidity and chaos (refer to Figure 3.2).

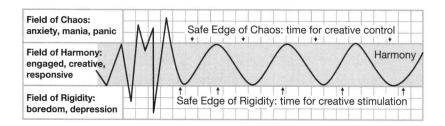

FIGURE 3.2: Chaos, Rigidity, and Harmony in a Complex System

Psychobiological systems indicate states of conflict or cooperation through emotions, behaviors, thoughts, beliefs, states of calm or distress, and feelings of sickness or health. The term "symptom" is generally used to describe things that indicate illness, but people also express symptoms of wellness. The challenge for a therapist is to find an explanation of the conflict, but from a systems perspective, there is also a challenge to facilitate appropriate conditions and circumstances for the system to self-organize a resolution of the conflict—that is, for the system to move *itself* toward order. The overt and observable activities of therapy are underpinned by changes in biological factors ranging from brain plasticity to anti-inflammatory activity to the activities of molecules that regulate emotions. All these changes are made with the supply of proteins that come from gene expression. To understand how DNA is affected and affects humans from a psychotherapeutic perspective requires first an understanding of DNA and how genetics works.

GENETICS

The literature about genetics is vast. A lot can be learned from videos that show real-time activity in the cell. Genetics has a comprehensive metalanguage, and the barrage of new words can feel overwhelming at first, but the rewards of being able to delve more comfortably into this fascinating subject will make learning the key terminology worthwhile.

DNA and RNA. DNA (*deoxyribonucleic acid*) is a molecular structure within the nucleus of almost all cells that contains the genetic instructions

FIGURE 3.3

for the development and function of living things. As described earlier, DNA has four bases that bond in specific pairs (A–T and C–G) to create a stable double helix. A simple memory key for the pairing is "Apples in the Tree; Car in the Garage."

RNA (*ribonucleic acid*) has one different nucleotide: uracil (U) instead of thymine. Thymine has a stronger bond with adenine, so it improves the stability of DNA. RNA is usually single stranded (Figure 3.3) but can also be double stranded.

Chromatin (Histones and Nucleosomes). Human DNA, if stretched out, is roughly 1.8 meters (6 feet) in length. There are several steps and phases as DNA is compacted in the nucleus. The first is the *nucleosome*: A small section of DNA (147 base pairs) wraps twice around an octamer (8) of basic protein molecules called *histones* (Quina et al. 2006). A ninth histone, called the linker histone, attaches to the outside to hold the structure together (Figure 3.4; Happel & Doenecke, 2009). The histone octamer is positively charged and thus attracts negatively charged DNA. At the molecular level, electrostatic attraction and repulsion is how cooperation and conflict, respectively, create and change the shapes of structures. In their loose state, nucleosomes look like beads on a string. This string is compacted further in

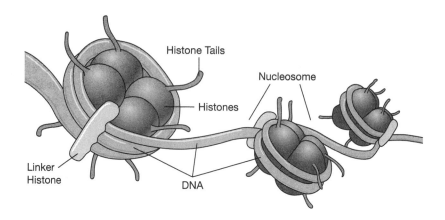

FIGURE 3.4: Histones and Nucleosomes

a step that draws nucleosomes together, again by electrostatic forces, to form a very compact fiber called *chromatin* (Figure 3.5). In the third step, chromatin is wound in a compact spiral to form a *chromatid* that is the compacted form of a chromosome (Figure 3.6).

Chromosomes. Each cell has 46 chromosomes consisting of 22 pairs plus the sex chromosomes X and Y—23 chromosomes from each parent. Each chromosome in the pair can carry dominant or recessive genes, which

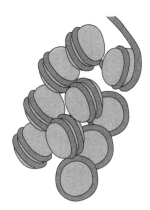

FIGURE 3.5: Section of Packed Nucleosomes Forming a Chromatid

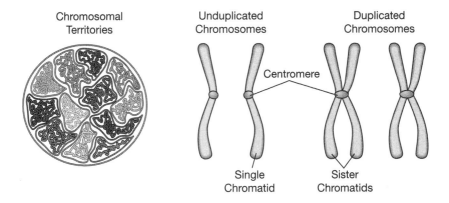

Chromosomal Territories

Unduplicated Chromosomes

Duplicated Chromosomes

Centromere

Single Chromatid

Sister Chromatids

FIGURE 3.6

determine which *chromatid* ("arm") of the chromosome pair provides the active gene. The familiar image of a chromosome is an X-like structure, but that is not a chromosome *pair*. It is a duplicated chromosome, and only one of three possible forms of a chromosome. The two duplicate arms (chromatids) are connected at the centromere as illustrated in Figure 3.6, ready for cell division. The two connected arms are called *sister chromatids*. In the phase just after cell division there is only one arm, or chromatid. Most of the time that the cell is active, chromosomes are unraveled into loose threadlike forms that gather in "chromosomal territories" in the nucleus. The unraveled chromosome has tight and loose sections, depending on whether a gene is available to be expressed or gene expression is being repressed.

CELL DIVISION
There are two types of cell division: cell duplication (*mitosis*) and cell *division* that creates the cells required for reproduction (*meiosis*). Both are important, but in the context of looking at genetic changes that can affect the person that someone will become, meiosis has the largest potential impact on the next generation. In the next two sections of this chapter we will talk more about what can happen to change DNA.

Mitosis has six phases and produces two identical *diploid* ("two sets") cells:

- **interphase:** As the cell approaches the time to divide, the uncoiled chromatin duplicates and begins to compact, forming sister chromatids. Two **centrosomes** form at the side of the nucleus, which will create the framework for chromosomes to divide.
- **prophase:** Sister chromatids condense; the centrosomes move to opposite sides of the cell, while extending **mitotic spindles**.
- **late prophase:** The nucleus wall disintegrates; centrosomes arrive at opposite positions; and spindles begin to attach to **centromeres** in the chromosomes.
- **metaphase:** Chromosomes line up across the center of the cell, held by spindles.
- **anaphase:** Spindles pull back toward the centrosome, dragging one of the sister chromatids away from the other.
- **telophase:** A nuclear membranes begin to form; and the cell begins to divide into two separate, but identical cells (**cytokinesis**).

Meiosis produces four *haploid* ("single set") cells that each contain half the number of chromosomes (23). Each chromosome has undergone some degree of change and restructuring that creates a unique set of chromosomes for reproduction. During fertilization, one cell from the mother (ova) and one from the father (sperm) combine to produce a complete 46-chromosome cell. Meiosis has eight phases, divided into two parts. The first set of four phases is where DNA can be altered, creating genetic diversity in offspring but also potentially creating genetic disadvantages (refer to Section 3.3). The first four phases are

- **prophase I:** Duplicated chromosomes are drawn near their original pairs (remember that 23 chromosomes from each parent combine to create 46 chromosomes in 23 pairings). Chromatids exchange genetic information through processes such as crossing-over, sharing, duplication, and deletion to create unique DNA structures.

This is the phase where diversity, but also genetic disorders, can be created.

- **metaphase I:** Chromosome pairs are drawn to the center line of the cell and connect to spindles at the centromeres.
- **anaphase I:** One of each chromosome pair is drawn to the outside of the cell—still as two chromatids connected at the centromere (i.e., only 23 chromosomes at each pole).
- **telophase I:** The cell divides into two haploid *daughter cells*.

The second set of four phases is similar to mitosis in that the two daughter cells divide, separating the sister chromatids to create four new haploid cells. Because of the genetic changes made in prophase I, each cell has a unique DNA code to carry into the next generation.

Gene Expression: Transcription and Translation

While producing proteins, DNA goes through two processes: transcription in the nucleus, and translation in the cytoplasm surrounding the nucleus. Here we briefly describe one of the most intriguing "dances" in the self-organizing choreography of the microscopic world.

TRANSCRIPTION

During *transcription*, the DNA sequence is "read" by an RNA polymerase. The RNA polymerase is a molecular structure that attaches to a gene's pro-motor region of the DNA, creating a transcription mechanism that does two things: First it separates the two strands of the DNA helix by breaking the hydrogen bonds between nucleotides; then it draws in free-floating nucleosides in the surrounding nucleic fluid to produce a complementary, reverse RNA strand called a *primary transcript*. The primary transcript is then processed further: *Capping* adds a methylated guanosine molecule to the leading end of the RNA to stop it from unraveling; *polyadenylation* adds a string of some 200 adenine nucleotides to the end of the RNA sequence to stabilize the tail; and *splicing* removes unnecessary parts of the gene sequence, called *introns*, leaving the functional *exons*, which are spliced together into the mRNA strand. The mRNA exits the nucleus into the cytoplasm through a *nuclear pore complex*.

TRANSLATION

Once the mRNA arrives in the cytoplasm, *translation*—the process of using the mRNA code to make proteins—is initiated. First, a small *ribosome* unit attaches to the cap; then a larger ribosome unit attaches to the smaller one. This is the "factory" in which the protein will be constructed. The mRNA passes through the ribosome like a computer tape. Amino acids are drawn into the ribosome to form the protein. Each amino acid is attached to a specific unit of RNA called *transfer RNA* (*tRNA*; M. Lambert et al., 2019). Transfer RNA has only three nucleotides that are different for each of the 20 amino acids. These three nucleotides match up to a trio of nucleotides in the mRNA strand called a *codon*. The tRNA nucleotide trio is called an *anticodon*. Transfer RNA molecules line up in the order determined by the codons in the mRNA, and the larger subunit of the ribosome removes each amino acid and joins them to a growing protein chain. The connected amino acid chain emerges from the ribosome and folds up into a precise shape that is determined by the exact order of amino acids. This is how the four "letters" of the DNA code are turned into flesh and blood. In Section 3.3 we will say more about the problems that can arise when mutations alter the codons.

Noncoding DNA and Regulating RNA

Only about 1%–2% of DNA is made up of protein-coding genes. Scientists once thought that noncoding DNA was junk, but a vast array of regulatory RNA and nucleotide regions in DNA assist in transcription. Some of the noncoding DNA regions that act as regulatory elements include (Maston et al., 2006; Plank & Dean, 2014)

- **promoter regions:** DNA segments that provide binding sites for the protein machinery that carries out transcription. Promoter regions are usually found just ahead of the gene on the DNA strand.
- **enhancers:** sequences of DNA that stimulate transcription and can be distant from the head of the gene. The DNA strand literally bends to bring the enhancer in contact with the polymerase unit.
- **silencers:** binding sites for molecules that repress transcription.
- **insulators:** binding sites for molecules that control transcription.

Insulators can function as both enhancer blockers and barriers to transcription.

Other regions of noncoding DNA include *ribosomal RNAs (rRNAs)* that are important for the production of proteins in the ribosome (in conjunction with tRNAs; M. Lambert, 2019); *microRNAs (miRNAs)* and *short interfering RNAs (siRNAs)*, which are short lengths of RNA that block or interfere with protein production in the cytoplasm by attaching to mRNA (Lam et al., 2015); and *long noncoding RNAs (lncRNAs)*, which are longer lengths of RNA that have diverse roles in regulating gene activity, especially in the transcription process in the nucleus (Fernandes et al., 2019).

Some stretches of noncoding DNA serve structural purposes. One of the most important is the repeated noncoding DNA sequence TTAGGG at the ends of chromosomes that form telomeres. *Telomeres* close off the ends of chromosomes to protect the integrity of the DNA. Each time a cell divides, some of the telomere is lost. Telomeres degrade over time and are important for cell health and as time limiters in programmed cell death. Sleep, diet, mindfulness, and meditation have all been found to promote the production of the enzyme telomerase, which acts to sustain and even repair telomere length.

What Does All This Mean for a Psychotherapist?

The therapeutic experience is an immediate event that activates gene expression both during and after the "in-room" session—for both client and therapist. Ernest Rossi explored this idea in his book *The Psychobiology of Gene Expression* (2002), where he established the concept of *psychosocial genomics*. Defined as "the study of how psychological and social experience modulates gene expression in health and illness" (Hill, 2014), the field has produced a number of studies that show increased activity in genes that promote beneficial anti-inflammatory processes and other immune system benefits, as well as down-regulation of genes that are associated with disease and schizophrenia (Atkinson et al., 2010; Cozzolino, 2014). In similar experiments, positive genetic responses have resulted from practices that include meditation (Venditti et al., 2020) and mindfulness (Fredrickson et al., 2013). These experiments show that psychotherapy and mentalizing processes do not just produce changes in mental states but literally create new proteins that alter the body's biomolecular construct.

The fundamental and vital process of memory reconsolidation (refer to Section 1.4) is possible only after gene expression creates the proteins that reconsolidate the neural connections in a different way that alters a memory's association with emotional and behavioral responses. Brain plasticity is the ability of the brain to build new synapses. These become the new connections that alter the energy and information flow within the brain. These synapses are created from proteins that are built in situ as a result of gene expression. In the rest of this chapter and in the chapters that follow, we will provide examples and descriptions of changes that occur in a person's neurobiology—some beneficial, some detrimental—that are possible only because of the activity, or in some cases nonactivity, of genes and the proteins that their expression creates. The psychotherapist is not just altering thoughts or emotional states but is literally stimulating protein construction within the neurons of the brain and, potentially, throughout the body. The effects can even include biological changes to the DNA itself (epigenetics; refer to Section 3.2). Psychotherapy is not an abstract, ethereal activity; it affects the entire complex "psycho-neuro-bio-immunological" system.

The gene expression that creates the proteins required to satisfy what is biologically needed on a daily and even hourly basis is a frantic, complex, self-organizing, adaptive system. The inner world of the body is a constantly shifting biochemical milieu that triggers and stimulates myriad inner functions in response to the nature of a person's experience every moment of the day and night. Gene expression is prompted because of and in concert with those experiences (Ridley, 2003; Rossi, 2002). Genes must be expressed to create the proteins that become the matter that enables the functions of human biology and the mentalizations of human psychology. One example illustrating psychological complexity is the particular genes that are expressed during sleep when there have been meaningful experiences during the day. When the immediate early gene (IEG) called *ZIF268* (or *EGR1*) is expressed, it creates associated proteins (Penke et al., 2014) that enable the interaction between the hippocampus and the cortex to store memories and create associations with past experiences (Riberio et al., 2008).

Genes are expressed in four main contexts:

- **functional-dependent** (F. Jacob & Monod, 1961; Nestler & Hyman, 2002): Normal cellular processes such as energy production and regular metabolic processes need to occur to maintain cell survival and sustain necessary specialized cell function.
- **experience-dependent** (Clayton et al., 2020): An individual's biology develops and constructs itself in concert with the inner and outer environment and psychosocial experiences. Experiences are remembered genetically by the addition of molecules to the DNA that affect the way genes are expressed—epigenetics (refer to Section 3.2). Neuronal pathways are strengthened through experiences, particularly psychosocial experiences like trauma and insecure attachment.
- **behavior state–dependent** (Manning et al., 2017; Rossi, 2002; Sinha et al., 2020): All behavior states, such as sleeping, stress, emotional arousal, and depression are associated with different patterns of gene expression. An affective state stimulates gene expression. In the brain, the neurochemical milieu is subject to adaptive and dynamicprocesses that constantly change with mood, where gene expression is a central element.
- **activity-dependent** (Rossi, 2002; Yap & Greenberg, 2018): Most gene expression is triggered by the immediate events occurring in the inner and outer environment that require an active response. How the DNA responds to immediate events is mediated by the biology that has developed over time and with experience.

CLINICAL NOTES

Our main goal in this section was to introduce the fundamental processes in genetics. The previous paragraphs on what genetics means for the therapist are also clinical notes, but they delve into the question of therapeutic relevance more deeply. In the next sections we will explore epigenetics and, then, how genes are involved when things go wrong in a person's psychology. Understanding what genetics means to the psychotherapist is still in an early stage, but we expect that knowing about genetics will become essential as research progresses to the point that biochemistry can be used as an indicator of how effective therapy is. Current research shows that some therapies produce distinct genetic responses that favor anti-inflammatory and stem cell activity. This is a very positive basis to inspire continued work and research.

3.2 Epigenetics

Laura Vega Garzon went with her friend, Janeth Paez, to buy some meat from a butcher's shop in Bogotá, Colombia. Janeth knew one of the butchers and expected to get a good cut of meat. When Laura entered the shop, she recognized one of the men behind the counter as Jorge, a coworker at her engineering firm. She wondered whether Jorge might have taken a second job. When Janeth introduced this man as her boyfriend's cousin, William, Laura was astounded because he was the spitting image of Jorge. William swore he knew nothing of Jorge. Initially, they passed it off as just an extraordinary coincidence. Laura later joked about it with Jorge, and eventually they began a thorough investigation. The story proved to be more surprising than anyone could have imagined.

Jorge and William were twin brothers born at the same time as another set of twins, Carlos and Wilbur. By a strange and complicated twist of fate, Carlos was switched with William in the hospital. Jorge and Carlos lived an urban, middle-class life in Bogotá, while William and Wilbur lived in a poor rural community far from the urban centers. Both pairs grew up believing they were fraternal twins. They reunited in 2014, when they were 26 years old. A video of their reunion went viral in 2015, bringing them to the attention of twins researcher, Nancy Segal. The full and fascinating story has been captured in her book *Accidental Brothers* (Segal & Montoya, 2018).

The story of twins Jorge and William, and Carlos and Wilbur, was an unprecedented opportunity to study twins that have been raised apart. Neither the brothers nor the parents had any idea the babies had been separated. Separated twins are known to have strong similarities, but also clear differences because of different life experiences. As monozygotic twins, the brothers have identical DNA, but there are distinct differences in appearance and attitudes toward life. Why? This question taps into the nature/nurture debate: Are humans determined by DNA (nature) or by the experiences of life (nurture)? These brothers are living examples that the answer is both.

Life experiences and the environment in which someone is raised, which include everything from attachment relationships to traumatic events to schooling and socioeconomic status, do not change the DNA code but do affect the *expression* of the DNA code. Experience "writes" itself onto the DNA as molecules of memory that can affect not only the biological profile but also the psychological profile. The study of this molecular overlay is called *epigenetics*. Epigenetic changes turn gene expression on or off (J. Kang et al., 2019).

Genotype and Phenotype

The DNA sequence is the complete inherited genetic identity, which is in every cell nucleus and is called the *genotype*. The *phenotype* is the composite of observable characteristics of the organism as it grows and develops. In the language of complex systems, the phenotype is comparable to the emergent property. In humans, phenotype's emergent properties include physical appearance, biological and biochemical composition, behavior, and psychological disposition. The phenotype is linked to the genotype (Nussinov et al., 2019), but the organism also develops in response to epigenetic patterns, environmental conditions, and molecular variations. So, similar genotypes that experience different environmental and developmental conditions may result in a different phenotype. This is exactly what we see in these "accidental brothers."

When they met at the age of 26, their faces were very similar, but William's face was more narrow and gaunt than that of the urban-raised Jorge. William was wary of life and believed that nothing in life was easy. He had been forced to leave school when he was 12, and take whatever job he could, eventually becoming a relatively poorly paid butcher. Jorge, however, had been able to complete his education and join an engineering firm, becoming an optimist and a dreamer who yearned to travel. Carlos's urban lifestyle had left him cynical but suave. He was very interested in women but also quite a loner. Wilbur was much more joyous and quick to laugh. He was uncomplicated and naïve, compared with his brother. Wilbur had a persistent speech impediment that Carlos had also had as a child but had resolved through speech therapy. The rural life had left William with a huskier voice than Jorge, plus an accent. William also referred to his brother as "sir," which was an attitude of social hierarchy that rural people held toward urban professionals. So much about them was the same, but also so much was different.

Epigenotype

Epigenetics is defined by Chuang and Jones (2007) as "the study of heritable modifications of gene regulation that does not involve changing the DNA sequence." The word "heritable" means simply that epigenetic changes are maintained during cell replication and division (mitosis). Some epigenetic changes can be maintained during meiosis and are, therefore, *in*heritable—that is, passed to the next generation (this is an important aspect of epigenetics, but we will not deal with it in this chapter; refer instead to Lacal & Ventura, 2018; Shen et al., 2019). Most epigenetic changes are an addition or subtraction of specific molecules and proteins on the DNA or on the histone tails in the nucleosome (Dupont et al., 2009). Some researchers consider epigenetic changes to include certain effects brought about by microRNA and siRNA that interfere with or disrupt mRNA translation (Aristizabal et al., 2019; Gibney & Nolan, 2010).

Conrad Waddington (1942/2012) introduced the term "epigenotype" and the study of "epigenetics" in the early 1940s. In 1968, Waddington defined epigenetics as "the branch of biology which studies the causal interactions between genes and their products which bring the phenotype into

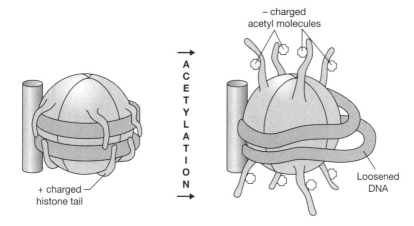

- charged
acetyl molecules

A
C
E
T
Y
L
A
T
I
O
N

+ charged
histone tail

Loosened
DNA

FIGURE 3.7

being" (pp. 9–10). Early definitions of epigenetics included all molecular pathways that modulated the expression of a genotype into a particular phenotype.

Adding a negatively charged acetyl molecule to a specific position on the histone tails in the nucleosome (acetylation) decreases the electrostatic difference between the histone octamer and the DNA, causing the DNA copied around the histones to loosen which makes the section of DNA that codes for that gene accessible for transcription. In other words, acetylation turns the gene on (Figure 3.7). Deacetylation has the reverse effect and turns the gene off. Another epigenetic addition is a methyl group molecule to specific sections of DNA. This methylation blocks the RNA polymerase complex from attaching to the DNA and transcribing the gene; that is, it turns the gene off (Figure 3.8).

These are two of the most common epigenetic additions possible, but turn your attention back to the client sitting opposite for a moment. It may be difficult to relate to these biochemical processes occurring at the molecular level. The truth remains, however, that the microscopic world of DNA and epigenetic markers is fundamental to how someone becomes a person who thinks and feels and believes. Everything about humans, large and small, is part of the complex system from which symptoms emerge as an observable, emergent message. Symptoms are the observable "phenotype"

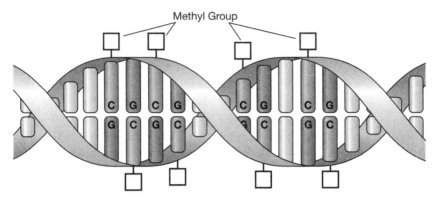

Methylation at CpG islands turns off gene expression

FIGURE 3.8

of something happening within the client that can be more than just mental activity.

Epigenetics is how the DNA remembers experiences. The *epigenome* creates itself to protect the organism by regulating gene expression and protein synthesis to produce a biology and psychology that is better able and suitably equipped to manage an individual's outer and inner environments. The goal is to improve chances of survival and achieve reproduction for continuation of the species (Dupont et al., 2009). Unfortunately, the epigenome is also an influential component in creating a body that "holds the score" (van der Kolk, 2014) on past trauma and difficulty. Early experiences affect children's future outcomes through biological embedding (lasting changes in the biological system produced by experiences), which has consequences for development, behavior, and health. Early-life social experiences that are measured in adverse-childhood-experience questionnaires (Finkelhor et al., 2013) include early caregiving, trauma, and maternal mental health. These aspects of early life are known to contribute to individual differences in susceptibility and resilience over a range of physical and mental health outcomes (Aristizabal et al., 2019). Facilitating a mental or emotional change may not be enough. The epigenome may need to be "convinced" that it is safe to allow selected genes to be turned on, or off, again.

In the context of complex systems, one of the organizing principles of gene regulation is that gene expression can be turned on or turned off. As already described, addition of a methyl group to a cytosine nucleotide near the promoter region of the gene (at what is described as CpG islands) turns gene expression off. Genes can also be turned on through acetylation of the histone tails in the nucleosome, which loosens the DNA coiled around the histone and also relaxes the chromatin. Chromatin that is tightly packed is called *heterochromatin*. Accessible chromatin is called *euchromatin*.

Epigenetic regulation of the chromosomes begins in utero (Naumova & Taketo, 2017). Initially, the fertilized egg divides and grows by producing identical copies, but as growth continues, cells begin to differentiate as they become specific cells of the body. *Cell differentiation* requires an epigenetic process (Arney & Fisher, 2004). A liver cell needs to remain a liver cell throughout the life of the organism. Epigenetic silencing in a liver cell turns off all the genes that are not liver cell genes. A second developmental process turns off one of the X chromosomes in females. This is necessary to prevent abnormal development that can occur because of a double dose of X genes (Payer et al., 2011). At about 4 days, when the embryo is a blastocyst of about 100 cells, the two X chromosomes come together briefly in a response that is triggered by long coding RNA (lcRNA). In an arbitrary fashion, one of the X chromosomes turns off to become heterochromatin through histone tail acetylation, DNA methylation, and the addition of structural proteins. Because inactivation of the extra X chromosome is entirely arbitrary, females end up with a mosaic of X chromosomes from the mother and the father, making for some curious variations in female biology (Shvetsova et al., 2019).

A number of disorders come from the X chromosome and thus are termed *X-linked disorders* (Skuse, 2005; Wu et al., 2014). Females are protected from the severity of some of these disorders because the "dosage" of proteins produced from gene expression is reduced by silencing one of the X chromosomes. Males receive only one X chromosome and are therefore more susceptible to X-linked disorders. Rett syndrome is a disorder of the *MECP2* gene that is usually fatal for afflicted males, who often do not survive to birth. Females may show deterioration that starts after several years as the "dose" of proteins from gene expression builds up. Intellectual and developmental difficulties are the main results of X-linked disorders. Other conditions are hemophilia and red–green color blindness (Migeon, 2020). X-linked genetic problems may also contribute to autism (Nguyen et al., 2020). Because females may exhibit only mild symptoms, a genetic disorder may not be considered. It is helpful to consider the possibility of a genetic condition when working with people, especially children, who are struggling to keep up with school or have other developmental delays.

Experiential Adaptation

Epigenetic changes are how gene expression adapts to current events and prepares, in a unique form of biochemical memory, for repetition of an experience in the future (Rothstein et al., 2009). This can be a two-edged sword in the modern world, which is environmentally and socially inconsistent with the evolutionary development of human DNA. Humans have different foods, sedentary lifestyles, performance and status stress, and socioeconomic anxiety that create epigenetic changes to their DNA. Some of these "protective" adaptations increase susceptibility to illness, disease, and dysfunction (Gibson, 2009). Adaptation to a dysfunctional world can produce a dysfunctional organism.

ATTACHMENT, ENVIRONMENT, AND EXPERIENCE

Attachment theory and complex-trauma theory maintain that early-life experiences can have long-lasting negative effects. Insecure attachments and trauma-based behavior are embedded in the neurology of the brain. Some of these neuronal activations are encoded epigenetically. Breakthrough research on attachment and epigenetics came in 2004 from a team led by Ian Weaver at McGill University in Montreal (Weaver et al., 2004). The team investigated what happens epigenetically to rat pups who have "good" mothers (exhibiting high levels of licking and grooming behaviors, referred to as "HLG") or "bad" mothers (exhibiting low levels of licking and grooming behaviors, referred to as "LLG"). The pleasant response to HLG maternal care increases serotonin and oxytocin, as well as other responses throughout the brain and body that are aligned with feeling comforted, safe, and well nourished. These responses stimulate the rat's biochemical milieu, which activates genes to produce the binding factors and growth factors that promote growth and connection to the mother. The safe relationship with the mother results in epigenetic changes that are the epigenetic "memory" of the quality of life the organism can expect.

The experience is different for rats with LLG mothers. They experience stress that is marked by increases in cortisols through activity of the HPA axis. Cortisols also return to the hippocampus as a biomarker to inform the HPA axis that the stress response is active, and the response can be moderated. The returning cortisols are "read" by glucocorticoid receptors in the hippocampus. The number of receptors depends on expression of the GR gene (Kino, 2015). The GR receptor genes for rat pups from LLG mothers were methylated, causing the number of glucocorticoid receptors in the hippocampus to be reduced and thereby altering the rat pup behaviors. LLG rat pups were epigenetically changed into animals that expected an insecure attachment and difficulty finding food. This epigenetic change made them less able to modulate the stress response, which means they were less able to handle stress, less able to enjoy life, and more likely to become distressed and anxious (Meaney & Szyf, 2005). This quality of behavior and emotion was written onto their DNA. Hyperactivity, anxiousness, and distress were adaptations to save their lives. If they did not make the extra effort to find their LLG mother, they would die. But is this epigenetic "memory" changeable? Fortunately, the answer is yes (McGowan & Szyf, 2010).

When the LLG pups were put in the care of an HLG mother, their biochemical milieu changed, eventually "convincing" the DNA to remove the methyl groups and acetylate the histone tails of the GR genes as if they had never had a difficult early life. This restoration took a little time, but a persistent, novel, positive, and beneficial experience revised their biological capacity to respond to stress.

In 2009 another team, led by Patrick McGowan (McGowan et al., 2009), was given permission to examine the genetic records from suicide death autopsies. They studied three groups: 12 suicides that had a history of childhood abuse, 12 without abuse, and 12 nonsuicide controls. The control group and the group without abuse had similar epigenetic profiles in relation to the GR gene. The group with a history of childhood abuse showed epigenetic silencing of the GR gene that was similar to the GR silencing observed in the rat pups with LLG mothers. The difficulties that each person experienced that led to suicide were affected by their limited capacity to regulate their stress response. Psychotherapy does so much more than just shifting behaviors and emotions. Over time, it is possible to shift the underlying biological orientation—just as happened with the stressed rat pups that were place with a caring mother. Understanding epigenetics can provide a deeper, more informed "felt sense" of the client.

Alcohol addiction provides another example of the need to be aware of an epigenetic contribution. Increased alcohol in the system triggers transcription factors and eventually establishes epigenetic mechanisms in response to the persistent flood of alcohol molecules (Nieratschker et al., 2013). The system needs to turn on genes that produce the enzymes that break down alcohol. At the same time, other genes are being turned on to adapt the system to cope with persistent high levels of alcohol. Over time, the system comes to require alcohol in order to function "normally." When alcohol is not present, the system has two primary options: (1) seek out alcohol or (2) change the biological structures back to a system in which alcohol is not required. The therapeutic phase shift to achieve option 2 is termed "rehabilitation" ("rehab") or "drying out." An important part of the therapeutic program is to alter the epigenetic profile. The epigenetic profile will change in response to persistent change in environmental conditions, but this alteration may take more time than some cognitive and affect regulation therapies take. The epigenetic processes need to be understood and incorporated into the therapeutic strategy.

Epigenetics will continue to be an area of study. Lester et al. (2011) suggested a specific field of "neuroepigenetics" or "behavioral epigenetics," which Day and Sweatt (2010) described as "the unique mechanisms and processes allowing dynamic experience-dependent regulation of the epigenome in nondividing cells of the nervous system" (p. 1320). Here is a small selection of topics under investigation:

- **child abuse** (Beach et al., 2010): An epigenetic investigation analyzed the relationship of child abuse to methylation of cytosine residues in the promoter region of the serotonin transporter gene in DNA from 96 male and 96 female subjects of the Iowa Adoption Studies. The **SLC6A4** serotonin transporter gene that produces the protein required for healthy serotonin distribution was down-regulated because of increased methylation of the DNA. The under-functioning serotonin system in these children manifests as an increased likelihood of PTSD and depression in later life.

- **memory formation** (Levenson & Sweatt, 2005; Zovkic et al., 2013): There are genes that enhance and suppress memory. As always, the system is complex and has many elements. The curiosity is that memory encoding, consolidation, and reconsolidation are turned off until there is an appropriate level of activity in the inner and outer environment to warrant that memory processes be turned on. Genes that produce memory suppressor proteins like protein phosphatase-1 (PP1) have been found to require increased methylation to be turned off. Genes that code for plasticity-associated proteins such as reelin and brain-derived neurotrophic factor are demethylated and deacetylated to turn on expression. Demethylation and deacetylation change chromatin from closed (heterochromatin) to open (euchromatin), and promoter regions are receptive to transcription factors and RNA polymerase transcription of mRNA. These factors are important in considering how best to treat problems stemming from the association of memories with emotions and behaviors. Epigenetic research shows that the first 3–5 hours after an event are important for reconsolidating memories of that event.

- **socioeconomic disadvantage in urban environments** (Olden et al., 2015; Reuben et al., 2020): The "accidental twins" expressed different phenotypes as a result of activity-dependent gene expression and epigenetic memory. Studies of urban, disadvantaged environments show increases in the activity of genes that produce inflammatory proteins such as NF-κB (nuclear factor kappa B) and IL-6 (interleukin-6), which lead to exaggerated activity of the adrenocorticoid systems. When such activity persists, the risk of chronic diseases is higher.

CLINICAL NOTES

Epigenetics is one of the ways that the body writes down and memorizes ongoing life experience. What a person does, when they do it, and how they feel about it while doing it contribute to the way experience uses the building materials in DNA to construct the individual that the person sees in the bathroom mirror and in the mirror of friends, family, and loved ones. People construct themselves with what they do and think and feel today, and they need to reconstruct those things built yesterday that are either overprotecting or were used to be protective but are now dysfunctional. Neuroplasticity is a familiar concept. Epigenetics shows that "geno-plasticity" is also possible.

3.3 Genetic Basis for Brain Dysfunction

Genetic *mutations* are changes to one or more of the nucleotides in DNA. Change to even a single nucleotide alters the genetic code. Translation of mRNA is based on the three-nucleotide group (codon) that codes for a specific amino acid. The codons determine the selection and order of the amino acids that will build a protein. When the genotype is altered, the phenotype can change too (Orgogozo et al., 2015). A psychotherapist, however, is not a medical practitioner or a geneticist, so what is the benefit of knowing about genetic mutations? With increased access to genetic testing, people are becoming more aware of what lies within. Whether a therapist is dealing with a client who has a mutation or family members who are trying to understand what is happening to their loved one, the more the therapist knows, the better able they are to respond to the needs of those who consult them.

Mutations can have little or no effect, or they can create changes that are very bad for the host. Equally, they can create changes that are very helpful. Mutations in DNA can manifest as emotional and behavioral variations in the phenotype (Griffiths et al., 2000). Changing a single nucleotide in the gene that produces the enzyme MTHFR can contribute to an increased risk of anxiety and depression, as well as cardiovascular diseases, some cancers, allergic reactions, migraines, and bipolar disorder (Wan et al., 2018). We will explore this important cycle later in the chapter, but first let us establish some of the technical elements of DNA mutation. There will be a lot of letters and numbers in this section, representing genes, molecules, and molecular compounds. These can be challenging, to say the least, but it can be even more challenging to read those abbreviated terms in full! We have included the technical terms to help you become familiar with the language of genetics, which will be useful if you choose to explore these topics further.

What Are Mutations?

Unlike epigenetic changes, which are chemical additions *over* DNA, mutations are heritable changes *to* DNA.

There are two classes of mutations:

- **germ mutations:** These are mutations in the reproductive cells that will be inherited by offspring; in other words, they will be in the DNA of every cell.
- **somatic mutations:** These mutations occur in the organism after conception in single cells or groups of cells that are not passed on to offspring. An example is mutations that make cells cancerous because of some form of environmental exposure.

Mutations occur in two regions:

- **gene:** changes in the nucleotides of a single gene
- **chromosome:** changes in chromosome structure that affect multiple genes

GENE MUTATIONS

Changes to one or more nucleotides within the gene are called *point mutations*. Point mutations alter the DNA sequence and therefore also the mRNA sequence. There are three types:

- **substitutions:** A base in the DNA sequence changes to a different base. For example, if the adenine base were changed to guanine, then the subsequent mRNA would include a cytosine base instead of uracil (remember that the pair for adenine in RNA is uracil, not thymine as in DNA). Alteration of only a single base is called a *single-nucleotide polymorphism*, or *SNP* (often pronounced "snip").
- **deletions:** A base is removed from the DNA sequence.
- **insertions:** A base is inserted into the DNA.

Deletions and insertions are known as *frameshift mutations* because they change the reading frames of some codons.

Here is a brief reminder of the translation process: During translation, mRNA is read by a ribosome in groups of three nucleotides called codons. These codons match anticodons (the opposite base triplet) in tRNA. The tRNA carries an amino acid, and as each codon of the DNA is read by the ribosome progressively from a start codon to a stop codon, the amino acid detaches from the tRNA, forming a chain of amino acids that becomes the protein that is the intended output of the gene's expression.

If, however, the nucleotide sequence has one more or one less base, then the order changes and the resulting codons change, disrupting the normal sequence of amino acids. The result is a variation in the protein. The normal sequence has been shifted, rendering an mRNA that is unreadable, has a premature stop codon, or creates a protein that either functions differently or does not function at all.

What Happens When the Letters Change?

Because there are 64 codons but only 20 amino acids, sometimes a mutation causes no change to the structure of the protein. Amino acids can have as many as six codons, so deletion, insertion, or a SNP may not change the intended protein. The "codon wheel" in Figure 3.9 shows the codon for each amino acid. A simple change from UAC (tyrosine) to UAG creates a stop codon that will prematurely stop the process and create a shortened protein (Mort et al., 2008). This change is likely to produce a nonfunctioning or

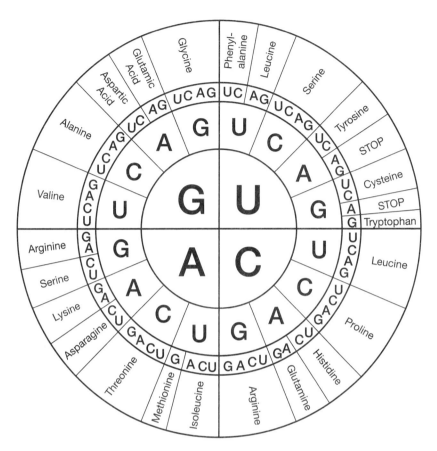

FIGURE 3.9: The Codon Wheel, Showing the Codons for Each Amino Acid

poorly functioning protein. For example, about 10% of people with cystic fibrosis have been found to have a false stop codon, sometimes called a "nonsense mutation," which affects the CFTR (cystic fibrosis transmembrane conductance regulator) protein (Gambari et al., 2015).

A number of DNA-altering mutations are relevant to mental health. Serotonin is generally known to be an important neurotransmitter involved in the process of calming brain regions like the amygdala. Interference to or reduction in the activity of serotonin can lead to increased anxiety, depression, and limitations to self-regulation during stressful experiences. Serotonergic processes are affected by the availability of transporter proteins that transport serotonin out of the synaptic cleft and back into the presynaptic axon terminal through reuptake transporters. This reuptake replenishes the supply of serotonin for future use and clears the synapse for another rapid firing across the synapse. An insertion mutation of tandem duplications in the promotor region of the serotonin transporter–linked polymorphic region (5-HTTLPR) of the *SLC6A4* transporter gene affects how many serotonin transporter (SERT) proteins are made.

The number of duplications in 5-HTTLPR determines whether a short or long allele of the *SLC6A4* gene is created. (An *allele* is the unique version of a gene on each of the paired chromosomes—one from the father and one from the mother.) The short allele transcribes fewer mRNA molecules, thereby reducing the number of SERT proteins. The lower number of SERT proteins negatively affects the activity of serotonergic neurons, thus increasing the risk for a variety of psychological disorders, including depression, anxiety, and alcoholism (Caspi et al., 2010). The long allele initiates the production of more SERT proteins, resulting in more effective and efficient transmission between neurons.

It may seem contradictory, but when serotonin reuptake is too fast, it reduces the movement of serotonin across the synapse, which reduces the calming effect on the amygdala and other limbic regions. A number of prescribed medications for depression inhibit reuptake to keep serotonin in the synapse longer. This inhibition helps serotonin reach the appropriate receptors on the postsynaptic neuron and maintain neuronal flow. These medications are called *selective serotonin reuptake inhibitors* (SSRIs) and include fluoxetine (Prozac), sertraline (Zoloft), paroxetine (Paxil), and citalopram (Celexa). Other medications that alter the activity of neurotransmitters and warrant a therapist's research include the tricyclics (norepinephrine reuptake inhibitors) and SNRIs (serotonin and norepinephrine reuptake inhibitors), which are used for anxiety and chronic pain (Artigas et al., 2002). When a client informs the psychotherapist that they have been prescribed medications, they are providing two important messages:

- that they have been diagnosed as having an affective disorder, and
- which neurotransmitters the prescribing physician believes require intervention.

This information gives a psychotherapist who has some knowledge of what happens at the molecular level a broader appreciation of what is contributing to the client's emotional and behavioral states. The therapist is more likely to feel confident to ask the client whether their medical practitioner has considered investigating gene mutations. From another perspective, a client who has received a genetic-based diagnosis will benefit from a psychotherapist who understands the science behind the diagnosis (Marteau & Croyle, 1998; Meiser, 2005). Here are some possibilities:

- **fragile X syndrome:** The mutation consists of multiple repeats of the CGG section of the fragile X mental retardation gene (*FMR1*). Without the FMR protein, symptoms include hand flapping, hyperactivity, recurrent ear infections, severe anxiety and tantrums, speech and language delays, behavioral challenges, and ASD symptoms (Schneider et al., 2020).
- *BRCA1/2* **breast cancer gene mutation:** Mutations include an 11-base-pair deletion, a 1-base-pair insertion, a stop codon, and a missense substitution. Someone with one of these mutations may need to consider preventive surgery.
- **cystic fibrosis:** The disease is caused by a mutation in the gene that codes for CFTR. The most common mutation is a deletion of three nucleotides (a single codon) that results in loss of the amino acid phenylalanine at the 508th position on the protein. It affects mostly the lungs, but also the pancreas, liver, kidneys, and intestine, causing difficulty breathing and the constant need to cough up mucus as a result of frequent lung infections (O'Sullivan & Freedman, 2009).
- **Rett syndrome:** Nonsense mutations (which produce interrupting stop codon) in the *MECP2* gene are due to deletion/insertion at the methyl-CpG-binding domain. Only females survive, often having a period of normal development until about 1 year, followed by a rapid regression with loss of acquired speech and motor skills, microcephaly, seizures, autism, ataxia, intermittent hyperventilation, and stereotypic hand movements. Despite these symptoms, patients often survive into adulthood (Kriaucionis & Bird, 2003).

- **worrier/warrior:** COMT (catechol-O-methyltransferase) is an enzyme that catalyzes the breakdown of catecholamines—including dopamine, epinephrine, and norepinephrine—in the synaptic cleft and presynaptic neuron. The gene that codes for COMT has a guanine-to-adenine SNP that is also referred to as "Val158Met." Met158 is 25% less effective, meaning that dopamine remains in the synaptic cleft. Met158 is known as the "worrier." Val158 is known as the "warrior." Met158 tends to be more anxious, less aroused by positive expectation, but also having advantages in memory and attention, which increases the likelihood of worry. Val158 is better able to process aversive stimuli (Craddock et al., 2006).
- **impulsive aggression, defiance/self-regulation:** MAO-A (mono-amine oxidase A) is an enzyme that catalyzes the breakdown of serotonin, dopamine, and norepinephrine in the synaptic cleft and the presynaptic neuron. The variable number of tandem repeat polymorphisms of the *MAOA* gene produces genotypes with low (*MAOA*-L) and high (*MAOA*-H) activity. The low-activity variant was present in subjects who were impulsive and showed more defiance, especially when paired with the short serotonin transporter *SLC6A4* variation (Williams et al., 2009).

CHROMOSOMAL MUTATIONS

Chromosomal mutations cause large areas of the chromosome to change. There are four types:

- **deletion:** losing all or part of a chromosome
- **duplication:** adding all or part of a chromosome
- **inversion:** reversing the direction of all or parts of the chromosome
- **translocation:** part of the chromosome breaking off and attaching to another chromosome

Chromosomal mutations are involved in a number of diseases and developmental problems. Again, the psychotherapist may work with both the individual and the family members, so having some insight into these problems is an important part of treatment and also important for establishing trust and rapport.

Chromosomal abnormalities include

- **Down syndrome, or trisomy 21:** duplication of chromosome 21, a condition that causes intellectual disabilities and delays, weak muscles, and flat facial features. It can also cause a heart defect, digestive problems, thyroid problems, and other health issues.
- **hemophilia:** an X-linked disorder caused by inversions in the factor VIII gene F8 at the distal end of the X chromosome. It is a blood coagulation defect that causes excessive bleeding.
- **Klinefelter's syndrome (XXY):** an additional X chromosome in males. Symptoms include taller-than-average stature; longer legs, shorter torso, and broader hips, compared with other boys; absent, delayed, or incomplete puberty; after puberty, less muscle and less facial and body hair, compared with other teens; small, firm testicles; small penis; and enlarged breast tissue.
- **triple X syndrome:** an extra X chromosome in females. Symptoms include learning disabilities, delayed language skills, and problems with motor skills and muscles.
- **Turner syndrome:** a missing or partly missing X chromosome in females. The mutation can cause a variety of medical and developmental problems, including short height, failure of the ovaries to develop, lack of fertility, and heart defects.

Methyl Groups and Mental Health: The MTHFR SNP Mutation

In this final section of the chapter we give an overview of one of the most significant molecules in human microbiology. A *methyl group* is a molecule of carbon with three hydrogen atoms (CH_3), and humans need it to do a lot of things. Availability of methyl groups is an important element in psychiatric disorders, neurodegenerative disorders, heart disease, autoimmune conditions, and even cancer. Methyl groups are vital for normal cell replication, and they are the means of turning gene expression on or off. Methyl groups are vital for phase II liver detoxification, protein methylation, homocysteine metabolism, neurotransmitter synthesis, and epigenetic processes. Methyl groups affect the processes involved in the removal and degeneration of neurotransmitters from the synapse and the presynaptic axon terminal (e.g., the enzymes COMT and MAO). Inadequate methylation capacity can lead to birth defects, affective disorders, executive cognition decline, diseases, and cancer. Methyl groups help to regulate histaminic concentrations, which affect allergic reactions and recovery. Methyl groups are used for a lot of things (Crider et al., 2012; Fava & Mischoulon, 2009; Gao et al., 2018; Gilbody et al., 2007; Holmes et al., 2011; A. L. Miller, 2003; Poduri et al., 2013; Shiran et al., 2015).

MTHFR SNP

Every cell has the capability to produce quantities of methyl groups, which it does continuously in a complex cycle involving molecules within the cell and molecules that are delivered to the cell from the food we eat. Methyl groups are required for "a multitude of cellular methylation reactions" (Bottiglieri, 2002, p. 1151S).

The following descriptions are limited, and further investigation is recommended, but we hope you can wonder at the intricate dance of self-organization happening in every cell, in millisecond time, every moment of the day. First, we will look at how the methylation system works, and then how it can go wrong and what can be done when it does.

THE METHYLATION SYSTEM

When the system is working naturally, the dynamic methylation cycle produces methyl groups: CH_3. Diet provides a fresh supply of methyl donors that carry and donate CH_3 into the process, including folate (vitamin B_9), B_{12}, B_6, B_2, serine, choline, betaine, and protein.

Three separate but interrelated mechanisms produce methyl groups (Mahmoud & Ali, 2019). As so often happens in the body's biochemistry, more than one mechanism develops. This is true for production cycles and utilization cycles. It makes sense in daily life to have backup systems and multiple uses of products. Nature worked that out a long time ago. The key element in the methylation cycle is the amino acid methionine. Once methionine is available, the process has only a few more steps: methionine combines with ATP (adenosine triphosphate, body energy) with the activating input of the enzyme MAT (methionine adenosyltransferase) to form SAMe (*S*-adenosyl methionine) which is the donor source of methyl groups. Specific enzymes activate methyl group transfer when and where required; for example, DNMT (DNA methyl transferase) is the activating enzyme when DNA requires a methyl group. When SAMe sheds a methyl group, it becomes SAH (*S*-adenosyl homocysteine) which is then broken down into homocysteine and adenosine. Homocysteine is then "restocked" with a methyl group extracted from food intake in one of two other pathways. Once the methyl group is converted back into methionine, the process is able to repeat (Gao et al., 2018). Here are the three methylation pathways:

- **Methionine pathway** (Figure 3.10): Methionine is produced directly from dietary proteins, which come from various foods, including turkey, beef, tuna, eggs, pork, tofu, Brazil nuts, and quinoa.

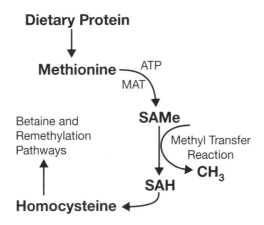

FIGURE 3.10: Methionine Pathway. ATP = adenosine triphosphate; MAT = methionine adenosyltransferase; SAH = *S*-adenosyl homocysteine; SAMe = *S*-adenosyl methionine.

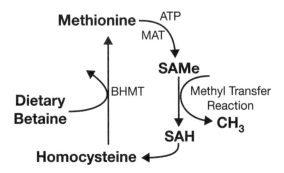

FIGURE 3.11: Betaine Pathway. ATP = adenosine triphosphate; BHMT = betaine homocysteine methyltransferase; MAT = methionine adenosyltransferase; SAH = S-adenosyl homocysteine; SAMe = S-adenosyl methionine.

- **Betaine pathway** (Figure 3.11; N. Zhang, 2015): Dietary betaine (from foods such as wheat, wheat germ, spinach, and beets) or betaine converted from dietary choline (found in fish, poultry, eggs, dairy products, and vegetables) provides the methyl group. Dietary betaine is activated by the enzyme BHMT (betaine homocysteine methyltransferase) to transfer a methyl group to homocysteine to convert it back to methionine. This pathway is particularly active in the liver and the kidney, which are the main organs that store large amounts of betaine (Obeid, 2013).
- **Remethylation pathway** (Figure 3.12; Crider et al., 2012): The chemical compound 5-MTHF donates a methyl group to homocysteine to turn it back into methionine. Dietary folate (and/or folic acid) is activated by the enzyme DHFR (dihydrofolate reductase) to become THF (tetrahydrofolate), which is activated by SHMT (serine hydroxymethyltransferase) and vitamin B_6 to become 5,10-MTHF (5,10-methylenetetrahydrofolate), which is activated by MTHFR (methylenetetrahydrofolate reductase) and B_2 to become 5-MTHF (5-methyltetrahydrofolate), the active form of folate. The final step of donating a methyl group to homocysteine is activated by the

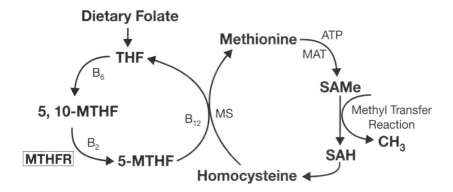

FIGURE 3.12: Remethylation Pathway. See the text for explanation of the abbreviations.

enzyme methionine synthase (MS) and coenzyme B_{12}. The key nutrient donor is "folate," the generic term for vitamin B_9, which is found in peas, broccoli, brussels sprouts, and cereals (also folic acid, which is the human-made version that is more resilient to heat and thus can be used to fortify baked foods like bread).

What can go wrong?

The most obvious problem with each of the three methylation pathways is the availability of dietary intake. Looking into what people eat is a very useful question for any psychotherapy. What clients eat and how they sleep, exercise, and breathe are fundamental lifestyle practices that are important for mental health. It is possible to appear obese and be undernourished. A genetic concern that can reduce the efficiency of the methylation cycle is a SNP mutation in the gene that encodes MTHFR. More than one SNP has been discovered, but the most concerning is the presence of homozygous alleles with the *C677T* SNP—where a cytosine is replaced by tyrosine at nucleotide 677 (Liew & Gupta, 2015).

This genetic mutation interferes with the efficiency of the step between 5,10-MTHF and the active form of folate, 5-MTHF (see Figure 3.12). Without the means to convert homocysteine to methionine, homocysteine can build up and have serious health implications. Other factors can also raise homo-cysteine levels, including lifestyle factors such as chronic alcohol intake, cigarette smoking, stress, and toxic environmental exposure. A high level of homocysteine, which can be measured in a blood test, is an indicator, and the potential cause, of a number of health problems. Most concerning are arteriosclerosis and heart disease (Barroso et al., 2017), but a high level of homocysteine as a biomarker also indicates concern for associated mental issues, as mentioned earlier. Many sources suggest adding folate, B_6, and B_{12} to the diet, but the MTHFR polymorphism causes a problem in creating the methyl-*activated* form of folate: 5-MTHF. If improvement in dietary intake does not have a positive effect, then it is necessary to take preactivated folate and B_{12}, which are indicated on packaging as *methyl*folate and *methyl* B_{12}.

Research continues to investigate the degree of impact of MTHFR poly-morphisms, but maintaining a good diet as preventive of methylation prob-lems is simple and, often, effective. We have already mentioned some of the dietary suggestions. It is not difficult to find reliable experts in the field who can advise with lifestyle, dietary, and supplement suggestions.

CLINICAL NOTES

The information in this and previous sections of this chapter helps psychotherapists understand that the client may have a genetic basis for their capacity to manage or not manage affective states. More to the point, the information provides an awareness that people are not all equal. There are variations in experience, environment, genotype, and epigenotype, as well as both inherited and heritable mutations. Knowledge that there are, potentially, a variety of biological bases to a client's problems is a reminder that each person is an individual, a unique phenotype, and this knowledge is an encouragement to explore a variety of therapeutic possibilities, including suggestions and recommendations made by those who understand the genetic, molecular, and protein environment of human biology. It has long been accepted that it is important to consider diet, sleep, exercise, and breathing when treating affective disorders. The deeper human biology affirms this by responding positively to what may seem like a simplistic therapeutic treatment. In our journey through these deep inner processes, we have described some of the building blocks of human microbiology in the unseen interplay that emerges as the mental states, behavior, affect, and emotions of human psychology. All this makes sense if the psychotherapist approaches the client as a mystery and, at the same time, a marvel. Therapy helps to produce the positive outcome that emerges from somewhere in between.

Conclusion

The search for a simple genetic answer to mental health has been robust, but largely unsuccessful. For psychiatric conditions like bipolar disorder and schizophrenia, plus neural conditions like autism, research papers focusing on new possible genetic influences continue to be published. We suggest that searching for a linear, causal connection is a large part of the problem. The genotype and epigenotype are part of a complex, systemic context from which the phenotype emerges. Still, the framework established in the genes must and does create predictable dispositions for the individual and for groups of individuals. At this stage it does not seem possible to establish definite outcomes of the phenotype, and it is likely that the unpredictability of a system that is based on something as complex as DNA will always be confounding. DNA is only the blueprint of what is possible for a living organism to become.

CHAPTER 4

Disorders

4.1 Affective Disorders

Each section of this chapter explores disorders that might lead someone to seek out a psychotherapist for help. Some of these disorders may require multiple practitioners. We hope you are discovering, as you work through this book, that mental health can be much more than what is going on in the skull-based brain, or any other single element of human biology. For the psychotherapist, the focus is assisting the client to recover a sense of well-being and find the mental state that enables them not only to manage their difficulties but to overcome them and discover how, as Martin Seligman (2012) describes, to flourish and thrive.

DEPRESSION, ANXIETY, BIPOLAR DISORDER

There are a host of therapeutic methods for affective disorders, but first, what do we mean by "affective disorder"? Is it a disease, a chemical imbalance, or an abstract mentalized emotional state? Someone who thinks that disorders like depression and anxiety are diseases will seek to cure the disease that is causing the symptomatology. Someone who thinks in a linear, cause-and-effect fashion will look for and resolve the things causing the disorder. Someone whose thinking is more systemic (refer to the Introduction), however, sees affective disorders as emergent expressions of a set of complex interacting elements. An emergent property is something different from the contributing elements, so it may not directly indicate what the elements are.

An affective disorder is an outcome, not a cause, and alerts the individual that a problem or problems need a response.

From the systems perspective, people become consciously aware of "symptoms" in order to stimulate deliberate, self-directed actions. There is a point at which our innate, nonconscious, problem-solving mechanisms need something more to solve the problem. For example, the feeling of hunger emerges into conscious awareness to stimulate a move toward food. Most of the time there is no awareness of what we need to eat. Systems thinking can seem confusing because the "hungry" message may not be just about the need to eat. The symptom can be an emergent message that means something other than the obvious. It can arise, for example, because of insulin resistance or perhaps a negative mood that is looking for an increase in serotonin levels by eating refined sugars, especially chocolate. The person's system is using eating-related mechanisms to sound the alarm. Another example is pain, which draws the attention to an area of the body or a behavior that warrants attention and a response. Pain is felt for a number of reasons—for example, injury, referred sensation, social rejection, and relational (heart) break. In this context, affective disorders are important messages that emerge into conscious awareness and/or as observable emotions and behaviors, urging the individual to attend to something that is disrupting and disturbing their sense of well-being and, because we also coregulate, to ask for help.

Affective disorders also provide a context for concern. Depression indicates issues of sadness, shame, self-worth, and a pointless future. Anxiety indicates concern and fear about the future, failure, and the pressure of expectation. An affective disorder is both a message and a starting point for therapeutic exploration.

In the British Psychological Society's report *Understanding Depression*, Bowden et al. (2020) argue that

> depression is best thought of as an experience, or a set of experiences, rather than as a disease. The experience we call depression is a form of *distress* [emphasis added]. The depth of distress itself, as well as the contributing events and circumstances, can be life-changing, and even

life-threatening. However, calling it an illness is only one way of think-ing about it, with advantages and disadvantages. For many people, depression is unlikely to be the result of an underlying biological dis-ease process or chemical imbalance in the brain and nervous system. Even if there are changes in the brain when people are depressed these are often consequences not primary causes. After all, all mental states have physiological and biochemical elements. . . . Whilst of course our brains are involved in all experiences, the reasons for depression are usually complex and include the events and circumstances of people's lives and the ways they can respond to them. (p. 16)

DISTRESS

Life consistently presents demands that must be responded to and resolved. This is the natural demand–stress–resolve cycle. Robert Sapolsky wrote about this cycle in *Why Zebras Don't Get Ulcers* (2004), where he showed that when demands are resolved, there is little residual or compounding stress. Unresolved demands create a chronic activation of the HPA axis that provides persistent pressure on the sympathetic nervous system to produce cortisol. The debilitating effect is not stress, but *distress*. Human biology automatically seeks to create a stable state,

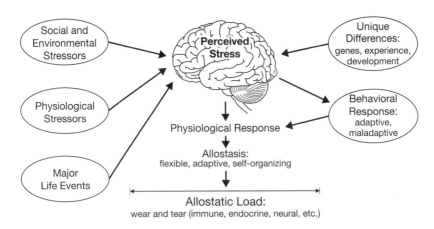

FIGURE 4.1: **Allostatic Load.** *Adapted from McEwen (2000).*

called *homeostasis*. When there is arousal from demands, desires, needs, and threats, that biology shifts to a flexible and adaptive process called *allostasis* to reestablish a stable state. The degree of impact on physiological and psychological systems is called *allostatic load* (Figure 4.1; McEwen, 2000).

When allostatic load is high and/or extends for long periods of time, it literally creates wear and tear on the body and its systems, including the immune system, the endocrine system, and the ANS. Too much load, for too long, leads to a deterioration in physiological and psychological systems (McEwen, 2005). Some people, as a result, become vulnerable to a range of neurobiological disruptions and dysfunctions, including major depression and anxiety (McEwen & Akil, 2020). In healthy situations the stressor is successfully dealt with, and the allostatic response is switched off. That is why zebras don't get ulcers, but all too many humans do.

We will explore depression and anxiety first, as the most common affective disorders. We include bipolar disorder here because the affective states of mania and depression are the two poles of bipolar disorder. We appreciate that bipolar disorder can be more complex, and some classify bipolar as more than an affective disorder. Remember, affective conditions are "best thought of as an experience, or a set of experiences, rather than as a disease," or perhaps even a disorder.

4.1.1 Depression

WHAT IS DEPRESSION?

Everyone feels low or sad at times, but when negative emotions are severe and prolonged, the problem may be clinical *depression*. Depression is a reactive response to difficult situations like abuse, bullying, loneliness, or family breakdown. It can run in families, indicating a genetic disposition (as discussed in Chapter 3). Depression can be comorbid with addiction, PTSD, trauma-related problems, insecure attachment, and, most commonly, anxiety (Groen et al., 2020). Janiri et al. (2019) found that mood disorders account for nearly 65% of psychosocial disability worldwide, with one in three Canadians affected by a mental illness in their lifetime.

According to the *DSM-5* (fifth edition of the *Diagnostic and Statistical Manual of Mental Disorders*), there are nine common symptoms of depression:

- sadness or depressed mood most of the time or almost every day
- loss of enjoyment in things once pleasurable
- major change in weight (gain or loss of more than 5% of weight within a month) or appetite
- insomnia or excessive sleep almost every day
- a state of physical restlessness or feeling rundown that is noticeable to others
- fatigue or loss of energy almost every day
- feelings of hopelessness or worthlessness or excessive guilt almost every day
- problems with concentration or making decisions almost every day
- recurring thoughts of death or suicide, suicide plan, or suicide attempt

Depression has been divided into subtypes:

- **major depression, or clinical depression:** at least 5 of the 9 common symptoms occurring daily for at least 2 weeks, with a depressed mood or loss of interest present each day.
- **chronic depression (dysthymia):** fewer symptoms, but experienced over a longer period, often 2 years or longer.
- **atypical depression:** an unusual group of symptoms, but with a positive mood reactivity (i.e., a positive response when something good happens).
- **melancholic depression:** no improvement when something positive happens.
- **postpartum depression:** beginning within 4 weeks of delivery of a baby, in association with a rapid drop in hormone levels of estrogen and progesterone. It is often resolved with medication.
- **seasonal affective disorder (SAD):** usually occurring in the winter months and related to a reduction of skin exposure to the sun.

Reduced sun exposure means lower availability of vitamin D, which has a wide range of activity in the body, including calcium metabolism and a number of important functions in the brain, including gene expression (Anjum et al., 2018).

- **treatment-resistant depression:** failure of at least two medications or (in some definitions) four therapies.

OTHER FACTORS

Brain Development. Cortical development during the teenage years affects an individual's capacity to manage their inner and outer worlds. There is a natural increase in gray matter around age 11, followed by a natural pruning and increase of myelination in the cortical neurons during the teen years as the brain organizes its structure in relation to the individual's life experience, attitudes, and behaviors (discussed in relation to schizophrenia in Section 4.7). Excessive and/or rapid loss of gray-matter volume makes it harder to regulate emotional states and leaves the person more likely to suffer from an affective disorder (Thompson et al., 2001).

Neurotransmitters. Neurotransmitters change in relation to affective states. The most notable changes are in the monoamines—serotonin, norepinephrine, and dopamine. Depression is associated with decreased serotonin (5-HT) transporter binding in the midbrain and amygdala; decreased serotonin receptor binding in frontal temporal and limbic regions; and increased density of monoamine oxidase (MAO), an enzyme that reduces serotonin in the synaptic cleft and presynaptic axon (Kaltenboeck & Harmer, 2018).

Genetics. Genetic mutations and some epigenetic patterns increase susceptibility to depression (reviewed in Chapter 3). Some epigenetic code from trauma can be inherited, creating an affective disposition independent of the individual's experience (Bogdan et al., 2014).

Sickness Behavior. Depression is also an indicator of chronic inflammatory processes. The immune system responds to bacterial and viral infection, as well as pollution, allergies, and chronic stress. A simple blood test for higher levels of C-reactive protein (CRP) indicates the presence of inflammatory molecules, such as tumor necrosis factor (TNF) and interleukin-6 (IL-6), which can enter the brain and trigger *sickness behavior*. This protective behavior includes wanting to lie down, keeping away from other people, and eating simple foods. These are natural ways both to recover and to protect others. Chronic stress increases inflammatory activity, but if there is no discernible illness, depression is often diagnosed. Some people on antidepressants would be more effectively treated with anti-inflammatories and psychotherapy for stress triggers. Consideration should also be made for histamine intolerances and/or mast cell overreactivity, stimulating the inflammatory process and possibly producing depressive symptoms.

Medication. Antidepressant treatments seek to reestablish balance in the neurobiochemical milieu. The idea is to shift the negative bias created when serotonin and dopamine levels are reduced. Medication combined with psychotherapy has been shown to be more effective than medication alone (Cuijpers et al., 2014).

Gut Microbiota. The symbiotic bacteria that live in the gut assist with digestion (microbiota), directly communicate with the brain, and can affect brain functions (refer to Section 2.2). Various gut-inhabiting bacteria influence the serotoninergic and GABAergic systems, which regulate the stress response. Patients with bipolar and major depressive disorders have been found to have an increase in Actinobacteria and Enterobacteriaceae, as well as a decrease in *Faecalibacterium* (Huang et al., 2019).

CLINICAL NOTES

The multiple systems and possible causal factors contributing to depression make this a very complex problem to deal with. Certainly, to think that a single antidepressant drug, such as an SSRI, is the silver bullet for depression is naïve at best and negligent at worst. The clinician should consider all of the elements described in this section (neural development, genetics, immune system/histamine reaction, gut health, etc.), as well as the psychosocial factors that can be triggers for depression.

4.1.2 Anxiety

Anxiety is an unnerving feeling of fear and/or dread that disrupts normal life. The U.S. National Institute of Mental Health (2017) reports that 31% of the population suffers from some type of anxiety in their lifetime. Annual U.S. statistics show an incidence of 18%–20% for all anxieties, including 6.8 million adults (3.1%) with general anxiety disorder, 15 million (6.8%) with social anxiety disorder, and 19 million (8.7%) with the anxiety of phobias. Anxiety is not the same as worry, concern, or being anxious. Feeling anxious is a normal up-regulation of the sympathetic nervous system in relation to reasonable concerns. The difference between this relatively normal up-regulation of the threat response system and an anxiety disorder is that once the difficult situation or threat is resolved—the exam is completed, the tax forms submitted—someone who is merely anxious is able to feel better and calm down, whereas someone with an *anxiety disorder* continues to feel fear or panic at the same level or even more strongly.

ANTICIPATION OF UNCERTAINTY

The human's ability to imagine into the future produces anticipation, prediction, and expectation. Accessing memories to predict the future increases the odds of achieving desired outcomes and avoiding, or preparing for, future adversity. This means of establishing a positive level of certainty in a capacity to manage future events strengthens resolve and a feeling of safety. The need for certainty, however, complicates matters by creating pressure. Being caught up in social demands such as educational success, employment, and financial commitments like a home mortgage establishes predetermined future outcomes that are often outside of the individual's control. Uncertainty in an ability to meet these and other "demands" can make it difficult to prepare for the future. This uncertainty increases the likelihood that even general living will lead to anxiety (Grupe & Nitschke, 2013).

Symptoms of an anxiety disorder include

- prolonged and severe feelings of fear or worry
- avoidance of anxious situations, such as by withdrawing from social activities
- persistent, specific phobias
- heart palpitations, chest pain, trembling, nausea, and panic attacks
- changes in appetite, activity levels, and sleep

Even though these symptoms interfere with an ability to be adaptive and enjoy life, only when these symptoms—struggling to focus attention on tasks, distracted by negative thoughts, fearful, and experiencing unpleasant bodily sensations—are persistent and pervasive are they considered to signify an anxiety disorder. When these behaviors continue beyond the triggering events or when the response is out of proportion with the triggering events, as in phobias and PTSD, is when people need help. An important life skill is to notice and resolve anxiousness before it becomes anxiety.

TYPES OF ANXIETY

According to the *DSM-5* (American Psychiatric Association, 2013; Europeans use the International Classification of Diseases—ICD-11), the five major types of anxiety disorder are generalized anxiety disorder, social anxiety disorder (social phobia), separation anxiety, panic disorders, and phobias.

General Anxiety Disorder. GAD (American Psychiatric Association, 2013) is characterized by excessive anxiety and worry (apprehensive expectation) about various events or activities experienced more days than not for at least 6 months, plus at least three of the following six behaviors:

- restlessness/being keyed up/feeling on edge
- being easily fatigued

- reduced concentration
- irritability
- muscle tension
- sleep disturbance

Social Anxiety Disorder. SAD (Rose & Tadi, 2020) negatively affects a person's ability to function successfully in social situations and is a significant risk factor for the development of other mood disorders, including bipolar disorder (Duffy et al., 2010), and substance abuse (J. D. Buckner et al., 2008). Symptoms and behaviors include

- marked and persistent fear of social/performance situations in which social scrutiny or negative evaluation may occur
- fear of humiliation or embarrassment
- avoidance of situations, or distress endured during them
- interference with routine functioning
- marked distress from phobia
- absence of substance abuse, underlying medical condition, or another psychiatric condition

Separation Anxiety. Although separation anxiety was previously considered only a childhood concern, adults also experience this type of anxiety when they are separated from loved ones and pets. Separation anxiety disorder is the fear of being away from a certain person or people, usually because of a fear that something bad might happen to either themselves or the other person. Symptoms can include headaches, nausea, difficulty sleeping, and nightmares. Separation anxiety may prompt panic attacks and a fear of leaving the home, which can be mistaken for agoraphobia (Bögels et al., 2013; Silove et al., 2010).

Panic Disorders. A *panic attack* is an abrupt surge of intense fear or discomfort that reaches a peak within minutes, during which time four (or more) of the following symptoms occur (American Psychiatric Association, 2013; note that the abrupt surge can occur from either a calm state or an anxious state):

- palpitations, pounding heart, or accelerated heart rate
- sweating
- trembling or shaking
- sensations of shortness of breath or smothering
- feelings of choking
- chest pain or discomfort
- nausea or abdominal distress
- feeling dizzy, unsteady, light-headed, or faint
- chills or heat sensations
- paresthesia (numbness or tingling sensations)
- derealization (feelings of unreality) or depersonalization (being detached from oneself)
- fear of losing control or "going crazy"
- fear of dying

Panic disorder is diagnosed when there are repeated attacks during the month following a panic attack, plus persistent concerns about more attacks, their consequences (heart attack, losing control), and negative behavioral changes to avoid more attacks.

CLINICAL NOTES

Certainly, affect and cognition play a significant role in panic attacks, often born from a past trauma and manifested as an overreaction to stay safe. But cognition and affect can come after a physiological driver initiates the panic. For example, too much histamine in the system can initiate an inflammatory response that includes palpitations, nausea, and a sense of dread that segues into a panic attack. Knowing some of the physiological causes of the 13 symptoms just listed will help to broaden the causal/systemic picture for the clinician, avoiding the assumption that it is all in the client's head as if only a cognitive construct.

TABLE 4.2 SYMPTOMS OF BIPOLAR DISORDER

MANIC-EPISODE SYMPTOMS	DEPRESSIVE-EPISODE SYMPTOMS
Feeling elated, "high," and sensitive	Feeling sad, anxious, or "down"
Being jumpy or overactive	Feeling slow or restless
Having racing thoughts	Having trouble concentrating or making decisions
Staying awake	Finding it hard to fall asleep, or sleeping too much
Talking fast and jumping topics	Talking slowly, having nothing to say, or forgetting the topic
Having a large appetite for pleasures like food, drinking, and sex	Being disinterested in almost any activity
Believing you can do everything at the same time	Struggling to do even simple things
Feeling important, talented, or powerful	Feeling hopeless or worthless, and thinking about death or suicide

Note. Adapted from Manning (2010).

Phobias. *Phobias* are unreasonable or excessive fears triggered by a specific object or situation, with a rapid anxiety response out of proportion to the danger. Those who suffer from phobias avoid the object/situation or endure it only with extreme distress; thus, phobias significantly affect activities of daily life. There are five main types of specific phobias:

- **natural/environment type:** These include a fear of thunder and lightning (astraphobia) or of water (aquaphobia).
- **injury type:** Fears of the dentist (dentophobia) or of injections (trypanophobia) are examples.
- **animal type:** These include a fear of dogs (cynophobia), of snakes (ophidiophobia), or of insects (entomophobia).
- **situational type:** Feared situations include washing (ablutophobia), enclosed spaces (claustrophobia), and open spaces or leaving the home (agoraphobia).
- **other types:** Some examples are choking, vomiting, or loud sounds.

4.1.3 Bipolar Disorder

Bipolar disorder is associated with episodes of mood swings ranging from depressive lows to manic highs. The exact cause of bipolar disorder is not known, but genetics, environment, altered brain structure, and chemistry all play a role. Depression is described as unipolar, but when there are two poles of symptoms, the experience is bipolar.

Bipolar disorder is subdivided into four types:

- **bipolar I disorder:** Manic episodes last more than 7 days or are so severe that hospital care is needed. Depressive episodes may also occur.
- **bipolar II disorder:** There is a pattern of depressive episodes and hypomanic episodes, but not as constant or intense as in bipolar I disorder.
- **cyclothymic disorder (cyclothymia):** Persistent hypomanic and depressive symptoms recur over 2 years in adults or 1 year in teens, but they are not intense enough to qualify as bipolar I or II.
- **other specified and unspecified bipolar and related disorders:** These disorders have symptoms that do not match those of any of the recognized categories.

Comorbidities with bipolar disorders include

- psychosis, which can occur during severe episodes of mania or depression, including hallucinations and/or delusions. Psychotic symptoms tend to match the person's extreme moods—for example, believing during a manic episode either that they are famous, have a lot of money, or possess special powers; or that they are financially ruined, are penniless, or have committed a crime.
- comorbid anxiety disorders, ADHD, and a tendency to misuse drugs and alcohol.

In the United States, about 40% of people presenting with depression are later found to be bipolar (Hirschfeld et al., 2003). Approximately 33%

of patients are misdiagnosed for 10 years or more (Singh & Rajput, 2006). Treatments for bipolar disorder vary for different types and include psychotherapies such as CBT and interpersonal and social-rhythm therapy (Novick & Swartz, 2019) plus medications such as lithium and valproate, sometimes used in combination (Missio et al., 2019). Side effects can be undesirable, including hand tremors, weight gain, diarrhea, and poor concentration. Some people choose to manage their condition with a minimal use of medication or reject medication altogether.

CLINICAL NOTES

Affective disorders have long been treated with combinations of medication and psychotherapy. The literature is still exploring what is effective and whether effectiveness has changed. The best starting point is to normalize sleep, exercise, diet, and thinking: take a 20-minute robust walk twice a day, regulate sleep patterns, direct dietary habits toward healthy foods, and encourage positive self-contemplation. We encourage you to explore the available literature on these important fundamentals (see, for example, Asnis et al., 2012; Briguglio et al., 2020; Hearing et al., 2016). Modern therapies seek to incorporate a better understanding of how to recognize and manage the symptoms. Tom Wootton has advocated for a change of attitude toward the management of bipolar disorder, developing self-managing protocols and introducing a more positive approach, applying the term "bipolar IN order" (Wootton, 2009).

Conclusion

It is not our intention to make affective disorders appear inordinately confusing or impossible to treat, but they are often complex. As a species, humans seem to be both finely balanced and robustly resilient. Sometimes people feel as if they are poised precariously on a precipice, but they may not be too distant from their resilient capacities. Assisting the client to access their own resilience—their natural problem-solving capacities—can lead to rapid recovery, although some clients may need more time and process to access their natural "mental health immune system." Affective disorders are not a disastrous collapse of the system, but an emergent quality that informs the host and the community to act. An affective disorder is not about an individual's emotional weakness, but a message from an age-old system that is seeking recovery.

4.2 Trauma Disorders

According to the *DSM-5*, trauma disorders caused by exposure to traumatic or stressful events include reactive attachment disorder, disinhibited social engagement disorder, PTSD, acute stress disorder, and adjustment disorders (American Psychiatric Association, 2013). Traumatic disorders are precipitated by severe or extreme traumatic events. Some are isolated one-off events; others can involve an entire childhood or life. As you learn about these traumatic conditions, it is important to keep in mind that the trauma spectrum is wide. As Dr. Robert Scaer details in his book *The Trauma Spectrum: Hidden Wounds and Human Resiliency* (2005), trauma spans events from war, rape, and other catastrophic violence to the vicarious trauma we can experience through film and TV. Even a fetus that suffers an avalanche of cortisol from a stressed-out mother has unwittingly taken part in the trauma spectrum.

This book is being written during the 2020–21 COVID-19 pandemic, where the trauma spectrum is unavoidable. Mental health issues, including suicides and depression, have increased—not only because of exposure to, or fear of exposure to, the virus, but also because of loss of employment, being in lockdown, and not having the social connections required for emotional and mental health (Giorgi et al., 2020; Pan et al., 2021). Only time will tell the full extent of the trauma inflicted by both the virus and the social measures implemented to contain it. Regardless, it is reasonably certain that both posttraumatic damage and posttraumatic growth will emerge from this pandemic.

In this section we will explore three of the disorders within the trauma spectrum: PTSD, complex trauma, and dissociative identity disorder.

4.2.1 PTSD

PTSD, according to the *DSM-5* (American Psychiatric Association, 2013) and the *ICD-10* (World Health Organization, 2004), is the result of a traumatic event of exceptional severity, such as war, terrorist bombing, natural disaster, or rape. The criteria do not specify what the event has to be, but rather that it is "exposure to actual or threatened death, serious injury, or sexual violence," either directly or vicariously (American Psychiatric Association, 2013, p. 271).

> The intensity and duration of symptoms are usually less severe if the trauma is caused by nature (e.g., hurricane) rather than by people (e.g., rape, torture). Single-event traumas are less likely to cause PTSD than complex traumas that repeat and persist. However, many single-event traumas (e.g., hurricanes) are associated with secondary adversities, such as loss of home, school, friends, and income, which transform them into complex traumas with indistinguishable clinical results. (Kilgus et al., 2016, p. 448)

There are, broadly, three cardinal features of PTSD:

- Avoidance of triggers (cues that bring the trauma back into memory), which may include a denial that anything actually happened.
- Intrusive recollections of the event, such as flashbacks when awake or nightmares when sleeping.
- Heightened autonomic arousal manifesting as hypervigilance, being easily startled, and insomnia.

Proximity to the trauma, the length of exposure, psychiatric history, attachment history, support network, genetic predispositions, and sense of control during the trauma are among the risk factors for developing PTSD. Fortunately, most people are resilient to even the most devastating traumas. About 80%–90% of people exposed to such extreme events will not develop PTSD (Koenen et al., 2017).

People with PTSD cannot, or have great difficulty, suppressing vivid and distressing memories of past trauma. People with PTSD may be confused over the temporal order of events, have gaps in memory, and give disorganized narratives of what actually happened (Ehlers, 2010). Individuals who do not suffer from PTSD when exposed to trauma employ an array of brain regions in an orchestrated manner to counteract any intrusive memories of the trauma (Mary et al., 2020), and they have a more coherent recall of events.

For PTSD sufferers, implicit emotional memories are uncoupled from the past and are felt as a here-and-now reality (Ehlers et al., 2004; Michael et al., 2005). These emotional memories of trauma are dissociated from the autobiographical memory of the event (Ehlers & Clark, 2000), and they lack *autonoetic awareness*, the self's awareness of the context of time produced in episodic memory (Tulving, 2002), so they are easily triggered (Ehlers et al., 2002; also refer to Frewen & Lanius, 2015, for an in-depth consideration of trauma-related altered states of consciousness). Essentially, these emotional memories are sensory and somatic impressions from the worst part of the trauma (Ehlers, 2010). The neural networks involved, which can be so easily triggered, run free from the constraints of other networks that are able to put the memory in its proper temporal context.

CLINICAL NOTES

There are many different ways to consider PTSD, but we will look at the intrinsic connectivity networks in the brain. These larger interconnected networks can be easier to conceptualize than drilling down to many smaller areas of the brain. You can review some of these networks in Section 1.1.

PTSD is marked by cognitive deficits that affect, among other things, short-term memory, declarative memory, attention, and executive functioning in general. These symptoms are generally manifestations of decreased activity within and between specific networks within the larger central executive network (CEN) and decreased capacity to switch between task-relevant and task-irrelevant networks (that is, between the CEN and the default mode network [DMN]; Lanius et al., 2015). Connectivity is also altered in the salience network (SN) between the anterior insula, amygdala, and areas within the SN (Tursich et al., 2015). These changes create a shift in threat sensitivity leading to heightened vigilance and arousal, and at the same time, dysfunctional activation of the insula points to both heightened *and* blunted emotional responses because of altered interoceptive awareness (Lanius et al., 2015). The DMN plays a key role in self-referential processing and maintaining a consistent sense of self in past, present, and future. It is important in autobiographical memory retrieval, and in conceiving the perspective of others, which is all altered when there is DMN dysfunction (Brewin, 2014; A. D. Brown et al., 2013).

Taken together, the complex picture of PTSD symptoms can be conceptualized as altered networks affecting cognition (CEN), arousal and interoception (SN), and sense of self (DMN). We will discuss treatments in Section 5.4. Let us continue now into complex trauma.

4.2.2 Complex Trauma

Affect regulation is a fundamental skill that everyone needs to live life well. Individuals who lack affect regulation are plunged into a dysregulated, chaotic state that produces feelings of fear, shame, anger, and an inability to connect in meaningful ways with others. Affect regulation is a primary reason why many clients come for therapy. Individuals develop affect regulation naturally when they have the right environment for secure attachment to unfold—attuned and regulating parents and an enriched environment—and they gain the capacity for flexibility, self-regulation, and a healthy sense of self. Complex trauma, however, can completely derail the ability to develop this sort of regulation, sense of self, and ability to relate to others. It can cause serious and debilitating dissociation and somatic dysregulation. Unfortunately, such trauma, and the havoc it wreaks, can be perpetuated across generations through persisting environments and even epigenetic inheritance. Trauma often begets more trauma.

So, what is *complex trauma*? According to Christine Courtois and Julian Ford (2009), complex psychological trauma results from exposure to severe stressors that (1) are repetitive or prolonged, (2) involve harm or abandonment by caregivers or other ostensibly responsible adults, and (3) occur at developmentally vulnerable times in the victim's life, such as early childhood or adolescence (when critical periods of brain development are rapidly occurring or being consolidated). (p. 13)

This type of trauma disrupts the emerging capacity for the individual to develop a normal secure attachment style and sufficient psychobiological self-regulation for a satisfying and productive life. Critical periods of early-childhood development can be hindered or distorted in often catastrophic ways in response to abuse by people who should be the nurturers and protectors. Interpersonal traumas in early childhood often come from caregivers; they include chronic and severe neglect, violence, sexual abuse, and emotional abuse. Some suggest that such trauma might be better described as "developmental trauma" (Spinazzola et al., 2018). The child is in the impossible situation of needing to find refuge in the arms of the caregiver, who is also the threat the child needs to escape from. Disruptions also come from nonattachment circumstances such as war, terrorism, and community violence (Ford, 2005).

The developing brain in early childhood is busy establishing the foundations of memory systems, personality formation, emotional and physiological regulation, and attachment—all of which are under threat by traumatic events. These foundations, once derailed or distorted, are difficult to reestablish in later life. The nervous system's focus on learning what is needed for survival creates a fundamental shift in the neural architecture. A brain primarily concerned with survival is more likely to be vigilant, anticipatory, and avoidant of anything that could be threatening. In a safe, nurturing environment the nervous system learns to be approach oriented, engaged in curiosity and exploration, and looking for novelty, which creates a richer neural architecture that is flexible, resilient, and self-controlling, with enhanced prefrontal cortical inhibition of subcortical responses.

Not only does the "survival/avoidant brain" operate in a vastly different way from the "learning/approach brain," but activation of the stress response system as a result of trauma can damage the nervous system functions that are responsible for managing distress, showing tolerance, seeking rewards, planning, and learning. Dopaminergic and serotonergic systems responsible for activating such responses are inhibited (refer to Section 3.2 for more on epigenetic changes). There are other serious health implications as well, such as depression of the immune system by a chronically activated stress response, resulting in a compromised ability to fight pathogens; activation of autoimmune diseases as a result of chronic inflammation caused by chronic levels of stress-related cortisol; and dysfunction of the HPA axis (refer to Section 1.2) as chronic cortisol damages hippocampal capacity to regulate the stress response.

The developmental trajectory is guided by survival in the experiential environment. The environment activates gene expression that produces the organism (refer to Section 3.2). Optimizing the foundational neural connections for a threatening environment paves the way for further development of neural architecture to deal with a dangerous environment. The biology and neurobiology increasingly lack "degrees of freedom" (Ford, 2009; M. D. Lewis, 2005). This fixedness of the traumatized psychobiological system not only defines the individual's identity and way of being in the world but becomes very difficult to shift as it reinforces itself, reducing the likelihood that new networks will emerge that might help in recovery and growth.

CLINICAL NOTES

Given the neural architecture of the traumatized psychobiological system, there is still hope. It is possible to change the brain throughout life, but changing deeply entrenched patterns of thought and emotional responses primed for danger is a task of many layers. It is more than just reframing thoughts or beliefs in the head, although this can be a good place to start if thoughts and beliefs are a readily accessible aspect of the problem. However, trauma often happens during transitional brain and body development, such as language formation (at about 2 years of age) and the process of myelination that enables higher order symbolic thought in late preadolescence (M. D. Lewis, 2005). The development and consolidation of many of the neural networks occurs throughout childhood as a one-off event, and it is not possible to go back and start again. With that in mind, there are positive, helpful, and successful therapeutic interventions that can make a difference to people who have suffered complex trauma. The brain can also develop other, unique alternative ways to achieve or simulate missing elements of brain development. We will cover some of those in Chapter 5.

4.2.3 Dissociative Identity Disorders

In 1985, Daniel Goleman wrote an article for *The New York Times* that told the story of playboy Peter and his socially charitable twin Paul; Davis, in his mid-20s, a sculptor; teenager Tom, who could pick locks with a bent paper clip; and 10-year-old Dorothy, who repeatedly ran away from home. They were interesting characters as individuals, but what made the story newsworthy is that they all existed within one person, John, an air traffic controller who broke down on the job one day, revealing his complex set of inner identities.

Normal individuals have an integrated sense of who they are (their identity), with a consciousness and memory to match. When these elements are not integrated, a disconnect can develop between memory, identity, and consciousness that produces a state of dissociation. There are a number of dissociative disorders, including

- **dissociative amnesia:** forgetting significant amounts of personal information. Dissociative amnesia often develops after an extreme stressor, causing the person to be unable to recall anything for hours or days after the time the stress occurred.
- **dissociative fugue:** forgetting who you are or where you come from. Like dissociative amnesia, dissociative fugue is typically triggered by a major stressor. In some elaborate cases, the person is in such an intense fugue state that they set up an entirely new life as a different person in a different city.

- **depersonalization:** feeling detached from the body, like an outside observer. This physical detachment produces a feeling of detachment from feelings, experiences, thinking, or memories, as if they somehow belonged to someone else.
- **derealization:** feeling that the world around, the people in it, and even colors are not real, or are distant or lifeless.

Probably the best-known dissociative disorder is *dissociative identity disorder* (*DID*), commonly referred to as "multiple personality disorder," although dissociative amnesia is the most common. In DID, two or more distinct personalities populate a single person. Popular books and films, such as *The Three Faces of Eve* (1957) and *Sybil* (1976), have increased public awareness of DID. However, someone who suffers from DID is not the same as a person who is quiet and introverted with her parents but becomes a "party animal" at friends' places on weekends. When the person is aware of deliberately acting out different parts of their personality, that is not DID. Someone with DID will manifest different personalities, each with a distinct memory, history, temperament, and even age, sex, or race. Research in the 1980s revealed some startling cases. Bennett Braun (1983) described a woman who was color-blind in only one of her "alters," as well as another individual who developed diabetes, but each alter required a different dosage of insulin. Dr. Frank Putnam presents his life's opus in the book *The Way We Are: How States of Mind Influence Our Identities, Personality and Potential for Change* (2016), which describes the extraordinary experience of living with "a collection of separate and distinct identity states that may have little or no awareness of each other and thus often behave in conflicting, contradictory, and self-defeating ways" (p. 159).

Secondary personalities (as opposed to the original or primary personality) are often aware of each other and of the primary personality, but the primary personality is often not aware of the others. These personalities can even converse with each other. Secondary personalities take on roles. One personality might be protective, and another might speak on behalf of the others.

CLINICAL NOTES

A therapist might not be aware that a client has DID because only the primary or one of the secondary personalities comes to see them. Experiencing dissociative memory lapses can mean a very difficult existence. People with DID might not remember certain purchases or weekends away, encounter people they do not know who insist they are friends, or be unable to understand why things turn up in the house that they do not recognize as theirs. DID is often associated with severe childhood sexual abuse (Ross et al., 1990) and seems to be a way to separate oneself from the horror. The abuse is compartmentalized to a certain personality, thereby protecting the "whole person."

If dissociation is a fragmentation of the "self," then it makes sense that a primary treatment goal is integration. Bringing these elements of self together can be challenging.

> Integration is an adaptive process involving mental and behavioral actions that help to assimilate experiences and sense of self over time and contexts. Well-integrated individuals have a consistent sense of who they are, realizing they can grow and change, while remaining the same person. Such a person experiences him or herself as "me," regardless of what he or she is thinking, feeling, or doing, and remains grounded in the present when remembering traumatizing events, and experiences the recall as an autobiographical narrative memory rather than a reliving of the past. Moreover, the person typically is able to recognize and accept reality for what it is, including his or her history and present circumstances, acting adaptively based on present circumstances rather than reacting with habituated dysfunctional patterns. (Courtois & Ford, 2009, p. 147)

According to Onno van der Hart and colleagues, from the Netherlands, dissociation is maintained by phobias related to trauma (van der Hart et al.,

2006). The core issue described by Steele, Boon, and van der Hart (2017) is *nonrealization*, the inability to accept, grasp, or realize experiences that are part of our reality. People exhibit nonrealization in many different ways, such as denying that the face in the mirror is actually theirs, or believing that their childhood was fine even if it was filled with abuse, or that their life is wonderful when it is clearly falling apart. Realization is a therapeutic step toward *integration*. Helping the client to become aware of reality, and then to able to accept it, makes it possible to adapt to it. Dissociation isolates the trauma into parts:

> Dissociation involves a division of the patient's personality into parts that each have their own sense of self and some degree of first-person perspective, with specific emotions, thoughts, beliefs, sensations, perceptions, predictions, physical actions, and behaviors. Each dissociative part of the patient's personality encompasses a unique perception of reality that can contradict the reality of other parts, with an amazing attitude of indifference toward profound inconsistencies. (Steele et al., 2017, p. 7)

Within a traumatized individual there can coexist many contradictory memories and perceptions, each in an insulated bubble of "reality." Some parts may try to shut down other parts that have an alternative take on reality. In their excellent book *Treating Trauma-Related Dissociation: A Practical, Integrative Approach*, Steele et al. (2017) open their chapter on principles of treatment like this:

> The treatment of dissociative disorders may seem very different than other psychotherapies, as it concerns work with a divided personality and sense of self. However, the best approach is simply good, solid psychotherapy, with the addition of an understanding of and ability to work with trauma and dissociation. While techniques are helpful, it is the ability to follow the essential principles of psychotherapy and to maintain a working relationship with the patient as a whole that truly makes treatment effective with dissociative patients. (p. 163)

They go on to describe the core attributes of effective psychotherapy for dissociative disorders and practical guidance for the application of phase-oriented treatment. Phase-oriented treatment aims to help clients integrate their personality from fragmented parts into a whole sense of self (Steele et al., 2005). This approach has been widely used for DID, and the International Society for the Study of Trauma and Dissociation (2011) provides guidelines for treatment; however, we highly recommend the books by Steele et al. (2017) and Dr. Frank Putnam (2016) for their case studies, highly accessible style, and deep understanding of dissociation.

4.3 Behavioral Disorders

We present behavioral disorders as a separate category because we feel it is important to distinguish these difficulties from behaviors that emerge from an emotional or cognitive context. A behavioral disorder is not something the person chooses or can easily stop. Many sufferers are extremely keen for the behavior to stop. We will introduce as many aspects of these disorders as possible, although we will be able to examine only a few in detail. We will describe the neurobiology where we can, although there is always more to every disorder. Emotional, traumatic, attachment, and sociocultural issues can underlie the development of most disorders, including behavioral ones. The most important contribution of the undesirable behavior is that it is a message from the "human system" that something is awry, and something needs to be done. Even though some behavioral disorders are difficult to resolve, that does not mean they are not manageable. Tourette's is one example.

It is frustrating to find it impossible to leave the house without returning over and over to check that the oven is turned off (obsessive–compulsive disorder). Aggressively resisting anything that seems like authority or control, even when it is in a person's best interests to accept help or instruction, can constantly sabotage school, home, and employment environments (oppositional defiant disorder). Lying awake at night because the muscles in your legs are twitching, sometimes so much that your partner cannot sleep with you (restless legs), is exhausting. It is awful when your brain almost feels like it is on fire and you want to explode when people, even your mother, are pressing you to think or pay attention (ADHD).

Therapists can help in many ways—first, by understanding *what* they are being asked to help.

4.3.1 Obsessive-Compulsive Disorder and Related Disorders

Obsessive-compulsive disorder (OCD) is a common anxiety condition found in about 2.5%–4% of the general population (Nazeer et al., 2020; Robbins et al., 2019). It is characterized by recurring upsetting thoughts (obsessions)—typically along the lines of contamination, doubts, the need to order things, impending doom, or aggression—that disrupt the person's life, sometimes severely.

These obsessions are managed by ritualistic actions (compulsions) such as hand-washing, checking, ordering, counting, praying, and other sequences of action or thought. People who suffer from OCD feel driven to act out specific compulsions to mitigate the anxiety generated by the obsessive thoughts. One of the more common OCD experiences is that of feeling contaminated and being compelled to wash hands or the entire body to be clean. Often the feeling of being clean either never happens or is fleeting, despite excessive washing. Another typical example is persistent doubt upon leaving the house that the house is locked and windows are closed, or that the oven has been turned off, and such persistent thoughts lead to compulsive checking—a distressing state that intrudes on the harmonious flow of life and torments the sufferer when they are not in a position to do the checking.

NEURAL UNDERPINNINGS OF OCD

The increasing sophistication of brain-imaging technology is making it possible to identify specific brain structures implicated in OCD, as well as some of the neurochemicals involved in modulating the OCD response. In this section we will consider the circuits involved in OCD and the ramifications for treatment; note, however, that the picture is much more complex than just neural wiring.

OCD-like behavior is significantly manifested in pediatrics with the autoimmune disorders known as "pediatric acute-onset neuropsychiatric syndrome" (PANS) and "pediatric autoimmune neuropsychiatric disorders associated with streptococcal infections" (PANDAS; Nazeer et al., 2020; refer to Section 4.8.1). In addition to the immunological connections with OCD, researchers have found pro-inflammatory cytokines implicated in the behavior, as well as a connection with the microbiome–gut–brain axis (refer to Section 2.2).

At a Parisian hospital in 1967, psychiatrist and neurosurgeon Jean Talairach and his team were investigating the origins of seizures in epileptic patients when they discovered that stimulation of the cingulum resulted in compulsive behaviors. The cingulum, located directly above the corpus callosum in the cingulate gyrus, is involved in complex repetitive movements and has been implicated in a bigger circuit involved in OCD. This more elaborate neural circuit has become known as the "OCD loop" and includes the orbitofrontal cortex (OFC), striatum, and thalamus (Alexander et al., 1986; Posner et al., 2014). Today, researchers are finding that hyperactivity of the cortico-striato-thalamo-cortical (CSTC) loop is deeply implicated in OCD. Information flow from the cortex to the striatum to the thalamus (via the globus pallidus) and back to the cortex can continue unhindered by the usual "gates" that would put the brakes on such looping flow of energy. These looping pathways can involve different regions and are commonly divided into sensorimotor, cognitive (associative), and limbic (affective/motivational) domains (Posner et al., 2014), with the obvious correlation between movement, thought, and emotional aspects of OCD.

The OFC (discussed in Section 1.2) is involved with the cognitive processing of decision-making and expectation. It is an emotionally attuned part of the frontal cortex that is sensitive to threatening situations. Fed to the OFC is information from the striatum, a major part of the basal ganglia involved in reward and habit formation. It is the striatum that enables multitasking, by running automatic behavior in the background, like playing with your hair while listening to a challenging lecture. The part of the striatum that is known as the caudate nucleus, working with the putamen, acts rather like an entrance/gate within the basal ganglia to activate or attenuate automatic responses. In OCD, part of what is believed to be happening is that when the striatum is not doing its gatekeeping job properly (i.e., the "entrance" is left open and unmanaged), obsessive thoughts and compulsions can flood the OFC uninhibited. For example, a "warning" from the amygdala about germs might prompt thoughts of washing hands. The OFC responds to such incoming information by reinforcing compulsive behaviors (such as hand-washing) to "make things right." A single action, however, fails to satisfy the OFC, because there is an open loop in operation that recycles the warning signal (e.g., that there is still contamination) to the OFC. This hyperactivity of the OFC and the lack of inhibition by the dorsolateral prefrontal cortex (dlPFC) of the striatum could be one of the main causes of OCD.

The OFC receives messages from the amygdala that are sent back to the lateral amygdala. This fear circuit is mediated by the HPA axis (see Section 1.2) and is further activated when sufferers of OCD do not engage in the compulsive behavior—in other words, when they consciously stop the compulsive behavior but the obsessive thoughts are still feeding back to the amygdala, letting the system know that things are still not OK. Engaging in the compulsive behavior brings a temporary measure of relief by downregulating the fear circuits. This management of fear and anxiety can lead to even more obsessive thinking and compulsive behaviors to avoid the uncomfortable consequences of an anxiety response.

Normally, a balance between the OFC, basal ganglia, and thalamus provides flexibility as responses to thoughts and the environment are activated or inhibited in a situationally appropriate way. When the balance breaks down and there is less inhibition, as in the case of Tourette's disorder, automatic behaviors become very difficult to inhibit. An OFC flooded with input from the basal ganglia needs help in inhibiting the automatic behavior that is trying to make things right. This help can come from the dlPFC—the part of the frontal cortex involved in positive, goal-orientated, reflective, and rational behavior—which can assist the more emotionally driven OFC in putting the brakes on the OCD loop. This inhibition of the OCD loop is achieved by strengthening the control the OFC has over the amygdala to attenuate the "fear network." The dlPFC can strengthen attentional skills (such as focusing on the present moment, reframing, tolerance, and acceptance) and override the automatic and habitual flow from the OFC, in effect distracting the OFC from autopilot and training it to engage in something more beneficial than the habitual OCD response. As clients in therapy learn to ignore the compulsive urges and see the behavior as nonfunctional, they can establish stronger connections from the OFC to the amygdala and regain control over what was an uninhibited autopilot of fear.

Some theory postulates a delayed maturation of the frontal cortex–striatum circuitry, where maturation of the cingulate is a causal factor in OCD (Rosenberg & Keshavan, 1998). Neuroimaging studies have shown higher activity in the OFC, anterior cingulate cortex (ACC), and striatum in OCD patients, compared with non-OCD subjects.

From a neurochemistry perspective, engaging in OCD behavior can down-regulate stress in an attempt to resolve internal anxiety while eliciting the reward of dopaminergic activity in the brain. A region of the basal forebrain called the "nucleus accumbens," also referred to as the "pleasure center" of the brain, is rich in dopaminergic neurons and plays a central role in reward behavior. Other neurotransmitter activity that seems to be important in the OCD loop is that of glutamate and GABA between the OFC and caudate nucleus, the globus pallidus, and the thalamus. Dopamine modulates the activity of the caudate nucleus, and serotonin modulates the activity of the globus pallidus.

CLINICAL NOTES

Although OCD patients do not typically show serotonin deficits, when they are placed on serotonin reuptake inhibitors (SRIs), 40%–60% show improvement of symptoms. Similarly, administering a dopamine antagonist can be effective in reducing motor tics, indicating dopamine as a possible modulator of behavioral compulsions in OCD.

Psychopharmacological therapy for OCD today revolves around the use of SRIs/SSRIs, even though there is no good explanation of why increasing serotonin levels improves OCD symptoms. Clomipramine (Anafranil) was the first SRI demonstrated to bring improvement in some cases of OCD. It blocks 5-HT (serotonin) and norepinephrine uptake and has some dopamine receptor–blocking function. This class of SRI has more side effects than do more recent SSRIs, such as fluoxetine (Prozac), sertraline (Zoloft), paroxetine (Paxil), and fluvoxamine (Luvox). Sometimes anxiolytics like benzodiazepines are used at the same time to combat the anxiety associated with OCD. It is difficult to judge how effective these pharmacological therapies are; most approaches are a combination of chemical intervention and some form of CBT.

An effective psychotherapeutic approach with a solid foundation in science was pioneered and developed by Jeffrey Schwartz and described best in his book, **Brain Lock** (2016).

As we have discussed, the dlPFC is the brain region that can attenuate the OCD loop by reorienting the OFC away from its obsessive–compulsive drive. Activation of the dlPFC (in conjunction with the hippocampus) to take executive control over thoughts and behavior, along with a recognition that OCD behavior is not adaptive, and the laying down of new neural traces that are more adaptive, can retrain the OFC. The most common approach to all this is to use CBT techniques such as "exposure and response prevention," first developed in the 1970s. Exposing clients gradually and systematically, with careful cognitive processing, can rewire the abnormal cortico-ganglia circuit to function in a much more adaptable and flexible way. Research has indicated that OCD patients who engage in such CBT do have decreased metabolism in the right caudate nucleus in the basal ganglia, a decrease in thalamus activity, and an increase in right-side ACC activity (Linden, 2006; Saxena et al., 2009). A practical and up-to-date workbook for clients is *Brain Based Therapy for OCD: A Workbook for Clinicians and Clients*, by John Arden (2014).

Other research into treating OCD revolves around deep brain stimulation (an invasive neuro–psychosurgical intervention (Tastevin et al., 2019) and deep transcranial magnetic stimulation (dTMS, a noninvasive technique; Roth et al., in press), which are both in early days of research but show promise for those who do not respond to other treatments (Rapinesi et al., 2019).

4.3.2 Impulse Control/Self-Control Issues

*She first ran away from home after an argument with her mother at age 16. Her immediate impulse was to throw some clothes in a garbage bag and go. Her disappearance lasted only 1 day because she became afraid, but many people who have that impulse are able to resist the temptation and override it. When she went out with friends, she was the one who would drink until she passed out. She would spend her pay on the first day, sometimes on herself, but often buying gifts or drinks for friends. She had unprotected sex without any thought of getting pregnant. Things got worse in adulthood. She described the situation as having "no space in my mind between thought and action" (G. Gill, 2019). She never hesitated to take a new drug. She would go to the store for one thing and return with 20. She left her relationship, only to return—six times. Her life became a revolving door of impulsive actions and disastrous consequences. "It was as if my brain was telling me I **had** to act" (G. Gill, 2019). Then came the inevitable shame.*

The large prefrontal cortex of the human brain gives us humans an exceptional capacity for self-governance or self-control. Such self-regulation, or self-restraint, affords us many benefits, from improving our health by keeping us from eating that doughnut, to helping us finish a Ph.D. when every fiber in our being wants to throw in the towel and go fishing! When self-control is impaired, the problem can be as mild as giving in to the doughnut temptation or as severe as psychopathologies that can lead to aggression, violence, and the violation of others' rights, known as "impulse control disorder" (ICD). Among such psychopathologies, according to the *DSM-5*, are oppositional defiant disorder (ODD), intermittent explosive disorder (with the unfortunate acronym IED), conduct disorder (CD), pyromania, and kleptomania. We might also include antisocial personality disorder and borderline personality disorder (see Section 4.6), which are part of a group of disorders called "cluster B personality disorders," since they also feature a lack of impulse control (American Psychiatric Association, 2013; Fossati et al., 2007; Herpertz, 2007). Impulsivity is an issue in Parkinson's disease, various movement disorders like restless legs syndrome, and ADHD, and extreme impulsivity has been observed in cases of PANS/PANDAS (refer to Section 4.8).

As with many psychopathologies, and in line with the view of complex systems that we have presented, multiple factors lead to a lack of impulse control. Genetics and environment both play a role, and separating them is difficult.

> Genetics may play a pertinent role as children with ODD are often the progeny of parents with mood disorders, whereas those with CD spawn from parents who have schizophrenia, ADHD, substance use disorder, or antisocial personality disorders. However, this association may manifest as a result of a confounding variable, as parents afflicted with the disorders mentioned above often provide a dysfunctional family environment, thus increasing ICD diathesis.
>
> Social factors implicated in the development of ICD include low socioeconomic status, community violence, lack of structure, neglect, abusive environment, and deviant peer relations. Lastly, some have postulated that those with ICD suffer from biological disturbances, distinguishable as reduced basal cortisol activity and functional abnormalities in frontotemporal-limbic circuits. Others have proposed cognitive deficits act as antecedents to ICD, such as learning disabilities. (Fariba & Gokarakonda, 2020)

Some clues as to the etiology of impulse control disorder come from the study of patients with Parkinson's disease who commence dopamine replacement therapy. About 15% of them develop such impulsivity and many more subclinical symptoms (Vriend, 2018). Similar manifestation of ICD is seen in patients who do not have Parkinson's but are being treated with dopaminergic drugs. In one such study, patients being treated for restless legs syndrome developed pathological gambling (Tippmann-Peikert et al., 2007).

So, what exactly is going on here? First, endogenous dopamine release in the ventral striatum, relating to reward, pauses when a negative outcome follows a behavior—signaling to the individual to avoid doing that again. Introducing dopamine D_2 receptor agonists increases impulsivity by preventing these natural pauses when there is a negative outcome (van Eimeren et al., 2009). Thus, the person does not get the encoding needed to avoid the negative behavior in the future, while leaving dopamine D_1 receptors to maintain any positive reinforcement intact. For ICD it is reasonable to speculate that something is going on in the reward-related pathways of the cortico-striatal-thalamo-cortical circuit, the brain circuit that controls movement execution, reward, and habits, to cause impulsivity.

Parkinson's disease also progresses to destroy serotonin- and norepinephrine-producing neurons, which can contribute to impulsivity. Increasing serotonin in the synaptic cleft through SSRIs has been shown to reduce impulsivity in OCD, although the effect is extremely varied with Parkinson's patients (Vriend, 2018, pp. 329–330). Similarly, increasing noradrenergic signaling can improve impulse control (Baarendse et al., 2013), yet the complex interactions between serotonin, dopamine, and norepinephrine make it difficult to get a clear causal picture of ICD. Does the cortico-striatal-thalamo-cortical circuitry contain genetic factors that predispose individuals to ICD, or to the development of ICD in difficult environmental/relational circumstances? The jury is still out.

Besides the research on Parkinson's disease, there are studies focused on executive function and impulsivity in borderline personality disorder (BPD) and ADHD, where the lack of impulse control is a marked feature. A systematic review by Sebastian et al. (2014) lay out the multiple components of impulsivity and the many variables that depend on the individual, disorder, environment, circumstances, and so on. As we continually emphasize, it is complex! What seems to be clear is that impulse control in BPD and ADHD revolves around the ventrolateral, ventromedial, and dorsal aspects of the prefrontal cortex (PFC), as well as the inferior frontal gyrus, insula, and ACC. In BPD, dealing with emotional stimuli may be accompanied by hypoactivation in the dorsal ACC and the dlPFC (Holtmann et al., 2013; Wingenfeld et al., 2009) that is also associated with negative emotionality in BPD (Ruocco et al., 2013). Hypoactivation of the orbital and medial PFC is also evident in BPD behavioral inhibition studies (G. A. Jacob et al., 2013; Silbersweig et al., 2007). It is not known, however, whether this hypoactivation is due to disturbed emotional processing in BPD (refer to Section 4.6) or to underlying impulse control deficits.

Similar hypoactivation of these executive functioning areas of the brain have been found in ADHD. Comparing studies of BPD with studies of ADHD, Sebastian et al. (2014) pointed out that

> across all components of impulse control, individuals with BPD exhibited frontal dysfunctions mainly in orbitofrontal, dorsomedial (dorsal ACC), and dorsolateral prefrontal regions, whereas individuals with ADHD displayed dysfunctional activation rather in ventrolateral prefrontal regions including IFG [inferior frontal gyrus] and insula, as well as in more dorsal medial frontal regions, particularly in ACC. (p. 11)

CLINICAL NOTES

This is still a nascent area of research, and given that impulse control is multifaceted across a number of psychopathologies, a full understanding of the neural foundations of impulse control disorder will require much more research. If hypoactivation of certain executive function systems is at the core of ICD, then there may be innovative stimulation or neurofeedback treatment methods that can address the deficit directly and beyond the use of dopamine agonists. As with OCD, techniques such as deep brain stimulation, which is used to treat Parkinson's disease, have proved helpful (Merola et al., 2017), as has more traditional CBT (Grant et al., 2011). Many more therapies supported by less research evidence have been helpful, but it is important to note that a therapist is useful in dealing with not only the disorder but the subsequent and consequent emotional issues of shame, distress, frustration, and social rejection. People with behavioral disorders often describe the feeling as "I couldn't help myself," so that is a good place to start—with some help.

4.4 Neurodevelopmental Disorders

Neurodevelopmental disorders occur when the development of the CNS is disrupted, manifesting as neuropsychiatric, motor, learning, language, or nonverbal communication problems. In this section we will briefly look at attention deficit hyperactivity disorder (ADHD), autism spectrum disorder (ASD), and Asperger's disorder.

4.4.1 Attention-Deficit/Hyperactivity Disorder

ADHD is a neurodevelopmental disorder characterized by short attention span, hyperactivity, and impulsivity that is age inappropriate and lasts at least 6 months. The condition typically is recognized during elementary school or earlier. Individuals with ADHD are the "active" children, the inattentive, impulsive, distracted ones who are always "on the go." The prevalence rate for ADHD is in the 3%–7% range for school-age children (Killgus et al., 2015).

Although we are discussing ADHD here as a "disorder," for the individual living with ADHD it is simply their experience. Some people generously share their stories, such as in the blog post "What ADHD Feels Like to Me" (MacKay, 2016):

> Like a pinball, my focus bounces from one thing to another. The lecture is the last thing my brain wants to pay attention to, even though I *want* to pay attention and I'm trying hard to. But I'm caught up in the chaos of the sounds of my fellow students—zippers, coughs, pens, keyboard clicks . . . there's no "before" and no "after" that can help. . . . It's just part of who you are. I realized around middle school that maybe I felt "different." But since "different" was my normal, I didn't think too much on it.

Like many developmental disorders, ADHD runs in families, with high heritability rates (about 70%–90% in twins studies), and it is 2–8 times more likely if a first-degree relative had ADHD (Thapar et al., 2013). However, genetic variation is not the whole picture. Commonly cited pre- and perinatal factors include smoking (Langley et al., 2005), exposure to illicit substances (Linnet et al., 2003), and exposure to other toxins (Nigg, 2008). Diet is implicated in the ADHD picture, but it is complicated, without strong evidence to conclude that nutrition is a causal factor (Thapar et al., 2013). However, studies looking at diet and ADHD give weight to the notion that diet does play a role in this disorder (Konikowska et al., 2012; Ríos-Hernández et al., 2017) and to the efficacy of diet-related treatments (Bloch & Mulqueen, 2014; Pellow et al., 2011; Pelsser et al., 2017), which affect gut microbiota and the gut–brain axis (Bull-Larsen & Mohajeri, 2019; Stobernack et al., 2019).

There is no doubt that ADHD can be extremely disruptive in families and environments like school. However, some children are diagnosed with ADHD because they have ADHD-like symptoms when they are very active and have trouble sitting still. Certainly, the classrooms of the last century or so have been difficult environments for the active child who has trouble focusing on logical, sequential, detailed, and abstract things, especially when they are not interested. Children who are more spontaneous, think more non-linearly, and are full of energy may not have a psychopathology at all but are wired to thrive in a different environment. There was a time when learning was a physical, on-the-job practical experience, as opposed to a classroom's sedentary, cognitive, and abstract learning. Thom Hartmann's book *ADHD and the Edison Gene: A Drug-Free Approach to Managing the Unique Qualities of Your Child* provides a unique discussion about ADHD-like behavior, cultural contexts, and a nonpathologizing way of looking at these children.

FUNCTIONAL CONNECTIVITY IN ADHD

As we discussed in Section 1.1, the default mode network (DMN) is associated more with daydreaming than with being on task and paying attention. When the DMN is active, attention-dependent tasks are more difficult (R. L. Buckner et al., 2008). To pay attention requires deactivating the DMN in favor of an active mode, and such deactivation is seen with increasing functional connectivity between the dlPFC and the DMN, where the dlPFC is, in effect, down-regulating the DMN. Failure to inhibit the DMN is seen as a neural signature of ADHD (Konrad & Eickhoff, 2010).

A recent study (McNorgan et al., 2020) looking at task-dependent connectivity in ADHD used machine learning to analyze the nonlinear relationships between different brain regions. In complex systems many regions interact, and at different levels and patterns. Machine learning using deep neural networks is the only way to make sense of the multitude of connections and resulting output. By applying machine learning to whole-brain fMRI functional connectivity studies, the researchers were able to come up with a predictive model that can identify ADHD with 99% accuracy. The model can even identify adults who were diagnosed with ADHD as children, suggesting that the underlying neural connectivity remains, even though the adult brain has matured, the connectivity is probably more integrated, and the person may have learned various strategies to limit the impact of ADHD. Machine learning also made it possible to identify typical and atypical ADHD patterns, where a linear perspective using paper tests would not correctly diagnose. For example, hypoconnectivity from the right visual network to a region within the anterior DMN was associated with ADHD when the individual performed poorly on a certain task (Iowa Gambling Task, IGT), but those who did well on that same task showed interhemispheric hypoconnectivity within the visual network—still associated with ADHD. The researchers say of such complexity that

> resting state hyperconnectivity but task-related hypoconnectivity may be characteristic of ADHD, indicating a general difficulty in task-appropriate engagement and disengagement of multiple functional networks, but that individuals with ADHD that perform atypically well on the IGT demonstrate a different connectivity profile within the visual processing network. (McNorgan et al., 2020, p. 13)

In 1997 the National Institute of Mental Health (NIMH) embarked on a landmark research project to evaluate the multimodal treatment of ADHD. The study (MTA Cooperative Group, 1999a, 1999b) and subsequent follow-up studies (Jensen et al., 2007; Molina et al., 2009; MTA Cooperative Group, 2004ab) looked at three fundamental questions about the treatment of ADHD:

1. How do behavioral and medication treatments compare with one another?
2. Are there benefits when behavioral and medication treatments are used together?
3. What is the most effective delivery of treatment?

The NIMH study focused on 579 children between the ages of 7 and almost 10 years old around the United States who were diagnosed with ADHD. These children were assigned to one of four different treatment groups for 14 months, after which the impact of the treatments was evaluated. The treatment groups were

- **medication management:** The only treatment was medication, and the study evaluated different doses of Ritalin (methylphenidate).
- **behavioral treatment:** Behavioral interventions delivered by parents, counselors, and schools were conducted in a coordinated manner.
- **combined treatment:** Children received both the medication and behavioral treatment.
- **community care:** This was the control (nontreatment) group.

The study found that core ADHD symptoms (intention and hyperactivity/impulsivity) were better treated by medication alone than by behavioral treatment alone. Interestingly though, on other measures—aggressive behavior, oppositional behavior, anxiety, sadness, social skills, parent–child relations, and academic achievement—there was not a significant difference between the first two groups. Unsurprisingly, the combined treatment—both medication and behavioral intervention—was statistically superior in terms of core symptoms and oppositional/defiant behaviors.

What may be puzzling is that the study's statistical analysis did not show a significant difference in the other domains compared to medication alone. However, any conclusion depends on how the data are analyzed. Children in the combined group did best in 12 of the 19 outcome measures, compared with children in the medication-only group, who did best in only 4.

Furthermore, parents rated children on the combined-treatment group better in terms of aggression, oppositional behavior, core ADHD symptoms, internalizing symptoms (anxiety, sadness, etc.), and reading.

So, what have we learned 20 years on? The basic findings seem to hold true: Medication in the form of stimulants seems superior to behavioral therapy, but a combination of medication and stimulants is better yet (Catalá-López et al., 2017). Unfortunately, the lack of robust studies on complementary and alternative medicines, including neurofeedback and nutrition, prevent these interventions from finding a place in the broad reviews that carry weight in this particular area. Reviews of specific alternative treatments reveal that mixed findings and alternatives to stimulants are, at best, seen as additions or complements to pharmacological intervention. Nevertheless, plenty of testimonies suggest that alternatives to stimulants can play a significant or even major role in treatment. For example, a recent systematic review on the sustained effects of neurofeedback concludes that "[neurofeedback] can be considered a non-pharmacological treatment option for ADHD with evidence of treatment effects that are sustained when treatment is completed and withdrawn" (Van Doren et al., 2019, p. 303). The gut–brain axis, discussed in Section 2.2, is also implicated with ADHD and the connection to specific mixes of microbiota in children who have the disorder (Boonchooduang et al., 2020; Mathee et al., 2020), and dietary changes, such as adhering to the Mediterranean diet (Ríos-Hernández et al., 2017; San Mauro Martín et al., 2018), may be, at the very least, a great complementary therapy. The "few-foods diet" (otherwise known as an "oligoantigenic diet"), a short-term elimination diet that is intended to identify foods that may be causing or exacerbating symptoms, has also been shown to significantly reduce symptoms (Pelsser et al., 2017; Stobernack et al., 2019).

CLINICAL NOTES

We come, as we have so many times in this book, to the fact that psychotherapists need to be aware of the diverse factors implicated in both etiology and treatment. Exploring therapeutic strategies like exercise and diet may not have been part of the therapist's training, but it may be a significant part of the client's clinical picture and should be addressed. For example, knowing that something in the diet can have significant effects on ADHD symptoms is motivation to look carefully at the client's diet for any red flags. It is wise to consider what is going on with the client's immune system, their histamine response, and their gut microbiome, as well as whether they are putting something into their body that is producing or amplifying symptoms.

4.4.2 Autism Spectrum Disorder

The term "autism spectrum disorder" (previously "pervasive developmental disorder"; Kilgus et al., 2016) is used to describe an emerging pattern of behavioral development between 6 and 30 months after birth. Although the developmental disorder may be well under way during fetal life, postpartum developmental delays may represent the completion of a foundation already laid. *ASD* is a heterogenous group of disorders. Severity can range from individuals who are nonverbal, with little awareness or interest in the social world, to high-functioning individuals who excel in many cognitive domains but have difficulty understanding social interactions and communication (Mierau & Neumeyer, 2019).

In terms of epidemiology, the prevalence of the disorder is about 2% (Frye et al., 2019; Mierau & Neumeyer, 2019; Mughal et al., 2020), with a bias toward males, in a male:female ratio ranging from 4:1 to 5:1. Typically, parents will notice a lack of social communication, interactions, and interest, along with repetitive behaviors like rocking, clapping, or head-banging. As these children grow, their impaired social interactions, fixations, and routines/rigidity become obvious as their developmental trajectory misses normal milestones by the third year (Mughal et al., 2020). The symptoms are on a spectrum and, at the extreme, can be severely disabling. At the "high-functioning" end of the spectrum, the capacity for focus in narrow fields (like the now clichéd young male computer coder) can be an advantage in some fields, but it is often at the detriment of a "normal" social life.

A high-functioning autistic individual can learn to fake it and even appear normal, but

> high-functioning autism . . . means that I usually look normal on the outside. But I'm here to tell you that I am fundamentally different on the inside. By the time I hit adulthood, I learned to hide my autism to avoid unintentionally upsetting or insulting neurotypical people (our word for non-autistic). . . . I wish I could shout from the rooftops: *You have no idea how hard I have to work to appear this way!* . . . If there's a loud TV, my brain cannot tune it out. Actually, I cannot tune out anything. Ever. That smell of popcorn from a co-worker's desk? It hijacks my brain to the point that I have to take my work to another room if I am to have any hope of concentrating. . . . Imagine having the acuity of your senses turned up to 11. (Condo, 2020)

Although the etiology of ASD is still unclear, the disorder is highly heritable (Colvert et al., 2015), with hundreds of associated genes, as well as twins studies demonstrating strong genetic correlations (Wiśniowiecka-Kowalnik & Nowakowska, 2019). Evidence suggests that synaptic dysfunction may be at the center of the problem, with genetic mutations highlighting deficits in excitatory and inhibitory synaptic function (Ebrahimi-Fakhari & Sahin, 2015) and in signaling networks that regulate synaptic development and plasticity (Ebert & Greenberg, 2013). Such synaptic dysfunction leads to not only developmental delays but atypical developmental trajectories (Johnson et al., 2015). Interestingly, in a review of brain adaptation during development, Johnson et al. (2015) speculated that

> in some cases that lead to autism, synaptic dysfunction leads to the early environment being sampled with poor fidelity, with a particular cost to the most dynamic and least easily predictable elements of the external environment. In many cases, these are associated with the social world and the complex and pseudo-predictable interactions with other humans. A mild degree of noisy sampling may lead to prolonged plasticity and delays in the subsequent steps of brain development that

may be specific to the most complex and dynamic aspects of the early environment. (p. 431)

Early disturbances of synaptic function could be compromising the processing of input from the environment at critical times of development, delaying typical trajectories, and resulting in atypical neural architecture that makes it more difficult to deal with the world. Neuroscientists have become rather adept at understanding the implications of damage or alterations to discrete brain areas, but the level of understanding is not good when the alterations are as widespread as they are in ASD. However, many genes implicated in ASD do seem to have patterns of peak expression during fetal life between Weeks 8 and 22 after conception (Parikshak et al., 2013; Willsey et al., 2013), with some of these gene mutations leading to excitation–inhibition imbalances in the maturing cortex later in life (Graf et al., 2004). The developmental timing of cortical areas is complex, with inhibitory/excitatory (GABAergic/glutamatergic) systems developing at different times, adding complexity to the picture. The understanding of how such widespread, diffuse, atypical changes in connectivity during development cause the sort of neural processing referred to as "ASD" is incomplete, and thus there is no known way of reversing the syndrome, if that is even possible.

In addition to synaptic changes, there are, according to Frye et al. (2019), some promising biomarkers of ASD, beyond simply observing behavior, that may lead to treatment interventions. Biomarkers fall into several major types—for example, behavioral, genetic, immune, medical history, metabolic, neuroimaging, neurophysiology, and nutritional (Frye et al., 2019). Even the gut–brain relationship (refer to Section 2.2) is implicated in autism, with researchers finding that some gene mutations affecting neuronal communication in autism also cause dysfunctions in the gut and in gut microbial interactions with the brain (Hosie et al., 2019).

It is still early days, and much more research needs to be done, but there may be pathways to treating the core symptoms of ASD and the disorder's progress. One interesting dietary approach for many neurodevelopmental disorders, including ASD, is the "gut and psychology syndrome" (GAPS) approach (Campbell-McBride, 2010). The basis of the approach is to heal the gut through good nutrition, reduce inflammation, and restore a healthy gut microbiome.

CLINICAL NOTES

Much of the literature about ASD is rather bleak in terms of treatment, so alternative or novel approaches such as metabolic interventions (Mierau & Neumeyer, 2019), many of which are being used in practice, are very welcome, and the hope is that more and better clinical trials are on the horizon.

Full recovery from ASD is uncommon but not unheard of (Helt et al., 2008). Mark Hedges claims he was cured of autism through diet and healing his gut (Hedges, 2016), giving credence to approaches like GAPS. Some research suggests that there can be movement along the spectrum to higher functioning, but shifts like this can also result in residual comorbidities such as depression, phobias, ADHD/attention difficulties, emotional immaturity, and impaired social functioning. A timely psychoeducational intervention can significantly improve the level of autonomy reached by the individual, and therefore favorably modify the outcome (Posar & Visconti, 2019).

4.4.3 Asperger's Disorder

You have likely heard about *Asperger's disorder*, although the DSM-5 now includes the condition as part of the spectrum of ASD. Children who have Asperger's are not impaired in cognition or language, and they have normal intelligence, but they do suffer from impaired social/empathic behavior and can have narrow, restrictive interests, be reliant on routines, and display some of the stereotyped behavior seen in autism, albeit in a milder state (Kilgus et al., 2016). About half of children with Asperger's who are a little late in speech development can speak fluently by age 5. They may also show some quirks in the way they use language in social contexts (Attwood, 1998), and they may have an odd prosody (peculiar voice characteristics). One affected individual spoke with a distinctly upper-class English accent when he was young, even though he came from a very middle-class Australian family. Although he was high functioning cognitively, his other mild ASD symptoms betrayed the fact that this unusual prosody was somehow connected to his place on the spectrum. In other examples of Asperger's symptoms, the child might open a conversation with a seemingly irrelevant comment or question about something interesting, but with no relevance to the current social interaction; they might interrupt the other speaker; they might not be able to adjust to the flow of conversation; or they might take things literally when it would be obvious to others that a literal interpretation was not intended.

The social awkwardness or "quirky" behavior of these children (and adults) can be addressed by teaching social skills (refer to Bowers, 2015, for a very accessible book on the topic). Such high-functioning children can be highly successful in domains they are keenly interested in. One company employs such young people to code computer games because they are highly focused on what is often narrow and tedious work, yet they do this work with enthusiasm and excellence. Social distractions in this sort of work environment are not a problem because individuals with Asperger's simply are not interested in socializing! It is not a "neurotypical workplace" but a workplace that understands and embraces Asperger's disorder and even capitalizes on the benefits. Often people at the high-functioning end of ASD will have poor short-term memory and diminished capacity to multitask, but great long-term memory and the capacity to make associations (Grandin & Panek, 2014).

CLINICAL NOTES

Computer programming, accounting, and engineering are all career paths that people with ASD can thrive in. Temple Grandin, one of the world's most famous and accomplished adults with ASD, suggests also commercial art, photography, and design, if the work is well defined and can be sold on its own merits and not on personality (Grandin, 1999). In addition, she notes that these jobs might be better done as freelancing. We know a person with Asperger's who is brilliant at commercial design in a freelance capacity but would be frustrated in a neurotypical workplace, having to work in a team environment. He definitely prefers something like the game-coding workplace described in this section.

Conclusion

The brain has a developmental journey that can falter or diverge. Congenital differences, genetic dispositions and mutations, childhood diseases, injury, and trauma are elements that can affect how an individual brain will develop. As the personal stories we presented in this section attest, the brain you have is the brain you have. The question is, What can the emergent qualities and quantities of an individual biological construct become? That is where a psychotherapist who understands what might be happening beneath the surface can help a client make the journey to the most they can be.

4.5 Neurocognitive Disorders

PARKINSON'S, ALZHEIMER'S/DEMENTIA, AND TRAUMATIC BRAIN INJURY

The conditions discussed in this section usually require specialist attention, including medical, psychological, and psychiatric. There is, however, an important place for the psychotherapist. Whenever someone faces difficulties, there will be emotional and behavioral issues that may not strictly be part of their condition but emerge because of the condition. The first consideration for a psychotherapist is *who* is requiring assistance. Certainly, there is the client, but there is also the human system surrounding the client, including family, spouse, friends at work or school, and a social community.

Each condition has unique aspects, but a common feature affecting all neurodegenerative disorders is cognitive impairment. Figure 4.2 indicates the scope of issues that affect cognitive performance. Changes in cognitive capacities affect the individual and everyone in their social system. Neural tissue is damaged by neurodegenerative diseases and by injury, and some

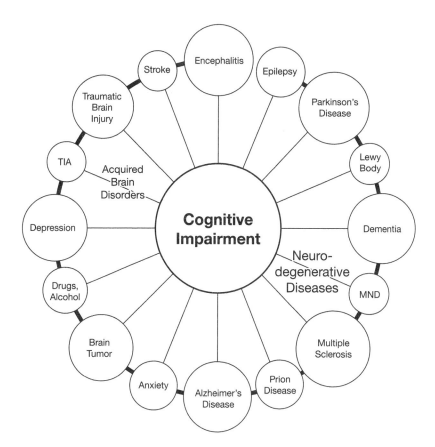

FIGURE 4.2: Array of Cognitive Impairments. MND = motor neuron disease; TIA = transient ischemic attack. *Adapted from Trojsi et al. (2018).*

treatments have side effects that exacerbate and even initiate other problems. The key is to be aware that these conditions are complex. A therapist needs to be informed and aware.

Sometimes a psychotherapist is recommended by another practitioner, but people also seek out psychotherapy independently. The client needs help managing their affective issues, building resilience, and handling practical lifestyle needs. It is valuable for the psychotherapist to know something about what is happening in the client's brain and body in order to understand how that affects their daily life and the lives of those around them. We will focus on the problems in the three cases just presented: Parkinson's disease, age-related dementia and Alzheimer's, and TBI and dysexecutive syndrome.

4.5.1 Parkinson's Disease

Mary is the wife of long-term client John, who was diagnosed with Parkinson's disease 3 years ago. She is now struggling to manage John's changing behavior and unpredictable moods. Initially, he needed help to deal with anxiety about the diagnosis, which was followed by depression. Most sessions with John involved talking about the symptoms and what he could expect as the disease progressed. He felt that the doctors were honest and forthright, but no one had the time to help him process the information. Now Mary needed help managing one of the medicinal side effects: John was having schizoidal-type delusions and hallucinations. She understood, but she needed help dealing with imaginary people who were telling John things that were not true about members of the family. She felt that the doctors were helpful but not heartful.

Parkinson's disease is the result of a reduction in dopamine in the motor regions of the basal ganglia (Figure 4.3). This decrease in dopamine is caused by a loss of dopaminergic cells in the *substantia nigra*, a dark cluster of cells in the midbrain. There are four distinct dopaminergic systems in the brain, each having a different effect. The main system affected in Parkinson's disease is the dopaminergic neurons that extend from the substantia nigra to the striatum, the *nigrostriatal* system. Dopamine and the striatum of the basal ganglia play a vital role in regulating movement of the body. Exactly what causes the loss of nerve cells is still unclear. Genetic and environmental factors are among the main areas of investigation. Parkinson's disease affects about 1 in 500 people. Symptoms generally develop after age 50, although approximately 1 in 20 people first experiences symptoms before age 40. Men are slightly more likely to get Parkinson's. Unfortunately, there

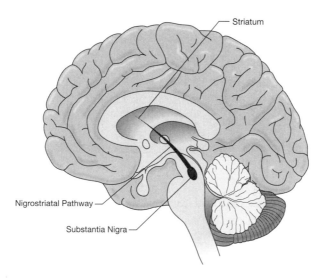

Striatum

Nigrostriatal Pathway

Substantia Nigra

FIGURE 4.3: Nigrostriatal Pathway. *Adapted from Ledonne & Mercuri (2017).*

is still no cure, although many treatments are available to help manage the symptoms and slow the progression.

The three main symptoms of Parkinson's disease are

1. involuntary shaking of parts of the body (tremor),
2. slow movement, and
3. stiff and inflexible muscles.

Many other symptoms are not only elements of the disease but also reactions to and complications of having the disease. Medications (e.g., Sinemet, which is carbidopa plus levodopa) increase available dopamine throughout the brain and thus can disrupt normal processes in the other dopaminergic pathways (Figure 4.4). Disruption to the *mesocortical pathway* affects mental activity in the frontal cortex (producing foggy thinking) and the medial PFC (which regulates emotions). Increased dopamine in the *mesolimbic pathway* can trigger psychotic-like episodes (conversely, antipsychotic medication that reduces dopamine can produce Parkinsonian symptoms; Pfeiffer, 2015; Tibar et al., 2018). (The fourth dopamine pathway is the *tuberoinfundibular pathway*, which extends from the arcuate nucleus of the hypothalamus to the median eminence on top of the pituitary stalk and is involved in the production of prolactin, enabling the production of breast milk. Some females and males on antipsychotic medication experience the side-effect of producing breast milk.)

Nonmotor symptoms include

- depression and/or anxiety.
- loss of the sense of smell (this can predate diagnosis by several years).
- memory problems.
- difficulty with heat regulation.
- problems with saliva and tear production.
- sleep disruption and fatigue during the day—partly because of the

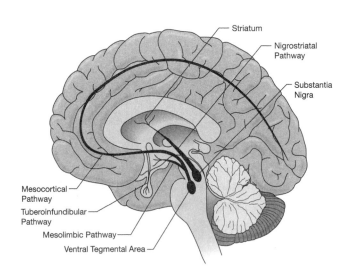

FIGURE 4.4: The Four Dopamine Pathways. *Adapted from Luo & Huang (2016).*

disease, partly because of a lack of sleep, and partly a side effect of the medication (levodopa has a side effect of sedation).

- acting out dreams (kicking, calling out, and talking, which is a serious concern for the bed partner). The patient can fall out of bed or injure themselves on bedside furniture.
- constipation and frequent urination and/or incontinence.
- sexual dysfunction (in up to 50% of cases).
- pain. Half of patients with Parkinson's disease experience pain that is nonspecific and might initially be suspected as arthritis or fibromyalgia. Parkinson's-based pain tends to occur on the side of the body that correlates with the side of the brain that is deteriorating most. Pain on just one side of the body is an indicator that warrants a test for Parkinson's.

COGNITIVE IMPACTS AND STRATEGIES

Cognitive problems, which are largely related to disruptions to the mesocortical pathway, as well as serotonergic and cholinergic neurotransmitter availability, are reported by family caregivers as the most distressing. Changes in personality, attitudes, and motivations are more disturbing than motor symptoms for many loved ones. Mary describes this aspect of Parkinson's as making her feel sometimes like she is caring for a stranger. Most patients will suffer from disorganization and confusion. Creating daily routines is very helpful, and cognitive training such as computer-based activities can improve attention and problem-solving skills (Glizer & MacDonald, 2016). Some 25%–30% of Parkinson's patients develop dementia (not Alzheimer's disease), which is related to executive dysfunction, causing daily confusion and language disruption.

Other cognitive issues will vary between individuals, on different days, and even at different times of the day. Mary would say, "We have good days and bad days." Attention and working memory—the holding of several elements of an activity in conscious focus—can fluctuate such that the client feels clear in one moment and then confused or foggy in another. This variability is related to fluctuations in the cholinergic system, specifically acetylcholine, which is necessary for regulation of attention in the PFC.

Disruption of processes in the PFC produces difficulties with problem-solving, planning, and organization. Difficulty in retrieving words and producing words is another frustration that results from losing these abilities to self-regulate. Patients feel frustration, anxiety, depression, and even anger. Another very frustrating cognitive problem is *perseveration*, the tendency of the brain to get "stuck" on a topic, which requires considerable patience from caregivers.

Dysfunction in the ability to self-motivate or self-activate is very distressing. For example, the individual might want to make a movement but the brain is simply unable to process the "request." Dance therapy, as well as music and singing, has had some success in overcoming the difficulty Parkinson's patients have of being unable to walk through a doorway or to speak the words they are thinking (Michels et al., 2018).

CLINICAL NOTES

There is much more to know about the effects of Parkinson's disease, but psychotherapy has been shown to be helpful (Hurwitz, 2001; Sproesser et al., 2010). Mary and John reported finding not only comfort from their psychotherapy, but also the support and confidence that they needed to continue.

4.5.2 The Problems of an Aging Brain: Alzheimer's and TIAs

Nancy struggles with the care of her aging mother, who has had a series of ministrokes (transient ischemic attacks, or TIAs) and was recently diagnosed with Alzheimer's disease. Nancy does not know how to manage her mother's sometimes outlandish behavior, but mostly she fears how she will cope as her mother deteriorates. Nancy wants to make the upcoming decisions herself, but she

does not want to do anything to negatively affect her mother's
life. The situation is causing her anxiety, and she is having trouble
sleeping.

Unfortunately, the cells in the body, which of course includes those in the brain, are not everlasting. Most areas of the body replace cells throughout life in varying cycles. It is colloquially said that the body is replaced every 7 years. White blood cells are the quickest to renew, sometimes lasting only a few hours, whereas brain neurons are not replaced by cell division at all. The brain can create new neurons, in a process called *neurogenesis*, from stem cells in the brain, but this is largely an activity in the process of learning and only in certain parts of the brain, predominantly the hippocampus. The formation of new connections, *synaptogenesis*, is an ongoing process that can compensate for neuronal loss and create new pathways to compensate for even severe neuronal loss. From the cellular perspective, however, once a brain cell dies, replacement is highly limited.

There are three forms of cell death:

- **apoptosis:** "programmed" cell death, occurring in response to established triggers, that includes depletion of the telomeres that act as a cap at the end of chromosomes to maintain stability of the DNA. At each cell division, the telomere is shortened until it is depleted and the DNA is unable to maintain integrity, resulting in cellular death. Telomere depletion is not an issue in brain neurons, because they do not undergo cell division.
- **necrosis:** the destruction of a cell as a result of an unexpected event such as a trauma, infection, or toxin exposure that causes premature death of the cell.
- **parthanatos:** a process of cell death resulting from overactivity of the enzyme poly (ADP-ribose) polymerase in a number of areas of the body, but particularly the brain, accelerates neurodegenerative conditions: stroke (thrombosis and embolism), trauma, Alzheimer's

disease, Parkinson's disease, Huntington's disease, amyotrophic lateral sclerosis, and spinal cord injury (Fatokun et al., 2014).

Aging is the most widely recognized risk factor for Alzheimer's disease, and the brain's "immune system" plays a role in neurodegeneration. Microglial cells (one of the brain's glial group of cells) are the brain's immune system that will attack invaders and also remove damaged or abnormal tissue. Unfortunately, microglial cells can become either overactive (contributing to cell death) or underactive (leaving damaging chemicals in the space between neurons and thus producing a toxic environment and cell death). In the same way that an autoimmune disease attacks healthy tissue in the body, microglial cells can damage neural tissue (Dheen et al., 2007).

Aging is characterized by a shift toward a more inflammatory expression as the immune system faces increasing challenges to remain healthy. When molecules of the inflammatory system, such as tumor necrosis factor (TNF) or interleukin-1 (IL-1), enter the brain, they trigger activity of the microglial cells. A normal microglial activity is to remove the buildup of dysfunctional cell groups called beta-amyloid plaques, but when microglial cells are overactivated by inflammatory chemicals, they are less effective in cleaning the interneuronal spaces, causing a buildup of plaque density. This increase in plaque interferes with normal cellular functions and results in cell death, which leads to a buildup of intercellular detritus, which triggers normal microglial functions that create a damaging dynamic of cell death and neurodegenerative diseases such as Alzheimer's.

In Alzheimer's disease, neurons are degraded by other means as well:

- Neurofibrillary tangles occur when abnormal accumulations of a protein called tau collect inside neurons, in the axon. Tau stabilizes the microtubules that are the transport highways for nutrients and neurotransmitters from the cell nucleus to the presynaptic space. In Alzheimer's disease, abnormal chemical changes cause tau to detach from microtubules and stick to other tau molecules, forming threads that eventually join to form tangles inside neurons. These tangles end up blocking the axonal transport system, thus stopping synaptic activity and leading to death of the neuron.

- The brain's vascular system transports essential nutrients, glucose, and most important, oxygen to the brain. Reduced blood flow can occur with atherosclerosis (hardening of the arteries), and with mini-strokes (TIAs) due to thrombosis (blockage) or embolism (bursting or leaking). Vascular problems may weaken the blood–brain barrier, allowing larger molecules into the brain that trigger a microglial response. In Alzheimer's, a faulty blood–brain barrier prevents the removal of the toxic beta-amyloid plaques in the fluid between neurons and of tau proteins found within neurons.

CLINICAL NOTES

What concerns Nancy are the changes that her mother will be going through. Nancy wants to be prepared for these changes so as not to be surprised or overwhelmed. To some extent, she needs some psychoeducation, but she can find facts and details in a good book. The psychotherapist needs to help her *understand* what is happening to her mother so that Nancy feels supported. It is important for the therapist to be psychoeducated as well. The modality that will be best for Nancy will depend on how she responds to her mother at any given time. Sometimes it may be cognitive, but other times it may be more affective or somatic. She may just need a mental break with something like mindfulness or another form of relaxation therapy. She may just need the relief of a holiday!

MILD COGNITIVE IMPAIRMENT

Neurodegenerative diseases often start with only mild features, called *mild cognitive impairment*. These mild features in conjunction with aging and other inflammatory health issues, such as diabetes type 1 or 2, arthritis, or cardiovascular problems can be important indicators that more serious problems are on the way.

Mild cognitive impairment is indicated by

- memory problems;
- language deficits;
- disorientation—in time and space;
- difficulty making decisions;
- apraxia—difficulty in self-directed actions (e.g., tying shoelaces, or connecting a zipper, or expressing thoughts through speech);
- apathy, especially about things that have usually been important or pleasurable; and
- irritability, especially when having trouble with what has always been a simple task (e.g., buttoning a shirt).

The likelihood of depression is doubled with dementia, so Nancy needs to maintain a positive lifestyle and an enriched environment for her mother in order to minimize depression. Doing so will probably be helpful for Nancy too.

Some simple measures are known to be very beneficial for someone who is developing dementia or Alzheimer's, as well as for carers and loved ones like Nancy, who will spend a lot of time with the patient:

- **sleep:** A program of sleep hygiene includes avoiding caffeine, nicotine, and alcohol in the few hours before sleep; keeping the bedroom calm and tidy and free of blue electronic lights from screens like computers and mobile phones; avoiding overly hot or overly cold temperatures (slightly cooler is the ideal); and trying to maintain regular times to sleep and wake.
- **diet:** A healthy diet of whole foods, a moderate amount of protein, and several servings of vegetables and fruits is fundamental for all. The ANS, brain health, and mood balance require folate and B_{12}. These vitamins are needed to produce methyl group molecules, which are essential for a host of chemical activities in the body, including gene expression and functions of the immune system.

- **exercise:** Walking 20 minutes twice a day is ideal. This routine will help sleep and also helps produce calmness through the release of endorphins. Exercise also promotes the production of one of the most important factors in promoting brain plasticity, including memory and a healthy hippocampus: brain-derived neurotrophic factor (K. I. Erickson et al., 2012). In addition, exercise reduces the inflammatory stress hormone cortisol (Tortosa-Martínez et al., 2018).
- **mindfulness:** Mindfulness has been shown to make small but significant changes in executive function and immune system performance, as well as to reduce age-related degradation of myelinated axons. It reduces stress and enhances feelings of self-worth and resilience (Laneri et al., 2016; Moynihan et al., 2013).

4.5.3 Traumatic Brain Injury and Dysexecutive Syndrome

Jenny and Wendy were involved in a car accident 5 months ago. Both were severely affected by whiplash. In addition, Jenny's head hit the steering wheel, and she was knocked unconscious. Wendy did not lose consciousness. Both were taken to the hospital and required remedial therapy. Wendy has had a steady recovery and is almost back to normal, but Jenny is having a lot of difficulties. They have been a couple for more than 10 years, and now Jenny is forgetful, finds it hard to keep focus, and sometimes does not seem to recognize Wendy. Jenny's balance falters, and she has had a couple of falls. Their doctors advised finding a psychotherapist who could help them manage the emotional difficulties of adjusting to Jenny's injury.

TBI is caused by a sudden blow or jolt to the head. This could be a blunt-force impact or a penetrating injury. For Jenny and Wendy it was a car accident, which is a common cause of TBI. Injuries vary according to the severity of the event because the damage is done when the brain smashes into the skull. The more the brain moves back and forth inside the skull, the more damage can be done. On the inside of the skull there is bruising, bleeding, and tearing of nerve fibers. The second jolt, when Jenny hit the steering wheel, amplified her injury, causing her to lose consciousness, whereas Wendy remained conscious.

The first injury is known as the primary injury. For Wendy, the injury most likely affected one area of the brain. Because Jenny's head was jolted twice on different sides of the skull, she suffered a global trauma; in other words, it involved the entire brain. Another danger is that after the initial event, the brain can swell, pushing into the skull, affecting the vascular system, and causing problems with oxygen flow. Surgery performed after a TBI is often to reduce the pressure inside the skull of this second phase of swelling. This second injury can be more damaging than the primary injury.

Jenny's behavioral issues are largely around her ability to regulate herself. This deficit indicates damage to the frontal lobe, which fits with the report that she struck the steering wheel with her forehead. Traumatic injury to the frontal lobe results in what is known as a *dysexecutive syndrome*.

The behavioral and mental impacts of dysexecutive syndrome include

- impulsivity,
- disorganized thinking,
- poor social judgement,
- inefficient planning,
- poor problem-solving,
- slow mental processing,
- forgetfulness, and
- passivity and aggression.

CLINICAL NOTES

These symptoms are disturbingly similar to the effects of a frontal lobotomy. Jenny has suffered damage to the frontal lobe, the area of the brain that is needed for self-regulation, organizing, planning, emotional regulation, and decision-making. Besides the continued rehabilitation work with a variety of therapists, the psychotherapist has important work to do for both parties. Jenny will still experience emotional pains and discomfort that can be amplified because of increased impulsivity. Wendy will need attention as she manages both the care of her injured partner and the difficulties of relating to a person who is likely to be very different from the Jenny she once knew. Equally, Jenny will have a different personal filter through which she is perceiving Wendy. People with dysexecutive syndrome often feel grief and confusion. They are less able to control their hostile behavior with family and friends as they struggle to rediscover their sense of identity. Therapy may need to be directive when dealing with immediate issues, and gentle, sensitive, and supportive when emotional fragility is at the fore.

Conclusion

We have explored just three neurodegenerative conditions, but when the brain becomes damaged, something happens to the "person." They need help managing the challenge of these changes in themselves and how they relate to family and friends. Their partner can feel as though they have lost the person they fell in love with. It is possible for couples and families to engage in the exciting experience of meeting each other anew. It is not that everything changes and everything is lost. It can be that there are many happy years to come. There is much for a sensitive, knowledgeable, and aware psychotherapist to do.

4.6 Personality Disorders

WHAT IS PERSONALITY?

Personality is something you *are*. It could be summarized as your relatively stable ways of behaving, thinking, feeling, and "being" in the world. It is the way you manage relationships, respond emotionally to people and circumstances, approach problems, and navigate life. One part of personality, often called *character*, develops over time in relation to life experiences

(Fountoulakis & Gonda, 2019). Another part, called *temperament*, is heritable, stable, and underpinned by genetic and biological dispositions (Kagan, 1998/2018). The interplay between character and temperament, between *nurture* and *nature*, is both dynamic and complex.

There are a number of different measures and definitions of personality, its types, and differentiated qualities. One of the most robust methodologies is the five-factor model that suggests a "Big Five" set of personality traits: openness, conscientiousness, extroversion, agreeableness, and neuroticism (McCrae & Oliver, 1992). These factors are relevant within Western culture, but personality factors can differ across cultures and political landscapes.

A personality disorder is considered when someone displays consistent rigid or marked deficits in cognitive, affective, or relational areas that cause distress to themselves or distress to others and are not explained by another psychopathology.

> Personality features may or may not be adaptive. Compulsiveness in a student is adaptive when it promotes orderly study habits, but it is maladaptive when the student spends hours sharpening pencils instead of studying. Personality traits turn into personality disorders when they (1) become inflexible and maladaptive, and (2) significantly impair social and occupational functioning or cause substantial subjective distress. People with personality disorders are not always in significant emotional distress. Often, the people they are living or working with are more distressed. Freud once defined a successful mature adult as someone "who is able to love and to work." People with personality disorders frequently fail at both. (Maxmen et al., 2009, p. 547)

Clearly, determining that someone has or does not have a personality disorder can be difficult. Even the word "disorder" is misleading, as if there were a definitive point between "normal" and "disordered." Some have tried to create clear definitions, such as in the *DSM*, but identifying a personality as dysfunctional is both contentious and somewhat "slippery." People who have "different" perceptions, espouse unusual beliefs, or deviate from social "norms," should not immediately be considered mentally ill. It is important to carefully consider individuality and context. Labeling can have serious social and economic consequences. For example, a Japanese man in a season of melancholy and lack of drive may be labeled "depressed" and require intervention in one culture, but in Japan his experience is valued as a sign of personal development. Cultural differences can be found not only at the national level but also at the micro level of communities and families, but if a personality issue is wreaking havoc within and without, whatever the cultural setting, there is probable cause for a closer look at a personality disorder.

The *DSM-5* lists 10 types of personality disorders (not including personality changes due to medical conditions or "unspecified" personality disorders). Personality disorders have a reputation of being difficult to treat with psychotherapy. For example, treating borderline personality disorder (BPD), which we will discuss in detail shortly, can be frustrating for client, family, and therapist. For some clients, BPD symptoms naturally diminish over time (Biskin, 2015). What is the evidence?

Two major longitudinal studies—the Collaborative Longitudinal Personality Study and the McLean Study of Adult Development—looked at the recovery rates of BPD clients in therapy over time (Gunderson et al., 2000; Skodol et al., 2005; Zanarini et al., 2015). The emerging picture suggested that remission of symptoms is more common than had previously been believed and that psychotherapies such as dialectical behavioral therapy and psychodynamic approaches are effective, although the effects may be small (Cristea et al., 2017). Anthony Bateman and Peter Fonagy (2012) explain their mentalization approach:

> This is not a therapy aiming to achieve structural/personality change or to alter cognitions and schemas. Rather, it is a therapy to enhance capacities of mentalization and to make them more stable and robust so that the individual is better able to solve problems and to manage emotional states (particularly within interpersonal relationships), or at least to feel more confident in doing so. (p. 274)

4.6.1 Attachment and Personality

Attachment theory, developed by John Bowlby and Mary Ainsworth, has had a huge impact on how personality development, affect regulation, and the way people see and interact with the world are understood. In a nutshell, early childhood experiences with the primary caregiver shape an "internal working model" of the self and the world. These early experiences can foster the development of either a secure attachment style or an insecure one. Insecure attachment patterns can share many similarities with personality disorders. For a complete understanding of attachment disorders and treatment, we recommend *Attachment Disturbances in Adults: Treatment for Comprehensive Repair*, by Daniel Brown and David Elliott (2016). Rather than attempt to rehash attachment theory, we will look briefly at the neurobiology of attachment and what might go wrong in a personality disorder.

Early attachment experience has a significant impact on the neurobiology and ultimate mental health of social mammals. Jaak Panksepp, a leading researcher in the neurobiology of affect, described a panic circuit that is activated when young animals are left alone in a strange environment (refer to Panksepp & Biven, 2010, Chapter 9, for more about the seven primary emotional systems). Distress signals can originate in the central gray matter, from the thalamus, ACC, and amygdala. These circuits, with considerable overlap, orchestrate the release of stress hormones (CRH and ACTH) and endorphins as a stress response. The neurotransmitters that modulate this circuit are glutamate, which activates the distress response, followed by the calming influence of oxytocin and prolactin.

When there is a good sense of attachment (warm, loving, protecting, and helpful interaction) with a primary attachment figure, there is a timely down-regulation (calming) of the fear response. This calming effect begins a cascade of chemical events that calm the child, inhibit the formation of negative memories, and both build and reinforce neurophysiological circuits of trust and social engagement that will later influence emotional regulation. This healthy process develops neurological pathways from the limbic areas via the ACC through to the OFC and PFC, with effective cortical blood flow and hippocampal functioning. These all act to enhance and reinforce healthy affect regulation. Such processes lead to *approach motivational schemata* (Dahlitz, 2015, 2017).

Children who do not have a sensitive and caring attachment figure to help down-regulate their stress response may experience prolonged stress and develop negative memories, emotions, and alternative coping patterns—suboptimal *avoidance motivational schemata* that result in an inability to regulate emotions. This inability to regulate negative affect is a common marker of many mental disorders—in particular, personality disorders like BPD.

Dysfunctional attachment relationships can result in cortical loops that typically overactivate limbic functioning, increasing the stress response; cause hippocampal maladaption and even atrophy; and stimulate negative feedback loops in the PFC, OFC, and ACC. These effects inhibit the cognitive regulating pathways in the left PFC. When caught in such loops, the person may feel as if caught in a rut and unable to effectively think through or rationalize a situation. Instead, they react in a recursive, fearful way that only reinforces (reconsolidates) avoidance schemata.

CLINICAL NOTES

The neural synaptic architecture that places people at risk for the emergence of mental disorders like depression and personality disorders is often laid down before explicit memory forms. Having no ability to consciously remember what happened leaves the person with seemingly inexplicable behaviors and emotions. Family and partners can suffer as they struggle to find who is to blame for these feelings. Therapy needs to find a way to repair and resolve implicit emotional memories and neural networks that developed in the first months of life. This can be a challenge.

4.6.2 Borderline Personality Disorder

"What have you done to your arm, Kath?" I asked, noticing a crimson trail of blood flowing from her elbow and down the arm of the couch.

"It's nothing . . . just a small cut," she offered, unconvincingly. Nothing Kath does to harm herself is done in half measures. I had learned that much after seeing her every week for over 2 years.

"Show me. You're bleeding. . . . It's seeping right through your shirt." She always wore long sleeves to cover up the latest knife work or the odd embedded rusty nail. As she rolled up her sleeve, I think she was as shocked as I was. Her bandaging had massively failed, was soaked in fresh blood, and was now leaving a crimson trail on the carpet. I reached for my first aid kit to add another compression bandage to slow the flow of blood while we waited for the ambulance.

I found out that Kath had narrowly avoided an accident while driving to the session and had been thrown into a state of being overwhelmed and hating herself. To numb the pain of the moment, she had taken a blade to her left arm while in the parking lot outside my practice. The depth of the cuts was too much for her quick bandaging attempt, and, to her great embarrassment, she was exposed. With gushing apologies and even greater self-loathing, she—and I—felt that our 2 years of work was completely undone. Kath could be described as a "quiet borderline," lacking the loud and dramatic gestures of the extroverted borderline. Kath kept her incredible sense of despair and pain to herself as much as possible. She punished herself with a strict and relentless exercise regime, was anorexic, self-mutilating, depressed, suicidal, empty, and always oscillating between self-improvement and self-annihilation.

According to the *DSM-5* (American Psychiatric Association, 2013), "the essential feature of borderline personality disorder is a pervasive pattern of instability of interpersonal relationships, self-image, and affects" (p. 663). According to the National Education Alliance for Borderline Personality

Disorder, the condition affects about 5.9% of Americans. To meet a diagnosis of BPD, according to the *DSM-5*, a person must have at least five of the following nine symptoms:

- frantic efforts to avoid real or imagined abandonment
- unstable and intense interpersonal relationships characterized by alternating between extremes of idealization and devaluation
- identity disturbance: unstable self-image or sense of self
- impulsivity in at least two areas that are potentially self-damaging (e.g., spending, sex, substance misuse, reckless driving, binge-eating)
- recurrent suicidal behavior or threats, or self-mutilating behavior
- instability of mood and marked reactivity of mood
- chronic feelings of emptiness
- inappropriate, intense anger or difficulty controlling anger
- transient, stress-related paranoid ideation or severe dissociative symptoms

The word "borderline" comes from an older psychoanalytic term, "borderline personality organization," which described a patient who was neither psychotic nor neurotic, but on the borderline between those two levels of organization (Stern, 1938). Unfortunately, the word has stuck, despite its lack of descriptive accuracy. "Emotional dysregulation" and "self-identity instability" would be more appropriate descriptions. There was support for the term "emotional dysregulation disorder" to replace BPD in the *DSM-5*, but that change was not adopted (Meares, 2012).

As with most personality typing, disordered personality types are complex and unique to the individual, emerging out of myriad genetic and environmental variables. The borderline personality, however, does have some general characteristics. Primarily, there is a lack of integration of the self. Typically, perception polarizes to a black-and-white or all-or-nothing approach to people, circumstances, and the self. This rigid stance leads disordered personalities to believe that their perception or opinion is the only truth, with no tolerance for differing views. There is often a pattern of unstable and intense relationships. Their black-and-white thinking can oscillate between idealizing others to devaluing them. Sudden and dramatic changes in how they feel about people causes ruptures in relationships. Often, only family members remain connected, albeit in a strained manner, as the borderline burns bridges in most of their relationships. The title of a popular book describes the difficulties that families face when they live with someone who has BPD: *Walking on Eggshells: Navigating the Delicate Relationship Between Adults, Children, and Parents* (Isay, 2008); and another title highlights the problems that therapists face in treating people with BPD: *Stop Walking on Eggshells: Taking Your Life Back When Someone You Care About Has Borderline Personality Disorder* (P. T. T. Mason & Kreger, 2010).

The person with BPD suffers an enduring sense of relational insecurity. There is a persistent underlying feeling of impending separation or rejection, with heightened alertness to any cues that might suggest rejection or abandonment, and they often interpret perceived abandonment as validation that they are bad or evil or that they are being unjustly treated as such. Perceived threats of separation, rejection, and thinking of themselves as being bad can lead to recurrent suicidal behavior, threats, self-mutilation, or some other form of self-punishment. In an effort to avoid real or imagined abandonment, the BPD sufferer can try to control relationships with explosive anger, sarcasm, bitterness, and other forms of manipulation. There is often a deep sense of shame and guilt after such explosions of emotion. The situation is complicated even more when there is a coexisting narcissistic personality trait.

Self-image for borderline personalities is unstable, shifting, or seemingly nonexistent. Changing roles—for example, from needy supplicant to righteous avenger, or from kindhearted friend to cold and harsh judge—is a result of an unstable sense of self. Risky behavior, changing aspirations, modified tastes, and fluctuating values can all be part of the borderline rollercoaster. At the core of BPD is emotional dysregulation in the face of psychosocial stressors (Meares, 2012). Fast and intense reactivity to social interactions, facial expressions, tones of voice—anything that would provoke feelings of shame, devaluation, or abandonment—erupt without control or regulation. As the neurobiology, discussed next, shows, there is a

disconnect between the production of intense emotions and the mechanisms to process and regulate them.

NEUROBIOLOGY OF BPD

Dr. Robert J. Gregory, professor of psychiatry at SUNY Upstate Medical
University, formulated a treatment paradigm for BPD called "dynamic
deconstructive psychotherapy" (Gregory, n.d.). This treatment integrates
translational neuroscience with object relations theory and Jacques Derrida's
deconstruction philosophy (Caputo, 1996). The neuroscience framework is
particularly helpful for understanding the neurobiological underpinnings of
BPD. We say "underpinnings" because the neurobiology is just one part of
the puzzle—neither the horse nor the cart. The etiology of BPD is controversial, and there are many views, but we feel that the lens of neuroscience
can provide a common "handle" on this complex disorder.

Gregory proposes an "emotion-processing hypothesis" that conceptual-
izes BPD not as a disorder of emotional dysregulation, but rather a disorder
of emotional processing. Here are some highlights of his hypothesis (Gregory, n.d., pp. 13–15):

- Because of interpersonal stress, emotion in BPD is not processed in
  normal fashion—lateral to medial movement of information through
  the PFC and integration with cortical and subcortical networks.
- BPD demonstrates less PFC activation and greater limbic system
  activation (ventral striatum, amygdala), as well as less integration
  of cortical and subcortical networks. These altered levels of involvement affect the capacity to label emotions, encode episodic memories, and interpret affect into language. In addition, awareness
  and reflection of the self and one's own personal character, as well
  as general attributions of self and others, are muted.
- In BPD, emotional experiences may be processed through subcortical limbic systems (amygdala, hippocampus, ventral striatum)
  rather than the usual verbal/symbolic processing of lateral-to-
  medial flow of information through the temporal lobe and the PFC
  and medial PFC. This different means of processing emotion may

limit the capacity for mentalization, empathy, tolerance of uncertainty, and even moral judgment.

Dissociation is used to down-regulate hyperarousal in the face of aversive stimuli. This down-regulation decreases activity in the amygdala, which increases dissociation.

When someone who suffers from BPD is exposed to strong emotional stimuli, the ACC and medial PFC are deactivated, and the limbic and cortical networks are decoupled. These effects cause difficulties with encoding emotional experience into language and with identifying, labeling, and acknowledging emotions.

When hyperaroused by emotional stimuli, BPD individuals have low levels of endogenous opioids and are less able to turn off the panic system. To alleviate the panic system, the BPD sufferer may use self-destructive or hostile actions, or self-soothing coping mechanisms to activate their ventral striatal region (the pleasure system).

CLINICAL NOTES

People with BPD use limbic solutions to interpersonal problems. More severe cases of BPD may have not only emotion-processing network deficits but diminished baseline tonic activity in certain brain regions. Treatment of BPD is almost always very challenging and is best done with support from local programs, good supervision, and thorough knowledge of the disorder. Therapists should receive specialist training in one or more of the treatment options targeting BPD; we outline five of them in the next section.

TREATMENT OPTIONS

A variety of approaches are used to treat BPD, including

- **dynamic deconstructive psychotherapy (DDP):** a 12-month treatment for BPD and other complex behavior problems, such as

alcohol or drug dependence, self-harm, eating disorders, and recurrent suicide attempts. DDP combines elements of translational neuroscience, object relations theory, and deconstruction philosophy
to encourage healing from negative self-image and maladaptive
processing of emotional experiences by helping clients connect with
their experiences and develop authentic and fulfilling connections
with others. Originators claim DDP is more effective for the treatment of BPD than are other common approaches. Approximately
90% of clients who undergo a full year of treatment achieve clinically
meaningful improvements. For more information, go to http://www
.upstate.edu/psych/education/psychotherapy/dynamic_decon.php.

- **dialectical behavior therapy (DBT):** probably the best-known
  intervention for BPD, DBT combines cognitive behavioral methods, interpersonal skills, and mindfulness. This approach is fundamentally different from DDP. DBT teaches skills to control intense
  emotions, reduce self-destructive behavior, manage distress, and
  improve relationships. BPD is treated as an affect regulation problem, so the goal is to enhance the ability to regulate. DBT seeks a
  balance between accepting and changing behaviors. This proactive,
  problem-solving approach was designed specifically to treat BPD.

- **mentalization-based therapy (MBT):** a psychodynamic psychotherapy that is less directive than DBT, focusing on enhancing mentalization, the capacity to understand behaviors and feelings and
  how they are associated with specific mental states in self and others. The therapy is designed to help people with BPD differentiate and
  separate their own thoughts and feelings from those around them.

- **schema therapy:** a therapy developed by Dr. Jeffrey Young that
  integrates elements of cognitive therapy, behavioral therapy, object
  relations, and gestalt therapy into a unified, systematic approach
  to treatment. There are four main concepts in the schema therapy
  model: early maladaptive schemata, core emotional needs, schema
  mode, and maladaptive coping styles. For more information, visit
  the International Society of Schema Therapy's website (https://
  schematherapysociety.org).

- **conversational model:** developed by Robert Hobson and expanded by Russell Meares, this therapy aims to develop the client's sense of self through a form of conversational relating. Such therapeutic relatedness helps the client develop the capacity to embody what is described as "aloneness-togetherness." The development of such a dialectic gives the BPD client a unique sense of personal being that was formerly deficient and at the root of much of the borderline pathology. The manualized form of the conversational model is presented in psychodynamic interpersonal therapy.

Conclusion

Kath dropped out of therapy after 2 years. It was the longest I (M. D.) had a regular BPD client, and I expect that her "quiet" borderline personality kept her faithful to her regular sessions. She felt she was doing much better and wanted to see how she would do on her own. I was (nervously) interested to see too, so we stopped our sessions. She promised to get back in touch if she needed to. She wrote about a year later and was, indeed, doing much better. Still anorexic, still addicted to exercise and diet pills, still cutting now and then, but nothing life-threatening. Her "dark cloud" of hopelessness was starting to break up. She spoke about her new job and how she projected less hatred toward herself. I think I would have felt better if she were still in therapy. Like an anxious parent, I worried about her capacity to self-regulate and be kind to herself. But she assured me that she was getting there by herself. A lot of understanding and patience from her mom and dad helped. They all lived in the same house. She said that there were many times she wanted to hurt herself really badly, but then she would remember me, see my face, and stop. It was not anything I had said—just a feeling. The progress in therapy had been slow over those 2 years but worth it, and it may still be going on without my being there.

4.7 Schizophrenia and Psychotic Behavior

The terms "psychosis" and "psychotic disorder" describe different things. A psychotic disorder is a diagnosable psychological *condition*, whereas psychosis is a describable *symptom* that can be present in not only psychotic disorders but also other disorders. It is not helpful when these words are used interchangeably, although they often are. Another issue is that when the topic of psychosis or psychotic disorders comes up, people think of schizophrenia. It can be confusing when the term "schizophrenia" is used colloquially or as an umbrella term for any mental health problems in which mental confusion, hallucination, or delusions are present. One of the intentions of this chapter is to expand our understanding of both terms. Another is to show what role the psychotherapist can play in what might otherwise be considered a psychiatric concern.

4.7.1 Psychosis

Psychosis affects the way the brain processes information. A psychotic episode, sometimes called a "psychotic break," can be short, temporary, or continue throughout life. It interferes with the perception of reality (Carey, 2018), but before psychosis becomes obvious, some symptoms can seem quite ordinary, as the following list of indicating behaviors shows:

- difficulty concentrating
- depressed mood
- sleeping too much or not enough
- anxiety
- suspiciousness
- withdrawal from family and friends
- delusions
- hallucinations
- disorganized speech, such as switching topics erratically
- depression
- suicidal thoughts or actions

People experiencing psychosis might see, hear, or believe things that are not real. Thoughts can become disorganized, and concentration can be difficult. These effects can lead to frustration, distrust, and suspicion of the world, which can lead to withdrawal from family and friends. All of these behaviors and symptoms can also be early warning signs of an impending and more serious psychotic break.

Psychosis can emerge during a number of conditions—alcohol and drug use, brain tumors or stroke, illnesses that result in high temperature (fever), and extreme stress or trauma—even though those disorders would not be classified as psychotic disorders. Psychosis can be part of the symptomatology of epilepsy and bipolar disorder. Psychosis can even be experienced as a result of streptococcal infection, as seen in PANDAS (refer to Section 4.8).

4.7.2 Psychotic Disorders

Psychotic disorders are the class of severe mental disorders that are marked by abnormal thinking and perceptions. Two of the main symptoms are delusions and hallucinations. Schizophrenia is a psychotic disorder with psychosis as a core symptom. There are a number of psychotic disorders:

- **schizophrenia** (most common): a long-term mental disorder that includes a number of symptoms that interfere with the capacity to successfully manage social and personal needs and demands. Characteristics include a dis-integration between thought, emotion, and behavior, leading to faulty perception, along with inappropriate actions and feelings. Reality is lost to fantasy and delusion, as well as a state of mental fragmentation (Picchioni & Murray, 2007).
- **schizoaffective disorder:** a condition involving both psychotic and mood symptoms. It has a high risk of self-harm and suicide. Symptoms of schizophrenia are experienced during hypomanic, manic, or major depressive episodes (Wy & Saadabadi, 2020).
- **schizophreniform disorder:** schizophrenia in which symptoms persist for less than 6 months. This disorder can also be an early stage of or precursor to schizophrenia. More than 65% of people that have schizophreniform experience will go on to develop schizophrenia (Poulton et al., 2000).
- **delusional disorder:** a condition in which the afflicted person cannot tell what is real from what is imagined, leading to erotomanic,

grandiose, jealous, persecutory, paranoid, or somatic delusions (Ibanez-Casas & Cervilla, 2012).

- **brief psychotic disorder:** a psychotic disorder whose symptoms continue for less than a month.
- **substance-induced psychotic disorder:** delusions or hallucinations caused by the taking of or withdrawal from a substance (Weibell et al., 2016).
- **bipolar psychosis, or bipolar disorder with psychotic features:** a disorder in which delusions and/or hallucinations are experienced along with an episode of mania or depression (Bellivier et al., 2013)
- **postpartum psychosis:** also known as "puerperal psychosis" or "postnatal psychosis" and very different from the colloquially known "baby blues," which is not an uncommon condition and often lasts only a few days. Symptoms can include delusions and hallucinations; manic moods; low moods—depressive feelings, tearfulness, loss of appetite, anxiety, sleeplessness; feeling fearful or suspicious; and confusion (Ghaedrahmati et al., 2017).
- **psychotic depression:** severe depression leading to delusions and/or hallucinations that are consistent with the depressive feelings—for example, worthlessness, failure, and shame (A. J. Rothschild, 2013).
- **age-related psychosis:** symptoms that can arise in the elderly as mood disorders (either depression or mania), late-onset schizophrenia, dementia, and hallucinations and/or delirium. Diagnosis is complicated by comorbidities, such as dementia complicated by delirium, or schizophrenia complicated by dementia (O'Connor, 2006).

DOPAMINE

One of the key neurobiological components of psychotic experiences is the neurotransmitter dopamine. We described the dopamine network in detail (refer to Section 4.5.1) in relation to Parkinson's disease. We also discussed the impact of dopamine distribution in affective disorders (refer to Figure 4.4). This is an impactful example of nature using the same element for multiple purposes. Complex utilization of limited resources is how humans have been able to develop such a complex biology. Complications arise, however, when the system is disrupted and counterproductive. Medications that change dopamine levels globally can have undesirable effects on one system or another.

Psychosis emerges when there is an increase in dopamine levels in the limbic area, distributed via the mesolimbic pathway from the dopamine source in the ventral tegmental area. There can also be a decrease in dopamine availability in the frontal cortex as distributed via the mesocortical pathway, again from the ventral tegmental area, which can result in "brain fog." Reducing dopamine levels globally with medication also reduces dopamine in the nigrostriatal pathway, triggering motor problems in the striatum, such as tardive dyskinesia, which is uncontrollable jerky movements of the face and body, blinking, and tongue rolling and protrusions. Reduced striatal dopamine can also produce Parkinsonian symptoms (refer to Section 4.5). There are a number of reasons for dysfunction in dopamine systems, including drug use (e.g., methamphetamines and cannabis), genetics, dopaminergic nuclei dysfunction, and poor lifestyle, including diet and sleep. Dopamine is an important neurotransmitter that has wide-ranging impacts on health and mental well-being (Rege, 2018).

CLINICAL NOTES

We will discuss other triggers for psychotic experiences in response to inflammation and autoimmune disorders in Section 4.8, which we mention now so that you keep your mind open as we discuss symptoms. Disruptions of the dopamine system may be at the heart of symptoms, but symptoms need to be explored carefully for the trigger, source, or cause that has allowed those symptoms to emerge. Whereas a psychiatrist might focus more on returning the patient to a manageable state, or the field worker might administer medication to calm a violent or suicidal person, the psychotherapist is likely to be helping a client or family outside of the acute stages. Having the time to explore the client's story and future possibilities to discover the nuanced life experiences that might be contributing to the problem is an opportunity not to be underestimated.

4.7.3 Psychotic Symptoms

Symptoms of psychotic disorders fall into three major categories (Schultze-Lutter, 2009):

- **positive symptoms** (those abnormally present): hallucinations, such as hearing voices or seeing things that do not exist; paranoia; exaggerated or distorted perceptions, beliefs, and behaviors.
- **negative symptoms** (those abnormally absent): a loss or decrease in the ability to initiate plans, speak, express emotion, or find pleasure.
- **disorganized symptoms:** confused and disordered thinking and speech, trouble with logical thinking, and sometimes bizarre behavior or abnormal movements.

Dr. Robert Freedman (Freedman et al., 2020), from the University of Colorado is one of the leading researchers into schizophrenia in the world today. He speaks empathetically of what it is like to manage in the world with schizophrenia as your lens (Brain & Behavior Research Foundation, 2018). He quotes the film *A Beautiful Mind* (Howard, 2001), which follows the life of the Nobel Prize–winning mathematician John Nash. The film shows the intense struggles with delusion and hallucination, as well as the impact of negative moods and anhedonia (inability to feel pleasure or enjoy pleasurable activities). One of the taglines for the film captures both the difficulty and the possibility within those who suffer from a mental illness: "He saw the world in a way that no one could have imagined."

Dr. Freedman describes the brain of someone with schizophrenia as "hyper-reactive to the world around it . . . bombarded with sounds and sights and smells that normally most of us are able to screen out" (Brain & Behavior Research Foundation, 2018). So, whether suffering the long-term disease of schizophrenia or having one of the other experiences with schizoid conditions, these people find it hard to focus as information floods their mental systems. They get more information than they can process, and the result is delusions and hallucinations as their brain tries to make sense of a seemingly impossible world.

Although dopamine is one of the primary concerns, Dr. Freedman (2014) found that there was also a concern with the neurotransmitter acetylcholine. He found a particular synapse where acetylcholine activates a nicotinic receptor that was, at the time, unknown. He visited the leading expert in nicotinic receptors, Jean-Pierre Changeux at Paris University and they began working on the problem. Eventually, they were able to isolate the receptor and find the gene that makes it. The next piece in the puzzle was the discovery that this gene is among the many genes affected in schizophrenia. In some patients one copy of the gene is entirely missing. A lot of work has been done at the genetic level to see what underlies the emergence of these disorders. One gene is named to show that it is an important candidate: *disrupted-in-schizophrenia 1* (*DISC1*; Gejman et al., 2010).

Researchers have sought to find straightforward causal pathways to schizophrenia, but a much more complex and varied landscape has been found. No doubt, research will continue because even though interesting culprits have been found in the environment, in heritable genetics and epigenetics, none have proved to be consistent enough to lead to highly effective new treatments.

Psychopharmacology is well established and continues to improve. Slow-release, injectable dosages can be effective from 14 to 28 days, potentially giving those who struggle with the symptoms an opportunity to find some stability. Very few pharmacological interventions are without side effects, and some of the antipsychotic medications can have side effects that are distressing enough for some people to resist medication. Decisions about medications and compliance are outside the purview of a psychotherapist, but someone suffering a psychotic disorder or a disorder involving psychosis still has to manage their day-to-day life, deal with their emotions, and try to make the best of their situation. Equally, some people suffering psychotic disorders are still in the prodrome (early symptom) stage when they seek out a psychotherapist with what they think is a far less severe condition. In such cases a psychotherapist is positioned at the point of first aid. Knowing what to recognize and how to respond needs to be an important part of every therapist's skill set.

The following case study comes from Seikkula et al. (2006).

Diagnosis: schizophrenia. Martti was 16 years when, during his first year in the vocational school, he started to show signs of problems to his parents. He became easily irritated and isolated himself in his room during weekends at home. He continued to go to school in another city, where he also lived in a flat. The following April everything seemed to fall apart. He stopped taking care of his hygiene, his talking went to a mumble, and his eyes were turned towards the Sky. He also had peculiar body movements, such as rocking. His parents were unable to have any contact with him and took him into primary care. At that point of time, his psychotic symptoms had continued for one month. He stayed overnight in the ward, and the following day a team consisting of a psychiatrist from the psychiatric hospital, a nurse, and a psychologist from the local psychiatric outpatient clinic met him at the primary care center together with his parents. It was decided that Martti would return home, and home visits were arranged. Meetings were held every day or second day. During the first meetings Martti most often sat with his knees under his jaw and his eyes turned towards the Sky. When asked a question, he did not answer. Only some mumbling was heard. His parents were very worried, and they both cried a lot; his sister returned home to support them. In many meetings neuroleptic medication was considered, but the parents did not like that idea, and the psychiatrist wanted to be careful. In these meetings a slight progress was noted in the sense that Martti started to sleep better, and he also started to give short answers to the team members. (p. 222)

The first point of interest is the case report itself. The elements that have been included relate mostly to diagnosable symptomatology. Reports are often truncated, and decisions have to be made about what is relevant— or at least most relevant. A psychotherapist may have other questions about affective states that are not answered by these predominantly behavioral observations. The second point of interest for a psychotherapist is whether Martti might have reasonably reported to a psychotherapist or school counselor. There is no indication that any early assistance was sought; only when "everything seemed to fall apart" in April was he hospitalized and attended to by psychiatrists.

Let us imagine that Martti presented to a psychotherapist in the early stages, when he was becoming "easily irritated and isolated himself in his room during weekends at home." It is not unreasonable to approach his problems from an affective, resilience, and perhaps attachment perspective. He was starting at a new school, which was the beginning of training for a future career. He was living away from home in a flat, although the case notes are a little unclear as to when he moved to "another city" and whether he was traveling home on the weekends from that city. Lack of clarity in case reports can be confusing for therapists joining the case. Regardless of these contentions, it would not have been unreasonable for a therapist to deal with Martti as someone who was having normal difficulties with beginning a new phase in life. Therapy might have sought to investigate his strengths, build self-efficacy, and even look for past traumas that might be exacerbating the situation.

The important question is this: When should a psychotherapist or school counselor have begun to be concerned that Martti was having problems indicating a psychotic disorder? The answer is certainly when symptoms like poor self-care, mumbling communication, and peculiar body movements began, but there may have been earlier indicators, not mentioned in the case report, that might have raised concerns. Having some knowledge about early indicators and risk factors is vital. It is too much to expect the parents to be knowledgeable enough to take early action.

4.7.4 Early Indicators and Risk Factors

Psychotic disorders often have a long period of development. The average age of onset for schizophrenia is the mid-20s, but the first episode may occur as early as the preteen years. Differences between genders also need to be considered. Li et al. (2016) showed that males have a clear peak age of onset between 21 and 25, whereas women have a peak onset between 25 and 30 and then another peak in the mid-40s (Figure 4.5).

Symptomatology can vary between gender, so treatments that include

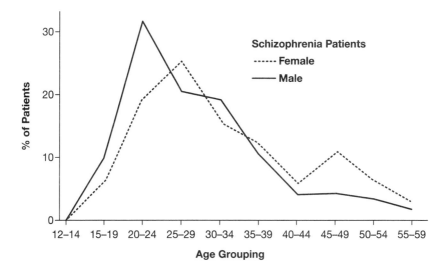

FIGURE 4.5: Gender and Age Peaks for Schizophrenia

pharmacology can vary in effectiveness. Although it is not a fixed rule, men tend to express more negative symptoms with more severe clinical features. Social withdrawal, substance abuse, and blunted or incongruent affect are seen more in men, as with Martti. Women with schizophrenia will often present with more mood disturbance and depressive symptoms. It is not hard to imagine that these symptoms can be mistakenly treated as emotional issues. A schizoaffective disorder can make it even more difficult to predict the onset of psychosis. These symptoms can appear over a number of years as indicators of a developmental flow toward psychosis and a psychotic disorder (see Figure 4.6).

Another symptom that can emerge early on in the developmental flow is the presence of cognitive deficits. Early onset can have a direct relationship to neural development, particularly gray-matter loss during the natural pruning and myelination of the brain that occurs between the ages of 12 and 16 (Gogtay, 2008). If these processes are delayed or interrupted, there is greater difficulty developing the neural organization and integration required for the PFC to successfully regulate behavior, emotion, learning, and self-control.

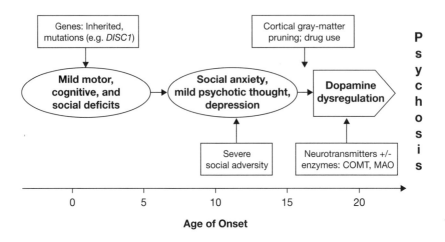

FIGURE 4.6: Developmental Flow Toward Schizophrenia. COMT = catechol-O-methyltransferase; MAO = monoamine oxidase. *Adapted from Di Forti et al. (2007).*

Medications can reduce positive symptoms but often are ineffective in improving cognitive deficits (Jahshan et al., 2017). There are a number of ways to help cognitive issues. Something as simple as exercise can make a difference to enhance cognitive function by activating neuroplasticity, and cognitive exercise has been shown to remediate some of the difficulties of schizophrenia. Exercise is essential in affective disorders, and it is helpful to be reminded here that natural benefits can be useful in many different situations (M. Fisher et al., 2010).

CLINICAL NOTES

As we have already described, it is not so much what you know in minute detail, but what you know *about* psychotic disorders. It is helpful for therapists to be prepared because they can encounter people in the early stages, or the prodrome phase, before serious symptoms emerge. They might encounter people who are in the midst of symptoms but present to a psychotherapist because they or their family do not realize how serious the situation is. Therapists who work with the highly disadvantaged and homeless community are very likely to encounter people with psychotic disorders and other morbidities and comorbidities.

We have not covered psychopharmacology because prescribing drugs is not the psychotherapist's task. It is, however, helpful to know something about medications in order to understand what the prescribing physician is thinking and what relief the patient is getting. When someone is hard to control, especially in homeless situations or with addicts, emergency staff might give an injection that has a rapid calming effect and can last for a period of time. Currently known as *long-acting injectables* or *depot injections*, these injections have effects that can last 14–28 days, depending on the medications included (Brissos et al., 2014). The medications include pharmaceuticals like olanzapine, paliperidone, and risperidone. These pharmaceuticals also have product names. For example, risperidone is an atypical antipsychotic marketed as Risperdal. Here is a brief list of the chemical base and brand names.

- **mood stabilizers:**
  - carbamazepine (Tegretol)
  - lithium (Lithicarb, Quilonum)
  - valproate (Epilim, Valpro)
- **antipsychotics:**
  - aripiprazole (Abilify)
  - chlorpromazine (Thorazine, Largactil)
  - olanzapine (Zyprexa)
  - quetiapine (Seroquel)

Conclusion

The search for better treatments and more effective therapies will, no doubt, continue, but establishing a foundation of knowledge is the first step on any journey. These conditions that blur into the psychiatric field can be difficult to navigate, especially when other practitioners are disinclined to include therapists. Because these conditions are so complex, have symptoms that take time to develop, or can seem to be just one-off occurrences, the best treatment can come from a cooperative group of practitioners, including therapists, who have different areas of focus. A psychotherapist who is well versed in the information about these conditions can be a very valuable bridge of understanding not only between other therapists, but also between the client and their family, friends, and community.

4.8 Autoimmune Encephalitis

There are a number of immune-mediated psychiatric disorders that psychotherapists need to be aware of because the symptoms can be confused with and easily absorbed by other diagnoses. The symptoms may look like those of a psychotic event or OCD, but they are only the observable symptoms. The cause of these disturbing mental behaviors is based not in a neurobiological cause but in an autoimmune assault on the CNS that causes an inflammation of the brain: *encephalitis*. A prominent autoimmune encephalitis is cause by an immune assault on NMDA receptors; thus, "anti-NMDA receptor encephalitis" describes a slew of symptoms from psychotic and delusional, to seriously life-threatening autonomic dysfunctions.

The 2018 film *Brain on Fire*—based on the book *Brain on Fire: My Month of Madness* (Cahalan, 2013)—recounts the story of Susannah Cahalan's experience with anti-NMDA receptor encephalitis. Cahalan, a writer for *The New York Post*, becomes suddenly ill and descends into mood changes, seizures, psychotic episodes, and eventually a catatonic state. She is misdiagnosed throughout the ordeal until Dr. Souhel Najjar, a Syrian-American neurologist, takes on her case and successfully diagnoses and treats her for anti-NMDA receptor encephalitis.

In a similar vein, the shocking documentary *My Kid Is Not Crazy: A Search for Hope in the Face of Misdiagnosis* (Sorel, 2018) is another exposé of the childhood autoimmune encephalitis called PANDAS. Although these disorders are considered rare, it is highly possible that immune-mediated psychiatric disorders may be more common than once thought. It is not hard to see how people are wrongly diagnosed with a psychotic disorder, when in fact they are suffering an autoimmune disorder. Once a correct diagnosis of autoimmune encephalitis has been made, the paths of treatment come into sharp focus. Although there are wildly varying degrees of efficacy for any one of the proposed treatments, at least people are saved from unnecessarily being labeled as schizophrenic, psychotic, delusional, or any other such thing. Most important is that they are saved from taking the often heavy medications that accompany those diagnoses.

4.8.1 PANS/PANDAS

Tamika was just turning 12 when she began to exhibit highly unusual behaviors. Although having general problems with focus and attention at school, something much more disruptive was happening. Her handwriting deteriorated, she became confused with numbers, and found it very hard to concentrate. She wasn't sleeping well, began to develop strange automatic movements with her arms and contortions of her body, and was prone to uncharacteristic outbursts of anger.

Over the next few weeks, she deteriorated rapidly. OCD-type repetitive behaviors and strange motor movements overtook her. She would bounce on her bed for hours, sometimes breaking down and crying, sometimes yelling in frustration, as her body betrayed her desire to just stop. Her arms would throw themselves out in front of her and twist and turn. She felt compelled to hold her breath, make strange noises, stomp with her feet, contort her body in a frenzy of activity. These distressing antics would continue for hours.

She was no longer able to go to school. Dressing became almost impossible because of the obsessive or uncontrolled arm and body movements. She couldn't even go to the toilet unassisted. She described it as being trapped in a body that was out of control. Her parents described one stretch of extreme jumping, bouncing, pacing, stomping, crying out and flailing around that lasted for 3 days. In that time, Tamika had almost no sleep, and hardly any food or water. Their doctor prescribed heavy doses of Valium that literally knocked her out. The parents expressed their guilt, but also felt that the Valium was a harsh but saving grace. Tamika revealed that she often thought she was going to have a heart attack.

Doctors could not pin down a biological cause; counselors did not help; psychiatrists put it all down to some unknown mental disturbance and ordered strong doses of antipsychotics and antidepressants. These drugs calmed Tamika down and reduced the intensity of her behavior, but not enough to stop it. For the next few years, she continued to struggle with bouts of OCD and outbursts of anger, unable to sleep for any length of time, and feeling trapped in a body that refused to be still. She put on a lot of weight because of the psychiatric drugs and became depressed. Her parents reported that she tried to jump out of their moving car and she would often cry out loud that she wanted to die so that it all would stop.

After a number of years of searching for answers, Tamika's parents found a pediatric neurologist in another state who thought the symptoms sounded like "pediatric autoimmune neuropsychiatric disorders associated with streptococcal infections"—PANDAS—a neuroinflammatory encephalitis that is caused by the body's immune inflammatory response to any of a number of infectious and noninfectious triggers.

Tamika and her parents flew interstate to visit the doctor and she was officially diagnosed with PANDAS. The doctor explained that this was still a controversial diagnosis that had critics within the broader medical profession. Tamika was prescribed a common antibiotic, erythromycin. The doctor explained that the main purpose of the medication was to modulate the immune response rather than just killing the infection.

Streptococcus is a common bacterium that is responsible for a wide group of infections from a sore throat to pneumonia. Severe strep infections can be fatal. The problem for Tamika was that killer T cells (T_H17) that attack the streptococcus infection can also attack parts of the brain (Chang et al., 2015). When certain parts of the brain are attacked, the result is the sort of symptoms that Tamika experienced.

The proposed theory for PANS and PANDAS postulates that serum antibodies produced against infectious and non-infectious agents cross the blood–brain barrier and cross-react with neuronal antigens. These antibodies then elicit injury and cause dysregulation to basal ganglia functions producing a variety of neurological and psychiatric manifestations. Anti-neuronal antibodies produced include anti-lysoganglioside, anti-tubulin, and anti-dopamine D1 and D2 receptor antibodies. Their effects on the brain include alterations to the enzyme tyrosine hydroxylase, resulting in increased synthesis of dopamine. In addition, dopaminergic and glutamatergic transmission and regulation are affected due to an increase in receptor sensitivity caused by antibody stimulation. Increased dopamine and glutamate in the basal ganglia may be responsible for the overstimulation and the many psychiatric symptoms associated with PANDAS. (Monteiro-Haig, 2017b, p. 8)

The response to erythromycin was almost immediate. After just one dose, literally overnight, Tamika changed dramatically. She had a long and sound sleep. After a second dose the next day, Tamika joined the family for a picnic at the local reserve. She was almost symptom-free within 48 hours. For Tamika, and the family, it was nothing short of miraculous.

Tamika's father called the doctor, who was pleased, but not surprised. He explained that this was often the response, although not every child responds to antibiotics, so there is more to learn about this problem.

In addition to the antibiotics, Tamika was taken off all his psychiatric medication and put on a regimen of herbal supplements to support her gut while she was taking strong doses of erythromycin to keep his autoimmune response at bay. Improving her gut health also acts to help heal the body, and combat infections (refer to Section 2.2).

Now 17, she still struggles with some OCD symptoms. She can have a "flare" of symptoms when she gets sick, but compared to the height of her crisis, the symptoms are very mild. She also works with a psychotherapist to manage her residual trauma and to catch up on the years lost to this debilitating illness.

CLINICAL NOTES

The impact of autoimmune disorders like this is not only tragically detrimental to the sufferers and their families but can present a huge challenge for mental health professionals to correctly diagnose and treat. At the time of writing this book, 2021, the diagnosis of PANS or

PANDAS is still fraught with difficulties for health professionals, some of whom do not accept that the severe symptoms could be the result of an autoimmune assault on the brain. However, the mechanisms of PANS, and the evaluation and management, have been articulated by Susan Swedo and colleagues in a series of landmark papers published in 2017 and a few formative papers published in 2015 (Chang et al., 2015; Cooperstock et al., 2017; Frankovich et al., 2017; Swedo et al., 2017; Thienemann et al., 2017). Parents have also brought this disorder into focus, with books like Beth Alison Maloney's *Saving Sammy: A Mother's Fight to Cure Her Son's OCD* (Maloney, 2009) and documentaries/films like the one mentioned earlier (Sorel, 2018). PANDAS can strike children as young as 4 or 5 years old. It is something that affects the afflicted person's whole family and possibly their community. Psychotherapists can do so much to help, but they will need to be sensitive on many levels to the needs of their client(s).

There is now, thankfully, a definitive test to help diagnose PANS/PANDAS called the Cunningham Panel. It is actually a set of five tests that provide laboratory results to assist in diagnosing infection-induced autoimmune neuropsychiatric disorders. The panel measures the level of circulating antibodies directed against antigens concentrated in the brain, as well as the ability of these and other autoantibodies to increase the activity of an enzyme (CaMKII) that up-regulates neurotransmitters in the brain (The Science of Psychotherapy, 2018a). The telltale signs of an autoimmune assault on key parts of the brain should inform physicians that there is an immune response to deal with and not just a mental disorder.

Treatment can be as simple as an antibiotic, along with some counseling and attention to good gut health. Sometimes the intervention needs to be multifaceted, incorporating a range of psychological and medical interventions such as anti-inflammatory drugs, corticosteroids, or intravenous immunoglobulin therapy. In extreme cases, therapeutic plasma exchange and high-dose intravenous corticosteroids can be used (Frankovich et al., 2017).

While underlying infectious and inflammatory processes in PANS and PANDAS patients are treated, psychiatric and behavioral symptoms need simultaneous treatment to decrease suffering and improve adherence to therapeutic intervention. Psychological, behavioral, and psychopharmacologic interventions tailored to each child's presentation can provide symptom improvement and improve functioning during both the acute and chronic stages of illness. In general, typical evidence-based interventions are appropriate for the varied symptoms of PANS and PANDAS. Individual differences in expected response to psychotropic medication may require marked reduction of initial treatment dose. Antimicrobials and immunomodulatory therapies may be indicated. (Thienemann et al., 2017, p. 566)

Apart from correctly diagnosing and treating autoimmune neuropsychiatric disorders, there may well be a need for the entire family to be engaged with a therapist in recovery. The trauma, financial stress, and social stressors induced by such a disorder can be intense and extended, leaving parents and siblings burned out. A family therapist with an understanding of the disorder can bring much-needed empathy and a space for expression that may not be available among other family or friends. Tamika's parents found that a few of their friends tried to sympathize by saying that they, too, had some OCD symptoms once, but unfortunately this is a misinterpretation of the nature and severity of the disorder. An informed therapist is important in assisting the family to feel understood.

Conclusion

We hope this discussion stays with you, especially as you come across clients presenting with OCD, psychotic behavior, uncharacteristic mood changes, uncontrollable motor movements, and the other symptoms we have touched on. Ruling in or out an autoimmune-mediated disorder like PANS/PANDAS for children or anti-NMDA receptor encephalitis for adults during the early stages can potentially relieve everyone from a traumatic journey through wrong medications and feelings of frustration and helplessness.

CHAPTER 5

What the Experts Do

A large number of experts could be included in this chapter, of course. We have selected just a handful whom we particularly admire, but not so much to isolate their practices from others. The types of work these experts do are relevant because they are effective for the sorts of conditions that psychotherapists regularly encounter. Equally, we want this chapter to act as an hors d'oeuvre that stimulates your hunger to explore what these practitioners do in the practice of their technique and the many others whom we do not have the space to include. There is so much we need to know *about*. We intend this chapter to be both a foundation and a springboard for your dynamic curiosity (refer to Section 6.5).

5.1 Anxiety and OCD

Reid Wilson is director of the Anxiety Disorder Treatment Center of Durham and Chapel Hill, North Carolina, and has been working with the problems of anxiety and OCD since the 1980s. In 2014 the Anxiety and Depression Association of America honored Wilson for a lifetime of service in treating anxiety disorders, awarding him the Jerilyn Ross Clinician Advocate Award at its annual conference in Chicago. Wilson developed *strategic therapy* (or paradoxical therapy) to help people struggling with anxiety and OCD. Wilson's work has serious intent, but he is also able to incorporate his natural humor to engage people with straightforward language. In an interview, he described strategic therapy as "messing with patterns . . . we . . . find the pattern, and then mess with it" (Yalom, 2012).

Strategic therapy acknowledges that many of the patterns and psycho-biological responses are based in natural protective processes, so trying to resist those impulses and implicit intentions is not only very hard to do but can be part of why people end up with unmanageable anxiety and OCD elevated to the level of a disorder. The process can seem paradoxical because the client is encouraged to stop trying to get rid of or resist the symptoms and do the opposite: invite more of the symptoms. The idea is that the important issue is not the anxiety itself but the relationship the client has with it. The focus is to redefine and modify that relationship.

Anxiety disorders (refer to Sections 4.1 and 4.2) stem from a natural anxious response to feeling threatened. The threat may be immediate or distal, the two extremes of temporal context for anxiety disorders: *Panic disorder* is an overwhelmed reaction to an immediate danger, whereas *generalized anxiety disorder* (GAD) is worry or distress about things coming far in the future. Anxiety is, essentially, an irrational fear of real or mentalized threats. People with anxiety disorders have an intolerance of uncertainty and distress, and their anxiety is, in part, their resistance, their fight to push away symptoms in order to avoid discomfort. Anxiety symptoms trigger feelings and thoughts of escape: "This is awful. I don't want this. I want to get away." Unfortunately, this response only makes the situation worse, and it is this response, this relationship with the symptom, that strategic therapy seeks to change.

Wilson utilizes a five-step treatment that he bases on the work of top clinicians and researchers:

1. Encourage clients to become anxious on purpose.
2. Once clients are anxious, persuade them to welcome that anxiety for as long as it lasts.
3. While clients are anxious, teach them to support themselves through positive self-talk and steer them away from catastrophic thinking.
4. Help clients to gradually forgo the use of relaxation exercises or other "safety crutches."
5. Introduce clients to this routine in safe places such as the therapist's

office, and then have them apply it in progressively more threatening situations.

Wilson is regularly challenged by therapists who use techniques that are
based around relaxation and calming the agitations of anxiety. Although
he can see a parallel in the intent—that the therapy is trying to help the
client manage the hyperreactive response—he clarifies the difference this
way: "I liken this approach to persuading a reluctant swimmer to get wet
by wading gradually into the water. What I'm suggesting is that you'll get
better results and get them more quickly if you can persuade that swimmer
to jump" (Wilson, n.d., para. 3).

Fears become habituated when there is sufficient frequency, duration,
and intensity of exposure. Relaxation techniques may reduce the intensity
element and interrupt habituation, but clients can become dependent upon
the techniques and still be vulnerable to an attack that is strong enough
to overcome them. Strategic therapy seeks to change clients' orientation to
their experience of fear of the uncertainty and distaste for the apprehension
and agitation of anxiety. It is not about simply tolerating the discomfort, but
about learning that it is not "bad" to be apprehensive and uncertain in a
fearful situation and how to confront the "cognitive set" that anxiety needs
to be resisted, avoided, and stopped.

Wilson sometimes describes the therapy as a "mental game," although
he is quick to point out that this is serious business. Much of the work is
cognitive, and the process of proactively regaining control of responses is
assisted by three mentalizations (Wilson, 2016):

- **personify:** Give your disordered thinking an identity. Call it "anxiety," or "the worry machine," or "Barry," if you wish.
- **externalize:** Perceive your disordered thinking not as a part of you
  but as something external that has a relationship with you.
- **simplify:** Reduce this relationship to its basic elements. What is anxiety doing *with/to* you (as different from the behavior or feelings you
  are having)? For example, anxiety is telling you that you are weak in
  the face of threat and that you are not capable of moving forward;

anxiety demands that you pay attention to it and follow its instructions and retreat from this threat, and you are listening and obeying.

Here is a case example:

*J. K. and his family moved in with his mother during her later years.
It was wonderful to have a grandmother readily at hand, but as the
years went on, she began to suffer age-related neural degradation
that affected her mental abilities (refer to Section 4.5). Anxiety and
panic attacks became a recurring problem. J. K. consulted with Reid
Wilson, eventually feeling confident to apply strategic therapy to
help his mother.*

She became increasingly concerned about leaving the house, even for
the simple task of shopping. Part of her frustration and apprehension was fear
of not being able to remember people or places. She was also anxious about
having a panic attack, which sometimes caused her to lose consciousness in a
vasovagal syncope (refer to Section 2.3). J. K. found it emotionally testing to
press his mother to defy her anxiety. She became expert at creating excuses
and inventing alternative tasks that were more important than going out.
The first time that J. K. really pressed her was upsetting and felt almost dis-
respectful, but ultimately it was successful. J. K. used a simple 1–10 scale to
describe the intensity of anxiety. She assessed herself to be at 6. When J. K.
pressed her to make the anxiety worse, to invite it in, she was not very keen
to do so, and J. K. reported that he could feel his voice getting louder and
more insistent. It was almost like he was shouting at his mother. "Where are
you now, Mum?" "At an 8!" she replied. "That's amazing, Mum. You're telling
your anxiety what to do! Let's bring it back down to where you were a minute
ago." To the surprise and relief of them both, she did so with little trouble.
Emphasizing that anxiety was something separate from her true self and
she had just shown that she could tell it what to do, rather than the other
way around, J. K. asked whether she could make the anxiety less. "Can I do
that?" she wondered half to herself and half to J. K. She was able to reduce

it almost 1 point in about 30 seconds. J. K. felt he should continue to trust the process and asked his mother to raise the anxiety level once more. "Let's take it back up to a 7, Mum. Do you think we can do that?" "Oh, dear . . ." was all she said as she raised her intensity again. "It's a 7!" she said, almost triumphantly. "That's amazing, Mum. You're kicking that anxiety all over the place. It's not in control of you. You're in control of it!" In that moment she suddenly seemed to calm down. Her eyes had that inward-sensing gaze. After a brief time, probably less than a minute, she focused back on J. K. and calmly announced, "We can go shopping now." And that was that.

Anxiety kept trying to interfere with J. K.'s mother. When it did, they would go through the same routine. Sometimes it was easy, and other times they had to work harder. Voices would rise, but together they were always able to greet the anxiety, play with it, and then get on with what she wanted to do. The process would begin as a struggle; then at some point she would suddenly let it all go. As she aged, new problems emerged, and as her cognitive capacities declined there were new fears and feelings of threat, but she was never defeated by anxiety again.

The Fear of the Fear

Obsessing about and being fearful of the next attack, whether it is anxiety panic or obsessive behavior, can be incredibly time-consuming and can expend a lot of energy that could well be directed to more useful things—like getting better! Considering that a panic attack may last less than 30 seconds and someone who engages in obsessive hand-washing may do that for only 20–30 minutes each day, worry and stress open the door for the anxiety that can pervade the entire day and persist into the night, disrupting sleep. Anxiety is very consuming mentally and physically. This is the problem that clients bring with them into the therapy session. Wilson teaches people what he does himself:

> That's my job—to find any and every mechanism to help change their mind. So, I'm going to work at the level of frame of reference and I'll use examples of other patients. I'll use metaphors, I'll give analogies, I'll use logic, whatever I can use. I told a woman the other day, "If your son were

in fifth grade and had to play the guitar every night, you could imagine him going, 'Darn, I have to practice now.' But if he sat down with his high-school cousin who plays in a rock band, and saw how cool it was, this fifth grader would begin to want to practice guitar every night. You can imagine the difference between a fifth grader having to practice for an hour, and a fifth grader wanting to practice for an hour." That is the kind of shift I'm seeking for my clients and I'll use these kinds of analogies to help them understand it on a deeper level. Every angle I can find to start loosening up their rigidity and resistance. (Yalom, 2012)

CLINICAL NOTES

Reid Wilson takes on what to some may seem an unusual trajectory for anxiety and OCD, but his experience is wide-ranging, and many people have benefited from his therapy and his training. He incorporates whatever is available and helpful to change the client's relationship with anxiety. He also incorporates psychoeducation and neuroscience to broaden the client's perspective and the ways in which therapist and client can discuss what is happening. People get caught up in obsessions and rigid belief systems. This can change when the elements within the system change. Strategic therapy has great success in doing just that—finding the patterns and messing with them.

5.2 Memory Reconsolidation in Coherence Therapy

Emily was rattled. As an advanced-care paramedic for 10 years, she had worked the toughest neighborhoods in the country across two states. But she could not shake what happened to her the previous week. Nightmares kept her awake, and for the first time in her life she had a panic attack. It was a frightening descent into fear and dread that she had previously only read about.

One week before meeting with a therapist, Emily was on the night shift, racing to an "unconscious male, early 20s," with her paramedic partner Elliot.

"We arrived; I grabbed my kit and went into the shop. It was one of those Asian supermarket places. An Asian woman at the door gestured frantically to the corner of the shop saying, 'He there, he there!' When I got to the far corner of the shop, this young Asian guy was sitting up, and he looked wasted. . . . I mean he had to be *on* something. I put my kit down, and before I knew what was happening, he got up and ran past me. He turned back and pulled a knife! It all happened so quickly. . . . I didn't see the knife at first." She was slowing down, searching her memory for the replay of that exact moment.

"Wow. A knife!" the therapist said to fill the space, concerned that this recall was going to be too intense for Emily. But her mind raced back to the scene. "Yeah, a knife, like one of those big army knives. . . . I backed up and then realized the aisle was a dead end! The shelves went right to the back wall and the only way out was the way I came in. It was crazy! Who sets a shop up like that? And then the woman who was at the door is at the top of the aisle yelling, and the guy is angry and yelling something back at her . . ."

After about 20 minutes, Emily had told the whole story: Held at knifepoint with no escape; the unpredictable 20-something guy stoned out of his brain; rescued by the Asian woman, who slapped the young man around the head (she was actually his mother, who was furious as hell and had launched into her son), causing him to run out of the store; and the ensuing trauma symptoms—nightmares, intruding thoughts, and the panic attack that landed her in the emergency department.

Emily was safe now, but her memory compelled her to stay in a state of alertness, pulling her back into that moment at the end of the supermarket aisle. She needed to reframe her emotional reactions to the event. The neurobiological mechanism to achieve such reframing is called *memory reconsolidation*.

Memory Reconsolidation

Bruce Ecker knew that something significant was happening with clients who experienced a sudden shift, transforming their traumatized distress. Their emotional reactions to their memory changed, sometimes eradicating it completely. Bruce decided to pay attention to when that transformational change took place. Thus began a long process of both scientific investigation and developing techniques to replicate therapeutic successes. The result was "depth-oriented brief therapy," which Ecker developed with his partner and coauthor Laurel Hulley.

> We examined thousands of our own therapy sessions with individu-als, couples, and families for key moments in which deep, symptom-dispelling change took place. What distinguished these hours from others? What was it that we as therapists had to know and had to do or not do in order to generate that kind of effectiveness *all the time?* (Ecker & Hulley, 1996, p. 1)

They wanted to understand the particular elements of the therapy that consistently led to positive transformation. Depth-oriented brief therapy was refined into "coherence therapy." Ecker and his colleagues describe the mechanisms of this transformative change in their groundbreaking book *Unlocking the Emotional Brain: Eliminating Symptoms at Their Roots Using Memory Reconsolidation* (Ecker et al., 2012).

Their work gives us a much clearer picture of what happens in the brain when clients have a transformative breakthrough. They describe memory reconsolidation as

> a type of neuroplasticity which, when launched by the specific series of experiences required by the brain, unlocks the synapses of a target emotional learning, allowing that learning to be re-encoded or "re-written" in memory (during a time period of several hours) accord-ing to new learning experiences, resulting in either full nullification (erasure), weakening, modification, or strengthening of the original

learning, depending on characteristics of the new learning. (Ecker et al., 2012, p. 204)

The memory of a traumatic event creates neurobiological connections to the emotional state. When the memory of that event is recalled, those emotional associations are also recalled. But the brain also does an extraordinary thing: It loosens (makes *labile*) the synaptic bonds to these associated memories so that it can update in relation to anything new in their current reality. If the emotional reaction is confirmed, such as having a panic attack, then the traumatized response is *reconsolidated*. This is why therapists are cautioned not to "retraumatize" a client by having them simply recall an event. If, however, there is new information about the memory—such as a bully is no longer able to get the client, or the shame felt while growing up is no longer happening to the adult client, or there is another way of thinking about the event—then new synaptic connections are created, and the memory of the event ceases to produce the same distressing feelings or behavior. The "target emotional learning" changes. Whatever has been the depression Sam feels every April, or Jamie's inability to get on an airplane without having a panic attack, or Dawn's unconscious sabotaging every opportunity she has at work, changes rapidly, in a transformative breakthrough. The key is that the synapses remain labile for only 3–4 hours. Processes like memory extinction are different. That is the development of a competing synaptic pathway establishing a preferred response—the mechanism used in therapies like CBT and explains why they often require 8–12 weeks to be effective.

Therapeutic Reconsolidation Process

Ecker lays out a process that therapists can follow to achieve a consistent result. It is the seven-step "therapeutic reconsolidation process" (Ecker, 2018, pp. 27–30) We will summarize each step which are fairly simple in their conceptual essence, but complex and subtle in their overall clinical implementation across clients who differ widely in personality, emotional tolerance, extent and depth of suppressed emotional distress, readiness to trust the therapist, and other variables (Ecker, 2018, p. 30).

PREPARATION PHASE

1. **symptom identification:** actively engaging the client in recognizing and labeling the specific behaviors, somatic responses, emotions, and/or thoughts that the client wants to eliminate, and identifying when these unwanted experiences happen—that is, the situations and perceptions that evoke or intensify them.

2. **retrieval of target schema:** an experiential process of eliciting into explicit awareness the emotional learning and memory that maintain a symptom, guiding the client to verbalize the emergent material while feeling it, and then integrating the newly conscious awareness into routine daily awareness as a personal emotional truth.

3. **identification of disconfirming knowledge:** finding past or present experience(s) in which the client has direct, living knowledge that are fundamentally contrary to the target learnings and memories retrieved in Step B.

ERASURE SEQUENCE

1. **reactivation of target schema:** using basic experiential methods to guide the client's attention toward key features of the target schema or memory, and inviting the client to allow and attend to the affective and somatic aspects of what arises.

2. **destabilization of target schema:** activating contrary knowledge mismatches to target schema (first juxtaposition) by guiding an initial experience of the contradictory knowledge that was found in Step C, while the target schema or memory remains reactivated from Step 1.

3. **nullification of target schema:** several repetitions of juxtaposition for counterlearning during the remainder of the session by guiding the client a few more times to attend to and affectively feel experiences, the target material, and the contrary knowledge.

VERIFICATION PHASE

1. **Verification of target schema erasure:** observing and documenting the markers of erasure in unambiguous reports from the client that
   — symptoms have ceased to occur completely,
   — there is no nonreactivation in response to any cues or contexts that previously evoked it, and
   — there is an effortless permanence of the change—no relapse.

As significant as memory reconsolidation is for the transformation of emotional memories it must be remembered that it is not a cure-all:

From the perspective of memory reconsolidation, the existence of a therapy client's symptomatology indicates the presence, outside of awareness, of distress-laden emotional learnings (schemas, mental models) generating the symptoms with adaptive intent; and the optimal process of psychotherapy consists of guiding the profound unlearning of the symptom-generating emotional learnings, nullifying and erasing them via the memory reconsolidation process. That perspective has been found applicable to a wide range of symptomatology. However, the clinician must be alert to recognize symptoms that are not based in learning and memory and therefore cannot be dispelled by MR [memory reconsolidation], such as Asperger's syndrome or depression due to hypothyroidism. (Ecker & Bridges, 2020, p. 298)

Memory reconsolidation is a complex phenomenon. Understanding how to use it can be easier than understanding the neurobiology behind it, but it is very helpful to have some grasp of the supporting science. Some misconceptions about memory reconsolidation have already emerged; Ecker highlighted 10 common ones in a paper titled "Memory Reconsolidation Understood and Misunderstood" (Ecker, 2015). There is also a wealth of information on the Coherence Therapy website (https://www.coherencetherapy.org).

"Emily, what would have made you feel much more in control and safe last week when you were being threatened?" asked her therapist, who wanted to discover a resource she could use to juxtapose her fearful response.

"I'm not sure what you mean," Emily said.

"Well, let's imagine that what happened was in a movie and you're the screenwriter. As the screenwriter you can change anything you like. What would you change about the character 'Emily' who is there, backed into a corner, being threatened by a knife-wielding, crazy guy?" The therapist hoped to draw out some creative imagination.

"OK, like I could have had my own weapon or something?"

"Sure. Anything! You could be a superhero, or have special powers, or a weapon. What comes to mind?"

"You probably think it's a bit childish, but I've always loved Wonder Woman," she blushed with a laugh.

"Cool! Wonder Woman . . . As the screenwriter, how would you incorporate Wonder Woman?"

"I guess I could defend myself like Wonder Woman. . . . I mean I, would just come up to the guy and go, Wham! Bam! You know? And just belt the crap out of him!" She laughed loudly at the thought, and at her own animation as she did a Wonder Woman move.

"Yes, OK. Cool. Now what would that feel like?"

From that point on, Emily's therapist had her imagine the *feeling* of being a Wonder Woman character in the market a week earlier. She refined her reimagination of the scene and came up with a feeling of complete confidence where she only had to make a gesture of defense, Wonder Woman style, to scare the guy off. The therapist took Emily back to the feeling of how the incident actually played out so that she could get back in touch with that feeling of helplessness and fear and allow her synapses to become labile; then they flipped back to Emily with Wonder Woman powers and imagined the scene with that feeling—a feeling that was a juxtaposition to helplessness and fear.

Emily's homework was to review the incident from both perspectives—the way it actually felt, and with the rescripted powers of Wonder Woman.

Her therapist also asked her to review the "scenes" as if she were watching them on two TVs, so that she could easily flip back and forth between them.

She returned 3 days later.

"I did the TV thing and the Wonder Woman invincibility thing as soon as I got home from our last session. . . . Well, . . . I slept all night! It was weird, but it was like something just turned off the edginess of what happened last week. And then the next day I couldn't really get the same intensity of fear, even when I tried to remember what happened. I mean, I can remember exactly what happened, but I just don't feel that upset about it."

Now she is able to remember that moment with a sense of detachment, even warmth and empathy for herself, rather than a fearful replay. Memory reconsolidation did its job in redefining the emotional timbre of her memory.

5.3 Somatic Therapy

He needed the pain to subside, to be manageable. The injury to his back would always give him some pain, but he knew he was making it worse in his own mind. He wanted to regain some control over his body. Other therapists, and he had visited many, had not succeeded in changing anything. R.H. suggested we might do better to ask his body. After some playful experiments, he found he wanted to hold the pain between his hands. He held his hands up about 12 inches apart and really focused on them. Then he suddenly dropped them to his side, saying, "Nothing."

We talked a little more, and his hands spontaneously rose in front of him, and he stared at them for about a minute. Again his hands dropped, "Nothing." We continued to talk. His hands repeated the rise and fall a few more times. Something was happening, but neither of us could explain it, so we just let the body continue with this strange conversation. Suddenly, his hands rose to either side of his head. He seemed very agitated. "I've got the pain!" His hands shook. This scenario did not fit any textbook description, so R. H. asked simply, "What do you want to do with it?" His hands jerked to the right of his head, and he vigorously threw away whatever was in them.

We paused for a moment as he got his breath. "OK," he said. "That worked. My pain has just dropped from 8 to 4." We talked about the experience for a few minutes, but he stopped and said, "This isn't about my brain knowing. My body seems to know what to do. I'm not going to fight it. I'm just going to let my body help me. Thank you very much." His pain is now something he can manage. We only ever had that one session.

Much of Western psychotherapy has focused primarily on a language-based narrative, talking about things in an often "logical," linear, and literal manner in the hope of resolving an inner conflict or healing a psychological wound. Psychotherapists who adopt the "talking cure" of psychodynamic, psychoanalytic, or cognitive therapies have been adept at listening to the language-based narrative of clients and offering interpretations and logical/cognitive avenues for healing. Nonverbal somatic (pertaining to the body, the "soma") and more integrated mind–body approaches have been observed for thousands of years in ancient contemplative healing traditions but had been largely overlooked in the formulation of Western 20th-century psychotherapy. However, because of a combination of advancing neuroscience, a more sophisticated psychology, and a return to the wisdom of ancient healing traditions, the latter part of the 20th century saw the emergence of an integrative somatic-focused therapy, particularly in the area of trauma. Allan Schore brought the importance of the brain's right hemisphere in emotional processing and the dominant implicit states within the brain–mind–body into sharp focus (Schore, 2003, 2012). This was a paradigm shift toward embodied psychology, as opposed to one that resided only within the cranium.

Many important contributors to the field of trauma and the body have advanced practitioners' understanding both theoretically and in clinical applications. In this section we touch on what has become known as *sensorimotor psychotherapy* and its originator, Pat Ogden.

Sensorimotor psychotherapy integrates what is known about traditional psychotherapeutic techniques but places the body firmly in the center of the therapy process. The foundation of this approach comes from Ron Kurtz, who pioneered a body-oriented psychotherapy in the mid-1970s called the Hakomi method. Kurtz (2009) was heavily influenced by gestalt therapy, bioenergetics, yoga and Eastern philosophy, and systems theory. He assimilated these influences into the Hakomi method, with an emphasis on enhancing personal awareness in a mindful state by evoking emotions, insights, and memories. He eventually deemphasized the gestalt and bioenergetics influences and emphasized mindful sensitivity, nonviolence, spirituality, and the importance of the body in psychotherapy.

Pat Ogden was an apprentice of Ron Kurtz in the early 1970s and was intimately involved in development of the Hakomi method as the educational director and designer of the original teaching curriculum.

> I met Ron in the early '70s. I was working in the psychiatric hospital, teaching yoga and dance. I was interested in the body, having practiced yoga for a very long time—and Ron was the first person I met who had the idea that the body was important in psychotherapy. He would talk about it as an "access route": The patterns and movements and sensations of the body would be an access route into implicit material. And I was fascinated. (Ogden, personal communication, January, 26, 2021)

In the early 1980s Ogden founded her own institute, Hakomi Bodywork (to be later named Hakomi Integrative Somatics), and continued pursuing her interests in trauma, movement, and posture in her work with survivors of sexual abuse.

> In 1981 I was sitting with Ron in a restaurant, and I said, "I love Hakomi, but I'm much more interested in the body than you are" . . . structural integration. I was teaching massage, I grew up dancing, you know, and so he said, "Well, start your own branch and call it Hakomi Bodywork." . . . Ron didn't work directly with trauma, and that was another huge influence for me in the late '70s. I was an adjunct therapist for the university clinic here in Boulder, and they were sending me women who were unresponsive sexually. I didn't know anything about trauma. Who was talking about trauma in '77, '78? So, I was

working with relationship issues and emotions, and my clients were getting worse! I was baffled. And I remember saying to my friend, "Well, maybe I can just keep them in their bodies." And that was the dawn of my own learning about trauma, from those clients. (Ogden, personal communication, January 26, 2021)

By 2002, Ogden had developed a body-based trauma intervention and renamed her school the Sensorimotor Psychotherapy Institute, with an emphasis on the things she had learned about the body and trauma, and the body's own posture and narrative in response to trauma.

The language of the body is important in so many ways. If you are tracking the body in nuanced ways, you will see the pulling in, the slight moving back, the squint of the eyes. It [the body] will show its opinion. (Ogden, personal communication, January 26, 2021)

Sensorimotor symptoms tell the story of trauma without words: bodily sensations, pain, numbing, and reactivity. These adaptations influence how a person responds to the environment and to internal cues and, in turn, inform them about the world and themselves. It is also these adaptations that can so easily derail someone with overwhelming and dysregulating emotions and bodily reactions (Ogden et al., 2006). Such sensorimotor processes are bottom-up processes that are largely unregulated by cortical or cognitive control (Schore, 1994).

Sensorimotor psychotherapy aims to nurture the resources that can regulate arousal and increase self-esteem, competency, and overall integration. There is a general three-phase approach:

- developing resources—stabilization and symptom reduction
- working with trauma memory
- moving forward, creating integration

Anyone working with clients must be flexible and sensitive to their individual challenges, choosing appropriate tools for the moment rather than stepping through a protocol. The workbook *Sensorimotor Psychotherapy: Interventions for Trauma and Attachment* (Ogden & Fisher, 2015) provides an extensive set of discrete exercises for therapist and client to work through. Because Ogden's approach is an extension of more traditional psychotherapy, I (M. D.) found these interventions easily integrated into therapy. I have been using this workbook since its publication to great effect, even though I have had no formal training in sensorimotor psychotherapy. The workbook is a clear road map for addressing physiology during therapy, both theoretically and experientially. Each chapter begins with a Therapist's Guide that outlines the purpose of the chapter and the types of clients who may benefit from it. Then it gives suggestions for clinical use, provides an overview of worksheets, and explains how the material can be adapted for dissociative clients. Finally, the workbook gives a succinct summary of the theory, followed by approximately five or six well-presented worksheets that can be easily integrated into therapy sessions.

In the first phase of therapy (developing resources), work might include identifying and appreciating client strengths, body awareness, grounding, posture, breathing, or identifying and developing missing resources. This work helps clients recognize and stay within their window of tolerance and become more sensitive to available coping resources. Simple awareness of movement, posture, and mindfulness equip the client to implement and develop regulatory resources.

The second phase addresses memory of past trauma. The thoughts, feelings, images, and words/language associated with the past are brought into the light, especially those implicit nonverbal memories of childhood. The aim is to shift awareness from explicit verbal descriptions of what happened in the past, to the legacy of the implicit mental–emotional–physical memory states established at that time. In an example from the worksheet "Identifying Implicit Memories" (Ogden & Fisher, 2015, p. 447), the client is asked to identify an implicit memory (e.g., "I get really upset when people are not there for me exactly when I want them to be.") and then a relevant past experience (e.g., "As a child, I was left on my own a lot, and neither of my parents really supported me."), and then think about resources that could change their experience of that implicit memory (e.g.,

"Containment—hug myself," "Call a supportive friend," "Hand on heart, hand on belly").

In the final phase—moving forward—parts of life that may have been neglected or disrupted because of the trauma are attended to. Utilizing, and further developing, the resources from earlier stages, the client learns to enrich everyday life, expand the window of tolerance, and overcome limiting beliefs. Some of this work might involve education about attachment, making sense of emotions, beliefs about self and body, how we physically move and posture ourselves, boundaries, and many other topics that integrate a mind–body awareness.

"The body speaks clearly to those who know how to listen" (Ogden & Fisher, 2015, p. 25).

5.4 Trauma Therapy

Trauma is so pervasive and covers such a broad spectrum that it is difficult to know what treatment modality or technique to use. Recognized techniques include imaginal exposure, sensorimotor therapy, variations of CBT, psychodynamic therapy, neuro- and biofeedback, EMDR (eye movement desensitizing and reprocessing), psychoeducation, memory reconsolidation, mentalizing, exercise, breathing, yoga, and more. Choosing a treatment can be daunting for both therapist and client, but the number of approaches available means it may be possible to find what is most suitable for each client and their unique situation.

Treating psychological trauma is very different from treating a medical event like a heart attack, which has clearly defined treatment protocols to deal with the blocked artery and medications to assist in recovery. In psychotherapy, things are rarely straightforward. What are observable, the symptoms, are not always a clear reflection of what needs to be resolved, as we saw with J. D. in Section 2.5. There is a theoretical understanding: that prolonged traumatized behavior has produced chronic levels of stress hormones that damage the hippocampus and the ability to integrate autobiographical and implicit emotional memories. This is a useful insight into why the war veteran with PTSD completely freaks out at the sound of a helicopter or a car backfiring. Unlike the cardiologist, psychotherapists cannot just give their clients aspirin, heparin, and coronary angioplasty as a fix for the problem. A hippocampus–memory dis-integration is only one possible piece of a very complex, nonlinear, systemic web of maladaptive states, as we discussed with preparatory sets in Section 2.5. So, which therapy is the right choice to deal with such complexity?

Therapists who work for an agency or for the government may be bound to apply only approved, evidence-based therapeutic methods. Typically, for PTSD the options are prolonged exposure (PE), cognitive processing therapy (CPT), trauma-focused CBT (CBT-T; Ursano et al., 2004; Watkins et al., 2018), and EMDR, which has been recognized by the World Health Organization (WHO, 2013) as a first-choice treatment for PTSD. The International Society for Traumatic Stress Studies, however, has compiled recommendations of the most effective therapies for trauma (Bisson et al., 2019), which include CBT-T, EMDR, CPT, and PE, but others as well—including nonpsychological and nonpharmacological treatments such as acupuncture, neurofeedback, TMS (transcranial magnetic stimulation), somatic experiencing, yoga, and saikokeishikankyoto (a traditional Japanese herbal formula; Numata et al., 2014)—that all show promise in treating PTSD, according to a combination of anecdotal evidence, limited journal publications, and nonjournal publications.

An evidence-based technique is a sensible choice but not the only option. One of the techniques that has been researched less but still shows good efficacy is coherence therapy. In the hands of trained practitioners, this protocol uses the well-researched mechanism of memory reconsolidation (refer to Sections 1.4 and 5.2).

Neurofeedback for developmental trauma is another good case in point. It has produced remarkable outcomes for the treatment of trauma symptoms with an approach completely different from some of the more established therapies. Similar comments can be made about TMS (Namgung et al., 2019), which is a noninvasive method to stimulate activity in specific brain regions. In our discussions with Sebern Fisher, who is at the forefront of treating complex trauma with neurofeedback (refer to Section 2.4), she reported transformational change with many clients but lamented the lack of rigorous research studies to validate such efficacy. Lanius et al. (2015), in their discussion of PTSD treatment, also point to neurofeedback and TMS as treatments showing encouraging signs of efficacy. We expect that neurofeedback and TMS will find a more prominent place in the future.

The best way to evaluate the most appropriate therapy is to first consider what the traumatized individual needs, as well as their disposition, or aptitude, for receiving and responding to the therapist's approach. What the client needs can be evaluated from a number of different conceptual perspectives: brain waves, networks, the nervous system, chemicals, and memory. There are more possibilities we could explore, but in our limited space we will focus on these five perspectives.

Brain Wave Perspective

From a brain wave perspective (refer to Section 2.4), complex developmental trauma has encoded the trauma in the lower delta and theta frequencies (0.1–3 Hz and 4–7 Hz). This brain activity is not readily accessible to the conscious mind, which operates at the higher alpha, beta, and gamma frequencies (8–12 Hz, 12–36 Hz, 36–45 Hz), yet the delta and theta frequencies can wield a strong negative influence. Anxiety and fear are easily evoked from seemingly benign cues from within and without. So, the lack of affect regulation in traumatized clients can be identified in an EEG: reduced alpha activity, increased theta:alpha ratio in the cortex, and general lack of integration and synchrony of such oscillations (van der Kolk et al., 2016). The goal, from a brain wave perspective, is to give the brain feedback about its own activity and send reward signals (in computer games, the reward is usually a win) when neuronal activation or connectivity patterns change in the right direction. This form of operant conditioning has been shown to reshape the neural architecture into a more coherent and self-regulatory system (Nicholson et al., 2017).

Network Perspective

From a network perspective, the neural nets that recall emotional memory and autobiographical memory can be maladapted. This connection is mediated by the hippocampus, which can be epigenetically affected by chronic and/or excessive stress hormones to inhibit receptivity to communicating hormones (refer to Section 1.4). Not only may the hippocampus have decreased functionality because of trauma but there may be decreased activation in the dorsolateral prefrontal, temporal, parietal, orbitofrontal, visual association, and parietal cortices, contrasting with the increased activity in the amygdala, posterior cingulate, and parahippocampal gyrus (Bremner et al., 1997). Maladaptation and dysfunction of the connectivity between the central executive, salience, and default mode networks (CEN, SN, and DMN; refer to Section 1.1)—which are the principal networks for consciousness, arousal, and self-orientation—can be observed in the traumatized client's difficulty switching between these mental states.

There is little doubt that the dysfunctions of these circuits in the cortex, and deeper into the subcortical regions, underlie many or all of the symptoms of the posttrauma survivor. As with the brain wave perspective, the goal is to bring back the proper balance of activity, connectivity, and function of all the networks into an integrated whole (refer to Section 2.4). To do so would mean interventions that help restore activity and connectivity in the CEN, improving working memory, decision-making, and selective attention. The disruption of emotional states, detachment, and lack of interoceptive awareness (alterations of the SN) require a restoration of salience detection. Related therapies might include mindfulness-based techniques such as body scans to enhance interoceptive awareness, and anxiety management skills to modulate hypervigilance and restore normal insula function. When the DMN is dysfunctional in PTSD, affecting sense of self, Lanius et al. (2015) suggest,

> Current PTSD treatments geared towards alleviating both cognitive and somatically-based disturbances in self-referential processing (including, but not limited to, cognitive processing therapy, exposure therapy, eye movement desensitization and reprocessing, mentalization based therapy, dialectical behavior therapy, trauma affect regulation: guide for education and therapy, emotion focused therapy, skill straining in affective and interpersonal regulation, psychodynamic approaches, and sensorimotor) may aid in the restoration of DMN function and in

reestablishing sense of self. . . . In theory, combination treatment may simultaneously target both cognitive and somatic-based self-dysfunction through top-down and bottom-up processing, respectively. (p. 6)

Nervous System Perspective

From a nervous system perspective, dysfunction of the ANS is a maladaptive regulation between the parasympathetic and sympathetic branches. The ANS is usually finely tuned to respond to both internal and external cues, but it becomes both overly sensitive and less flexible in traumatized individuals. Neuroception, the nonconscious assessment of safety in the nervous system, can trigger the flight/fight/freeze response (refer to Section 2.3). Inflexibility between the parasympathetic and sympathetic nervous systems causes low heart rate variability (HRV; refer to Section 2.3). HRV can be increased and vagal tone restored through breathing exercises, moderate physical exercise, socializing and laughter, and certain massages. Mindful techniques and biofeedback are also documented to help restore HRV. The HeartMath Institute has been on the leading edge of biofeedback for HRV optimization and has some great tools for therapists and clients alike. Many trauma therapies are somatically (bodily) oriented; examples include Pat Ogden's sensorimotor psychotherapy (Ogden & Fisher, 2015), Babette Rothschild's emphasis on somatic techniques (B. Rothschild, 2000, 2003), Bessel van der Kolk's focus on physical movement like yoga (van der Kolk, 2014), and Peter Levine's somatic experiencing (Payne et al., 2015).

Chemical Perspective

From a chemical perspective, both the HPA axis (which activates a stress response) and the regulatory system (which modulates the stress response) can break down. High levels of glucocorticoids in prolonged stress damage the regulatory system—more specifically, the hippocampus and its capacity to identify and regulate circulating cortisol and act as a "thermostat" for the stress response (refer to Section 1.2). Stress-related damage also inhibits new learning, heightens the potentiation of noradrenergic responsiveness to subsequent stressors, and increases the release of norepinephrine in the hippocampus and other brain regions (Jankord & Herman, 2008; Kino, 2015). When a breakdown of the HPA axis makes it hyperresponsive, the system often overreacts to even mild stressors. Such underregulated and overly intense responses can readily manifest as anxiety and panic attacks.

The therapeutic aim is to rebalance the neurochemical–hormonal system. The task is to reduce cortisol levels, increase serotonin levels (which is the intended purpose of SSRI medications), reduce inflammatory agonists like histamine, and stabilize the gut microbiome (refer to Section 2.2). A combination of diet, exercise, nutritional supplements, mindfulness and relaxation exercises, biofeedback, and talk and somatic therapies has a positive impact on the disrupted neurochemical milieu of the traumatized client.

Memory Perspective

From a memory perspective, the goal is to affect the intrusive, often implicit, emotional memories that give rise to a strong experiential recall of past trauma. As discussed in Section 4.2, PTSD is very much a memory recall problem. Intrusive memories that are highly vivid and emotionally strong steal people away from current reality and back into the most intense moments of a past trauma.

CLINICAL NOTES

Effective therapies need to shift intrusive trauma memories back into the historical archives. Reframing traumas as past events enables top-down processes to suppress or overrule out-of-context reactions. Effective therapies include trauma-focused CBT coupled with somatic and experiential therapies that address more of the body (Ogden & Fisher, 2015; Solomon & Siegel, 2003; van der Kolk, 2014). These therapies help identify the context of the trauma and the meaning that has been attached to the trauma, then update those meanings to create new perspectives. Equally important is to identify sensory triggers, become consciously aware of them, and reframe them in an appropriate context.

5.5 Addiction and Recovery

Dr. Sherif Darwish is an Egyptian psychiatrist who founded an enormously successful addiction recovery clinic in Alexandria. His approach to recovery is founded on love and acceptance. Darwish started his medical career in cardiology but shifted to psychiatry. Here is what he told us about those early days of training:

> An important motivation was the hospital where I would be training. Mamoura Hospital for Psychiatry and Addiction is the largest Ministry of Health hospital in northern Egypt. There are about 1,000 psychiatry and addiction inpatient beds and an outpatient clinic that covers some 400 patients per day. I still remember my first day when I stood in the middle of the very long corridor of the wards and how intimidating it was. Yet, in less than a year, I was playing football with the patients and having friendly conversations with them. This taught me much more than any textbook. My passion for psychiatry grew day after day. I could see it clearly. Every person is different, and managing each case is like taking a journey in human experiences and lives. It is not only challenging on the professional level but also very nourishing on the personal level.

In 2003, standard addiction treatments in Egypt were largely ineffective. There was a huge drug addiction problem, and Darwish decided this was where he wanted to make a difference. He was inspired by the changes he saw in his patients simply through interpersonal relationships. Darwish and a colleague started to develop a program for addicts that was very different.

> Working closely with addicts and listening to their stories and experiences made me believe that people, when they are given a true second chance and treatment, can really change. . . . This empowers them and helps them achieve abstinence. Using, or not using, drugs is just a symptom of the bigger problem of dependency.

With just a small group of people, Darwish started to build a recovery program and a recovery center that was more akin to building a family than an institutionalized program. They created a welcoming environment by painting the walls, furnishing the place, and holding barbecues, which was not the usual practice for a psychiatrist in Egypt, but Darwish was passionate to make a difference in his community.

Darwish saw that many of the addicts had traumatic backgrounds and realized that underneath the chemical addiction was a deep-seated need to be seen, accepted, and loved. This became the bedrock principle for his work: bring the patients into a "family" where they can be accepted and loved, while also attending to their chemical dependency and other issues that accompany their drug addiction.

Over the years those foundational principles have remained the context in which therapy is practiced. Darwish's team uses CBT, DBT, psychodynamic, and other modalities in a truly integrated approach. Everything is individually tailored. A patient might be exposed to CBT, some play therapy, some psychodynamic therapy, and whatever else emerges as appropriate and beneficial. These approaches, from different angles, seek to achieve an effective change and recovery, all the while emphasizing love and acceptance from peers and professionals at the center.

What is the priority for the patient? Often, they come into therapy and *everything* is an "emergency" and "urgent." The first task is to sort out what is not important, what is important, and what is urgent. When the patient feels like everything is urgent, the treatment is seen as urgent, and they want to get through it as fast as possible. Helping the client develop an awareness of what may be important but not an urgent emergency is invaluable. Learning this distinction helps the patient and the therapist with planning and executing activities and, importantly, reducing anxiety.

Unfortunately, patients often do not come into the program until they have hit rock bottom. On the positive side, being at such a low point also acts as a motivation to change: They have nothing more to lose. Darwish's approach is to take time to sit with the patient and contemplate the losses they have suffered from drug abuse. This exercise reinforces their motivation to change. A common stumbling block, however, is the belief some patients have that when they stop taking drugs, they will get immediate benefits. Such thinking is usually demotivating because benefits do not magically materialize. The program helps patients to understand that after managing the losses from taking drugs, they need to deal with the losses from *not* taking drugs, including withdrawal, their addiction lifestyle, and their addiction community. Recovery comes with a personal and social cost.

The length of engagement for each patient is open-ended. It all depends on the patient and their responsiveness to the program. Darwish is careful not to prejudge people, so they purposely ignore "on paper" predictions in the referral or the initial intake:

> I have seen people who, on paper, would have the easiest and most smooth treatment and they would die of an overdose. And I've had people, when you see them on paper, you'd say this is nearly impossible, and they go one trial, one way, and they never come back [i.e., they recover quickly and do not need to return to the program].

The most important part of the program is relationship. The program involves lots of communal activities, such as playing volleyball, breaking the Ramadan fast together, and encouraging the forming of strong bonds with others who are recovering. Patients are also encouraged to form new friendships beyond the walls of the center to satisfy attachment needs.

Darwish recalled events of the upheaval during the Arab Spring in a conversation with me (R. H.). In the midst of the crisis, the police disappeared, leaving the military, which was not very concerned about maintaining general law and order. Local neighborhoods had to organize their own checkpoints to protect their families and community. Even more unfortunate was that the loss of law enforcement opened the door to drug merchants. Darwish could see them setting up near the neighborhood checkpoints. The whole situation was a recipe for disaster. To his surprise, none of the recovered addicts from the recovery center relapsed. When he finally asked them why, the answer could be summarized as, "We did not relapse because what we were doing to protect our families and community was *too important*."

This says it all. When an ex-addict's motivation to protect families and community overrides any enticement to relapse, this is evidence that deep healing has taken place.

Another author and therapist, Dr. Oliver Morgan, has been on a similar track with addiction recovery therapy. His recent book *Addiction, Attachment, Trauma, and Recovery: The Power of Connection* (2019) has a telling title that emphasizes the importance of attachment as both causal and vital for recovery. Morgan's work is born out of academic, clinical, and personal experience in the arena of addiction.

He contends that the psychobiological and social developments that form attachments in early childhood are the foundation for addictive disorders when secure attachment fails to develop:

> While human connection is essential for development and buffers us from life's travails, disconnection creates fertile ground for the emergence of addiction and other troubles later in life. I view addiction in large measure as a disorder of attachment and human connection. Unfulfilled interpersonal needs can be shifted toward bonding and relationship—building with a drug, an activity, or a behavior that partially fulfils the role of a substitute. All that is required is for the drug or activity to "have what it takes" in order to fill the role of substitute. . . . Unmet attachment needs can be addressed, even if only partially, by a relationship to addiction. (Morgan, 2019, p. 104)

When secure attachment does not develop, internal states fail to regulate behavioral responses—sometimes significantly. This is especially true in the critical first 18–24 months of rapid brain development, when attachment bonds are particularly important. Without a robust internal regulatory system to navigate the often turbulent world, extrinsic forces are employed to substitute for the absence of secure attachment. These substitutes may be drugs, food, gambling, sex, work, or some other activity that activates neurobiological processes equating relationship and attachment.

The lust for power or wealth can be every bit as addicting as heroin, and just as deadly. And while it is tempting to limit our thinking to psychoactive chemicals and compulsive activities, human beings have the capability of utilizing many other elements of living into counterfeit substitutes for true relationships. (Morgan, 2019, p. 119)

These substitutes for attuned human connection provide momentary emotional management, but the side effects are often worse than the "cure." The reward system in the brain can become so sensitized to drug cues that it becomes disconnected from higher prefrontal cortical control. The addict goes back to the addictive behavior or substance "mindlessly"—that is, without activating their much-needed cognitive appraisal.

Are insecurely attached addicts, however, forever stuck with only substitutes for real connection? Can they achieve emotional regulation and stability? Morgan goes back to the work of Mary Main, who described "attachment repair" and "earned-secure attachment" (Roisman et al., 2002). This is the capacity for adults, despite the lack of secure attachment in childhood, to make sense of their history and why they do and feel the way they do today. This exercise in understanding the past helps them create a new narrative that has the power to alter their neural architecture and autobiographical memories that have trapped them in insecurity.

Attachment repair is the focus of Morgan's therapeutic process, as it is with Darwish. The best way to change the default narrative of an addicted patient is in the context of secure relationships—the "family" that Darwish nurtures and the interpersonal sensitivity, empathy, and love that Morgan demonstrates with his clients. Within this context of human connection, it is possible to activate coregulation between the client and therapist, and to reengage prefrontal, cognitive appraisal of what the addiction is doing to the client. The reward system, which is also wired to respond to attuned human connection, starts to respond to cues other than the addiction. Understanding is gained, narratives are altered, and positive feedback loops are established that align neural architecture with the new narrative. Part of this new narrative is making sense of the past. Other parts of the narrative revolve around the newly experienced reality that they are someone of worth; someone seen, heard, and valued; someone loved and accepted. Love and acceptance are indeed powerful drugs! Morgan (2019) describes the important goal for counseling as

> the co-creation of a new, safe, and more secure interaction. Over time, this may supply a corrective (reparative) relational experience. The same kind of attunement, mis-attunement (rupture), and re-attunement (repair) process that can cultivate synchrony in a new healing dance brings healing and openness to learning from experience once again. Social engagement, as opposed to defensiveness, takes over the process. (p. 128)

Once there is a safe and secure process of coregulation between client and therapist, Morgan suggests there is an opportunity to revisit painful memories and juxtapose them with the new narrative and understanding that the client has about themselves. This is the circumstance in which memory reconsolidation (refer to Sections 1.4 and 5.2) can fundamentally change old mental schemata about self-worth and disarm defensive mechanisms.

CLINICAL NOTES

These experts are not necessarily revealing something new about the neurobiology of attachment or chemical dependence. What they have done is shift the spotlight from chemical dependencies and the reward system and to the entire attachment paradigm. Sherif Darwish and Oliver Morgan, just to showcase two of the experts, are taking the science and practice to another level, and we think this is significant for the field of addiction. The obvious takeaway here is to consider attachment issues whenever you are faced with a client struggling with addiction.

CHAPTER 6

Innovations for the 21st-Century Therapist

In this final chapter we delve into some of the concepts that we believe will both underpin and drive the 21st-century psychotherapist and modern psychotherapy. Some of these sections do not introduce new concepts but rather focus on concepts that were ahead of their time. Now it is possible for these ideas to be embraced. Some are familiar concepts that have been updated, and some are new. Collectively, these are the activators for a phase shift in the way psychotherapy is practiced and perhaps in the fundamental perception of what psychotherapy is.

6.1 Mind to Body

The idea that a mental state or a mentalization, such as a thought, can affect the body is not new, but it can still be difficult to fully grasp, especially the implications of such a possibility (Kirsch & Hyland, 1987). It is also possible for someone else or an event or the environment to induce or activate a mental state or mentalization that can then affect the body (Anjum et al., 2018). For centuries people have been healers and medicine men (and women) with no more than rituals, incantations, and ideas to heal and, in some cases, to harm. The past few decades have produced a large array of practices that can have therapeutic benefits ranging from simple acts of motivation and positive affirmation to complex practices including mindfulness, as well as compassion and forgiveness therapies.

Ernest Rossi has been one of the most impactful investigators and developers of the principles involved in mind-to-body therapy. His work with Milton Erickson in the 1970s continued to develop after Erickson's death in 1980. Rossi's book with David Cheek, *Mind-Body Therapy: Ideodynamic Healing in Hypnosis* (Rossi & Cheek, 1988), continues to be popular in the field. The next important milestone for Rossi was his book *The Psychobiology of Mind-Body Healing: New Concepts of Therapeutic Hypnosis* (1993), followed with what must be considered his opus, *The Psychobiology of Gene Expression: Neuroscience and Neurogenesis in Hypnosis and the Healing Arts* (2002). Collectively, these volumes survey the mind-to-body therapeutic process from simple behavioral responses (ideomotor and ideodynamic) to the activity generated in genes in response to noninvasive psychotherapies. Rossi developed a therapeutic process, called "mirroring hands" (Hill & Rossi, 2017), that facilitates the client's ability to open and use "mind-to-body healing."

A number of research breakthroughs have provided deeper understanding (and altered people's perceptions) of the connections within and between human beings:

- The belief that each individual is an entity isolated from other human beings has been displaced by the discovery of mirror neurons and the neurobiology of empathy (refer to Section 1.5).
- There is a wide range of activity from brain to body through the vagus nerve (refer to Section 2.3), and that is just one pathway where mental activity communicates with the body to change and regulate biological functions.
- Activity of the immune system is altered by stress, anxiety, or depression, as it is by calm, contentment, and comfort (refer to Section 4.1).
- The activations from mind to body trigger gene expression and epigenetic encoding, all in response to mentalizations and emotional states (refer to Sections 3.1 and 3.2).
- Almost every section of this book leads us here: The mind interacts "top down" with the body. Antonio Damasio explained in ***Descartes' Error*** (2005) that the body and how it processes emotion is

critical for the mind, and the mind is vitally important for how the body functions. Ernest Rossi took that knowledge and applied it to therapeutic practice.

Rossi was among the early pioneers who connected the activity of therapy to the activation of gene expression. This link provides a biological basis for recovery from illness, whether physical or psychological. In an article titled "Art, Truth, and Beauty" (2004), Rossi remarked on "the psychobiology of mind-body healing and rehabilitation via activity-dependent gene expression":

> Neuroscience research is now documenting how facilitating gene expression and brain plasticity (involving synaptogenesis as well as neurogenesis . . .) via activity-dependent cognitive-emotional-behavioral experiences is a basic mechanism of molecular healing that makes rehabilitation possible. . . . Until recently, this molecular-genomic mechanism of rehabilitative healing by behavioral activation was not understood. The new neuroscience hypothesis is that cognition and behavioral action initiates activity-dependent gene expression. This activity-dependent gene expression initiates healing by the generation of proteins that facilitate brain plasticity and stem cell differentiation into new tissues that can be initiated within minutes and continue for the hours, days, and weeks required for full rehabilitation. (pp. 12–13)

Rossi found that Erickson encouraged the client to be the more active partner in the therapeutic relationship. Therapy was most effective when the activity was primarily with or within the patient. The therapist was more effective as a facilitator of the client's process, rather than the instigator or controller. By enabling the client to be the activator in the therapeutic experience, the client is able to amplify their own natural healing processes. In conversations with me (R. H.), Rossi discussed the idea that although many modes of therapy were being developed, they were all activities that clients would naturally generate. Most therapies are not inventions but observations, by very capable people, of what people do naturally to repair and resolve problems. Clients have difficulty because of blocks and barriers to their natural healing processes. These blocks and barriers are part of the cause of their mental and emotional distress. Humans are an interpersonal species that has evolved to coregulate, so it is natural to involve other people in the process of recovery. The difficulty for the therapist is to have the sensitivity to know when to assist, when to facilitate, and when to step back and allow the client to proceed without interruption or influence. At the 1985 Milton H. Erickson Foundation conference, Rossi explained:

> Creative moments are the essence of all forms of psychotherapy. They are the moments when there is an aha! experience. The first clue is when the client pauses and looks off. . . . That's the moment for the therapist to shut up. (Rossi, 1985)

Thirty-two years later, in a conversation with R.H., Rossi added,

> We have to learn to cast the burden . . . of effective therapy back to the client . . . because it's the *client* that has to activate their own creative activity . . . develop their own insight . . . insights that no therapist can ever know. (personal communication, June, 2017)

Natural Problem-Solving

Rossi described two essential natural cycles and rhythms that are poorly understood and largely disregarded: the four-stage creative cycle and the ultradian rhythm. The four-stage creative cycle is a natural organizing principle of nature. Knowing which stage of the cycle the client is working through helps the therapist to be more sensitive to the ebb and flow of the client's needs. The stages are as follows:

Stage 1—Information: gathering information and data. *What is this all about?*

Stage 2—Incubation: working out what the problem is really all about. *How does this affect me? What does this mean to me?*

Stage 3—Breakthrough and illumination: a flash of insight, resolution,

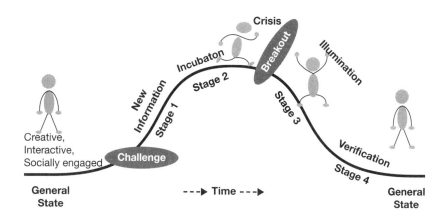

FIGURE 6.1: Ernest Rossi's Four-Stage Creative Cycle

or revelation (an "aha" moment), followed by an expansive and creative response to change. *Things makes sense now, and I can create something better in my life!*

Stage 4—Verification: quiet review and consideration of the whole experience, and integration of the benefits into everyday life. *I understand, appreciate, and accept what I have learned.*

Most clients come to us in Stage 2, where they are struggling with a problem and needing a breakthrough. The therapeutic process also has its stages. The client and therapist begin with exchanging information before beginning to delve into the heart of the problem. The "creative moment" is something that can be easily missed, and the therapist might continue working on the problem even though the client's natural problem-solving capacities have made a breakthrough and the client is ready to proceed without further assistance.

Ultradian rhythms (rhythms that are shorter than the daily circadian rhythm) are the brain's natural rhythms of energetic flow, which repeat about every 90–120 minutes (Hill & Rossi, 2017; Rossi & Cheek, 1988). This rhythm was discovered by a sleep researcher, Nathaniel Kleitman (1957, 1982), who called it the "basic rest–activity cycle." This revelation about ultradian rhythms answered Rossi's curiosity as to why Erickson would allow sessions to last 90–120 minutes. Erickson's response was simply, "Because it takes that long to get something done!" (M. H. Erickson, 2015). Rossi found that the creative moment was often a low-energy moment (Figure 6.2). The client would pause, take a breath, shift their eyes, or make some body adjustment. These actions indicated that the client's natural systems were ready to work. Rossi later found that this creative part of the cycle, about 10–20 minutes long, involved a shift in gene expression toward an up-regulation of the immune system and chemicals that foster brain plasticity (Atkinson et al., 2010; Rossi & Nimmons, 1991). He called this period of the cycle the "ultradian healing pause." The four stages of the creative cycle can be plotted against the ultradian rhythm. Unfortunately, ending a therapeutic session within an hour is likely to interrupt the client's natural rhythm. Many therapists will be familiar with the client who finally starts talking about their deeper feelings just as they are being ushered out.

Ultradian Stress Syndrome

When the client, or therapist, persistently ignores the natural call for rest and restoration—the ultradian healing pause—that Ernest Rossi's research revealed, they are likely to develop *ultradian stress syndrome*. The absence of healing pauses can lead to psychosomatic symptoms and affective disorders

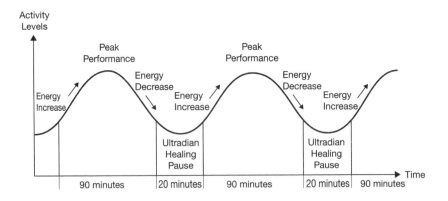

FIGURE 6.2: 90- to 120-Minute Ultradian Rhythm

such as depression or anxiety. The current world presses individuals to push through the ultradian healing pause, and the 55-minute therapy session denies clients the opportunity to complete the four stages of the creative cycle and enjoy the restorative benefits of the ultradian healing pause.

The ultradian healing pause occurs as many as seven or eight times a day, and four or five times each night. Hill and Rossi (2017) suggest that, over evolutionary time, a daily opportunity for taking this pause regularly was at sunset, when the loss of light heralded the time to stop work. The wondrous, spectacular, and numinous vision that appeared on the horizon produced an overwhelming sense of wonder and grandeur. At that time people would gather for a meal and share stories to explore the day's experience for learning, meaning, and purpose. This may be the evolutionary history of the practice that now requires purposeful activation: mindfulness. Taking advantage of the ultradian healing pause, even if only a few times a day— utilizing mindfulness, meditation, or a therapeutic practice such as Rossi's mirroring hands—is a wonderful and simple way for the client to reduce ultradian stresses and benefit from regular daily engagement with their own natural problem-solving and mind–body healing.

To help a client whose session has ended before they are ready, Hill and Rossi suggest a simple acknowledgment that even though the session has ended, they can still enjoy the benefits of the ultradian healing pause and allow their natural mind-to-body healing to continue.

> I can see/hear that you are suddenly aware of some wonderful thoughts and feelings you wish to share, but unfortunately our session has to conclude. I wonder if you might be able to take a few moments before you head home to write these down, or perhaps do a voice recording on your phone? It's a great idea to journal your thoughts between sessions anyway. Not only can we look at these when you arrive for the next session, but you can review them yourself when you have a quiet moment. Maybe next session you can begin by telling me the amazing things that emerged into your mind, just because you listened to, or reread, your own thoughts. (Hill & Rossi, 2017, pp. 85–86)

CLINICAL NOTES

As a complex system, mind-to-body processes will both self-organize and utilize feedback to effect beneficial change—when given the opportunity and the appropriate circumstances. Rossi has shown that the essential element is activity, and that the activity needs to be predominantly within the client as they marshal their own natural problem-solving and mind–body healing resources. The task of the therapist is to enable and facilitate the client's process *and* know when to get out of the way.

6.2 Effective Therapy Through Deliberate Practice

Scott Miller has been an important researcher and advocate for improving clinical effectiveness. He has sought to understand what lies behind the research that shows there has been little to no improvement in psychotherapeutic effectiveness over the past 40 years (S. D. Miller et al., 2014). Arguments about the effectiveness of psychotherapy and psychotherapists began many years ago. In a review of 24 studies, Hans J. Eysenck (1952) concluded that psychotherapy was not only ineffective but potentially harmful. This damning judgment prompted robust argument from a number of people, including Hans H. Strupp's article in the first issue of *Psychotherapy* (Strupp, 1963). Fifty years later Miller agrees with others that the efficacy of psychotherapy compared with no treatment has been well established (Duncan et al., 2010), but the issue of inconsistent results between practitioners, regardless of therapeutic technique, remains.

Miller highlights several fundamentally important areas that require investigation, including

- what creates effective therapy,
- how therapists can improve, and
- reliable tools for measurement and monitoring.

The goal is to find what works in psychotherapy: "valuing 'what works' rather than working with what we value" (S. D. Miller, 2018).

Effective Therapy

In careful examinations of the literature and across broad-ranging reviews, Miller and colleagues have shown that many of the assumptions made about the effectiveness of therapies, especially the effectiveness of one therapy over another, are not reliable. In an extensive review of CBT in comparative studies, Bruce Wampold et al. (2017) concluded "that the effects demonstrating the superiority of CBT are small, nonsignificant for the most part, limited to targeted symptoms, or are due to flawed primary studies" (p. 14). The article was not saying that CBT was ineffective, but that the use of CBT was no more effective than the other compared therapies. A review of the superiority of trauma-based treatments compared with non-trauma-focused treatments in PTSD (Benish et al., 2008; Wampold et al., 2010) found that all bona fide psychotherapies had an equivalent effect on patients with PTSD. This result was not without debate. Anke Ehler et al. (2010) determined that the Benish study was flawed and

> that there is good evidence that trauma-focused psychological treatments (trauma-focused cognitive behavior therapy and eye movement desensitization and reprocessing) are effective in PTSD; but that treatments that do not focus on the patients' trauma memories or their meanings are either less effective or not yet sufficiently studied. (p. 269)

At the very least, these studies are questioning the established dogma that there is a superiority of particular therapies. This debate has led to the reexamination of other elements in therapy that may be influential but have been considered nonspecific or just common factors. What do the client and the therapist each bring to the therapeutic experience, and how is that relevant? (Refer to the Introduction.) It is now well established that one of the most important elements of effective therapy is the quality of the relationship between therapist and client (Baldwin et al., 2007). Also important are the humanistic and interpersonal skills of the therapist

(Anderson et al., 2009). Miller and colleagues propose that "psychotherapy is implemented one person at a time, on the basis of that unique individual's perceptions of the progress and fit of the therapy and therapist" (Duncan et al., 2010, abstract).

Improving the Therapist

In drawing practitioners' attention to the research, Scott Miller has often stimulated, and challenged, the minds of therapists attending his lectures and workshop presentations. Many have been surprised, for example, to learn that the evidence shows that clients of the best therapists improve at a rate at least 50% higher and with a dropout rate at least 50% lower than those of average clinicians (Wampold & Brown, 2005). Questions that persisted in Miller's mind included "What makes a better therapist?" and "Why are some therapists more effective?"

A breakthrough came in a serendipitous event on an airplane in 2006. Bored with the movie entertainment, Miller opened a magazine left in the seat pocket. The October 2006 issue of *Fortune* magazine ran a collection of articles on "What It Takes to Be Great." Psychologist K. Anders Ericsson had written about a topic he first introduced in a paper in 1993 (Ericsson et al., 1993), concerning the role of "deliberate practice" in achieving excellence. Excellence was closely tied to intense practice, over a number of years, but more than just mindless repetition, valuable practice was directly related to five key elements:

- establishing a reliable and valid assessment of performance,
- the identification of and striving toward objectives just beyond an individual's current level of ability,
- development and engagement in exercises specifically designed to reach new performance milestones,
- ongoing corrective feedback, and
- successive refinement over time via repetition.

Miller and Irish psychologist Brendan Madden founded an international nonprofit dedicated to promoting excellence in behavioral health:

the International Center for Clinical Excellence (ICCE). Three components became the basic formula for teaching programs and research initiatives to create a "cycle of excellence":

- determining a baseline of effectiveness,
- engaging in deliberate practice, and
- getting feedback.

Feedback-Informed Treatment

Feedback-informed treatment (FIT) is the use of measures to "solicit feedback about progress and the quality of the therapeutic relationship" (S. D. Miller, 2019). Miller has established that clients whose therapists use FIT on an ongoing basis are 2.5 times more likely to experience benefit from treatment. When therapists are asked whether therapy is going well, their answer is often the opposite of the client's opinion. That discrepancy highlighted the need for workable tools that clients would be comfortable with and that could be reliably assessed and used to improve therapy.

Miller and colleagues developed two reliable measurement scales that can be used to establish a baseline and receive progressive feedback: the Outcome Rating Scale (ORS) and the Session Rating Scale (SRS). Both are available on the ICCE website, which includes assessment tools for the scales and other assistance in utilizing the scales effectively (and they are freely available to solo practitioners). These provide a mechanism for ongoing feedback that gives the client the opportunity to become more involved in the progress of their therapeutic experience, as well as a simple mechanism that enables them to feel comfortable giving feedback to the therapist.

The evidence shows that with these tools, clients are less likely to deteriorate, more likely to stay longer, and twice as likely to achieve a clinically significant change.

The mere act of measuring yields improved outcomes. In fact, it is the first and among the most potent forms of feedback available to clinicians seeking excellence. Several recent studies demonstrate convincingly that monitoring client progress on an ongoing basis improves effectiveness dramatically. (S. D. Miller et al., 2006, p. 7)

A study of 75 therapists and 6,424 clients over a 2-year period, using the ORS and the SRS, found that providing therapists with real-time feedback improved outcome by nearly 65% (Psychotherapy Networker, n.d.).

If relationship is a key element of therapeutic effectiveness, then it seems reasonable to try to determine how that relationship is progressing. Miller and colleagues have shown this to be resoundingly true.

Deliberate Practice

Deliberate practice can be as much of a challenge for therapists as it is for anyone seeking to achieve excellence in their chosen endeavor. Developing the skills and practicing the application of relational engagement during therapy is not a major focus of training, compared with the concentrated focus on learning techniques and methodologies. This lack of emphasis on relational engagement is evident even though the "pinnacle of therapists' aspiration . . . [is to be] engaging, affirming, highly empathetic, staying flexible, and dealing constructively with difficulties encountered in the therapeutic interaction" (S. D. Miller et al., 2014, p. 69). It is certainly important to learn the content of professional practice, but Miller expands the conventional view of psychotherapy in light of the research: "The evidence is incontrovertible. *Who* provides the therapy is a much more important determinant of success than *what* treatment approach is provided" (Duncan & Miller, 2008).

The key difference between therapists who are highly knowledgeable and therapists who have well-honed social skills is deliberate practice. The five key elements of valuable practice described earlier are fundamental to deliberate practice, and more interesting elements are emerging in Miller's research, including the value of a mentor or coach who is able to provide comments, make critiques, and facilitate improvement. In a study of 69 therapists and 4,580 clients, a group led by Miller's colleague Daryl Chow (Chow et al., 2015) confirmed the established results showing that the contribution of the therapist was 5.1%. But when they explored the best-performing quartile, there were obvious differences in the quantity and qualities of the therapists' deliberate practice process. A key element was spending time alone considering the cases, reviewing recordings, and using "cognitive effort" (Chow et al., 2015, p. 341). The more effective group also spent more than 2.8 times the amount of time in deliberate practice each week.

CLINICAL NOTES

Scott Miller encourages therapists to adopt ideas and ideals that are more suitable to being foundations and fundamentals: paying attention to the research, achieving better outcomes, informing therapy with feedback, seeking practitioner excellence, and doing this with deliberate practices. His work is shared by numerous colleagues around the globe. He presents his FIT program in Finland in fluent Finnish. Therapists can access the ICCE website for the ORS and SRS feedback forms and implement them into regular practice. Miller's contributions are changing the way therapy is viewed and practiced. Everyone can achieve degrees of performance and effectiveness beyond their basic training and even beyond just years of repetitive practice. The methods are the same for any skill. In Miller's words, "In the end, you may not become the Frank Sinatra, Tiger Woods, or Melissa Etheridge of the therapy world, but you will be able to sing, swing, and strum along with the best" (Psychotherapy Networker, n.d., p. 7).

6.3 The Clinical Biopsychological Model

The problem of pain is as old as humanity itself. It is obvious that pain wields great utility in warning that something is wrong, to cause a person to recoil from the source of pain or to attend to an injured limb or organ. So, the goal is not to eliminate pain altogether and be deprived of a valuable sensation. The same may be argued for emotional pain. When pain becomes chronic, long after it has fulfilled its function of warning that something is wrong, eliminating the pain becomes the goal. Such chronic pain can crush a person, reducing them to a depressed shell and susceptible to other health issues that can emerge from a myriad of social, psychological, and physiological complications. Such chronic and complex pain syndromes are maladaptive at best, and practitioners of medicine and psychology have been on a long journey to help people deal with this sort of pain.

Robert A. Moss, a clinical neuropsychologist, has worked for decades as a practitioner and researcher in the area of chronic pain. In his recent book *Psychotherapy in Pain Management: New Perspectives and Treatment Approaches Based on a Brain Model* (Moss, 2020a), he offers both a theoretical model of higher cortical functions and a practical model for the treatment of pain. We covered some of his theory in Section 1.6, on cortical columns; now we would like to apply that theory to pain.

A primary motivator for human behavior is to activate positive emotions and avoid negative ones. Positive emotions are associated with thriving; negative ones, with threats. Strong emotional memories activated in the cortex connect to subcortical structures that, in turn, activate the physiological and motivational responses.

When people find themselves in a negative situation beyond their control, as may be perceived with chronic pain, this sense of uncontrollability activates negative memory systems and, in turn, associated subcortical structures. Uncontrollable pain can result in an increased sensitivity to that pain. What the cortical-column understanding of this situation offers is a way to divert the flow of information so that it does not activate subcortical regions that would exacerbate pain sensitivity (Moss, 2020a, p. 121). For example, focusing attention so that something external would reduce connectivity between the medial PFC (implicated in the transition from acute to chronic pain) and the anterior insular, ACC, and inferior parietal lobe. The external focus (dlPFC attention) would reduce connectivity to the anterior insula and thalamus because these are not part of the task at hand—external attention. In addition to shifting focus in this way, helping people have more resilience (an internal perception of being able to cope) is important to mitigate against the right-medial PFC aspects of perceived uncontrollability and inadequacy. Right-cortical negative memories have the most influence in maladaptive emotional states and reactions and can be relatively untouched by psychotherapy that engages the left-cortical verbal-thinking areas without direct access to right-posterior processing and memories. When there are past emotional memories of personal inadequacy and loss of control, chronic pain seems more likely.

The core of what Moss is aiming for is a change in the dominance of right-hemisphere negative emotions that channel pathways of neural activity that exacerbate chronic pain. If these negative emotional memories can be changed, or at least prevented from running the show, then the pain sensitivity networks can be altered.

Because right-frontal-lobe emotional memory is key, Moss proposes a structured assessment to identify all potentially relevant relationships and experiences that contribute to the client's emotional functioning and then experiential techniques to reach the right cortex. One such treatment method is emotional restructuring (Moss, 2007, 2013), which involves six steps for each influential relationship that has been identified (for details, see Moss, 2020a):

- **negative emotional memory recall:** recalling specific negative events or situations that have occurred in the past to activate autobiographical negative emotional sensory memories in the right-posterior lateral and medial cortex. (It is important not to traumatize or create false memories.)
- **interpersonal relationship behavior description:** describing why the target individual acted the way they did, with a recognition of the interactions displayed. This step can lead to increased congruence between the hemispheres and less perceived internal conflict.
- **role reversal/role play:** taking the target individual's place, with the therapist acting as the client. Acting like the other person can activate the client's frontal lateral and medial action columns and evoke a deep emotional response.
- **imagery for anger release and self-nurturance:** visualizing scenes (refer to Moss, 2020a, for details) described by the therapist that involve interaction with the target individual. Imagery can cause the most pronounced and rapid change. "Throughout imagery, the

left and right vlPFC [ventrolateral PFC] are being provided with new dialogues with verbal and emotional information, with the most important ones being related to the self-nurturing statements. This assists in hemispheric congruence" (Moss, 2020a, p. 128).

- **origins of the relationship pattern description:** using images to elicit an empathic view of the target individual, creating new schemata in right-receptive columns and action columns.
- **role-played forgiveness sequence:** expressing pity for the target individual and making a statement of forgiveness.

The whole process described here engages the right and left posterior and frontal areas, creating new frontal action columns where there is more perceived control, personal adequacy, self-compassion, and other-compassion.

Another aspect of the clinical biopsychological treatment is educating the client as to the nature of their problem. Understanding what is going on in their brain can normalize the symptoms for the client. This part of the process can be thought of as a bridge between assessment and treatment. The therapist explains the negative emotional response system designed to ensure survival but also notes that this survival response is maladaptive in many situations that the client experiences.

Then comes an explanation of the cortex and the two hemispheres: the left, processing analytical and detailed information slowly; and the right, quickly processing global information. Some details of exactly what the two hemispheres specialize in are also described, and the therapist might even demonstrate the different analysis of an angry voice and a calm voice but the same words—how these are encoded very differently by the right hemisphere. Then comes an explanation of how one of the hemispheres will step up to give a response—whichever one is likely to get the best results (if there is danger, the right; otherwise, it is likely to be the left).

Next, the therapist describes the storage of memory on both sides of the brain, in that the left will store the memory of a new word, but the right will store a nonverbal emotional memory. So, it is possible to think about a situation verbally one way but have a different feeling about it as two memory systems work together.

An explanation of negative mood states is also in order. Here is what Moss (2020a) says:

> Based on this design, negative mood states can come from one of three sources. The first involves reactions to current or ongoing situations. For example, if you get into an argument, it can create negative emotions. If you are in pain, the pain can cause negative emotions. Therefore, current factors must always be considered in psychological treatment and treatment must include healthier ways to more effectively deal with current factors. The second source of negative emotions involves loss issues. If you cannot activate positive emotional memories tied to activities or objects you enjoy, the result is a depressive or grieving state tied to the loss. This can involve loss of relationships, or even a loss of an ability to do previously enjoyable activities. . . . The third source of negative mood states involves the activation of previously stored negative emotional memories. There are two aspects tied to negative emotional memories that determine if they later have significant impact on our current functioning. The first has to do with controllability, and the other is tied to feelings of personal responsibility or inadequacy. The more the negative memory has one or both of these aspects, the more influential it will be on us later in life. (p. 152)

Highlighting the influence of emotional memories, the therapist explains that new memories are built on the foundations of early ones. How these emotional memories are accumulated has an impact on how someone responds to others and to themselves and can even cause conflict between how the right hemisphere produces a feeling about an interaction and the left hemispheres tries to analyze an interaction. The continual impact of negative emotional memories in the present—the fact that the right hemisphere can pick up cues in the environment that elicit a negative emotional memory and response, even if the environment is not exactly the same as the circumstance that initially laid down the negative memory—can be emphasized.

The therapist then explains the concept of exposure therapy: activating negative memory systems in an environment that is safe. A safe environment is essential when recalling negative experiences and distressing past relationships as the therapist works through the six steps of the emotional restructuring process. Here is how Moss (2020a) introduces the process:

> As this term implies, this procedure allows a change in the stored negative emotional memories such that the goal is to render them neutral. If successful, current day situations still reactivate the memories, but there are fewer negative emotional reactions tied to these memories. The result is that a person will experience lessened negative emotions tied to current day situations that reactivate the memories. (pp. 158–159)

CLINICAL NOTES

After running through the six steps, the therapist describes the process as removing roadblocks from past situations and allowing the two hemispheres to work in harmony. Taking the time to do the psychoeducation and explain the process not only normalizes the symptoms the client is experiencing but gives them a greater sense of control and therefore more likelihood of positive emotions toward the therapy.

6.4 A Client-Responsive Approach

I (R. H.) was both student of and, later, coauthor with Ernest Rossi for more than 15 years. Rossi spent nearly 10 years learning and writing with Milton Erickson. A client-responsive approach emerged and developed over time from Erickson's nondirective approach; Rossi's mind–body work, including the natural rhythms and cycles; and my experience with responsive improvisation from an early theatrical career. Both Rossi and Hill have proposed that a client-responsive approach to therapy is a necessary advance in how therapy is practiced. The *client-responsive approach* is founded in concepts that many therapists already use in one way or another, but not necessarily collectively or as fundamental to effective therapy.

Carl Rogers was radical when he brought the "person" back into the center of therapy. Client responsiveness is a more nuanced shift, but even in these times of person-centered practices, training and practice protocols still have a strong methodology base. The therapist is expected to initiate the work and advance the direction of therapy. I call this "the tail wagging the dog."

Client responsiveness is based on a bold assumption: The therapist and the client have equal knowledge and capacity to enable recovery and resolution. The client is the better informed, but the client's knowledge is implicit, whereas the therapist's is explicit. Therapeutic methods and techniques are not invented but are based on natural healing and recovery processes already within human behavior and biology. The client is implicitly imbued with a natural "mental health recovery system." Psychotherapies are existing behaviors that have been observed, explicitly recorded, studied, refined, and reintroduced publicly as a therapeutic method.

Francine Shapiro, the developer of EMDR (eye movement desensitizing and reprocessing), noticed that when she was having disturbing thoughts, her eyes moved spontaneously from side to side. On further recall, those thoughts were not as disturbing (Luber & Shapiro, 2009). The Hollywood film *It's a Wonderful Life* has Jimmy Stewart's character considering suicide because he believes that he is the cause of everyone's problems. An angel appears and proves that his belief is wrong by taking him through his hometown as if he had never been born. He experiences a cognitive reframing of his negative self-belief. This is classic CBT, in a film that was made in 1946, 20 years before Aaron Beck began to publish his first papers on a cognitive theory of depression and 10 years before Albert Ellis proposed "rational emotive behavior therapy."

When the therapist *responds* to the client's implicit and explicit "messages," there is a mutual attunement to what is most naturally beneficial for the client. I (R. H.) explained in a conversation with M.D. (October, 2020):

It is amazing what the client will reveal that I might never have thought of, at least not without a lot of time. One client had a paranoid fear and anxiety about something happening to her children. As we talked, she began to describe an image she was imagining. We began to work with these images as our therapeutic approach. It was a bit like imagery therapy or metaphor therapy. That didn't matter. It was *her* therapy, it worked, and it worked really quickly. Another client was struggling with long-term anhedonia. Coincidentally, I was writing positive messages on a chalkboard outside the clinic. This day it was an image of a set of scales and a mobile with words to the effect of "life isn't simply like scales; it's more complex, like a mobile." My client liked that idea, and we decided to draw a "mobile" structure of his life. Slowly, we added the good and the bad. The really bad influence was a heavy weight at one end of the mobile. He stopped and stared at the mobile for some time and then asked, "Can I move the fulcrum?" When I did, the whole center of balance of the mobile changed. He had one of those flashbulb moments that totally shifted him. He reported the next week that he hadn't stopped smiling. Together we invented "mobile therapy," but I've never used it again. It was perfect for him, in that moment and that was all that mattered.

The key elements of a client-responsive approach are that

- clients implicitly (and explicitly) express therapeutic opportunities, patterns, and forms during what Rossi called "creative moments" (refer to Section 6.1);
- given the opportunity and appropriate conditions, human beings will seek to move toward health and well-being;
- sensitive observation precedes response, producing real-time feedback that both informs and generates the therapeutic process;
- curiosity stimulates change of state, including psycho-neuro-geno-biology; and
- client and therapist cocreate the therapeutic experience.

Naturalness

These elements orient the therapist into a curious, responsive engagement with the client. Erickson would say that the task of the therapist was to return the activity of therapy *to the client* (M. H. Erickson, 1964/2008a). Client-responsive therapy seeks (a) to create the opportunity and appropriate circumstances for the client's natural capacities to emerge (Hill & Rossi, 2017); (b) to allow the client to explore their process without overt interpretation or opinion from the therapist; (c) to activate dynamic curiosity (Hill, 2018); and (d) to follow the natural rhythms and cycles (Hill & Rossi, 2017; Rossi & Lippincott, 1992).

Natural responsiveness is the purest form of utilization. As happens in artistic improvisation, therapeutic responsiveness can feel like it is coming from "somewhere else," but it is an emergent property/activity from *all that is within* interacting with *all that is around*, which happens simultaneously for both client and therapist.

Sensitive Observation

Sensitive observation begins the moment the client arrives and continues until they leave. So much information comes from the client: how they walk, how they sit, where they sit, where they look, how their vocal tone fluctuates, what words they use, how they breathe, when and how they shift position, what kinds of little body movements they exhibit, and how their facial expression changes. Equally, what the therapist does affects the client: where you sit, when you move, how you conduct the initial intake, what your first question is, and so on. The client is noticing all these things implicitly and explicitly.

Client-Responsive Language Style

A number of simple language techniques enhance client responsiveness.

- **curious interest:** Therapists ask questions and make statements that can push the client in a particular direction. Being curious about what the client is saying and doing, maybe just repeating interesting words or phrases, makes the client the most important person in the room.

- **the incomplete sentence:** Directive verbs or opinionated nouns can interrupt the client's process. Leaving a sentence unfinished allows the client to complete it. People will often fill the silence, especially when the therapist seems curious. For example, a client was clearly quite agitated and distressed, showing all the signs of anxiety. The therapist uttered an incomplete sentence. "I have been watching and listening carefully, and I can see that you are feeling very . . ." In the language vacuum, the client looked up with relief and said, "Oh, thank you, I really need to use the bathroom!" What might have happened if her therapist had told her that she was anxious? Curiously, when she returned, she sat down with relief and declared, "And, of course, I'm feeling very anxious!" The difference is that she owned the feeling *and* the opinion *and* where the therapy was focused.

- **silence:** Clients are sometimes happy to be in their own process. Therapists are inclined to try to activate the session. When a client seems to want some space but the therapist is not sure, the best thing is simply to ask. I (R. H.) recommend this question: "I can see you seem to be working on something. You are welcome to share a word or two with me if that will help, or you might like to continue with your own private work?" Whether the client speaks or remains silent, they have made their needs clear and are holding the response-ability for the session. The tail is *not* wagging the dog.

CLINICAL NOTES

We are surprised by the number of colleagues who respond to a description of a client-responsive approach by saying that they use this in their own work. Equally, when watching therapists demonstrate, we often see client responsiveness employed at one time or another. These random examples, however, are not quite the same as implementing client responsiveness as a foundation of therapeutic practice. Therapists may encourage a client in a particular direction or to a particular state of mind and then allow the client to explore that place or space in their own way. As effective as this approach might be sometimes, there is always the question, Would the client have gone to this particular place or space if they had been in the driver's seat from the beginning of the process? Something as simple as allowing the client to choose where they feel comfortable sitting and where they feel comfortable for the therapist to sit can give the client the sense of having a strong position in the therapeutic alliance and also orient the therapist to being a cocreator of the experience with a bias toward the client's preferences. Sometimes the client may not wish to choose which chair to sit in. A client-responsive therapist will then offer a recommendation. The client is still a functional influence in the dyad.

6.5 Dynamic Curiosity

Einstein said that a problem cannot be solved with the same mindset that created it. You cannot *make* a depressed person cheer up or *make* an anxious person calm down. Something needs to shift their state of mind first. I (R. H.) propose that curiosity, more than any other single mindset, facilitates the courage to explore the damaged parts within and the future possibilities at the growing edge. The medical model has sought to find ways to intervene and impose into the system things that will change the biochemical milieu with the intent of changing the state of the client from depression to something else. There is both research and anecdotal evidence suggesting that medications are able to do just that, but there are also side effects, which can include failure to get a response, as well as the emergence of more serious symptoms. Imposing something on the natural systems to achieve a specific change risks having a broad impact (refer to Sections 4.5.1 and 4.7.2 for the dopamine systems).

Milton Erickson was an ardent advocate of the therapist taking a keen interest in the client—to be curious and even fascinated at what the client is doing, how they have managed so far, and what qualities they possess that can help them resolve the issue. As we noted in the Introduction, client resources can account for as much as 87% of the therapeutic process. One of the biggest problems for therapists, especially in mental health, is burnout, in which the therapist becomes physically and emotionally distressed and cannot continue practicing. If the therapist adopts a curiosity-framed orientation, then the therapist's brain is adopting the qualities imbued in curiosity. Before describing the three facets of dynamic curiosity, we will look at the neurobiological functions of the curiosity system.

Curiosity in the Brain

Depression has a biochemical milieu that has been described as a "chemical imbalance." This phrase implies that there is a determinable balance that is the measure of a healthy brain. In systems thinking, however, depression is more usefully seen as the emergent, observable message that something needs attention. We know that, among other things, depression registers as low levels of dopamine, serotonin, and norepinephrine (refer to Section 4.1.1). The first thing a client-responsive therapist does is to turn on their own curiosity by asking, "I wonder what your depression is telling us?" The next step is to turn on the client's curiosity to shift their mental state to a more responsive "therapeutic consciousness" that will generate a different distribution of neurochemicals (Hill & Rossi, 2017, p. 43). The neurochemical distribution changes in response to the shift in mental state not because one causes the other but because the two are coexistent. The biochemical milieu that exists when someone is depressed is the biochemical milieu that has to exist for someone to be depressed. Conscious awareness of the *feeling* of being depressed occurs after the biology has created the conditions. This is because the first order representation (refer to the discussion of LeDoux and emotions in Section 1.7) takes about half a second to be experienced as a higher order representation in conscious thought or awareness (Dylan, 2006).

Although safety, empathic engagement, mindfulness, happiness, and comfort are important in therapeutically helpful ways, a curious mental state creates the most complete shift of neurochemicals. It creates a sense of anticipation; focus, attention, and arousal; a reduction in negative affect and fearfulness; a shift from feeling isolated to interpersonal relationship; and a satisfying, euphoric reward at points of resolution, insight, or realization (Kidd & Hayden, 2015). These states collectively produce an engaged, "toward" sense of exploration that is ideal for effective therapy. A neurobiology correlates with each of these states (Figure 6.3):

- **positive anticipation:** dopaminergic activity from the substantia nigra/ventral tegmental area and nucleus accumbens (Gruber et al., 2014; Knutson et al., 2001) which receive nicotinic modulation by cholinergic neurons from the mesopontine tegmentum (Maskos, 2008)
- **focus and attention:** norepinephrine from the locus coeruleus (Ashton-Jones & Cohen, 2005) and acetylcholine from the nucleus basalis (Buzsaki & Gage, 1989)
- **calming of stress and hypersensitivity:** serotonergic activity from the raphe nuclei (Hornung, 2003)

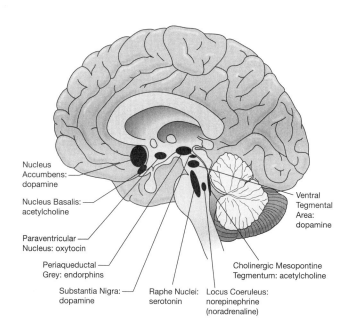

FIGURE 6.3: The Nuntius Nuclei

- **shifting from feeling isolated toward trust and social engagement:** increased receptivity in oxytocin receptors in the paraventricular nucleus
- **pleasure from playful satisfaction:** endogenous rewards from endorphins in the periaqueductal gray (Blood & Zatorre, 2001)

These nuclei project neurons out into midbrain and cortex from the upper brainstem and lower midbrain. I (R. H.) suggests that they are, collectively, the functional structures of curiosity, which I have named the "nuntius nuclei" in acknowledgment of the Latin word *nuncio*, meaning "messenger."

DYNAMIC CURIOSITY EXPLAINED

This conceptual frame and proposed neurobiological mechanism for curiosity set the conditions for the question of why the recent cultural drive of curiosity for "new" has not achieved a massive improvement in mental health. It has been argued that the current methods of school education are actually detrimental to mental health (Fazel et al., 2014; Mental Health Foundation, n.d.). If the only thing needed were more information, then this should be the happiest society in the history of humanity. According to *Forbes* magazine, 2.5 quintillion bytes of data are created each day (Marr, 2018), and 90% of the data in the world were generated over the last 2 years. At every point of daily experience, new information, commentary, social criticism, and self-serving agendas are being pushed at every person in a relentless torrent, trying to win people's attention, loyalty, and, more often than not, money.

"Dynamic curiosity" as a separate semantic term has been necessary to distinguish the multifaceted effect from the restricted colloquial acceptance of "curiosity" as only to do with the revelation of information, and the discovery of how things work. This is an important aspect of curiosity, but limited. Discovery also comes through serendipity, accident, and simply mucking about. Some of the most important discoveries have emerged in this way. Playfulness, however, is often considered less serious, childlike, and, in some eyes, unprofessional, not befitting something as serious as psychotherapy. It is the second aspect of dynamic curiosity. The third aspect has been largely isolated to studies in philosophy—the curiosity for meaning. Viktor Frankl, the Austrian neurologist best known for his book *Man's Search for Meaning* (1959/2006), reminded all people (but he also spoke as a therapist) of the importance of finding the personal relevance of what you know and what you do. Making the connection to your "self" is what enables you to adopt, adapt, and creatively expand on the information that comes to you through life.

A linguistic heuristic for dynamic curiosity ranges across a spectrum from *that's interesting* (information that explains and informs); to *that's surprising, unexpected, and amazing* (serendipitous information emerges from play); to *that's wonderful* and/or an aha moment (the moment of realization, self-relevance, and/or self-oriented revelation—meaning). We propose that dynamic curiosity includes all three of these *wonder-full* domains. Each domain produces something novel and expansive—a form of information.

- **the wonder of new information:** what we can learn;
- **the wonder of play:** the fascinating things that emerge serendipitously and unexpectedly from unregulated activity and a lightness of being; and
- **the wonder of meaning:** the discovery of what new information from learning and play *means to me* that sparks a creative and transformational experience that is often experienced as excitement, creative ideas, a new perspective, a sense of expansiveness and shift toward something now possible that was not before.

The client-responsive therapist begins in a state of curiosity about the client, sensitive to the client and observing them carefully in order to be responsive in both explicit and implicit ways. All this can be quite contagious, as the client's natural therapeutic systems, including the nuntius nuclei, respond. Turning on all three elements of curiosity creates a dynamic interplay in which each element activates and informs the others, leading to an open system that continually energizes itself, producing a positive state of repair and growth.

Systems that dissipate or fracture are generally closed systems that are unable to develop, gradually dissipating their energy until destruction. Undue focus on just one of the elements of dynamic curiosity can be problematic. Restricting focus to new information is one of the destructive aspects of modern society because it discourages people from investigating what more they can learn, thus confining the mind to the task of seeking out the next "new thing." Excessive reliance on play and playfulness is a problem because play can be experienced only in the moment. Play can be useful and delightful for a while, but eventually if nothing interesting emerges for a lengthy period of time, even play can become tiring and boring. If a persistent search for meaning becomes frustrating or annoying that can turn off the other curiosities, leading to a resistance to new information or to the joyfulness of play that produces negative meanings that are based on a rigid or chaotic orientation. The benefits of the fluid interplay and the dynamic expansion created when all three elements of curiosity are engaged are what protect against the problematic issue of overemphasis on just one aspect. This is why curiosity warranted a new term to represent all three elements and the activity they generate: *dynamic curiosity.*

Conclusion

We began with two human beings in a therapy room at the beginning of a journey that was shrouded in mystery. Then, like a jigsaw puzzle, we carefully and meticulously separated the elements of these complex beings to discover what might be learned by examining each piece, exploring the details, and opening our minds to the possibilities that lie hidden within their individual elements. We also discussed the ways in which individual elements can malfunction, disrupt, and interfere with how the puzzle appears and functions. In the end, we sought to instill a better understanding *about* these pieces and to explain how that understanding can help therapists engage in the therapeutic activity that, in the end, re-creates the whole human being—connected, integrated, and possible.

Throughout the book we have done our best to make it clear that what you have been reading and learning from is not a complete and detailed investigation. We have also pointed out that we do not ever expect a single individual to possess the complete and detailed knowledge of every topic in this book. What we suggest, right from the Introduction, is that there is a need for those who work in the areas of mental health and well-being to have not only specialist knowledge but also a broad knowledge about the many jigsaw pieces that connect beside, above, below, and beyond.

The references used throughout the book are there to establish the credibility of the information we have presented, but more important, they provide an extensive resource for your personal, ongoing investigations in response to your curiosity. So, when a particular topic piques your interest, we encourage you to look it up, check it out, be curious, wonder; find a lecture, a conference, a webinar, a video; seek out excellence; be cautious of knowledge that is presented without basis or backup; and deliberately practice to enhance your knowledge, your sensitivity, your observation, and your connection to what is within you and what is without.

All human beings have natural capacities to heal, natural capacities to learn, and natural capacities to access and engage the minds of others to deepen their own mind. Humans are a cocreative species. That is one of the prime principles that underpin this book. This book, itself, was cocreated.

As the authors of this book, we hope you have learned some things, confirmed some other things, and discovered some things you were not expecting. John Arden threw down the challenge, as quoted in the Introduction: A "therapist in the 21st century [needs to make] . . . an effort to keep pace of all this." We hope this book is a springboard for that recommendation and we look forward to where this might take us all next.

CLINICAL NOTES

Taking It Further. For many years, The Science of Psychotherapy has been gathering resources for therapists to aid them in the broad perspectives we have advocated in this book. For your continued learning, go to https://www.thescienceofpsychotherapy.net for expanded resources on all the topics we have presented here, and more.

References

Acharya, S., & Shukla, S. (2012). Mirror neurons: Enigma of the metaphysical modular brain. *Journal of Natural Science, Biology, and Medicine, 3*(2), 118–124. https://doi.org/10.4103/0976-9668.101878

Ackerman, S. J., & Hilsenroth, M. J. (2003). A review of therapist characteristics and techniques positively impacting the therapeutic alliance. *Clinical Psychology Review, 23*, 1–33.

Adolphs, R., & Andler, D. (2018). Investigating emotions as functional states distinct from feelings. *Emotion Review, 10*(3), 191–201. https://doi.org/10.1177/1754073918765662

Akashi, Y. J., Goldstein, D. S., Barbaro, G., & Ueyama, T. (2008). Takotsubo cardiomyopathy: A new form of acute, reversible heart failure. *Circulation, 118*(25), 2754–2762. https://doi.org/10.1161/CIRCULATIONAHA.108.767012

Alba, G., Vila, J., Rey, B., Montoya, P., & Muñoz, M. Á. (2019). The relationship between heart rate variability and electroencephalography functional connectivity variability is associated with cognitive flexibility. *Frontiers in Human Neuroscience, 13*, Article 64. https://doi.org/10.3389/fnhum.2019.00064

Albert, P. R., Vahid-Ansari, F., & Luckhart, C. (2014). Serotonin-prefrontal cortical circuitry in anxiety and depression phenotypes: Pivotal role of pre- and post-synaptic 5-HT1A receptor expression. *Frontiers in Behavioral Neuroscience, 8*, Article 199. https://doi.org/10.3389/fnbeh.2014.00199

Alegre, M., Guridi, J., & Artieda, J. (2011). The mirror system, theory of mind and Parkinson's disease. *Journal of the Neurological Sciences, 310*(1–2), 194–196. https://doi.org/10.1016/j.jns.2011.07.030

Alexander, G. E., DeLong, M. R., & Strick, P. L. (1986). Parallel organization of functionally segregated circuits linking basal ganglia and cortex. *Annual Review of Neuroscience, 9*, 357–381.

Allen, N. J., & Lyons, D. A. (2018). Glia as architects of central nervous system formation and function. *Science, 362*(6411), 181–185. https://doi.org/10.1126/science.aat0473

Alshami, A. M. (2019). Pain: Is it all in the brain or the heart? *Current Pain and Headache Reports, 23*(12), 88. https://doi.org/10.1007/s11916-019-0827-4

American Psychiatric Association. (2013). *Diagnostic and statistical manual of mental disorders* (5th ed.).

American Psychological Association, Presidential Task Force on Evidence-Based Practice. (2006). Evidence-based practice in psychology. *The American Psychologist, 61*(4), 271–285. https://doi.org/10.1037/0003-066X.61.4.271

Anderson, T., Ogles, B. M., Patterson, C. L., Lambert, M. J., & Vermeersch, D. A. (2009). Therapist effects: Facilitative interpersonal skills as a predictor of therapist success. *Journal of Clinical Psychology, 65*, 755–768. https://doi.org/10.1002/jclp.20583

Anjum, A., Ming, X., Siddiqi, A. F., & Rasool, S. F. (2018). An empirical study analyzing job productivity in toxic workplace environments. *International Journal of Environmental Research and Public Health, 15*(5), 1035. https://doi.org/10.3390/ijerph15051035

Arden, J. B. (2014). *Brain based therapy for OCD: A workbook for clinicians and clients*. PESI Publishing & Media.

Arden, J. B. (2015). *Brain2Brain: Enacting client change through the persuasive power of neuroscience*. Wiley.

Arden, J. B. (2019). *Mind-brain-gene: Toward psychotherapy integration*. W. W. Norton.

Ardito, R. B., & Rabellino, D. (2011). Therapeutic alliance and outcome of psychotherapy: Historical excursus, measurements, and prospects for research. *Frontiers in Psychology, 2*, Article 270.

Aristizabal, M., Anreiter, I., Halldorsdottir, T., Odgers, C., McDade, T., Goldenberg, A., Mostafavi, S., Kobor, M., Binder, E., Sokolowski, M., & O'Donnell, K. (2019). Biological embedding of experience: A primer on epigenetics. *Proceedings of the National Academy of Sciences of the United States of America, 117*(38), 23261–23269. https://doi.org/10.1073/pnas.1820838116

Armour, J. A. (1991). Intrinsic cardiac neurons. *Journal of Cardiovascular Electrophysiology, 2*, 331–341. https://doi.org/10.1111/j.1540-8167.1991.tb01330.x

Armour, J. A. (2008). Potential clinical relevance of the "little brain" on the heart. *Experimental Physiology, 93*, 165–176. https://doi.org/10.1113/expphysiol.2007.041178

Arney, K. L., & Fisher, A. G. (2004). Epigenetic aspects of differentiation. *Journal of Cell Science, 117*, 4355–4363. https://doi.org/10.1242/jcs.01390

Artigas, F., Nutt, D. J., & Shelton, R. (2002). Mechanism of action of antidepressants. *Psychopharmacology Bulletin, 36*(Suppl. 2), 123–132.

Asay, T. P., & Lambert, M. J. (1999). The empirical case for the common factors in therapy: Quantitative findings. In M. A. Hubble, B. L. Duncan, & S. D. Miller (Eds.), *The heart & soul of change: What works in therapy* (pp. 33–56). American Psychological Association.

Ashton-Jones, G., & Cohen, J. D. (2005). An integrative theory of locus coeruleus-norepinephrine function: Adaptive gain and optimal performance. *Annual Review of Neuroscience, 28*, 403–450. https://doi.org/10.1146/annurev.neuro.28.061604.135709

Asnis, G. M., Caneva, E., & Henderson, M. A. (2012). Treatment of insomnia in anxiety disorders. *Psychiatric Times, 29*(1), 1–8.

Atkinson, D., Iannotti, S., Cozzolino, M., Castiglione, S., Cicatelli, A., Vyas, B., Mortimer, J., Hill, R., Chovanec, E., Chiamberlando, A., Cuadros, J., Virot, C., Kerouac, M., Kallfass, T., Krippner, S., Frederick, C., Gregory, B., Shaffran, M., Bullock, M., Soleimany, E., . . . Rossi, E. (2010). A new bioinformatics paradigm for the theory, research, and practice of therapeutic hypnosis. *American Journal of Clinical Hypnosis, 53*(1), 27–46. https://doi.org/10.1080/00029157.2010.10401745

Atladóttir, H. O., Thorsen. P., Østergaard, L., Schendel, D. E., Lemcke, S., Abdallah, M., & Parner, E. T. (2010). Maternal infection requiring hospitalization during pregnancy and autism spectrum disorders. *Journal of Autism and Developmental Disorders, 40*(12), 1423–1430. https://doi.org/10.1007/s10803-010-1006-y

Atladóttir, H. O., Thorsen, P., Schendel, D. E., Østergaard, L., Lemcke, S., & Parner, E. T. (2010). Association of hospitalization for infection in childhood with diagnosis of autism spectrum disorders: A Danish cohort study. *Archives of Pediatrics and Adolescent Medicine, 164*, 470–477.

Attwood, T. (1998). *Asperger's syndrome: A guide for parents and professionals.* Jessica Kingsley Publishers.

Azevedo, F. A., Carvalho, L. R., Grinberg, L. T., Farfel, J. M., Ferretti, R. E., Leite, R. E., Jacob Filho, W., Lent, R., & Herculano-Houzel, S. (2009). Equal numbers of neuronal and nonneuronal cells make the human brain an isometrically scaled-up primate brain. *The Journal of Comparative Neurology, 513*(5), 532–541. https://doi.org/10.1002/cne.21974

Baarendse, P. J., Winstanley, C. A., & Vanderschuren, L. J. (2013). Simultaneous blockade of dopamine and noradrenaline reuptake promotes disadvantageous decision making in a rat gambling task. *Psychopharmacology, 225*(3), 719–731. https://doi.org/10.1007/s00213 -012-2857-z

Badenoch, B. (2008). *Being a brain-wise therapist: A practical guide to interpersonal neurobiology.* W. W. Norton.

Baldwin, S. A., Wampold, B. E., & Imel, Z. E. (2007). Untangling the alliance-outcome correlation: Exploring the relative importance of therapist and patient variability in the alliance. *Journal of Consulting and Clinical Psychology, 75*(6), 842–852.

Ballerini, M., Cabibbo, N., Candelier, R., Cavagna, A., Cisbani, E., Giardina, I., Orlandi, A., Parisi, G., Procaccini, A., Viale, M., & Zdravkovic, V. (2008). Empirical investigation of starling flocks: A benchmark study in collective animal behaviour. *Animal Behaviour, 76*(1), 201–215. https://doi.org/10.1016/j.anbehav.2008.02.004

Barroso, M., Handy, D., & Castro, R. (2017). The link between hyperhomocysteinemia and hypomethylation: Implications for cardiovascular disease. *Journal of Inborn Errors of Metabolism and Screening, 5*, 1–15. https://doi.org/10.1177/2326409817698994

Bartsch, R. P., Liu, K. K. L., Bashan, A., & Ivanov, P. C. (2015). Network physiology: How organ systems dynamically interact. *PLOS ONE, 10*(11), Article e0142143. https://doi.org/10.1371/journal.pone.0142143

Bateman, A. W., & Fonagy, P. (2012). *Handbook of mentalizing in mental health practice.* American Psychiatric Publishing.

Beach, S., Brody, G. H., Todorov, A. A., Gunter, T. D., & Philibert, R. A. (2010). Methylation at SLC6A4 is linked to family history of child abuse: An examination of the Iowa Adoptee sample. *American Journal of Medical Genetics. Part B, Neuropsychiatric Genetics, 153B*(2), 710–713. https://doi.org/10.1002/ajmg.b.31028

Beauchaine, T. P., Bell, Z., Knapton, E., McDonough-Caplan, H., Shader, T., & Zisner, A. (2019). Respiratory sinus arrhythmia reactivity across empirically based structural dimensions of psychopathology: A meta-analysis. *Psychophysiology, 56*(5), Article e13329. https://doi.org/10.1111/psyp.13329

Becchio, C., Cavallo, A., Begliomini, C., Sartori, L., Feltrin, G., & Castiello, U. (2012). Social grasping: From mirroring to mentalizing. *NeuroImage, 61*(1), 240–248. https://doi.org/10.1016/j.neuroimage.2012.03.013

Bellivier, F., Geoffroy, P. A., Scott, J., Schurhoff, F., Leboyer, M., & Etain, B. (2013). Biomarkers of bipolar disorder: Specific or shared with schizophrenia? *Frontiers in Bioscience, 5*, 845–863. https://doi.org/10.2741/e665

Bender, K. J., & Trussell, L. O. (2012). The physiology of the axon initial segment. *Annual Review of Neuroscience, 35*, 249–265. https://doi.org/10.1146/annurevneuro-062111-150339

Benedek, M., & Kaernbach, C. (2011). Physiological correlates and emotional specificity of human piloerection. *Biological Psychology, 86*(3), 320–329. https://doi.org/10.1016/j.biopsycho.2010.12.012

Benish, S. G., Imel, Z. E., & Wampold, B. E. (2008). The relative efficacy of bona fide psychotherapies for treating post-traumatic stress disorder: A meta-analysis of direct comparisons. *Clinical Psychology Review, 28*(5), 746–758. https://doi.org/10.1016/j.cpr.2007.10.005

Bercik, P., Denou, E., Collins, J., Jackson, W., Lu, J., Jury, J., Deng, Y., Blennerhassett, P., Macri, J., McCoy, K. D., Verdu, E. F., & Collins, S. M. (2011). The intestinal microbiota affect central levels of brain-derived neurotropic factor and behaviour in mice. *Gastroenterology, 141*, 599–609. https://doi.org/10.1053/j.gastro.2011.04.052

Berger, M., Gray, J. A., & Roth, B. L. (2009). The expanded biology of serotonin. *Annual Review of Medicine, 60*, 355–366. https://doi.org/10.1146/annurev.med.60.042307.110802

Berthoud, H. R., & Neuhuber, W. L. (2000). Functional and chemical anatomy of the afferent vagal system. *Autonomic Neuroscience, 85*(1–3), 1–17. https://doi.org/10.1016/S1566-0702(00)00215-0

Bertsou, E. (2019). Rethinking political distrust. *European Political Science Review, 11*(2), 213–230. https://doi.org/10.1017/S1755773919000080

Bianconi, E., Piovesan, A., Facchin, F., Beraudi, A., Casadei, R., Frabetti, F., Vitale, L.,

Pelleri, M. C., Tassani, S., Piva, F., Perez-Amodio, S., Srippoli, P., & Canaider, S. (2013). An estimation of the number of cells in the human body. *Annals of Human Biology, 40*, 463–471. https://doi.org/10.3109/03014460.2013.807878

Biskin, R. S. (2015). The lifetime course of borderline personality disorder. *Canadian Journal of Psychiatry, 60*(7), 303–308. https://doi.org/10.1177/070674371506000702

Bisson, J. I., Berliner, L., Cloitre, M., Forbes, D., Jensen, T. K., Lewis, C., Monson, C. M., Olff, M., Pilling, S., Riggs, D. S., Roberts, N. P., & Shapiro, F. (2019). The International Society for Traumatic Stress Studies new guidelines for the prevention and treatment of PTSD: Methodology and development process. *Journal of Traumatic Stress, 32*, 475–483. https://doi.org/10.1002/jts.22421

Blasé, K. L., van Dijke, A., Cluitmans, P. J., & Vermetten, E. (2016). Effectiviteit van hartrit-mevariabiliteitbiofeedback als aanvulling bij behandeling van depressie en posttrauma-tische stressstoornis [Efficacy of HRV-biofeedback as additional treatment of depression and PTSD]. *Tijdschrift voor psychiatrie, 58*(4), 292–300.

Bloch, M. H., & Mulqueen, J. (2014). Nutritional supplements for the treatment of ADHD. *Child and Adolescent Psychiatric Clinics of North America, 23*(4), 883–897. https://doi .org/10.1016/j.chc.2014.05.002

Blood, A. J., & Zatorre, R. J. (2001). Intensely pleasurable responses to music correlate with activity in brain regions implicated in reward and emotion. *Proceedings of the National Academy of Sciences of the United States of America, 98*, 11818–11823. https://doi.org/10 .1073/pnas.191355898

Bogdan, R., Agrawal, A., Gaffrey, M. S., Tillman, R., & Luby, J. L. (2014). Serotonin transporter-linked polymorphic region (5-HTTLPR) genotype and stressful life events interact to predict preschool-onset depression: A replication and developmental exten-sion. *The Journal of Child Psychology and Psychiatry, 55*(5), 448–457. https://doi.org/10 .1111/jcpp.12142

Bögels, S., Knappe, S., & Clark, L. (2013). Adult separation anxiety disorder in DSM-5. *Clin-ical Psychology Review, 33*(5), 663–674. https://doi.org/10.1016/j.cpr.2013.03.006

Bonaz, B., Bazin, T., & Pellissier, S. (2018). The vagus nerve at the interface of the microbiota-gut-brain axis. *Frontiers in Neuroscience, 12*, Article 49. https://doi.org/10.3389/ fnins.2018.00049

Boonchooduang, N., Louthrenoo, O., Chattipakorn, N., & Chattipakorn, S. C. (2020). Possible links between gut-microbiota and attention-deficit/hyperactivity disorders in children and adolescents. *European Journal of Nutrition, 59*(8), 3391–3403. https://doi .org/10.1007/s00394-020-02383-1

Bottiglieri, T. (2002). S-Adenosyl-l-methionine (SAMe): From the bench to the bedside: Molecular basis of a pleiotrophic molecule. *The American Journal of Clinical Nutrition, 76*(5), 1151S–1157S. https://doi.org/10.1093/ajcn/76.5.1151S

Bowden, G., Holttum, S., Shankar, R., Cooke, A., & Kinderman, P. (Eds.). (2020, October).

Understanding depression: Why adults experience depression and what can help. The British Psychological Society.

Bowers, M. (2015). *8 keys to raising the quirky child: How to help a kid who doesn't (quite) fit in.* W. W. Norton.

Bradfield, L. A., Bertran-Gonzalez, J., Chieng, B., & Balleine, B. W. (2013). The thalamostriatal pathway and cholinergic control of goal-directed action: Interlacing new with existing learning in the striatum. *Neuron, 79*(1), 153–166, https://doi.org/10.1016/j.neuron.2013.04.039

Brain & Behavior Research Foundation. (2018). Healthy minds—409—Schizophrenia: Potential breakthroughs, treatment, and prevention. [Video]. YouTube. https://www.youtube.com/watch?v=71aPbY3ufMY

Braun, B. G. (1983). Neurophysiologic changes in multiple personality due to integration: A preliminary report. *The American Journal of Clinical Hypnosis, 26*(2), 84–92. https://doi.org/10.1080/00029157.1983.10404148

Bravo, J. A., Forsythe, P., Chew, M. V., Escaravage, E., Savignac, H. M., Dinan, T. G., Bienenstock, J., & Cryan, J. F. (2011). Ingestion of *Lactobacillus* strain regulates emotional behaviour and central GABA receptor expression in a mouse via the vagus nerve. *Proceedings of the National Academy of Sciences of the United States of America, 108,* 16050–16055. https://doi.org/10.1073/pnas.1102999108

Breen, M., Tylee, D., Maihofer, A. X., Neylan, T. C., Mehta, D., Binder, E. B., Chandler, S. D., Hess, J. L., Kremen, W. S., Risbrough, V. B., Woelk, C. H., Baker, D. G., Nievergelt, C. M., Tsuang, M. T., Buxbaum, J. D., & Glatt, S. J. (2018). PTSD blood transcriptome mega-analysis: Shared inflammatory pathways across biological sex and modes of trauma. *Neuropsychopharmacology, 43,* 469–481. https://doi.org/10.1038/npp.2017.220

Bremner, J. D., Innis, R. B., Ng, C. K., Staib, L. H., Salomon, R. M., Bronen, R. A., Duncan, J., Southwick, S. M., Krystal, J. H., Rich, D., Zubal, G., Dey, H., Soufer, R., & Charney, D. S. (1997). Positron emission tomography measurement of cerebral metabolic correlates of yohimbine administration in combat-related posttraumatic stress disorder. *Archives of General Psychiatry, 54*(3), 246–254. https://doi.org/10.1001/archpsyc.1997.01830150070011

Bretherton, B., Atkinson, L., Murray, A., Clancy, J., Deuchars, S., & Deuchars, J. (2019). Effects of transcutaneous vagus nerve stimulation in individuals aged 55 years or above: Potential benefits of daily stimulation. *Aging, 11*(4), 4836–4857. https://doi.org/10.18632/aging.102074

Brewin, C. R. (2014). Episodic memory, perceptual memory, and their interaction: Foundations for a theory of posttraumatic stress disorder. *Psychological Bulletin, 140*(1), 69–97. https://doi.org/10.1037/a0033722

Briguglio, M., Vitale, J. A., Galentino, R., Banfi, G., Zanaboni Dina, C., Bona, A., Panzica, G., Porta, M., Dell'Osso, B., & Glick, I. D. (2020). Healthy eating, physical activity, and sleep hygiene (HEPAS) as the winning triad for sustaining physical and mental health in patients at risk for or with neuropsychiatric disorders: Considerations for clinical practice. *Neuropsychiatric Disease and Treatment, 16*, 55–70. https://doi.org/10.2147/NDT .S229206

Brissos, S., Veguilla, M. R., Taylor, D., & Balanzá-Martinez, V. (2014). The role of long-acting injectable antipsychotics in schizophrenia: A critical appraisal. *Therapeutic Advances in Psychopharmacology, 4*(5), 198–219. https://doi.org/10.1177/2045125314540297

Brook, C. A., & Schmidt, L. A. (2008). Social anxiety disorder: A review of environmental risk factors. *Neuropsychiatric Disease and Treatment, 4*(1), 123–143. https://doi.org/10 .2147/ndt.s1799

Brown, A. D., Root, J. C., Romano, T. A., Chang, L. J., Bryant, R. A., & Hirst, W. (2013). Overgeneralized autobiographical memory and future thinking in combat veterans with posttraumatic stress disorder. *Journal of Behavior Therapy and Experimental Psychiatry, 44*(1):129–134. https://doi.org/10.1016/j.jbtep.2011.11.004

Brown, D., & Elliot, D. (2016). *Attachment disturbances in adults: Treatment for comprehensive repair.* W. W. Norton.

Brumariu, L. E., & Kerns, K. A. (2008). Mother-child attachment and social anxiety symptoms in middle childhood. *Journal of Applied Developmental Psychology, 29*(5), 393–402. https://doi.org/10.1016/j.appdev.2008.06.002

Buccino, G., Vogt, S., Ritzl, A., Fink, G. R., Zilles, K., Freund, H. J., & Rizzolatti, G. (2004). Neural circuits underlying imitation learning of hand actions: An event-related fMRI study. *Neuron, 42*(2), 323–334. https://doi.org/10.1016/s0896-6273(04)00181-3

Buckner, J. D., Schmidt, N. B., Lang, A. R., Small, J. W., Schlauch, R. C., & Lewinsohn, P. M. (2008). Specificity of social anxiety disorder as a risk factor for alcohol and cannabis dependence. *Journal of Psychiatric Research, 42*(3), 230–239. https://doi.org/10.1016/j .jpsychires.2007.01.002

Buckner, R. L., Andrews-Hanna, J. R., and Schacter, D. L. (2008). The brain's default network: Anatomy, function, and relevance to disease. *Annals of the New York Academy of Sciences, 1124*(1), 1–38. https://doi.org/10.1196/annals.1440.011

Budd, G. E. (2015). Early animal evolution and the origins of nervous systems. *Philosophical Transactions of the Royal Society of London. Series B, Biological Sciences, 370*(1684), Article 20150037. https://doi.org/10.1098/rstb.2015.0037

Buetow, S. A., & Mintoft, B. (2011). When should patient intuition be taken seriously? *Journal of General Internal Medicine, 26*(4), 433–436. https://doi.org/10.1007/s11606-010-1576-6

Bullard, D. (2014). *Bessel van der Kolk on trauma, development and healing* [Interview]. Psychotherapy.net. https://www.psychotherapy.net/interview/bessel-van-der-kolk-trauma

Bull-Larsen, S., & Mohajeri, M. H. (2019). The potential influence of the bacterial microbiome on the development and progression of ADHD. *Nutrients, 11*(11), 2805. https://doi .org/10.3390/nu11112805

Bundespsychotherapeutenkammer. (2011). *Psychotherapy in Europe: Disease manage-*

ment strategies for depression. http://www.npce.eu/mediapool/113/1137650/data/Nat._
Development/Reader_National_Concepts.pdf

Buzsáki, G. (1996). The hippocampo-neocortical dialogue. *Cerebral Cortex*, 6(2), 81–92.
https://doi.org/10.1093/cercor/6.2.81

Buzsáki, G., & Gage, F. H. (1989). The cholinergic nucleus basalis: A key structure in neocortical arousal. *Experientia Supplementum*, 57, 159–171.

Cahalan, S. (2013). *Brain on fire: My month of madness*. Simon & Schuster.

Campbell-McBride, N. (2010). *Gut and psychology syndrome*. Medinform Publishing.

Caputo, J. D. (Ed.). (1996). *Deconstruction in a nutshell: A conversation with Jacques Derrida*.
Fordham University Press.

Carabotti, M., Scirocco, A., Maselli, M. A., & Severi, C. (2015). The gut-brain axis: Interactions between enteric microbiota, central and enteric nervous systems. *Annals of Gastroenterology*, 28(2), 203–209.

Carey, E. (2018, September 28). *Psychosis*. Healthline. https://www.healthline.com/health/
psychosis

Cartwright, P., Halgedahl, S. L., Hendricks, J. R., Jarrard, R. D., Marques, A. C., Collins,
A. G., & Lieberman, B. S. (2007). Exceptionally preserved jellyfishes from the Middle
Cambrian. *PLOS ONE*, 2(10), Article e1121. https://doi.org/10.1371/journal.pone.0001121

Carvalho, D., Teixeira, S., Lucas, M., Yuan, T. F., Chaves, F., Peressutti, C., Machado, S., Bit-
tencourt, J., Menéndez-González, M., Nardi, A. E., Velasques, B., Cagy, M., Piedade, R.,
Ribeiro, P., & Arias-Carrión, O. (2013). The mirror neuron system in post-stroke rehabilitation. *International Archives of Medicine*, 6(1), 41. https://doi.org/10.1186/1755-7682-6-41

Caspi, A., Hariri, A. R., Holmes, A., Uher, R., & Moffitt, T. E. (2010). Genetic sensitivity
to the environment: The case of the serotonin transporter gene and its implications for
studying complex diseases and traits. *The American Journal of Psychiatry*, 167(5), 509–527.
https://doi.org/10.1176/appi.ajp.2010.09101452

Catalá-López, F., Hutton, B., Núñez-Beltrán, A., Page, M. J., Ridao, M., Macías Saint-Gerons,
D., Catalá, M. A., Tabarés-Seisdedos, R., & Moher, D. (2017). The pharmacological and
non-pharmacological treatment of attention deficit hyperactivity disorder in children
and adolescents: A systematic review with network meta-analyses of randomised trials.
PLOS ONE, 12(7), Article e0180355. https://doi.org/10.1371/journal.pone.0180355

Chang, K., Frankovich J., Cooperstock, M., Cunningham, M., Latimer, E., Murphy, T.,
Pasternack, M., Thienemann, M., Williams, K., Walter, J., & Swedo, S. (2015). Clini-
cal evaluation of youth with pediatric acute-onset neuropsychiatric syndrome (PANS):
Recommendations from the 2013 PANS Consensus Conference. *Journal of Child and
Adolescent Psychopharmacology*, 25(1), 3–13. https://doi.org/10.1089/cap.2014.0084

Chen, Y., & Lyga, J. (2014). Brain-skin connection: Stress, inflammation and skin
aging. *Inflammation & Allergy Drug Targets*, 13(3), 177–190. https://doi.org/10
.2174/1871528113666140522104422

Chial, H. (2008). DNA sequencing technologies key to the Human Genome Project. *Nature Education, 1*(1), 219.

Chow, D. L., Miller, S. D., Seidel, J. A., Kane R. T., Thornton, J. A., & Andrews, W. P. (2015). The role of deliberate practice in the development of highly effective therapists. *Psychotherapy, 52*(3), 337–345. https://doi.org/10.1037/pst0000015

Chuang, J., & Jones, P. (2007). Epigenetics and microRNAs. *Pediatric Research, 61,* 24–29. https://doi.org/10.1203/pdr.0b013e3180457684

Clapp, M., Aurora, N., Herrera, L., Bhatia, M., Wilen, E., & Wakefield, S. (2017). Gut microbiota's effect on mental health: The gut-brain axis. *Clinics and Practice, 7*(4), 987. https://doi.org/10.4081/cp.2017.987

Clarke, G., Grenham, S., Scully, P., Fitzgerald, P., Moloney, R. D., Shanahan, F., Dinan, T. G., & Cryan, J. F. (2013). The microbiome-gut-brain axis during early life regulates the hippocampal serotonergic system in a sex-dependent manner. *Molecular Psychiatry, 18,* 666–673.

Clayton, D. F., Anreiter, I., Aristizabal, M., Frankland, P. W., Binder, E. B., & Citri, A. (2020). The role of the genome in experience-dependent plasticity: Extending the analogy of the genomic action potential. *Proceedings of the National Academy of Sciences of the United States of America, 117*(38), 23252–23260. https://doi.org/10.1073/pnas.1820837116

College of Psychotherapy & Psychotherapy and Counselling Federation of Australia. (n.d.). *Definition of psychotherapy.* https://www.pacfa.org.au/common/Uploaded%20files/PCFA/Documents/Definition-of-Psychotherapy.pdf

Colvert, E., Tick, B., McEwen F., Stewart, C., Curran, S. R., Woodhouse, E., Gillan, N., Hallet, V., Lietz, S., Garnett, T., Ronald, A., Plomin, R., Rijsdijk, F., Happé, F., & Bolton, P. (2015). Heritability of autism spectrum disorder in a UK population-based twin sample. *JAMA Psychiatry, 72*(5), 415–423. https://doi.org/10.1001/jamapsychiatry.2014.3028

Condo, C. M. (2020, March 3). "You don't look autistic": The reality of high-functioning autism. *The Washington Post: Inspired Life.* https://www.washingtonpost.com/lifestyle/2020/03/03/you-dont-look-autistic-reality-high-functioning-autism

Cooperstock, M., Swedo, S., Pasternack, M., Murphy, T., & PANS/PANDAS Consortium. (2017). Clinical management of pediatric acute-onset neuropsychiatric syndrome: Part III, Treatment and Prevention of Infections. *Journal of Child and Adolescent Psychopharmacology, 27*(7). https://doi.org/10.1089/cap.2016.0151

Costa, M., Brookes, S. J. H., & Hennig, G. W. (2000). Anatomy and physiology of the enteric nervous system. *Gut, 47*(Suppl. 4), iv15–iv19.

Courtois, C. A., & Ford, J. D. (Eds.). (2009). *Treating complex traumatic stress disorders: Scientific foundations and therapeutic models.* The Guilford Press.

Cowen, A. S., & Keltner, D. (2017). Self-report captures 27 distinct categories of emotion bridged by continuous gradients. *Proceedings of the National Academy of Sciences of the United States of America, 114*(38), E7900–E7909. https://doi.org/10.1073/pnas.1702247114

Cozolino, L. J. (2006). *The neuroscience of human relationships: Attachment and the developing brain*. W. W. Norton.

Cozolino, L. J. (2014). *The neuroscience of human relationships: Attachment and the developing social brain* (2nd ed.). W. W. Norton.

Cozzolino, M. (2014). The creative psychosocial and cultural genomic healing experience: A new top-down epigenomic psychotherapeutic protocol. *The International Journal of Psychosocial and Cultural Genomics, Consciousness & Health Research, 1*, 18–26.

Craddock, N., Owen, M., & O'Donovan, M. (2006). The catechol-O-methyl transferase (COMT) gene as a candidate for psychiatric phenotypes: Evidence and lessons. *Molecular Psychiatry, 11*, 446–458. https://doi.org/10.1038/sj.mp.4001808

Craig, A. D. (2010). The sentient self. *Brain Structure and Function, 214*, 563–577. https://doi.org/10.1007/s00429-010-0248-y

Craik, F. I. M., & Lockhart, R. S. (1972). Levels of processing: A framework for memory research. *Journal of Verbal Learning and Verbal Behaviour, 11*, 671–684.

Crider, K. S., Yang, T. P., Berry, R. J., & Bailey, L. B. (2012). Folate and DNA methylation: A review of molecular mechanisms and the evidence for folate's role. *Advances in Nutrition, 3*(1), 21–38. https://doi.org/10.3945/an.111.000992

Cristea, I. A., Gentili, C., Cotet, C. D., Palomba, D., Barbui, C., & Cuijpers, P. (2017). Efficacy of psychotherapies for borderline personality disorder: A systematic review and meta-analysis. *JAMA Psychiatry, 74*(4), 319–328. https://doi.org/10.1001/jamapsychiatry.2016.4287

Cryan, J. F., & O'Mahony, S. M. (2011). The microbiome-gut-brain axis: From bowel to behaviour. *Neurogastroenterology and Motility, 23*, 187–192. https://doi.org/10.1111/J.1365-2982.2010.01664.X

Cuijpers, P., Sijbrandij, M., Koole, S. L., Andersson, G., Beekman, A. T., & Reynolds, C. F., III. (2014). Adding psychotherapy to antidepressant medication in depression and anxiety disorders: A meta-analysis. *World Psychiatry, 13*(1), 56–67. https://doi.org/10.1002/wps.20089

Cummings, E. M., Koss, K. J., & Davies, P. T. (2015). Prospective relations between family conflict and adolescent maladjustment: Security in the family system as a mediating process. *Journal of Abnormal Child Psychology, 43*(3), 503–515. https://doi.org/10.1007/s10802-014-9926-1

Dahlitz, M. J. (2015). Neuropsychotherapy: Defining the emerging paradigm of neurobiologically informed psychotherapy. *International Journal of Neuropsychotherapy, 3*(1), 47–69.

Dahlitz, M. J. (2017). *The psychotherapist's essential guide to the brain*. Dahlitz Media.

Damasio, A. R. (2000). *The feeling of what happens: Body and emotion in the making of consciousness*. Mariner Books.

Damasio, A. R. (2005). *Descartes' error: Emotion, reason, and the human brain*. Putnam.

Damasio, A. R., Everitt, B., and Bishop, D. (1996). The somatic marker hypothesis and the possible functions of the prefrontal cortex. *Philosophical Transactions of the Royal Society of London. Series B, Biological Sciences, 351*, 1413–1420. https://doi.org/10.1098/rstb.1996 .0125

Dantzer, R. (2009). Cytokine, sickness behavior, and depression. *Immunology and Allergy Clinics of North America, 29*(2), 247–264. https://doi.org/10.1016/j.iac.2009.02.002

Dapretto, M., Davies, M. S., Pfeifer, J. H., Scott, A. A., Sigman, M., Bookheimer, S. Y., & Iacoboni, M. (2006). Understanding emotions in others: Mirror neuron dysfunction in children with autism spectrum disorders. *Nature Neuroscience, 9*(1), 28–30. https://doi .org/10.1038/nn1611

Dattola, A., Silvestri, M., Bennardo, L., Passante, M., Scali, E., Patruno, C., & Nisticò, S. P. (2020). Role of vitamins in skin health: A systematic review. *Current Nutrition Reports, 9*(3), 226–235. https://doi.org/10.1007/s13668-020-00322-4

Davis, K. L., & Montag, C. (2019). Selected principles of Pankseppian affective neuroscience. *Frontiers in Neuroscience, 12*, Article 1025. https://doi.org/10.3389/fnins.2018.01025

Day, J., & Sweatt, J. (2010). DNA methylation and memory formation. *Nature Neuroscience, 13*, 1319–1323. https://doi.org/10.1038/nn.2666

Decety, J., & Jackson, P. L. (2006). A social-neuroscience perspective on empathy. *Current Directions in Psychological Science, 15*(2), 54–58. https://doi.org/10.1111/j.0963-7214.2006 .00406.x

de Laet, S. J., Dani, A. H., Lorenzo, J. I., & Nunoo, R. B. (Ed.). (1994). *History of humanity: Vol. 1. Prehistory and the beginning of civilization*. Routledge. https://unesdoc.unesco.org/ ark:/48223/pf0000119149

Desbonnet, L., Garrett, L., Clarke, G., Bienenstock, J., & Dinan, T. G. (2008). The probiotic *Bifidobacteria infantis*: An assessment of potential antidepressant properties in the rat. *Journal of Psychiatric Research, 43*, 164–174. https://doi.org/10.1016/j.jpsychires.2008 .03.009

Desbonnet, L., Garrett, L., Clarke, G., Kiely, B., Cryan, J. F., & Dinan, T. G. (2010). Effects of the probiotic *Bifidobacterium infantis* in the maternal separation model of depression. *Neuroscience, 170*, 1179–1188. https://doi.org/10.1016/j.neuroscience.2010.08.005

De Vadder, F., Grasset, E., Holm, L. M., Karsenty, G., Macpherson, A. J., Olofsson, L. E., & Bäckhed, F. (2018). Gut microbiota regulates maturation of the adult enteric nervous system via enteric serotonin networks. *Proceedings of the National Academy of Sciences of the United States of America, 115*(25), 6458–6463. https://doi.org/10.1073/pnas.1720017115

Dheen, S. T., Kaur, C., & Ling, E. A. (2007). Microglial activation and its implications in the brain diseases. *Current Medicinal Chemistry, 14*(11), 1189–1197.

Diamond, A. (2013). Executive functions. *Annual Review of Psychology, 64*, 135–168. https:// doi.org/10.1146/annurev-psych-113011-143750

Di Bernardo, M. (2010). Natural selection and self-organization in complex adaptive systems. *Rivista di Biologia, 103*(1), 89–110.

Dickerson, F. B., Stallings, C., Origoni, A., Katsafanas, E., Savage, C. L. G., Schweinfurth, L. A., Goga, J., Khushalani, S., & Yolken, R. H. (2014). Effect of probiotic supplementation on schizophrenia symptoms and association with gastrointestinal functioning: A randomized, placebo-controlled trial. *The Primary Care Companion for CNS Disorders, 16*, 1. https://doi.org/10.4088/PCC.13m01579

Di Forti, M., Lappin, J., & Murray, R. (2007). Risk factors for schizophrenia: All roads lead to dopamine. *European Neuropsychopharmacology, 17*, S101–S107. https://doi.org/10.1016/j.euroneuro.2007.02.005

Dinan, T. G., & Cryan, J. F. (2012). Regulation of the stress response by the gut microbiota: Implications for psychoneuroendocrinology. *Psychoneuroendocrinology, 37*, 1369–1378. https://doi.org/10.1016/j.psyneuen.2012.03.007

di Pellegrino, G., Fadiga, L., Fogassi, L., Gallese, V., & Rizzolatti, G. (1992). Understanding motor events: A neurophysiological study. *Experimental Brain Research, 91*, 176–180.

Drachman, D. A. (2005). Do we have brain to spare? *Neurology, 64*, 2004–2005. https://doi.org/10.1212/01. WNL.0000166914.38327.BB

Drummond, P., & Lance, J. (1997). Facial flushing and sweating mediated by the sympathetic nervous system. *Brain, 110*, 793–803.

Duffy, A., Alda, M., Hajek, T., Sherry, S. B., & Grof, P. (2010). Early stages in the development of bipolar disorder. *Journal of Affective Disorders, 121*, 127–135. https://doi.org/10.1016/j.jad.2009.05.022

Dulak, D., & Naqvi, I. A. (2020, July 31). Neuroanatomy, cranial nerve 7 (facial). *StatPearls* [Internet]. https://www.ncbi.nlm.nih.gov/books/NBK526119

Duncan, B., & Miller, S. D. (2008). *Super shrinks: What is the secret of their success?* Psychotherapy.net. https://www.psychotherapy.net/article/successful-psychotherapists

Duncan, B. L., Miller, S. D., Wampold, B. E., & Hubble, M. A. (Eds.). (2010). *The heart and soul of change: Delivering what works in therapy* (2nd ed.). American Psychological Association. https://doi.org/10.1037/12075-000

Dupont, C., Armant, D. R., & Brenner, C. A. (2009). Epigenetics: Definition, mechanisms and clinical perspective. *Seminars in Reproductive Medicine, 27*(5), 351–357. https://doi.org/10.1055/s-0029-1237423

Durães Campos, I., Pinto, V., Nuno Sousa, N., & Vitor H. Pereira, V. H. (2018). A brain within the heart: A review on the intracardiac nervous system. *Journal of Molecular and Cellular Cardiology, 119*, 1–9.

Dylan, W. (2006). The half-second delay: What follows? *Pedagogy, Culture & Society, 14*(1), 71–81. https://doi.org/10.1080/14681360500487470

Ebert, D. H., & Greenberg, M. E. (2013). Activity-dependent neuronal signalling and autism spectrum disorder. *Nature, 493*, 327–337.

Ebrahimi-Fakhari, D., & Sahin, M. (2015). Autism and the synapse: Emerging mechanisms

and mechanism-based therapies. *Current Opinion in Neurology, 28*(2), 91–102. https://doi
.org/10.1097/WCO.0000000000000186

Ecker, B. (2015). Memory reconsolidation understood and misunderstood. *International Journal of Neuropsychotherapy, 3,* 2–46.

Ecker, B. (2018). Clinical translation of memory reconsolidation research: Therapeutic methodology for transformational change by erasing implicit emotional learnings driving symptom production. *International Journal of Neuropsychotherapy, 6*(1), 1–92. https://doi.org/10.12744/ijnpt.2018.0001-0092

Ecker, B., & Bridges, S. K. (2020). How the science of memory reconsolidation advances the effectiveness and unification of psychotherapy. *Clinical Social Work Journal, 48,* 287–300. https://doi.org/10.1007/s10615-020-00754-z

Ecker, B., & Hulley, L. (1996). *Depth-orientated brief therapy: How to be brief when you were trained to be deep and vice versa.* Jossey-Bass.

Ecker, B., Ticic, R., & Hulley, L. (2012). *Unlocking the emotional brain: Eliminating symptoms at their roots using memory reconsolidation.* Routledge.

Ehlers, A. (2010). Understanding and treating unwanted trauma memories in posttraumatic stress disorder. *Zeitschrift für Psychologie, 218*(2), 141–145. https://doi.org/10.1027/0044
-3409/a000021

Ehlers, A., Bisson, J., Clark, D. M., Creamer, M., Pilling, S., Richards, D., Schnurr, P. P., Turner, S., & Yule, W. (2010). Do all psychological treatments really work the same in posttraumatic stress disorder? *Clinical Psychology Review, 30*(2), 269–276. https://doi
.org/10.1016/j.cpr.2009.12.001

Ehlers, A., & Clark, D. M. (2000). A cognitive model of posttraumatic stress disorder. *Behaviour Research and Therapy, 38*(4), 319–345. https://doi.org/10.1016/s0005
-7967(99)00123-0

Ehlers, A., Hackmann, A., & Michael, T. (2004). Intrusive re-experiencing in post-traumatic stress disorder: Phenomenology, theory, and therapy. *Memory, 12*(4), 403–415. https://doi
.org/10.1080/09658210444000025

Ehlers, A., Hackmann, A., Steil, R., Clohessy, S., Wenninger, K., & Winter, H. (2002). The nature of intrusive memories after trauma: the warning signal hypothesis. *Behaviour Research and Therapy, 40*(9), 995–1002. https://doi.org/10.1016/s0005-7967(01)00077-8

Ekman, P. (1992). Facial expressions of emotion: New findings, new questions. *Psychological Science, 3*(1), 34–38. https://doi.org/10.1111/j.1467-9280.1992.tb00253.x

Ekman, P. (2003). *Emotions revealed.* Times Books.

Ekman, P. (n.d.). *Universal emotions.* Paul Ekman Group. https://www.paulekman.com/
universal-emotions/

El-Ansary, A. K., Ben Bacha, A., & Kotb, M. (2012). Etiology of autistic features: The persisting neurotoxic effects of propionic acid. *Journal of Neuroinflammation, 9,* 74.

El-Ansary, A., Shaker, G. H., & Rizk, M. Z. (2013). Role of gut-brain axis in the aetiology of neurodevelopmental disorders with reference to autism. *Journal of Clinical Toxicology, S6*, 005. https://doi.org/10.4172/2161-0495.S6-005

Elkins, D. N. (2009). The medical model in psychotherapy: Its limitations and failures. *Journal of Humanistic Psychology, 49*(1), 66–84. https://doi.org/10.1177/0022167807307901

Erickson, K. I., Miller, D. L., & Roecklein, K. A. (2012). The aging hippocampus: Interactions between exercise, depression, and BDNF. *The Neuroscientist, 18*(1), 82–97. https://doi.org/10.1177/1073858410397054

Erickson, M. H. (2008a). The burden of responsibility in effective psychotherapy. In E. Rossi, R. Erickson-Klein, & K. Rossi (Eds.), *The collected works of Milton H. Erickson: Vol. 3. Opening the mind: Innovative psychotherapy* (pp. 67–71). Milton H. Erickson Foundation. (Original work published 1964)

Erickson, M. H. (2008b). *The collected works of Milton H. Erickson: Vol. 3: Opening the mind: Innovative psychotherapy.* Milton H. Erickson Foundation. (Original work published 1964)

Erickson, M. H. (2015). *The collected works of Milton H. Erickson: Vol. 15. Mind-body communication in hypnosis.* Milton H. Erickson Foundation.

Erickson, M. H., & Rossi, E. (1981). *Experiencing hypnosis.* Irvington.

Ericsson, K. A., Krampe, R. T., & Tesch-Romer, C. (1993). The role of deliberate practice in the acquisition of expert performance. *Psychological Review, 100*(3), 363–406.

Erman, A. B., Kejner, A. E., Hogikyan, N. D., & Feldman, E. L. (2009). Disorders of cranial nerves IX and X. *Seminars in Neurology, 29*(1), 85–92. https://doi.org/10.1055/s-0028-1124027

Eysenck, H. J. (1952). The effects of psychotherapy: An evaluation. *Journal of Consulting and Clinical Psychology, 16*, 319–324.

Faraguna, U., Ferrucci, M., Giorgi, F. S., & Fornai, F. (2019) Editorial: The functional anatomy of the reticular formation. *Frontiers in Neuroanatomy, 13*, Article 55. https://doi.org/10.3389/fnana.2019.00055

Fariba, K., & Gokarakonda, S. B. (2020, October 6). Impulse control disorders. *StatPearls* [Internet]. https://www.ncbi.nlm.nih.gov/books/NBK562279

Farina, E., Baglio, F., Pomati, S., D'Amico, A., Campini, I. C., Di Tella, S., Belloni, G., & Pozzo, T. (2017). The mirror neurons network in aging, mild cognitive impairment, and Alzheimer disease: A functional MRI study. *Frontiers in Aging Neuroscience, 9*, Article 371. https://doi.org/10.3389/fnagi.2017.00371

Farmer, D. G., Dutschmann, M., Paton, J. F., Pickering, A. E., & McAllen, R. M. (2016). Brainstem sources of cardiac vagal tone and respiratory sinus arrhythmia. *The Journal of Physiology, 594*(24), 7249–7265. https://doi.org/10.1113/JP273164

Fatokun, A. A., Dawson, V. L., & Dawson, T. M. (2014). Parthanatos: Mitochondrial-linked mechanisms and therapeutic opportunities. *British Journal of Pharmacology, 171*, 2000–2016, https://doi.org/10.1111/bph.12416

Fava, M., & Mischoulon, D. (2009). Folate in depression: Efficacy, safety, differences in formulations, and clinical issues. *Journal of Clinical Psychiatry, 70*(Suppl. 5), 12–17.

Fazel, M., Hoagwood, K., Stephan, S., & Ford, T. (2014). Mental health interventions in schools 1: Mental health interventions in schools in high-income countries. *The Lancet. Psychiatry, 1*(5), 377–387. https://doi.org/10.1016/S2215-0366(14)70312-8

Fedorowski, A. (2019). Postural orthostatic tachycardia syndrome: Clinical presentation, aetiology and management. *Journal Internal Medicine, 285,* 352– 366.

Feistel, R., & Eberling, R. (2011). *The physics of self-organization and evolution.* Wiley-VCH.

Fenker, D. B., Schott, B. H., Richardson-Klavehn, A., Heinze, H.-J., & Düzel, E. (2005). Recapitulating emotional context: Activity of amygdala, hippocampus and fusiform cortex during recollection and familiarity. *European Journal of Neuroscience, 21,* 1993–1999. https://doi.org/10.1111/j.1460-9568.2005.04033.x

Fenster, R. J., Lebois, L., Ressler, K. J., & Suh, J. (2018). Brain circuit dysfunction in post-traumatic stress disorder: From mouse to man. *Nature Reviews Neuroscience, 19*(9), 535–551. https://doi.org/10.1038/s41583-018-0039-7

Fenton, A. M., Hammill, S. C., Rea, R. F., Low, P. A., & Shen, W.-K. (2000). Vasovagal syncope. *Annals of Internal Medicine, 133,* 714–725. https://doi.org/10.7326/0003-4819-133-9-200011070-00014

Fernandes, J., Acuña, S. M., Aoki, J. I., Floeter-Winter, L. M., & Muxel, S. M. (2019). Long non-coding rnas in the regulation of gene expression: Physiology and disease. *Non-Coding RNA, 5*(1), 17. https://doi.org/10.3390/ncrna5010017

Ferreira S., Pêgo J. M., & Morgado P. (2019). The efficacy of biofeedback approaches for obsessive-compulsive and related disorders: A systematic review and meta-analysis. *Psychiatry Research, 272,* 237–245. https://doi.org/10.1016/j.psychres.2018.12.096

Finegold, S. M. (2011). State of the art; microbiology in health and disease. Intestinal bacterial flora in autism. *Anaerobe, 17,* 367–368.

Finkelhor, D., Shattuck, A., Turner, H., & Hamby, S. (2013). Improving the Adverse Childhood Experiences Study scale. *JAMA Pediatrics, 167*(1), 70.

Fisher, M., Holland, C., Subramaniam, K., & Vinogradov, S. (2010). Neuroplasticity-based cognitive training in schizophrenia: An interim report on the effects 6 months later. *Schizophrenia Bulletin, 36*(4), 869–879. https://doi.org/10.1093/schbul/sbn170

Fisher, S. (2014). *Neurofeedback in the treatment of developmental trauma: Calming the fear-driven brain.* W. W. Norton.

Flückiger, C., Del Re, A. C., Wampold, B. E., & Horvath, A. O. (2018). The alliance in adult psychotherapy: A meta-analytic synthesis. *Psychotherapy, 55*(4), 316–340. http://.doi.org/10.1037/pst0000172

Ford, J. D. (2005). Treatment implications of altered affect regulation and information processing following child maltreatment. *Psychiatric Annals, 35*(5), 410–419. https://doi.org/10.3928/00485713-20050501-07

Ford, J. D. (2009). Neurobiological and developmental research: Clinical implications. In C. A. Courtois & J. D. Ford (Eds.), *Treating complex traumatic stress disorders: Scientific foundations and therapeutic models* (pp. 31–58). The Guilford Press.

Fossati, A., Barratt, E. S., Borroni, S., Villa, D., Grazioli, F., & Maffei, C. (2007). Impulsivity, aggressiveness, and DSM-IV personality disorders. *Psychiatry Research, 149*(1–3), 157–167. https://doi.org/10.1016/j.psychres.2006.03.011

Fountoulakis, K. N., & Gonda, X. (2019). Modeling human temperament and character on the basis of combined theoretical approaches. *Annals of General Psychiatry, 18*, 21. https://doi.org/10.1186/s12991-019-0247-1

Frankl, V. (2006). *Man's search for meaning.* Beacon Press. (Original work published 1959)

Frankovich, J., Swedo, S., Murphy, T., Dale, R., Agalliu, D., Williams, K., Daines, M., Hornig, M., Chugani, H., Sanger, T., Muscal, E., Pasternack, M., Cooperstock, M., Gans, H., Zhang, Y., Cunningham, M., Bernstein, G., Bromberg, R., Willett, T., Brown, K., . . . PANS/PANDAS Consortium. (2017). Clinical management of pediatric acute-onset neuropsychiatric syndrome: Part II: Use of immunomodulatory therapies. *Journal of Child and Adolescent Psychopharmacology, 27*(7). https://doi.org/10.1089/cap.2016.0148

Fredrickson, B. L. (2004). The broaden-and-build-theory of positive emotions. *Philosophical Transactions of the Royal Society of London. Series B, Biological Sciences, 359,* 1367–1377. https://doi.org/10.1098/rstb.2004.1512

Fredrickson, B. L. (2013a). Chapter one: Positive emotions broaden and build. *Advances in Experimental Social Psychology, 47,* 1–53. https://doi.org/10.1016/B978-0-12-407236-7.00001-2

Fredrickson, B. L. (2013b). *Love 2.0: How our supreme emotion affects everything we feel, think, do, and become.* Hudson Street Press.

Fredrickson, B. L., Grewen, K. M., Coffey, K. A., Algoe, S. B., Firestine, A. M., Arevalo, J. M. G., Ma, J., & Cole, S. W. (2013). Gene expression and well-being. *Proceedings of the National Academy of Sciences of the United States of America, 110*(33), 13684–13689. https://doi.org/10.1073/pnas.1305419110

Freedberg, D., & Gallese, V. (2007). Motion, emotion and empathy in esthetic experience. *Trends in Cognitive Sciences, 11*(5), 197–203. https://doi.org/10.1016/j.tics.2007.02.003

Freedman, R. (2014). α7-Nicotinic acetylcholine receptor agonists for cognitive enhancement in schizophrenia. *Annual Review of Medicine, 65*(1), 245–261.

Freedman, R., Olsen-Dufour, A. M., & Olincy A. (2020). P50 inhibitory sensory gating in schizophrenia: Analysis of recent studies. *Schizophrenia Research, 218,* 93–98, https://doi.org/10.1016/j.schres.2020.02.003

Frewen, P., & Lanius, R. (2015). *Healing the traumatized self: Consciousness, neuroscience, treatment.* W. W. Norton.

Frye, R. E., Vassall, S., Kaur, G., Lewis, C., Karim, M., & Rossignol, D. (2019). Emerging biomarkers in autism spectrum disorder: A systematic review. *Annals of Translational Medicine, 7*(23), 792. https://doi.org/10.21037/atm.2019.11.53

Furness, J. B. (2006). *The enteric nervous system*. Blackwell.

Furness, J. B. (2012). The enteric nervous system and neurogastroenterology. *Nature Reviews Gastroenterology and Hepatology, 9*, 286–294. https://doi.org/10.1038/nrgastro.2012.32

Gallese, V. (2001). The "shared manifold" hypothesis: From mirror neurons to empathy. *Journal of Consciousness Studies, 8*(5–7), 33–50.

Gallese, V. (2003). The roots of empathy: The shared manifold hypothesis and the neural basis of intersubjectivity. *Psychopathology, 36*, 171–180.

Gallese, V. (2009). Mirror neurons, embodied simulation, and the neural basis of social identification. *Psychoanalytic Dialogues, 19*(5), 519–536. https://doi.org/10.1080/10481880903231910

Gallese, V., Fadiga, L., Fogassi, L., & Rizzolatti, G. (1996). Action recognition in the premotor cortex. *Brain, 119*(2), 593–609. https://doi.org/10.1093/brain/119.2.593

Gambari, R., Breveglieri, G., Salvatori, F., Finotti, A., & Borgatti, M. (2015). Therapy for cystic fibrosis caused by nonsense mutations. In D. Wat (Ed.), *Cystic fibrosis in the light of new research* (Chap. 13). IntechOpen. https://doi.org/10.5772/61053

Gao, J., Cahill, C., Huang, X., Roffman, J., Lamon-Fava, S., Fava, M., Mischoulon, D., & Rogers, J. T. (2018). S-Adenosyl methionine and transmethylation pathways in neuropsychiatric diseases throughout life. *Neurotherapeutics, 15*(1), 156–175. https://doi.org/10.1007/s13311-017-0593-0

Gazzola, V., Aziz-Zadeh, L., & Keysers, C. (2006). Empathy and the somatotopic auditory mirror system in humans. *Current Biology, 16*(18), 1824–1829. https://doi.org/10.1016/j.cub.2006.07.072

Gejman, P. V., Sanders, A. R., & Duan, J. (2010). The role of genetics in the etiology of schizophrenia. *Psychiatric Clinics of North America, 33*(1), 35–66. https://doi.org/10.1016/j.psc.2009.12.003

Gershon, M. (1998). *The second brain*. Harper Collins

Gershon, M., & Gershon, A. (2018). Varicella-zoster virus and the enteric nervous system. *The Journal of Infectious Diseases, 218*(Suppl. 2), S113–S119. https://doi.org/10.1093/infdis/jiy407

Ghaedrahmati, M., Kazemi, A., Kheirabadi, G., Ebrahimi, A., & Bahrami, M. (2017). Postpartum depression risk factors: A narrative review. *Journal of Education and Health Promotion, 6*, 60. https://doi.org/10.4103/jehp.jehp_9_16

Gibney, E., & Nolan, C. (2010). Epigenetics and gene expression. *Heredity, 105*, 4–13. https://doi.org/10.1038/hdy.2010.54

Gibson, G. (2009). *It takes a genome: How a clash between our genes and modern life is making us sick*. Pearson Education.

Gilbert, W. (1986). Origin of life: The RNA world. *Nature, 319*, 618. https://doi.org/10.1038/319618a0

Gilbody, S., Lewis, S., & Lightfoot, T. (2007). Methylenetetrahydrofolate reductase

(MTHFR) genetic polymorphisms and psychiatric disorders: A HuGE review. *American Journal of Epidemiology, 165*(1), 1–13.

Gill, G. (2019, July 9). Life with impulse control disorder. *Publishous.* https://medium.com/publishous/life-with-impulse-control-disorder-99c4eb7722e3

Gill, S. R., Pop, M., Deboy, R. T., Eckburg, P. B., Turnbaugh, P. J., Samuel, B. S., Gordon, J. I., Relman, D. A., Fraser-Liggett, C. M., & Nelson, K. E. (2006). Metagenomic analysis of the human distal gut microbiome. *Science, 312*(5778), 1355–1359. https://doi.org/10.1126/science.1124234

Gilligan, C. (1993). *In a different voice: Psychological theory and women's development.* Harvard University Press. (Original work published 1982)

Giorgi, G., Lecca, L., Alessio, F., Finstad, G., Bondanini, G., Lulli, L., Arcangeli, G., & Mucci, N. (2020). COVID-19-related mental health effects in the workplace: A narrative review. *International Journal of Environmental Research and Public Health, 17*(21), 7857. https://doi.org/10.3390/ijerph17217857

Gleiser, M. (2012). From cosmos to intelligent life: The four ages of astrobiology. *International Journal of Astrobiology, 11*(4), 345–350. doi:10.1017/S1473550412000237

Glizer, D., & MacDonald, P. A. (2016). Cognitive training in Parkinson's disease: A review of studies from 2000 to 2014. *Parkinson's Disease,* Article 9291713. https://doi.org/10.1155/2016/9291713

Goessl, V. C., Curtiss, J. E., & Hofmann, S. G. (2017). The effect of heart rate variability biofeedback training on stress and anxiety: A meta-analysis. *Psychological Medicine, 47*(15), 2578–2586. https://doi.org/10.1017/S0033291717001003

Gogtay, N. (2008). Cortical brain development in schizophrenia: Insights from neuroimaging studies in childhood-onset schizophrenia. *Schizophrenia Bulletin, 34*(1), 30–36.

Goleman, D. (1985, May 21). New focus on multiple personality. *New York Times,* https://www.nytimes.com/1985/05/21/science/new-focus-on-multiple-personality.html

Graf, E. R., Zhang, X., Jin, S. X., Linhoff, M. W., & Craig, A. M. (2004). Neurexins induce differentiation of GABA and glutamate postsynaptic specializations via neuroligins. *Cell, 119*(7), 1013–1026. https://doi.org/10.1016/j.cell.2004.11.035

Grandin, T. (1999, November). *Choosing the right job for people with autism or Asperger's syndrome.* Indiana Resource Center for Autism. https://www.iidc.indiana.edu/irca/articles/choosing-the-right-job-for-people-with-autism-or-aspergers-syndrome.html

Grandin, T., & Panek, R. (2014). *The autistic brain: Exploring the strength of a different kind of mind.* Rider.

Grant, J. E., Donahue, C. B., & Odlaug, B. L. (2011). *Treating impulse control disorders: A cognitive-behavioral therapy program, therapist guide.* Oxford University Press.

Grawe, K. (2007). *Neuropsychotherapy: How the neurosciences inform effective psychotherapy.* Psychology Press.

Gregory, R. J. (n.d.). *Remediation for treatment-resistant borderline personality disorder: Manual*

of dynamic deconstructive psychotherapy. SUNY Upstate Medical University. http://www
.upstate.edu/psych/pdf/education/psychotherapy/ddp_manual.pdf

Grewal, S. I. S., and Jia S. (2007). Heterochromatin revisited. *Nature Reviews Genetics, 8*(1),
35–46. https://doi.org/10.1038/nrg2008

Griffiths, A. J. F., Miller, J. H., Suzuki, D. T., Lewontin, R. C., & Gelbart, W. M. (2000). How
DNA changes affect phenotype. In *An introduction to genetic analysis* (7th ed., Chap. 15).
W. H. Freeman. https://www.ncbi.nlm.nih.gov/books/NBK21955

Groen, R. N., de Clercq, N. C., Nieuwdorp, M., Hoenders, H. J., & Groen, A. K. (2018).
Gut microbiota, metabolism and psychopathology: A critical review and novel perspectives. *Critical Reviews in Clinical Laboratory Sciences, 55*(4), 283–293. https://doi.org/10
.1080/10408363.2018.1463507

Groen, R. N., Ryan, O., Wigman, J. T. W., Riese, H., Penninx, B. W. J. H., Giltay, E. J.,
Wichers, M., & Hartman, C. A. (2020). Comorbidity between depression and anxiety:
Assessing the role of bridge mental states in dynamic psychological networks. *BMC
Medicine, 18,* 308. https://doi.org/10.1186/s12916-020-01738-z

Grossman, P., & Taylor, E. W. (2007). Toward understanding respiratory sinus arrhythmia:
Relations to cardiac vagal tone, evolution and biobehavioral functions. *Biological Psychology, 74*(2), 263–285. https://doi.org/10.1016/j.biopsycho.2005.11.014

Gruber, M. J., Gelman, B. D., & Ranganath, C. (2014). States of curiosity modulate
hippocampus-dependent learning via the dopaminergic circuit. *Neuron, 84,* 486–496.
https://doi.org/10.1016/j.neuron.2014.08.060

Grupe, D. W., & Nitschke, J. B. (2013). Uncertainty and anticipation in anxiety: An integrated neurobiological and psychological perspective. *Nature Reviews Neuroscience, 14*(7),
488–501. https://doi.org/10.1038/nrn3524

Gunderson, J. G., Shea, M. T., Skodol, A. E., McGlashan, T. H., Morey, L. C., Stout, R. L.,
Zanarini, M. C., Grilo, C, M., Oldham, J. M., & Keller, M. B. (2000). The Collaborative
Longitudinal Personality Disorders Study: Development, aims, design, and sample char-
acteristics. *Journal of Personality Disorders, 14*(4), 300–315.

Hannah-Shmouni, F., Stratakis, C. A., & Koch, C. A. (2016). Flushing in (neuro)endocri-
nology. *Reviews in Endocrine and Metabolic Disorders, 17*(3), 373–380. https://doi.org/10
.1007/s11154-016-9394-8

Happel, N., & Doenecke, D. (2009). Histone H1 and its isoforms: Contribution to chromatin
structure and function. *Gene, 431*(1–2), 1–12. https://doi.org/10.1016/j.gene.2008.11.003

Harari, Y. N. (2014). *Sapiens: A brief history of humankind.* Harvill Secker.

Harlow, J. M. (1868). Recovery from the passage of an iron bar through the head. *Publications
of the Massachusetts Medical Society, 2,* 327–347.

Haskå, L., Andersson, R., & Nyman, M. (2011). The effect of dietary fiber from wheat processing streams on the formation of carboxylic acids and microbiota in the hindgut of
rats. *Journal of Agricultural and Food Chemistry, 59,* 3406–3413.

Håvås, E., Svartberg, M., & Ulvenes, P. (2015). Attuning to the unspoken: The relationship between therapist nonverbal attunement and attachment security in adult psychotherapy. *Psychoanalytic Psychology, 32*(2), 235–254. https://doi.org/10.1037/a0038517

Hayano, J., & Yuda, E. (2019). Pitfalls of assessment of autonomic function by heart rate variability. *Journal of Physiological Anthropology, 38*(1), 3. https://doi.org/10.1186/s40101 -019-0193-2

Hayden, B., & Gargett, G. (1988). Specialization in the Paleolithic. *Lithic Technology, 17*(1), 12–18.

Hayes, A. M., & Andrews, L. A. (2020). A complex systems approach to the study of change in psychotherapy. *BMC Medical, 18*, 197. https://doi.org/10.1186/s12916-020-01662-2

Hearing, C. M., Chang, W. C., Szuhany, K. L., Deckersbach, T., Nierenberg, A. A., & Sylvia, L. G. (2016). Physical exercise for treatment of mood disorders: A critical review. *Current Behavioral Neuroscience Reports, 3*(4), 350–359. https://doi.org/10.1007/s40473 -016-0089-y

Hedges, M. (2016). Losing autism. *The Neuropsychotherapist, 4*(11), 28–30.

Helt, M., Kelley, E., Kinsbourne, M., Pandey, J., Boorstein, H., Herbert, M., & Fein, D. (2008). Can children with autism recover? If so, how? *Neuropsychology Review, 18*(4), 339–366. https://doi.org/10.1007/s11065-008-9075-9

Hergeth, S. P., & Schneider, R. (2015). The H1 linker histones: Multifunctional proteins beyond the nucleosomal core particle. *EMBO Reports, 16*(11), 1439–1453. https://doi .org/10.15252/embr.201540749

Herpertz, S. (2007). Impulskontrollstörungen frühzeitig erkennen. Wechselt sie ständig den Job, oder ritzt sie schon die Adern auf? [Impulse control disorders in borderline and antisocial personality disorder]. *MMW: Fortschritte der Medizin, 149*(3), 33–36.

Hill, R. (2012). Psychosocial genomics: A new vision of the psychotherapeutic arts. *Energy Psychology Journal, 4*(2). https://doi.org/10.9769/EPJ.2012.4.2.RH

Hill, R. (2014). Psychotherapy with non-fatal bilateral thalamic thrombosis: A case study. *The Neuropsychotherapist*, no. 5, 22–28.

Hill, R. (2018, March 1). The nuntius nuclei: A new neuroscience for curiosity. The Science of Psychotherapy. https://www.thescienceofpsychotherapy.com/nuntius-nuclei-new -neuroscience-curiosity

Hill, R., & Rossi, E. L. (2017). *The practitioner's guide to mirroring hands: A client-responsive therapy that facilitates natural problem-solving and mind-body healing.* Crown House Publishing.

Hindocha, C., Freeman, T. P., Schafer, G., Gardner, C., Bloomfield, M. A. P., Bramon, E., Morgan, C. J. A., & Curran, H. V. (2019). Acute effects of cannabinoids on addiction endophenotypes are moderated by genes encoding the CB1 receptor and FAAH enzyme, *Addiction Biology, 25*(3), Article e12762. https://doi.org/10.1111/adb.12762

Hirschfeld, R. M., Lewis, L., & Vornik, L. A. (2003). Perceptions and impact of bipolar disorder: How far have we really come? Results of the National Depressive and Manic-Depressive Association 2000 survey of individuals with bipolar disorder. *Journal of Clinical Psychiatry, 64*(2), 61–74.

Hofmann, S. G., Curtiss, J., & McNally, R. J. (2016). A complex network perspective on clinical science. *Perspectives on Psychological Science, 11*(5), 597–605. https://doi.org/10.1177/1745691616639283

Høglend, P. (1999). Psychotherapy research: New findings and implications for training and practice. *The Journal of Psychotherapy Practice and Research, 8*(4): 257–263.

Holmes M. V., Newcombe P., Hubacek J. A., Sofat R., Ricketts, S. L., Cooper, J., Breteler, M. M. B., Bautista, L. E., Sharma, P., Whittaker, J. C., Smeeth, L., Fowkes, F. G. R., Algra, A., Shmeleva, V., Szolnoki, Z., Roest, M., Linnebank, M., Zacho, J., Nalls, M. A., Singleton, A. B., . . . Casas, J. P. (2011). Effect modification by population dietary folate on the association between *MTHFR* genotype, homocysteine, and stroke risk: A meta-analysis of genetic studies and randomised trials. *The Lancet, 378*(9791), 584–594. https://doi.org/10.1016/S0140-6736(11)60872-6

Holtmann, J., Herbort, M. C., Wüstenberg, T., Soch, J., Richter, S., Walter, H., Roepke, S., & Schott, B. H. (2013). Trait anxiety modulates fronto-limbic processing of emotional interference in borderline personality disorder. *Frontiers in Human Neuroscience, 7*, Article 54. https://doi.org/10.3389/fnhum.2013.00054

Hornung, J. P. (2003). The human raphe nuclei and the serotonergic system. *Journal of Chemical Neuroanatomy, 26*, 331–343.

Horvath K., Papadimitriou J. C., Rabsztyn A., Drachenberg C., & Tildon J. T. (1999). Gastrointestinal abnormalities in children with autistic disorder. *Journal of Pediatrics, 135*, 559–563.

Hosie, S., Ellis, M., Swaminathan, M., Ramalhosa, F., Seger, G. O., Balasuriya, G. K., Gillberg, C., Råstam, M., Churilov, L., McKeown, S. J., Yalcinkaya, N., Urvil, P., Savidge, T., Bell, C. A., Bodin, O., Wood, J., Franks, A. E., Bornstein, J. C., & Hill-Yardin, E. L. (2019). Gastrointestinal dysfunction in patients and mice expressing the autism-associated R451C mutation in neuroligin-3. *Autism Research, 12*, 1043–1056. https://doi.org/10.1002/aur.2127

Howard, R. (Director). (2001). *A beautiful mind* [Film]. Universal Studios; Dreamworks Pictures; Imagine Entertainment.

Huang, T. T., Lai, J. B., Du, Y. L., Xu, Y., Ruan, L. M., & Hu, S. H. (2019). Current understanding of gut microbiota in mood disorders: An update of human studies. *Frontiers in Genetics, 10*, Article 98. https://doi.org/10.3389/fgene.2019.00098

Human Microbiome Project Consortium. (2012). Structure, function and diversity of the healthy human microbiome. *Nature, 486*, 207–214. https://doi.org/10.1038/nature11234

Hunter, S., Hurley, R. A., & Taber, K. H. (2013). A look inside the mirror neuron system. *The Journal of Neuropsychiatry and Clinical Neurosciences, 25*(3), vi–175.

Hurwitz, T. A. (2001). Depression, anxiety, and psychosis in Parkinson's disease. *British Columbia Medical Journal, 43*(4), 214–218.

Iacoboni, M. (2007). Face to face: The neural basis of social mirroring and empathy. *Psychiatric Annals, 37*(4), 236–241.

Iacoboni, M. (2008). *Mirroring people: The new science of how we connect with others.* Farrar, Straus and Giroux.

Iacoboni, M., Molnar-Szakacs, I., Gallese, V., Buccino, G., Mazziotta, J. C., & Rizzolatti, G. (2005). Grasping the intentions of others with one's own mirror neuron system. *PLoS Biology, 3*, e79, https://doi.org/10.1371/journal.pbio.0030079

Iacoboni, M., Woods, R. P., Brass, M., Bekkering, H., Mazziotta, J. C., & Rizzolatti, G. (1999). Cortical mechanisms of human imitation. *Science, 286*(5449), 2526–2528. https://doi.org/10.1126/science.286.5449.2526

Ianì, F. (2019). Embodied memories: Reviewing the role of the body in memory processes. *Psychonomic Bulletin & Review, 26*, 1747–1766. https://doi.org/10.3758/s13423-019-01674-x

Ibanez-Casas, I., & Cervilla, J. A. (2012). Neuropsychological research in delusion disorder: A comprehensive review. *Psychopathology, 45*, 84–101.

International Human Genome Sequencing Consortium. (2004). Finishing the euchromatic sequence of the human genome. *Nature, 431*(7011), 931–945. https://doi.org/10.1038/nature03001

International Society for the Study of Trauma and Dissociation. (2011). Guidelines for treating dissociative identity disorder in adults, third revision. *Journal of Trauma & Dissociation, 12*(2), 115–187. https://doi.org/10.1080/15299732.2011.537247

Isay, J. (2008). *Walking on eggshells: Navigating the delicate relationship between adults, children, and parents.* Anchor.

Jacob, F., and Monod, J. (1961). Genetic regulatory mechanisms in the synthesis of proteins. *Journal of Molecular Biology, 3*, 318–356. https://doi.org/10.1016/s0022-2836(61)80072-7

Jacob, G. A., Zvonik, K., Kamphausen, S., Sebastian, A., Maier, S., Philipsen, A., Tebartz van Elst, L., Lieb, K., & Tüscher, O. (2013). Emotional modulation of motor response inhibition in women with borderline personality disorder: An fMRI study. *Journal of Psychiatry & Neuroscience, 38*, 164–172. https://doi.org/10.1503/jpn.120029

Jaffe, E. (2007). Mirror neurons: How we reflect on behavior. *Observer, 20*(5). https://www.psychologicalscience.org/observer/mirror-neurons-how-we-reflect-on-behavior

Jahnke, R., Larkey, L., Rogers, C., Etnier, J., & Lin, F. (2010). A comprehensive review of health benefits of qigong and tai chi. *American Journal of Health Promotion, 24*(6), e1–e25. https://doi.org/10.4278/ajhp.081013-LIT-248

Jahshan, C., Rassovsky, Y., & Green, M. F. (2017). Enhancing neuroplasticity to augment cognitive remediation in schizophrenia. *Frontiers in Psychiatry, 8*, Article 191. https://doi.org/10.3389/fpsyt.2017.00191

Jäkel, S., & Dimou, L. (2017). Glial cells and their function in the adult brain: A journey through the history of their ablation. *Frontiers in Cellular Neuroscience, 11,* Article 24. https://doi.org/10.3389/fncel.2017.00024

James, W. (1890). *The principles of psychology.* Dover.

Janiri, D., Moser, D. A., Doucet, G. E., Luber, M. J., Rasgon, A., Lee, W. H., Murrough, J. W., Sani, G., Eickhoff, S. B., & Frangou. S. (2019). Shared neural phenotypes for mood and anxiety disorders: A meta-analysis of 226 task-related functional imaging studies. *JAMA Psychiatry, 77*(2), 172–179. https://www.doi.org/10.1001/jamapsychiatry.2019.3351

Jankord, R., & Herman, J. P. (2008). Limbic regulation of hypothalamo-pituitary-adrenocortical function during acute and chronic stress. *Annals of the New York Academy of Sciences, 1148,* 64–73. https://doi.org/10.1196/annals.1410.012

Jeffers, C. S. (2009). On empathy: The mirror neuron system and art education. *International Journal of Education and the Arts, 10*(15). http://www.ijea.org/v10n15

Jensen, P. S., Arnold, L. E., Swanson, J. M., Vitiello, B., Abikoff, H. B., Greenhill, L. L., Hechtman, L., Hinshaw, S. P., Pelham, W. E., Wells, K. C., Conners, C. K., Elliott, G. R., Epstein, J. N., Hoza, B., March, J. S., Molina, B., Newcorn, J. H., Severe, J. B., Wigal, T., Gibbons, R. D., . . . Hur, K. (2007). 3-year follow-up of the NIMH MTA study. *Journal of the American Academy of Child and Adolescent Psychiatry, 46*(8), 989–1002. https://doi.org/10.1097/CHI.0b013e3180686d48

Johns Hopkins Medicine. (n.d.). The brain-gut connection. Retrieved August 2020 from https://www.hopkinsmedicine.org/health/wellness-and-prevention/the-brain-gut-connection

Johnson, M., Jones, E., & Gliga, T. (2015). Brain adaptation and alternative developmental trajectories. *Development and Psychopathology, 27*(2), 425–442. https://doi.org/10.1017/S0954579415000073

Junichiro, H., & Fumihiko, Y. (2003). Hypothesis: Respiratory sinus arrhythmia is an intrinsic resting function of cardiopulmonary system. *Cardiovascular Research, 58*(1), 1–9. https://doi.org/10.1016/S0008-6363(02)00851-9

Kagan, J. (2018). *Galen's prophecy: Temperament in human nature.* Routledge. (Original work published 1998)

Kaltenboeck, A., & Harmer, C. (2018). The neuroscience of depressive disorders: A brief review of the past and some considerations about the future. *Brain and Neuroscience Advances, 2.* https://doi.org/10.1177/2398212818799269

Kandel, E. R. (1998). A New Intellectual Framework for Psychiatry, *American Journal of Psychiatry, 155*(4), 457–469. https://doi.org/10.1176/ajp.155.4.457

Kandel, E. R., Schwartz, J. H., Jessell, T. M., Siegelbaum, A., & Hudspeth, A. J. (Eds.). (2012). *Principles of neural science* (5th ed.). McGraw-Hill.

Kang, D., Adams, J. B., Gregory, A. C., Borody, T., Chittick, L., Fasano, A., Khoruts, A., Geis, E., Maldonado, J., McDonough-Means, S., Pollard, E. L., Roux, S., Sadowsky, M. J., Schwarzberg Lipson, K., Sullivan, M. B., Caporaso, J. G., & Rajmalnik-Brown, R.

(2017). Microbiota transfer therapy alters gut ecosystem and improves gastrointestinal and autism symptoms: An open-label study. *Microbiome, 5*(1):10. https://doi.org/10.1186/s40168-016-0225-7

Kang, J., Daines, J. R., Warren, A. N., & Cowan M. L. (2019). Epigenetics for the 21st-century biology student. *Journal of Microbiology & Biology Education, 20*(3), 1–5. https://doi.org/10.1128/jmbe.v20i3.1687

Kashou, A. H., Basit, H., & Chhabra, L. (2019, June 23). Physiology, sinoatrial node (SA node). *StatPearls* [Internet]. https://www.ncbi.nlm.nih.gov/books/NBK459238

Keltner, D., & Anderson, C. (2000). Saving face for Darwin: The functions and uses of embarrassment. *Current Directions in Psychological Science, 9*(6), 187–192.

Kettenmann, H., Backus, K. H., & Schachner, M. (1984). Aspartate, glutamate and gamma-aminobutyric acid depolarize cultured astrocytes. *Neuroscience Letters, 52*(1–2), 25–9. https://doi.org/10.1177/1073858411403317

Kidd, C., & Hayden, B. Y. (2015). The psychology and neuroscience of curiosity. *Neuron, 88,* 449–460. https://doi.org/10.1016/j.neuron.2015.09.010

Kilgus, M. D., Maxmen, J. S., & Ward, N. G. (2016). *Essential psychopathology & its treatment* (4th Ed.). W. W. Norton.

Kiliaan, A. J., Saunders, P. R., Bijlsma, P. B., Berin, M. C., Taminiau, J. A., Groot, J. A., & Perdue, M. H. (1998). Stress stimulates transepithelial macromolecular uptake in rat jejunum. *American Journal of Physiology, 275,* G1037–G1044. https://doi.org/10.1152/ajpgi.1998.275.5.G1037

Killgus, M. D., Maxmen, J. S., & Ward, N. G. (2015). *Essential psychopathology and its treatment* (4th ed.). W. W. Norton.

Kino, T. (2015). Stress, glucocorticoid hormones, and hippocampal neural progenitor cells: implications to mood disorders. *Frontiers in Physiology, 6,* Article 230. https://doi.org/10.3389/fphys.2015.00230

Kirsch, I., & Hyland, M. (1987). How thoughts affect the body: A metatheoretical framework. *The Journal of Mind and Behavior, 8*(3), 417–434. http://www.jstor.org/stable/43853418

Kitamura, T., Ogawa, S. K., Roy, D. S., Okuyama, T., Morrissey, M. D., Smith, L. M., Redondo, R. L., & Tonegawa, S. (2017). Engrams and circuits crucial for systems consolidation of a memory. *Science, 356*(6333), 73–78. https://doi.org/10.1126/science.aam6808

Kleitman, N. (1957). Sleep, wakefulness, and consciousness. *Psychological Bulletin, 54,* 354–359.

Kleitman, N. (1982). Basic rest-activity cycle—22 years later. *Sleep, 5,* 311–317.

Knowles, E. (Ed.). (1999). *Oxford dictionary of quotations.* Oxford University Press, p. 290.

Knutson, B., Adams, C. M., Fong, G. W., & Hommer, D. (2001). Anticipation of increasing monetary reward selectively recruits nucleus accumbens. *The Journal of Neuroscience, 21*(16). https://www.jneurosci.org/content/21/16/RC159

Koenen, K. C., Ratanatharathorn, A., Ng, L., McLaughlin, K. A., Bromet, E. J., Stein, D.

J., Karam, E. G., Meron Ruscio, A., Benjet, C., Scott, K., Atwoli, L., Petukhova, M., Lim, C., Aguilar-Gaxiola, S., Al-Hamzawi, A., Alonso, J., Bunting, B., Ciutan, M., de Girolamo, G., Degenhardt, L., . . . Kessler, R. C. (2017). Posttraumatic stress disorder in the World Mental Health Surveys. *Psychological Medicine, 47*(13), 2260–2274. https://doi .org/10.1017/S0033291717000708

Kok, B. E., Coffey, K. A., Cohn, M. A., Catalino, L. I., Vacharkulksemsuk. T., Algoe, S. B., Brantley, M., & Fredrickson, B. L. (2013). How positive emotions build physical health: Perceived positive social connections account for the upward spiral between positive emotions and vagal tone. *Psychological Science, 24,* 1123–1132. https://doi.org/10 .1177/0956797612470827

Konikowska, K., Regulska-Ilow, B., & Rózańska, D. (2012). The influence of components of diet on the symptoms of ADHD in children. *Roczniki Panstwowego Zakladu Higieny, 63*(2), 127–134.

Konrad, K., and Eickhoff, S. B. (2010). Is the ADHD brain wired differently? A review on structural and functional connectivity in attention deficit hyperactivity disorder. *Human Brain Mapping, 31*(6), 904–916. https://doi.org/10.1002/hbm.21058

Kottmeier, R., Bittern, J., Schoofs, A., Scheiwe, F., Matzat, T., Pankratz, M., & Klambt, C. (2020). Wrapping glia regulates neuronal signaling speed and precision in the peripheral nervous system of *Drosophila. Nature Communications, 11,* Article 4491. https://doi.org/10 .1038/s41467-020-18291-1

Kregel, J., Meeus, M., Malfliet, A., Dolphens, M., Dannels, L., Nijs, J., & Cagnie, B. (2015). Structural and functional brain abnormalities in chronic low back pain: A systematic review. *Seminars in Arthritis and Rheumatism, 45*(2), 229–237. https://doi.org/10.1016/j .semarthrit.2015.05.002

Kriaucionis, S., & Bird, A. (2003). DNA methylation and Rett syndrome. *Human Molecular Genetics, 12*(Suppl. 2), R221–R227. https://doi.org/10.1093/hmg/ddg286

Kurtz, R. (2009). *A little history: Beginnings: Eastern philosophy, psychotherapeutic technique, and systems theory.* Ron Kurtz Hakomi Educational Materials: History of the Hakomi Method. http://hakomi.com/history

Laborde, S., Mosley, E., & Thayer, J. F. (2017). Heart rate variability and cardiac vagal tone in psychophysiological research: Recommendations for experiment planning, data anal-ysis, and data reporting. *Frontiers in Psychology, 8,* Article 213. https://doi.org/10.3389/ fpsyg.2017.00213

Lacal, I., & Ventura, R. (2018). Epigenetic inheritance: Concepts, mechanisms and per-spectives. *Frontiers in Molecular Neuroscience, 11,* Article 292. https://doi.org/10.3389/ fnmol.2018.00292

Lach, G., Schellekens, H., Dinan, T. G., & Cryan, J. F. (2018). Anxiety, depression, and the microbiome: A role for gut peptides. *Neurotherapeutics, 15,* 36–59. https://doi.org/10.1007/ s13311-017-0585-0

Lam, J. K. W., Chow, M. Y. T., Zhang, Y., & Leung, S. W. S. (2015). siRNA versus miRNA as therapeutics for gene silencing. *Molecular Therapy—Nucleic Acids, 4*, Article e252. https://doi.org/10.1038/mtna.2015.23

Lambert, M., Benmoussa, A., & Provost, P. (2019). Small non-coding RNAs derived from eukaryotic ribosomal RNA. *Non-Coding RNA, 5*(1), 16. https://doi.org/10.3390/ncrna5010016

Lambert, M. J., & Barley, D. E. (2001). Research summary on the therapeutic relationship and psychotherapy outcome. *Psychotherapy, 38*(4), 357–361. https://doi.org/10.1037/0033-3204.38.4.357

Lamm, C., & Majdandžić, J. (2015). The role of shared neural activations, mirror neurons, and morality in empathy: A critical comment. *Neuroscience Research, 90*, 15–24. https://doi.org/10.1016/j.neures.2014.10.008

Lamy, D., Salti, M., & Bar-Haim, Y. (2009). Neural correlates of subjective awareness and unconscious processing: An ERP study. *Journal of Cognitive Neuroscience, 21*(7), 1435–1446. https://doi.org/10.1162/jocn.2009.21064

Lane, A. M., & Godfrey, R. (2010). Emotional and cognitive changes during and post a near fatal heart attack and one-year after: A case study. *Journal of Sports Science & Medicine, 9*(3), 517–522.

Laneri, D., Schuster, V., Dietsche, B., Jansen, A., Ott, U., & Sommer, J. (2016). Effects of long-term mindfulness meditation on brain's white matter microstructure and its aging. *Frontiers in Aging Neuroscience, 7*, Article 254. https://doi.org/10.3389/fnagi.2015.00254

Langley, K., Rice, F., van den Bree, M. B., & Thapar, A. (2005). Maternal smoking during pregnancy as an environmental risk factor for attention deficit hyperactivity disorder behaviour: A review. *Minerva Pediatrica, 57*(6), 359–371.

Lanius, R. A., Frewen, P. A., Tursich, M., Jetly, R., & McKinnon, M. C. (2015). Restoring large-scale brain networks in PTSD and related disorders: A proposal for neuroscientifically-informed treatment interventions. *European Journal of Psychotraumatology, 6*, Article 27313. https://doi.org/10.3402/ejpt.v6.27313

Lazar, V., Ditu, L.-M., Gradisteanu Pircalabioru, G., Gheorghe, I., Curutiu, C., Holban, A. M., Picu, A., Petcu, L., & M. C. Chifiriuc. (2018). Aspects of gut microbiota and immune system interactions in infectious diseases, immunopathology, and cancer. *Frontiers in Immunology, 9*, Article 1830. https://doi.org/10.3389/fimmu.2018.01830

Ledonne, A., & Mercuri, N. (2017). Current concepts on the physiopathological relevance of dopaminergic receptors. *Frontiers in Cellular Neuroscience, 11*, Article 27. https://doi.org/10.3389/fncel.2017.00027

LeDoux, J. E. (2003). *Synaptic self: How our brains become who we are.* Penguin.

LeDoux, J. E. (2019). *The deep history of ourselves: The four-billion-year story of how we got conscious brains.* Viking.

LeDoux, J. E. (2020). Thoughtful feelings. *Current Biology, 30*, R1–R5.

LeDoux, J. E., & Brown, R. (2017). A higher-order theory of emotional consciousness. *Proceedings of the National Academy of Sciences of the United States of America, 114*(10), E2016–E2025. https://doi.org/10.1073/pnas.1619316114

Lee, E., Nam, Y., Kang, S., Choi, E., Kim, J., Kim, D., An, J., Lee, S., Lee, M. H., & Chung, J. (2020). The local hypothalamic–pituitary–adrenal axis in cultured human dermal papilla cells. *BMC Molecular and Cell Biology.* Advance online publication. https://doi.org/10.21203/rs.2.21076/v2

Lee, R., Corley, M. J., Pang, A., Arakaki, G., Abbott, L., Nishimoto, M., Miyamoto, R., Lee, E., Yamamoto, S., Maunakea, A. K., Lum-Jones, A., & Wong, M. (2018). A modified ketogenic gluten-free diet with MCT improves behavior in children with autism spectrum disorder. *Physiology & Behavior, 188,* 205–211. https://doi.org/10.1016/j.physbeh.2018.02.006

Lenzen, M. (2005). Feeling our emotions. *Scientific American Mind, 16*(1), 14–15. https://doi.org/10.1038/scientificamericanmind0405-14

Lester, B. M., Tronick, E., Nestler, E. J., & Abel, T. (2011). Behavioral epigenetics. *Annals of the New York Academy of Sciences, 1226*(1), 14–33. https://doi.org/10.1111/j.1749-6632.2011.06037.x

Levenson, J. M., & Sweatt, J. D. (2005). Epigenetic mechanisms in memory formation. *Nature Reviews Neuroscience, 6,* 108–118. https://doi.org/10.1038/nrn1604

Levine, P. A. (1997). *Walking the tiger: Healing trauma.* North Atlantic Books.

Lewis, M. D. (2005). Self-organising individual differences in brain development. *Developmental Review, 25,* 252–277.

Lewis, R., Asplin, K. E., Bruce, G., Dart, C., Mobasheri, A., & Barrett-Jolley, R. (2011). The role of the membrane potential in chondrocyte volume regulation. *Journal of Cellular Physiology, 226,* 2979–2986. https://doi.org/10.1002/jcp.22646

Ley, R. E., Peterson, D. A., & Gordon, J. I. (2006). Ecological and evolutionary forces shaping microbial diversity in the human intestine. *Cell, 124*(4), 837–848. https://doi.org/10.1016/j.cell.2006.02.017

Li, R., Ma, X., Wang, G., Yang, J., & Wang, C. (2016). Why sex differences in schizophrenia? *Journal of Translational Neuroscience, 1*(1), 37–42. https://journal.hep.com.cn/jtn/EN/10.3868/j.issn.2096-0689.01.006

Liang, S., Wu, X., & Jin, F. (2018). Gut-brain psychology: Rethinking psychology from the microbiota-gut-brain axis. *Frontiers in Integrative Neuroscience, 12,* Article 33. https://doi.org/10.3389/fnint.2018.00033

Liew, S. C., & Gupta, E. D. (2015). Methylenetetrahydrofolate reductase (MTHFR) C677T polymorphism: Epidemiology, metabolism and the associated diseases. *European Journal of Medical Genetics, 58*(1), 1–10. https://doi.org/10.1016/j.ejmg.2014.10.004

Lindauer, R. J., Vlieger, E. J., Jalink, M., Olff, M., Carlier, I. V., Majoie, C. B., Den Heeten, G. J., & Gersons, B. P. (2005). Effects of psychotherapy on hippocampal volume in out-patients with post-traumatic stress disorder: A MRI investigation. *Psychological Medicine*, 35(10), 1421–1431. https://doi.org/10.1017/S0033291705005246

Linden, D. E. J. (2006). How psychotherapy changes the brain: The contribution of functional neuroimaging. *Molecular Psychiatry*, 11, 528–538. https://doi.org/10.1038/sj.mp.4001816

Linnet, K. M., Dalsgaard, S., Obel, C., Wisborg, K., Henriksen, T. B., Rodriguez, A., Kotimaa, A., Moilanen, I., Thomsen, P. H., Olsen, J., & Jarvelin, M. R. (2003). Maternal lifestyle factors in pregnancy risk of attention deficit hyperactivity disorder and associated behaviors: Review of the current evidence. *The American Journal of Psychiatry*, 160(6), 1028–1040. https://doi.org/10.1176/appi.ajp.160.6.1028

Lipps. T. (1903). Einfühlung, innere Nachahmung und Organempfindungen. *Archive für die gesamte Psychologie*, 3(Heft 2–3), 185–204.

Locher, C., Meier, S., & Gaab, J. (2019). Psychotherapy: A world of meanings. *Frontiers in Psychology*, 10, Article 460. https://doi.org/10.3389/fpsyg.2019.00460

Lopetuso, L. R., Scaldaferri, F., Petito, V., & Gosbarrini, A. (2013). Commensal clostridia: Leading players in the maintenance of gut homeostasis. *Gut Pathogens*, 5, 23. https://doi.org/10.1186/1757-4749-5-23

Luber, M., & Shapiro, F. (2009). Interview with Francine Shapiro: Historical overview, present issues, and future directions of EMDR. *Journal of EMDR Practice and Research*, 3(4), 217–232.

Luo, S. X., & Huang, E. J. (2016). Dopaminergic neurons and brain reward pathways: From neurogenesis to circuit assembly. *The American Journal of Pathology*, 186(3), 478–488. https://doi.org/10.1016/j.ajpath.2015.09.023

MacKay, K. (2016, January 12). What ADHD feels like to me. *Understood by Us*. https://www.understood.org/en/young-adults/what-is-like/what-adhd-feels-like-to-me

Mahmoud, A. M., & Ali, M. M. (2019). Methyl donor micronutrients that modify DNA methylation and cancer outcome. *Nutrients*, 11(3), 608. https://doi.org/10.3390/nu11030608

Maloney, B. A. (2009). *Saving Sammy: A mother's fight to cure her son's OCD*. Crown Publishing.

Manning, J. S. (2010). Tools to improve differential diagnosis of bipolar disorder in primary care. *Primary Care Companion Journal of Clinical Psychiatry*, 12(Suppl. 1), 17–22.

Manning, C. E., Williams, E. S., & Robison, A. J. (2017). Reward Network Immediate Early Gene Expression in Mood Disorders. *Frontiers in Behavioral Neuroscience*, 11, Article 77. https://doi.org/10.3389/fnbeh.2017.00077

Marr, B. (2018, May 21). How much data do we create every day? The mind-blowing stats everyone should read. *Forbes*. https://www.forbes.com/sites/bernardmarr/2018/05/21/how-much-data-do-we-create-every-day-the-mind-blowing-stats-everyone-should-read/?sh=524d715460ba

Marteau, T. M., & Croyle, R. T. (1998). The new genetics: Psychological responses to genetic testing. *BMJ, 316*(7132), 693–696. https://doi.org/10.1136/bmj.316.7132.693

Mary, A., Dayan, J., Leone, G., Postel, C., Fraisse, F., Malle, C., Vallée, T., Klein-Peschanski, C., Viader, F., de la Sayette, V., Peschanski, D., Eustache, F., & Gagnepain, P. (2020). Resilience after trauma: The role of memory suppression. *Science, 367*(6479), Article eaay8477. https://doi.org/10.1126/science.aay8477

Maskos U. (2008). The cholinergic mesopontine tegmentum is a relatively neglected nicotinic master modulator of the dopaminergic system: relevance to drugs of abuse and pathology. *British journal of pharmacology, 153 Suppl 1*(Suppl 1), S438–S445. https://doi.org/10.1038/bjp.2008.5

Mason, P. T. T., & Kreger, R. (2010). *Stop walking on eggshells: Taking your life back when someone you care about has borderline personality disorder.* New Harbinger Publications.

Mason, W. A., & Capitanio, J. P. (2012). Basic emotions: A reconstruction. *Emotion Review, 4*(3), 238–244. https://doi.org/10.1177/1754073912439763

Maston, G. A., Evans, S. K., & Green, M. R. (2006). Transcriptional regulatory elements in the human genome. *Annual Review of Genomics and Human Genetics, 7*, 29–59. https://doi.org/10.1146/annurev.genom.7.080505.115623

Mathee, K., Cickovski, T., Deoraj, A., Stollstorff, M., & Narasimhan, G. (2020). The gut microbiome and neuropsychiatric disorders: Implications for attention deficit hyperactivity disorder (ADHD). *Journal of Medical Microbiology, 69*(1), 14–24. https://doi.org/10.1099/jmm.0.001112

Mawe, G. M., & Hoffman, J. M. (2013). Serotonin signalling in the gut: Functions, dysfunctions and therapeutic targets. *Nature Reviews Gastroenterology & Hepatology, 10*(8), 473–486. https://doi.org/10.1038/nrgastro.2013.105

Maxmen, J. S., Ward, N. G., & Kilgus, M. D. (2009). *Essential psychopathology and its treatment* (3rd ed.). W. W. Norton.

May A. (2008). Chronic pain may change the structure of the brain. *Pain, 137*, 7–15.

Mayer, E. A. (2011). Gut feelings: The emerging biology of gut-brain communication. *Nature Reviews Neuroscience, 12*(8), 453–466. https://doi.org/10.1038/nrn3071

Mayer, E. A., Knight, R., Mazmanian, S. K., Cryan, J. F., & Tillisch, K. (2014). Gut microbes and the brain: Paradigm shift in neuroscience. *The Journal of Neuroscience, 34*(46), 15490–15496. https://doi.org/10.1523/JNEUROSCI.3299-14.2014

McCrae, R. R., & Oliver P. J. (1992). An introduction to the five-factor model and its applications. *Journal of Personality, 60*(2), 175–215.

McCraty, R. (2014). Heart-brain neurodynamics: The making of emotions. *The Neuropsychotherapist, 6*, 68–89.

McCraty, R. (2017). New frontiers in heart rate variability and social coherence research: Techniques, technologies, and implications for improving group dynamics and outcomes. *Frontiers in Public Health, 5*, Article 267. https://doi.org/10.3389/fpubh.2017.00267

McEwen, B. S. (2000). Allostasis and allostatic load: Implications for neuropsychopharmacology. *Neuropsychopharmacology, 22,* 108–124. https://doi.org/10.1016/S0893-133X(99)00129-3

McEwen, B. S. (2005). Stressed or stressed out: What is the difference? *Journal of Psychiatry & Neuroscience, 30*(5), 315–318.

McEwen, B. S., & Akil, H. (2020). Revisiting the stress concept: Implications for affective disorders. *The Journal of Neuroscience, 40*(1), 12–21. https://doi.org/10.1523/jneurosci.0733-19.2019

McGilchrist, I. (2009). *The master and his emissary: The divided brain and the making of the Western world.* Yale University Press.

McGowan, P. O., Sasaki, A., D'Alessio, A. C., Dymov, S., Labonté, B., Szyf, M., Turecki, G., & Meaney, M. J. (2009). Epigenetic regulation of the glucocorticoid receptor in human brain associates with childhood abuse. *Nature Neuroscience, 12*(3), 342–348. https://doi.org/10.1038/nn.2270

McGowan, P. O., & Szyf, M. (2010). The epigenetics of social adversity in early life: Implications for mental health outcomes. *Neurobiology of Disease, 39*(1), 66–72. https://doi.org/10.1016/j.nbd.2009.12.026.

McNorgan, C., Judson, C., Handzlik, D., & Holden, J. G. (2020). Linking ADHD and behavioral assessment through identification of shared diagnostic task-based functional connections. *Frontiers in Physiology, 11,* Article 583005. https://doi.org/10.3389/fphys.2020.583005

Meaney, M. J., & Szyf, M. (2005). Maternal care as a model for experience-dependent chromatin plasticity? *Trends in Neuroscience, 28*(9), 456–463.

Meares, R. (2012). *A dissociation model of borderline personality disorder.* W. W. Norton.

Meiser, B. (2005). Psychological impact of genetic testing for cancer susceptibility: An update of the literature. *Psycho-Oncology, 14*(12), 1060–1074.

Mental Health Foundation. (n.d.). *Iain's story: How school affected my mental health.* https://www.mentalhealth.org.uk/stories/iains-story-how-school-affected-my-mental-health

Merola, A., Romagnolo, A., Rizzi, L., Rizzone, M. G., Zibetti, M., Lanotte, M., Mandybur, G., Duker, A. P., Espay, A. J., & Lopiano, L. (2017). Impulse control behaviors and subthalamic deep brain stimulation in Parkinson disease. *Journal of Neurology, 264*(1), 40–48. https://doi.org/10.1007/s00415-016-8314-x

Michael, T., Ehlers, A., Halligan, S. L., & Clark, D. M. (2005). Unwanted memories of assault: What intrusion characteristics are associated with PTSD? *Behaviour Research and Therapy, 43*(5), 613–628. https://doi.org/10.1016/j.brat.2004.04.006

Michels, K., Dubaz, O., Hornthal, E., & Bega, D. (2018). "Dance therapy" as a psychotherapeutic movement intervention in Parkinson's disease. *Complementary Therapies in Medicine, 40,* 248–252. https://doi.org/10.1016/j.ctim.2018.07.005.

Mierau, S. B., & Neumeyer, A. M. (2019). Metabolic interventions in Autism Spectrum Disorder. *Neurobiology of Disease, 132*, 104544. https://doi.org/10.1016/j.nbd.2019.104544

Migeon, B. R. (2020). X-linked diseases: Susceptible females. *Genetics in Medicine, 22*, 1156–1174. https://doi.org/10.1038/s41436-020-0779-4

Miller, A. L. (2003). The methionine-homocysteine cycle and its effects on cognitive diseases. *Alternative Medicine Review, 8*(1), 7–19.

Miller, G. A. (1956). The magical number seven, plus or minus two: Some limits on our capacity for processing information. *Psychological Review, 63*, 81–97.

Miller, S. D. (2018, November 2). What works in psychotherapy? Valuing "what works" rather than working with what we value. https://www.scottdmiller.com/what-works-in-psychotherapy-valuing-what-works-rather-than-working-with-what-we-value

Miller, S. D. (2019, May 6). How does feedback informed treatment work? I'm not surprised. https://www.scottdmiller.com/how-does-feedback-informed-treatment-work

Miller, S. D., Duncan, B. L., Brown, G. S., & Chalk, M. B. (2006). Using formal client feedback to improve retention and outcome. *Journal of Brief Therapy, 5*(1), 5–22.

Miller, S. D., Hubble, M. A., Chow, D., & Seidel, J. (2014). The outcome of psychotherapy: Yesterday, today and tomorrow. *Psychotherapy in Australia, 20*(3), 64–75.

Missio, G., Moreno, D. H., Demetrio, F. N., Soeiro-de-Souza, M. G., dos Santos Fernandes, F., Boschesi Barros, V., & Moreno, R. A. (2019). A randomized controlled trial comparing lithium plus valproic acid versus lithium plus carbamazepine in young patients with type 1 bipolar disorder: The LICAVAL study. *Trials, 20*, 608. https://doi.org/10.1186/s13063-019-3655-2

Mitchell, M. (2011). *Complexity: A guided tour.* Oxford University Press.

Molina, B. S. G., Hinshaw, S. P., Swanson, J. M., Arnold, L. E., Vitiello, B., Jensen, P. S., Epstein, J. N., Hoza, B., Hechtman, L., Abikoff, H. B., Elliott, G. R., Greenhill, L. L., Newcorn, J. H., Wells, K. C., Wigal, T., Gibbons, R. D., Hur, K., Houck, P. R., & The MTA Cooperative Group. (2009). The MTA at 8 years: Prospective follow-up of children treated for combined-type ADHD in a multisite study. *Journal of the American Academy of Child & Adolescent Psychiatry, 48*(5), 484–500. https://doi.org/10.1097/CHI.0b013e31819c23d0

Monkhouse, S. (2006). *Cranial nerves: Functional anatomy.* Cambridge University Press.

Montag, C., & Panksepp, J. (2017). Primary emotional systems and personality: An evolutionary perspective. *Frontiers in Psychology, 8*, Article 464. https://doi.org/10.3389/fpsyg.2017.00464

Monteiro, D. A., Taylor, E. W., Sartori, M. R., Cruz, A. L., Rantin, F. T., Leite, C. A. C. (2018). Cardiorespiratory interactions previously identified as mammalian are present in the primitive lungfish. *Science Advances, 4*(2), Article eaaq0800. https://doi.org/10.1126/sciadv.aaq0800

Monteiro-Haig, M. (2017a). The gut as a key player in neuroscience. *The Neuropsychotherapist*, 5(4), 16–31.

Monteiro-Haig, M. (2017b). Understanding PANS & PANDAS: The interplay of immune system and mental health. *The Neuropsychotherapist*, 5(12), 6–14.

Montiel-Castro, A. J., Gonzalez-Cervantes, R. M., Bravo-Ruiseco, R., & Pacheco-Lopez, G. (2013). The microbiota-gut-brain axis: Neurobehavioral correlates, health and sociality. *Frontiers in Integrative Neuroscience*, 7, Article 70. https://doi.org/10.3389/fnint.2013.00070

Morgan, O. J. (2019). *Addiction, attachment, trauma and recovery: The power of connection*. W. W. Norton.

Mort, M., Ivanov, D., Cooper, D. N., & Chuzhanova, N. A. (2008). A meta-analysis of nonsense mutations causing human genetic disease. *Human Mutation*, 29, 1037–1047. https://doi.org/10.1002/humu.20763

Moss, R. A. (2007). Negative emotional memories in clinical treatment: Theoretical considerations. *Journal of Psychotherapy Integration*, 17(2), 209–224.

Moss, R. A. (2013). Psychotherapy and the brain: The dimensional systems model and clinical biopsychology. *The Journal of Mind and Behavior*, 34(1), 63–89.

Moss, R. A. (2016). The hippocampus and memory: The binding of parallel cortical circuits. *The Neuropsychotherapist*, 4(2), 16–19.

Moss, R. A. (2020a). *Psychotherapy in pain management: New perspectives and treatment approaches based on a brain model*. Cambridge Scholars Publishing.

Moss, R. A. (2020b). Psychotherapy in pain management: New viewpoints and treatment targets based on a brain theory. *AIMS Neuroscience*, 7(3), 194–270. https://doi.org/10.3934/Neuroscience.2020013

Moynihan, J. A., Chapman, B. P., Klorman, R., Krasner, M. S., Duberstein, P. R., Brown, K. W., & Talbot, N. L. (2013). Mindfulness-based stress reduction for older adults: Effects on executive function, frontal alpha asymmetry and immune function. *Neuropsychobiology*, 68(1), 34–43. https://doi.org/10.1159/000350949

MTA Cooperative Group. (1999a). A 14-month randomized clinical trial of treatment strategies for attention-deficit/hyperactivity disorder. *Archives of General Psychiatry*, 56(12), 1073–1086. https://doi.org/10.1001/archpsyc.56.12.1073

MTA Cooperative Group. (1999b). Moderators and mediators of treatment response for children with attention-deficit/hyperactivity disorder: The Multimodal Treatment Study of Children With Attention-Deficit/Hyperactivity Disorder. (1999a). *Archives of General Psychiatry*, 56(12), 1088–1096. https://doi.org/10.1001/archpsyc.56.12.1088

MTA Cooperative Group. (2004a). National Institute of Mental Health Multimodal Treatment Study of ADHD follow-up: Changes in effectiveness and growth after the end of treatment. *Pediatrics*, 113(4), 762–769. https://doi.org/10.1542/peds.113.4.762

MTA Cooperative Group. (2004b). National Institute of Mental Health Multimodal Treatment Study of ADHD follow-up: 24-month outcomes of treatment strategies for attention-deficit/hyperactivity disorder. *Pediatrics, 113*(4), 754–761. https://doi.org/10.1542/peds.113.4.754

Mughal, S., Faizy, R. M., & Saadabadi, A. (2020, November 18). Autism spectrum disorder. *StatPearls* [Internet]. https://www.ncbi.nlm.nih.gov/books/NBK525976

Munoz-Bellido, J. L., Munoz-Criado, S., & Garcia-Rodriguez, J. A. (2000). Antimicrobial activity of psychotropic drugs: Selective serotonin reuptake inhibitors. *International Journal of Antimicrobial Agents, 14*, 177–180.

Nader, K., & Hardt, O. (2009). A single standard for memory: The case for reconsolidation. *Nature Reviews Neuroscience, 10*(3), 224–234. https://doi.org/10.1038/nrn2590

Nagai, N., Hamada, T., Kimura, T., & Moritani, T. (2004). Moderate physical exercise increases cardiac autonomic nervous system activity in children with low heart rate variability. *Child's Nervous System, 20*, 209–214. https://doi.org/10.1007/s00381-004-0915-5

Namgung, E., Kim, M., & Yoon, S. (2019). Repetitive transcranial magnetic stimulation in trauma-related conditions. *Neuropsychiatric Disease and Treatment, 15*, 701–712. https://doi.org/10.2147/NDT.S189498

National Institute of Mental Health. (2017, November). *Any anxiety disorder.* https://www.nimh.nih.gov/health/statistics/any-anxiety-disorder.shtml

National Institutes of Health. (2017, May 23). New role discovered for the thalamus. *NIH Research Matters.* https://www.nih.gov/news-events/nih-research-matters/new-role-discovered-thalamus

Naumova, A. K., & Taketo, T. (Eds.). (2017). *Epigenetics in human reproduction and development.* WSPC. https://doi.org/10.1142/10146

Nazeer, A., Latif, F., Mondal, A., Azeem, M. W., & Greydanus, D. E. (2020). Obsessive-compulsive disorder in children and adolescents: Epidemiology, diagnosis and management. *Translational Pediatrics, 9*(Suppl. 1), S76–S93. https://doi.org/10.21037/tp.2019.10.02

Neander, K., & Skott, C. (2008). Bridging the gap—the co-creation of a therapeutic process: Reflections by parents and professionals on their shared experiences of early childhood interventions. *Qualitative Social Work, 7*(3), 289–309. https://doi.org/10.1177/1473325008093703

Nejati, R., Kovacic, D., & Slominski, A. (2013). Neuro-immune-endocrine functions of the skin: An overview. *Expert Review of Dermatology, 8*(6), 581–583. https://doi.org/10.1586/17469872.2013.856690

Nestler, E. J., & Hyman, S. E. (2002). Regulation of gene expression. In K. L. Davis, D. Charney, J. T. Coyle, & C. B. N. (Eds.), *Neuropsychopharmacology: The fifth generation of progress* (Chap. 17). American College of Neuropsychopharmacology. http://www.acnp.org/asset.axd?id=38de5fb3-17ef-47f2-a203-57080417d4ec

Nguyen, T. A., Lehr, A. W., & Roche, K. W. (2020). Neuroligins and neurodevelopmental disorders: X-linked genetics. *Frontiers in Synaptic Neuroscience, 12*, Article 33. https://doi.org/10.3389/fnsyn.2020.00033

Nicholson, A. A., Rabellino, D., Densmore, M., Frewen, P. A., Paret, C., Kluetsch, R., Schmahl, C., Théberge, J., Neufeld, R. W., McKinnon, M. C., Reiss, J., Jetly, R., & Lanius, R. A. (2017). The neurobiology of emotion regulation in posttraumatic stress disorder: Amygdala downregulation via real-time fMRI neurofeedback. *Human Brain Mapping, 38*(1), 541–560. https://doi.org/10.1002/hbm.23402

Nieratschker, V., Batra, A., & Fallgatter, A. J. (2013). Genetics and epigenetics of alcohol dependence. *Journal of Molecular Psychiatry, 1*, Article 11. https://doi.org/10.1186/2049 -9256-1-11

Nigg, J. T. (2008). ADHD, lead exposure and prevention: How much lead or how much evidence is needed? *Expert Review of Neurotherapeutics, 8*(4), 519–521. https://doi.org/10 .1586/14737175.8.4.519

Novick, D. M., & Swartz, H. A. (2019). Evidence-based psychotherapies for bipolar disorder. *Focus, 17*(3), 238–248. https://doi.org/10.1176/appi.focus.20190004

Numata, T., Gunfan, S., Takayama, S., Takahashi, S., Monma, Y., Kaneko, S., Kuroda, H., Tanaka, J., Kanemura, S., Nara, M., Kagaya, Y., Ishii, T., Yaegashi, N., Kohzuki, M., & Iwasaki, K. (2014). Treatment of posttraumatic stress disorder using the traditional Japanese herbal medicine saikokeishikankyoto: A randomized, observer-blinded, controlled trial in survivors of the great East Japan earthquake and tsunami. *Evidence-Based Complementary and Alternative Medicine, 2014*, Article 683293. https://doi.org/10 .1155/2014/683293

Nussinov, R., Tsai, C.-J., & Jang, H. (2019). Protein ensembles link genotype to phenotype. *PLOS Computational Biology, 15*(6), Article e1006648. https://doi.org/10.1371/journal.pcbi .1006648

Obeid, R. (2013). The metabolic burden of methyl donor deficiency with focus on the betaine homocysteine methyltransferase pathway. *Nutrients, 5*(9), 3481–3495. https://doi.org/10 .3390/nu5093481

O'Connor, D. (2006). Psychotic symptoms in the elderly: Assessment and management. *Australian Family Physician, 35*(3), 106–108.

Ogden, P., & Fisher, J. (2015). *Sensorimotor psychotherapy: Interventions for trauma and attachment.* W. W. Norton.

Ogden, P., Minton, K., & Pain, C. (2006). *Trauma and the body: A sensorimotor approach to psychotherapy.* W. W. Norton.

O'Keefe, J., & Dostrovsky, J. (1971). The hippocampus as a spatial map: Preliminary evidence from unit activity in the freely moving rat. *Brain Research, 34*, 171–175. https://doi.org/10 .1016/0006-8993(71)90358-1

Olden, K., Olden, H. A., & Lin, Y. (2015). The role of the epigenome in translating neighborhood disadvantage into health disparities. *Current Environmental Health Report, 2*, 163–170. https://doi.org/10.1007/s40572-015-0048-x

O'Mahony, S. M., Clarke, G., Borre, Y. E., Dinan, T. G., & Cryan, J. F. (2015). Serotonin, tryptophan metabolism and the brain-gut-microbiome axis. *Behavioural Brain Research*, *277*, 32–48. https://doi.org/10.1016/j.bbr.2014.07.027

Orgogozo, V., Morizot, B., & Martin, A. (2015). The differential view of genotype-phenotype relationships. *Frontiers in Genetics*, 6, Article 179. https://doi.org/10.3389/fgene.2015.00179

O'Sullivan, B. P., & Freedman, S. D. (2009). Cystic fibrosis. *The Lancet*, *373*(9678), 1891–1904. https://doi.org/10.1016/s0140-6736(09)60327-5

Pan, K., Kok, A., Eikelenboom, M., Horsfall, M., Jörg, F., Luteijn, R., Rhebergen, D., van Oppen, P., Giltay, E. J., & Phenninx, B. W. J. H. (2021). The mental health impact of the COVID-19 pandemic on people with and without depressive, anxiety, or obsessive-compulsive disorders: A longitudinal study of three Dutch case-control cohorts. *The Lancet. Psychiatry*, 8(2), 121–129. https://doi.org/10.1016/s2215-0366(20)30491-0

Panisch, L. S., & Hai, A. H. (2020). The effectiveness of using neurofeedback in the treatment of post-traumatic stress disorder: A systematic review. *Trauma Violence Abuse*, *21*(3), 541–550. https://doi.org/10.1177/1524838018781103

Panksepp, J. (1998). *Affective neuroscience: The foundations of human and animal emotions.* Oxford University Press.

Panksepp, J., and Biven, L. (2010). *The archaeology of mind: Neuroevolutionary origins of human emotion.* W. W. Norton.

Parfrey, L. W., Lahr, D. J. G., & Katz, L. A. (2008). The dynamic nature of eukaryotic genomes. *Molecular Biology and Evolution*, *25*(4), 787.

Parikshak, N. N., Luo, R., Zhang, A., Won, H., Lowe, J. K., Chandran, V., Horvath, S., & Geschwind, D. H. (2013). Integrative functional genomic analyses implicate specific molecular pathways and circuits in autism. *Cell*, *155*(5), 1008–1021. https://doi.org/10.1016/j.cell.2013.10.031

Park, K. (2015). Role of micronutrients in skin health and function. *Biomolecules & Therapeutics*, *23*(3), 207–217. https://doi.org/10.4062/biomolther.2015.003

Patestas, M. A., & Gartner, L. P. (Eds.). (2016). *A textbook of neuroanatomy* (2nd ed.). Wiley-Blackwell.

Paus, R., Theoharides, T. C., & Arck, P. C. (2006). Neuroimmunoendocrine circuitry of the "brain-skin connection." *Trends in Immunity*, *27*(1), 32–39.

Payer, B., Lee, J. T., & Namekawa, S. H. (2011). X-inactivation and X-reactivation: Epigenetic hallmarks of mammalian reproduction and pluripotent stem cells. *Human Genetics*, *130*(2), 265–280. https://doi.org/10.1007/s00439-011-1024-7

Payne, P., & Crane-Godreau, M. A. (2015). Preparatory set: A novel approach to understanding stress, trauma, and the bodymind therapies. *Frontiers in Human Neuroscience*, 9, Article 178. https://doi.org/10.3389/fnhum.2015.00178

Payne, P., Levine, P. A., & Crane-Godreau, M. A. (2015). Somatic experiencing: Using interoception and proprioception as core elements of trauma therapy. *Frontiers in Psychology*, 6, Article 93. https://doi.org/10.3389/fpsyg.2015.00093

Pellow, J., Solomon, E. M., & Barnard, C. N. (2011). Complementary and alternative medical therapies for children with attention-deficit/hyperactivity disorder (ADHD). *Alternative Medicine Review, 16*(4), 323–337.

Pelsser, L. M., Frankena, K., Toorman, J., & Rodrigues Pereira, R. (2017). Diet and ADHD, reviewing the evidence: A systematic review of meta-analyses of double-blind placebo-controlled trials evaluating the efficacy of diet interventions on the behavior of children with ADHD. *PLOS ONE, 12*(1), Article e0169277. https://doi.org/10.1371/journal.pone .0169277

Penke, Z., Morice, E., Veyrac, A., Gros, A., Chagneau, C., LeBlanc, P., Samson, N., Baumgärtel, K., Mansuy, I. M., Davis, S., & Laroche, S. (2014). Zif268/Egr1 gain of function facilitates hippocampal synaptic plasticity and long-term spatial recognition memory. *Philosophical Transactions of the Royal Society of London. Series B, Biological Sciences, 369*(1633), Article 20130159. https://doi.org/10.1098/rstb.2013.0159

Pfeifer, J. H., Iacoboni, M., Mazziotta, J. C., & Dapretto, M. (2008). Mirroring others' emotions relates to empathy and interpersonal competence in children. *NeuroImage, 39*(4), 2076–2085. https://doi.org/10.1016/j.neuroimage.2007.10.032

Pfeiffer, R. F. (2015). Non-motor symptoms in Parkinson's disease. *Parkinsonism & Related Disorders, 22*(Suppl. 1), S119–S122. https://doi.org/10.1016/j.parkreldis.2015.09.004

Picchioni, M. M., & Murray, R. M. (2007). Schizophrenia. *BMJ, 335*(7610), 91–95. https:// doi.org/10.1136/bmj.39227.616447.BE

The Picower Institute for Learning and Memory. (2014, December 10). Dr. Joseph LeDoux: Rethinging emotion [2012 Fall Symposium]. YouTube. https://www.youtube.com/ watch?v=qFcT0ZZLnUg

Pinel, P. J., & Barnes, S. J. (2014). *Introduction to biopsychology* (9th ed.). Pearson Education.

Piovesan, A., Antonaros, F., Vitale, L., Strippoli, P., Pelleri, M. C., & Caracausi, M. (2019). Human protein-coding genes and gene feature statistics in 2019. *BMC Research Notes, 12*(1), Article 315. https://doi.org/10.1186/s13104-019-4343-8

Pizzimenti, C. L., & Lattal, K. M. (2015). Epigenetics and memory: Causes, consequences and treatments for post-traumatic stress disorder and addiction. *Genes, Brain, and Behavior, 14*(1), 73–84. https://doi.org/10.1111/gbb.12187

Plank, J. L., & Dean, A. (2014). Enhancer function: Mechanistic and genome-wide insights come together. *Molecular Cell, 55*(1), 5–14. https://doi.org/10.1016/j.molcel.2014.06.015

Plutchik, R. (2001). The nature of emotions: Human emotions have deep evolutionary roots, a fact that may explain their complexity and provide tools for clinical practice. *American Scientist, 89*(4), 344–350. https://www.jstor.org/stable/27857503

Poduri, A., Evrony, G. D., Cai, X., & Walsh, C. A. (2013). Somatic mutation, genomic variation, and neurological disease. *Science, 341*(6141), Article 1237758. https://doi.org/10 .1126/science.1237758

Porges, S. W. (1992). Vagal tone: A physiologic marker of stress vulnerability. *Pediatrics, 90,* 498–504.

Porges, S. W. (1995). Orienting in a defensive world: Mammalian modifications of our evolutionary heritage: A polyvagal theory. *Psychophysiology, 32,* 301–318.

Porges, S. W. (2004). Neuroception: A subconscious system for detecting threats and safety. *Zero to Three, 24*(5), 19–24.

Porges, S. W. (2009). The polyvagal theory: New insights into adaptive reactions of the autonomic nervous system. *Cleveland Clinic Journal of Medicine, 76*(Suppl. 2), S86–S90. https://doi.org/10.3949/ccjm.76.s2.17

Porges, S. W. (2011). *Polyvagal theory: Neurophysiological foundations of emotions, attachment, communication, and self-regulation.* W. W. Norton.

Posar, A., & Visconti, P. (2019). Long-term outcome of autism spectrum disorder. *Turkish Archives of Pediatrics, 54*(4), 207–212. https://doi.org/10.14744/TurkPediatriArs.2019.16768

Posner, J., Marsh, R., Maia, T. V., Peterson, B. S., Gruber, A., & Simpson, H. B. (2014). Reduced functional connectivity within the limbic cortico-striato-thalamo-cortical loop in unmedicated adults with obsessive-compulsive disorder. *Human Brain Mapping, 35*(6), 2852–2860. https://doi.org/10.1002/hbm.22371

Poulton, R., Caspi, A., Moffitt, T. E., Cannon, M., Murray, R., & Harrington, H. (2000). Children's self-reported psychotic symptoms and adult schizophreniform disorder: A 15-year longitudinal study. *Archives of General Psychiatry, 57*(11), 1053–1058. https://doi.org/10.1001/archpsyc.57.11.1053

Pray, L. (2008). Discovery of DNA structure and function: Watson and Crick. *Nature Education, 1*(1), 100.

Prüfer, K., Munch, K., Hellmann, I., Akagi, K., Miller, J., Walenz, B., Koren, S., Sutton, G., Kodira, C., Winer, R., Knight, J., Mullikin, J., Meader, S., Ponting, C., Lunter, G., Higashino, S., Hobolth, A., Dutheil, J., Karakoç, E., Alkan, C., . . . Pääbo, S. (2012). The bonobo genome compared with the chimpanzee and human genomes. *Nature, 486*(7404), 527–531.

Psychotherapy Networker. (n.d.). *The secrets of supershrinks: Pathways to excellence.* https://www.scottdmiller.com/wp-content/uploads/2014/06/Supershrinks-Free-Report-1.pdf

Puri, N. (2012). A study on cutaneous manifestations of thyroid disease. *Indian Journal of Dermatology, 57*(3), 247–248. https://doi.org/10.4103/0019-5154.96227

Putnam, F. W. (2016). *The way we are: How states of mind influence our identities, personality and potential for change.* IP Books.

Qin, J., Li, R., Raes, J., Arumugam, M., Burgdorf, K. S., Manichanh, C., Nielsen, T., Pons, N., Levenez, F., Yamada, T., Mende, D. R., Li, J., Xu, J., Li, S., Li, D., Cao, J., Wang, B., Liang, H., Zheng, H., Xie, Y., . . . Wang, J. (2010). A human gut microbial gene catalogue established by metagenomic sequencing. *Nature, 464*(7285), 59–65. https://doi.org/10.1038/nature08821

Quina, A. S., Buschbeck, M., & Di Croce, L. (2006). Chromatin structure and epigenetics. *Biochemical Pharmacology, 72*(11), 1563–1569. https://doi.org/10.1016/j.bcp.2006.06.016

Ramachandran, V. S. (2000, May 31). *Mirror neurons and imitation learning as the driving force behind the great leap forward in human evolution.* Edge. http://www.edge.org/conversation/mirror-neurons-and-imitation-learning-as-the-driving-force-behind-the-great-leap-forward-in-human-evolution

Rao, M., & Gershon, M. D. (2016). The bowel and beyond: The enteric nervous system in neurological disorders. *Nature Reviews Gastroenterology & Hepatology, 13,* 517–528.

Rapinesi, C., Kotzalidis, G. D., Ferracuti, S., Sani, G., Girardi, P., & Del Casale, A. (2019). Brain stimulation in obsessive-compulsive disorder (OCD): A systematic review. *Current Neuropharmacology, 17*(8), 787–807. https://doi.org/10.2174/1570159X17666190409142555

Read, D. & Stoll, W. (2009). Healthy behavior: The implications of a holistic paradigm of thinking through bodymind research. In J. M. Black, S. R. Furney, H. M. Graf, & A. E. Nolte (Eds.), (pp. 145–168). John Wiley & Sons.

Rege, S. (2018, January 27). The dopamine hypothesis of schizophrenia: Advances in neurobiology and clinical application. *Psyche Scene Hub.* https://psychscenehub.com/psychinsights/the-dopamine-hypothesis-of-schizophrenia

Relman, D. A. (2012). The human microbiome: Ecosystem resilience and health. *Nutrition Reviews, 70*(Suppl. 1), S2–S9. https://doi.org/10.1111/j.1753-4887.2012.00489.x

Reuben, A., Sugden, K., Arseneault, L., Danese, A., Fisher, H., Moffitt, T., Newbury, J., Odgers, C., Prinze, J., Rasmussen, L., Williams, B., Mill, J., & Caspi, A. (2020). Association of neighborhood disadvantage in childhood with DNA methylation in young adulthood. *JAMA Network Open, 3*(6), Article e206095. https://doi.org/10.1001/jamanetworkopen.2020.6095

Revlin, R. (2012). *Cognition: Theory and practice.* Worth.

Rhee, S. H., Pothoulakis, C., & Mayer, E. A. (2009). Principles and clinical implications of the brain-gut-enteric microbiota axis. *Nature Reviews Gastroenterology & Hepatology, 6*(5), 306–314. https://doi.org/10.1038/nrgastro.2009.35

Riberio, S., Simões, C., & Nicolelis, M. (2008). Genes, sleep and dreams. In D. Lloyd & E. Rossi (Eds.), *Ultradian rhythms from molecule to mind* (pp. 413–430). Springer.

Ridley, M. (2003). *Nature via nurture: Genes, experience, and what makes us human.* Fourth Estate.

Ríos-Hernández, A., Alda, J. A., Farran-Codina, A., Ferreira-García, E., & Izquierdo-Pulido, M. (2017). The Mediterranean diet and ADHD in children and adolescents. *Pediatrics, 139*(2), Article e20162027. https://doi.org/10.1542/peds.2016-2027

Rizzolatti, G., & Craighero, L. (2004). The mirror-neuron system. *Annual Review of Neuroscience, 27,* 169–192. https://doi.org/10.1146/annurev.neuro.27.070203.144230

Robbins, T. W., Vaghi, M. M., & Banca, P. (2019). Obsessive-compulsive disorder: Puzzles and prospects. *Neuron, 102*(1), 27–47. https://doi.org/10.1016/j.neuron.2019.01.046

Rodriguez-Raecke, R., Niemeier, A., Ihle, K., Ruether, W., & May, A. (2013). Structural brain changes in chronic pain reflect probably neither damage nor atrophy. *PLOS ONE*, 8, Article e54475.

Rogers, C. R. (1951). *Client-centered therapy*. Houghton Mifflin.

Roisman, G., Padrón, E., Sroufe, L., & Egeland, B. (2002). Earned-secure attachment status in retrospect and prospect. *Child Development*, 73(4), 1204–1219. http://www.jstor.org/stable/3696280

Rose, G. M., & Tadi, P. (2020, November 19). Social anxiety disorder. *StatPearls* [Internet]. https://www.ncbi.nlm.nih.gov/books/NBK555890

Rosenberg, D. R., & Keshavan, M. S. (1998). Toward a neurodevelopmental model of obsessive–compulsive disorder. *Biological Psychiatry*, 43, 623–640. https://doi.org/10.1016/S0006-3223(97)00443-5

Rosenzweig, S. (1936). Some implicit common factors in diverse methods of psychotherapy. *American Journal of Orthopsychiatry*, 6(3), 412–415.

Ross, C. A., Miller, S. D., Reagor, P., Bjornson, L, Fraser, G. A., & Anderson, G. (1990). Structured interview data on 102 cases of multiple personality disorder from four centres. *The American Journal of Psychiatry*, 147, 596–601.

Rossi, E. L. (1985, December 11). *Facilitating "creative moments" in hypnotherapy* [Conference presentation]. The Evolution of Psychotherapy, Milton H. Erickson Foundation. https://www.erickson-foundation.org

Rossi, E. L. (1993). *The psychobiology of mind-body healing: New concepts of therapeutic hypnosis*. W. W. Norton.

Rossi, E. L. (2002). *The psychobiology of gene expression: Neuroscience and neurogenesis in hypnosis and the healing arts*. W. W. Norton.

Rossi, E. L. (2004). Art, truth, and beauty: The psychosocial genomics of consciousness, dreams, and brain growth in psychotherapy and mind-body healing. *Annals of the American Psychotherapy Association*, 7(3), 10–17.

Rossi, E. L., & Cheek, D. B. (1988). *Mind-body therapy: Ideodynamic healing in hypnosis*. W. W. Norton.

Rossi, E. L., & Lippincott, B. M. (1992). The wave nature of being: Ultradian rhythms and mind-body communication. In D. Lloyd & E. L. Rossi (Eds.), *Ultradian rhythms in life processes* (pp. 371–402). Springer. https://doi.org/10.1007/978-1-4471-1969-2_18

Rossi, E. L., & Nimmons, D. (1991). *The 20-minute break: Reduce stress, maximise performance, and improve health and emotional well-being using the new science of ultradian rhythms*. Jeremy P Tarcher.

Roth, Y., Tendler, A., Arikan, M. K., Vidrine, R., Kent, D., Muir, O., MacMillan, C., Casuto, L., Grammer, G., Sauve, W., Tolin, K., Harvey, S., Borst, M., Rifkin, R., Sheth, M., Cornejo, B., Rodriguez, R., Shakir, S., Porter, T., Kim, D., . . . Zangen, A. (in press). Real-world efficacy of deep TMS for obsessive-compulsive disorder: Post-marketing data collected from twenty-two clinical sites. *Journal of Psychiatric Research.* https://doi.org/10.1016/j.jpsychires.2020.11.009

Rothschild, A. J. (2013). Challenges in the treatment of major depressive disorder with psychotic features. *Schizophrenia Bulletin, 39*(4), 787–796. https://doi.org/10.1093/schbul/sbt046

Rothschild, B. (2000). *The body remembers: The psychophysiology of trauma and trauma treatment.* W. W. Norton.

Rothschild, B. (2003). *The body remembers casebook: Unifying methods and models in the treatment of trauma and PTSD.* W. W. Norton.

Rothstein, M. A., Cai, Y., & Marchant, G. E. (2009). The ghost in our genes: Legal and ethical implications of epigenetics. *Health Matrix Cleveland, 19*(1), 1–62.

Ruocco, A. C., Amirthavasagam, S., Choi-Kain, L. W., & McMain, S. F. (2013). Neural correlates of negative emotionality in borderline personality disorder: An activation-likelihood-estimation meta-analysis. *Biological Psychiatry, 73*, 153–160. https://doi.org/10.1016/j.biopsych.2012.07.014

Sabikhi, L., Kumar, M. H., & Mathur, B. N. (2014). *Bifidobacterium bifidum* in probiotic Edam cheese: Influence on cheese ripening. *Journal of Food Science and Technology, 51*(12), 3902–3909. https://doi.org/10.1007/s13197-013-0945-7

Salem, I., Ramser, A., Isham, N., & Ghannoum, M. A. (2018). The gut microbiome as a major regulator of the gut-skin axis. *Frontiers in Microbiology, 9*, Article 1459. https://doi.org/10.3389/fmicb.2018.01459

San Mauro Martín, I., Blumenfeld Olivares, J. A., Garicano Vilar, E., Echeverry López, M., García Bernat, M., Quevedo Santos, Y., Blanco López, M., Elortegui Pascual, P., Borregon Rivilla, E., & Rincón Barrado, M. (2018). Nutritional and environmental factors in attention-deficit hyperactivity disorder (ADHD): A cross-sectional study. *Nutritional Neuroscience, 21*(9), 641–647. https://doi.org/10.1080/1028415X.2017.1331952

Sansone, R. A., & Sansone, L. A. (2013). Sunshine, serotonin, and skin: A partial explanation for seasonal patterns in psychopathology? *Innovations in Clinical Neuroscience, 10*(7–8), 20–24.

Sapolsky, R. M. (2004). *Why zebras don't get ulcers.* Holt Paperbacks.

Sathyanarayana Rao, T. S., Basavaraj, K. H., & Das, K. (2013). Psychosomatic paradigms in psoriasis: Psoriasis, stress and mental health. *Indian Journal of Psychiatry, 55*(4), 313–315. https://doi.org/10.4103/0019-5545.120531

Saxe, J. G. (1872). *The poems of John Godfrey Saxe.* James B. Osgood. https://openlibrary.org/works/OL5684635W/The_poems_of_John_Godfrey_Saxe

Saxena, S., Gorbis, E., O'Neill, J., Baker, S. K., Mandelkern, M. A., Maidment, K. M., Chang, S., Salamon, N., Brody, A. L., Schwartz, J. M., & London, E. D. (2009). Rapid effects of brief intensive cognitive–behavioral therapy on brain glucose metabolism in obsessive–compulsive disorder. *Molecular Psychiatry, 14,* 197–205. https://doi.org/10.1038/sj.mp.4002134

Scaer, R. (2005). *The trauma spectrum: Hidden wounds and human resiliency.* W. W. Norton.

Schneider, A., Winarni, T. I., Cabal-Herrera, A. M., Bacalman, S., Gane, L., Hagerman, P., Tassone, F., & Hagerman, R. (2020). Elevated *FMR1*-mRNA and lowered FMRP: A double-hit mechanism for psychiatric features in men with *FMR1* premutations. *Translational Psychiatry, 10,* 205. https://doi.org/10.1038/s41398-020-00863-w

Schore, A. N. (1994). *Affect regulation and the origin of the self: The neurobiology of emotional development.* Erlbaum.

Schore, A. N. (2003). *Affect dysregulation and disorders of the self.* W. W. Norton.

Schore, A. N. (2012). *The science of the art of psychotherapy.* W. W. Norton.

Schultze-Lutter, F. (2009). Subjective symptoms of schizophrenia in research and the clinic: The basic symptom concept. *Schizophrenia Bulletin, 35*(1), 5–8. https://doi.org/10.1093/schbul/sbn139

Schwartz, J. M. (2016). *Brain lock: Free yourself from obsessive-compulsive disorder.* Harper Perennial.

Schwartz, J. M., & Begley, S. (2003). *The mind and the brain: Neuroplasticity and the power of mental force.* HarperCollins.

The Science of Psychotherapy. (2018a, September 23). *Cunningham Panel.* https://www.thescienceofpsychotherapy.com/glossary/cunningham-panel

The Science of Psychotherapy [Podcast]. (2018b, December 18). *How does a therapist keep up with all this new knowledge?* [Video]. YouTube. https://youtu.be/jQ88mfxV5vM

Scoville, W. B., & Milner, B. (1957). Loss of recent memory after bilateral hippocampal lesions. *Journal of Neurology, Neurosurgery and Psychiatry, 20,* 11–21.

Sebastian, A., Jung, P., Krause-Utz, A., Lieb, K., Schmahl, C., & Tüscher, O. (2014). Frontal dysfunctions of impulse control: A systematic review in borderline personality disorder and attention-deficit/hyperactivity disorder. *Frontiers in Human Neuroscience, 8,* Article 698. https://doi.org/10.3389/fnhum.2014.00698

Segal, N. L., & Montoya, Y. S. (2018). *Accidental brothers: The story of twins exchanged at birth and the power of nature and nurture.* St. Martin's Press.

Seikkula, J., Aaltonen, J., Alakare, B., Haarakangas, K., Keränen, J., & Lehtinen, K. (2006). Five-year experience of first-episode nonaffective psychosis in open-dialogue approach: Treatment principles, follow-up outcomes, and two case studies. *Psychotherapy Research, 16*(2), 214–228. https://doi.org/10.1080/10503300500268490

Seligman, M. (2012). *Flourish.* William Heinemann Australia.

Seminowicz, D. A., & Moayedi, M. (2017). The dorsolateral prefrontal cortex in acute and chronic pain. *Journal of Pain, 18,* 1027–1035.

Shaffer, F., McCraty, R., & Zerr, C. L. (2014). A healthy heart is not a metronome: An integrative review of the heart's anatomy and heart rate variability. *Frontiers in Psychology*, 5, Article 1040. https://doi.org/10.3389/fpsyg.2014.01040

Sharon, G., Sampson, T. R., Geschwind, D. H., & Mazmanian, S. K. (2016). The central nervous system and the gut microbiome. *Cell*, *167*, 915–932. https://doi.org/10.1016/j.cell .2016.10.027

Shen, L., Li, C., Wang, Z., Zhang, R., Shen, Y., Miles, T., Wei, J., & Zou, Z. (2019). Early-life exposure to severe famine is associated with higher methylation level in the *IGF2* gene and higher total cholesterol in late adulthood: The Genomic Research of the Chinese Famine (GRECF) study. *Clinical Epigenetics*, *11*, Article 88. https://doi.org/10.1186/s13148 -019-0676-3

Shiran, A., Remer, E., Asmer, I., Karkabi, B., Zittan, E., Cassel, A., Barak, M., Rozenberg, O., Karkabi, K., & Flugelman, M. Y. (2015). Association of vitamin B12 deficiency with homozygosity of the TT MTHFR C677T genotype, hyperhomocysteinemia, and endo- thelial cell dysfunction. *Israeli Medical Association Journal*, *17*(5), 288–292.

Shvetsova, E., Sofronova, A., Monajemi, R., Gagalova, K., Draisma, H., White, S., Santen, G., Chuva de Sousa Lopes, S., Heijmans, B., van Meurs, J., Jansen, R., Franke, L., Kiełbasa, S., den Dunnen, J., & 't Hoen, P. (2019). Skewed X-inactivation is common in the general female population. *European Journal of Human Genetics*, *27*(3), 455–465.

Siegel, D. J. (2012). *The developing mind: How relationships and the brain interact to shape who we are*. Guilford Press.

Siegel, D. J. (2015). *The developing mind: How relationships and the brain interact to shape who we are* (2nd ed.). Guilford Press.

Siegel, D. J. (2020). *The developing mind: How relationships and the brain interact to shape who we are* (3rd ed.). Guilford Press

Sielski, R., Rief, W., & Glombiewski, J. A. (2017). Efficacy of biofeedback in chronic back pain: A meta-analysis. *International Journal of Behavioral Medicine*, *24*(1), 25–41. https:// doi.org/10.1007/s12529-016-9572-9

Silbersweig, D., Clarkin, J. F., Goldstein, M., Kernberg, O. F., Tuescher, O., Levy, K. N., Bren- del, G., Pan, H., Beutel, M., Pavony, M. T., Epstein, J., Lenzenweger, M. F., Thomas, K. M., Posner, M. I., & Stern, E. (2007). Failure of frontolimbic inhibitory function in the context of negative emotion in borderline personality disorder. *The American Journal of Psychiatry*, *164*, 1832–1841. https://doi.org/10.1176/appi.ajp.2007.06010126

Silove, D. M., Marnane, C. L., Wagner, R., Manicavasagar, V. L., & Rees, S. (2010). The prevalence and correlates of adult separation anxiety disorder in an anxiety clinic. *BMC Psychiatry*, *10*, 21. https://doi.org/10.1186/1471-244X-10-21

Singh, T., & Rajput, M. (2006). Misdiagnosis of bipolar disorder. *Psychiatry*, *3*(10), 57–63.

Sinha, S., Jones, B. M., Traniello, I. M., Bukhari, S. A., Halfon, M. S., Hofmann, H. A., Huang, S., Katz, P. S., Keagy, J., Lynch, V. J., Sokolowski, M. B., Stubbs, L. J., Tabe- Bordbar, S., Wolfner, M. F., & Robinson, G. E. (2020). Behavior-related gene regulatory networks: A new level of organization in the brain. *Proceedings of the National Academy of Sciences of the United States of America, 117*(38), 23270–23279. https://doi.org/10.1073/pnas.1921625117

Singh, R. B., Fedacko, J., Pella, D., Pella, D., Jarcuska, P., Mojito, V., Al-bawareed OA, Chibisov, S., Kharlitskaya, E. V., & Abramova, M. (2018). The gut-brain-axis and the heart. *MOJ Public Health, 7*(3),129–138. https://doi.org/10.15406/mojph.2018.07.00218

Skodol, A. E., Gunderson, J. G., Shea, M. T., McGlashan, T. H., Morey, L. C., Sanislow, C. A., Bender, D. S., Grilo, C. M., Zanarini, M. C., Yen, S., Pagano, M. E., & Stout, R. L. (2005). The Collaborative Longitudinal Personality Disorders Study (CLPS): Overview and implications. *Journal of Personality Disorders, 19*(5), 487–504. https://doi.org/10.1521/pedi.2005.19.5.487

Skuse, D. H. (2005). X-linked genes and mental functioning. *Human Molecular Genetics, 14*(Suppl. 1), R27–R32. https://doi.org/10.1093/hmg/ddi112

Slominski, A. [T.], Wortsman, J., Tuckey, R. C., & Paus, R. (2007). Differential expression of HPA axis homolog in the skin. *Molecular and Cellular Endocrinology, 265–266*, 143–149. https://doi.org/10.1016/j.mce.2006.12.012

Slominski, A. T., Zmijewski, M. A., Skobowiat, C., Zbytek, B., Slominski, R. M., & Steketee, J. D. (2012). *Advances in anatomy, embryology, and cell biology: Vol. 212. Sensing the environment: Regulation of local and global homeostasis by the skin's neuroendocrine system.* Springer. https://doi.org/10.1007/978-3-642-19683-6_1

Slominski, A. T., Zmijewski, M. A., Zbytek, B., Tobin, D. J., Theoharides, T. C., & Rivier, J. (2013). Key role of CRF in the skin stress response system. *Endocrine Reviews, 34*(6), 827–884. https://doi.org/10.1210/er.2012-1092

Smith, C. D., Sawyer, C. R., & Behnke, R. R. (2005). Physical symptoms of discomfort associated with worry about giving a public speech. *Communication Reports, 18*(1–2), 31–41. https://doi.org/10.1080/08934210500084206

Smith, S. M., & Vale, W. W. (2006). The role of the hypothalamic-pituitary-adrenal axis in neuroendocrine responses to stress. *Dialogues in Clinical Neuroscience, 8*(4), 383–395. https://doi.org/10.31887/DCNS.2006.8.4/ssmith

Solomon, M. F., & Siegel, D. J. (2003). *Healing trauma: Attachment, mind, body, and brain.* W. W. Norton.

Sorel, T. (Director). (2018). *My kid is not crazy: A search for hope in the face of misdiagnosis* [Vimeo]. 4 the Kids Films.

Sotodeh-Asl, N., Tamadon, M. R., Malek, F., & Zahmatkesh, M. (2014). Vitamin D deficiency and psychological disorders. *Journal of Parathyroid Disease, 2*(1), 21–25.

Spencer, J., Goode, J., Penix, E. A., Trusty, W., & Swift, J. K. (2019). Developing a collaborative relationship with clients during the initial sessions of psychotherapy. *Psychotherapy, 56*(1), 7–10. https://doi.org/10.1037/pst0000208

Spinazzola, J., van der Kolk, B., & Ford, J. D. (2018). When nowhere is safe: Interpersonal trauma and attachment adversity as antecedents of posttraumatic stress disorder and developmental trauma disorder. *Journal of Traumatic Stress, 31*(5), 631–642. https://doi .org/10.1002/jts.22320

Sperry, R. (1983). *Science and moral priority: Merging mind, brain and human values.* Basil Blackwell.

Sproesser, E., Viana, M. A., Quagliato, E. M. A. B., & de Souza, E. A. P. (2010). The effect of psychotherapy in patients with PD: A controlled study. *Parkinsonism & Related Disorders, 16*(4), 298–300. https://doi.org/10.1016/j.parkreldis.2009.08.008

Steele, K., Boon, S., & van der Hart, O. (2017). *Treating trauma-related dissociation: A practical, integrative approach.* New York, NY: W. W. Norton & Co.

Steele, K., van der Hart, O., & Nijenhuis, E. R. (2005). Phase-oriented treatment of structural dissociation in complex traumatization: Overcoming trauma-related phobias. *Journal of Trauma & Dissociation, 6*(3), 11–53. https://doi.org/10.1300/J229v06n03_02

Sterling, P. (2004). Principles of allostasis: Optimal design, predictive regulation, pathophysiology, and rational therapeutics. In J. Schulkin (Ed.), Allostasis, homeostasis, and the costs of physiological adaptation (pp. 17–64). Cambridge University Press. https://doi .org/10.1017/CBO9781316257081.004

Stern, A. (1938). Psychoanalytic investigation of and therapy in the border line group of neuroses. *Psychoanalytic Quarterly, 7,* 467–489.

Stilling, R. M., Dinan, T. G., & Cryan, J. F. (2014). Microbial genes, brain & behaviour: Epigenetic regulation of the gut-brain axis. *Genes, Brain and Behavior, 13,* 69–86. https:// doi.org/10.1111/gbb.12109

Stobernack, T., de Vries, S., Rodrigues Pereira, R., Pelsser, L. M., Ter Braak, C., Aarts, E., van Baarlen, P., Kleerebezem, M., Frankena, K., & Hontelez, S. (2019). Biomarker Research in ADHD: The Impact of Nutrition (BRAIN)—study protocol of an open-label trial to investigate the mechanisms underlying the effects of a few-foods diet on ADHD symptoms in children. *BMJ Open, 9*(11), e029422. https://doi.org/10.1136/bmjopen-2019 -029422

Strupp, H. H. (1963). The outcome problem in psychotherapy revisited. *Psychotherapy, 1*(1), 1–13. https://doi.org/10.1037/h0088565

Sudo, N., Chida, Y., Aiba, Y., Sonoda, J., Oyama, N., Yu, X. N., Kubo, C., & Koga, Y. (2004). Postnatal microbial colonization programs the hypothalamic-pituitary-adrenal system for stress response in mice. *The Journal of Physiology, 558*(Pt. 1), 263–275. https://doi.org/10 .1113/jphysiol.2004.063388

Swedo, S., Frankovich, J., & Murphy, T. (2017). Overview of treatment of pediatric acute-onset neuropsychiatric syndrome. *Journal of Child and Adolescent Psychopharmacology, 27*(7), 562–565. https://doi.org/10.1089/cap.2017.0042

Szanto, T., & Krueger, J. (2019). Introduction: Empathy, shared emotions, and social identity. *Topoi, 38,* 153–162. https://doi.org/10.1007/s11245-019-09641-w

Tahsili-Fahadan, P., & Geocadin, R. G. (2017). Heart-brain axis: Effects of neurologic injury on cardiovascular function. *Circulation Research, 120*(3), 559–572. https://doi.org/10.1161/CIRCRESAHA.116.308446

Tastevin, M., Spatola, G., Régis, J., Lançon, C., & Richieri, R. (2019). Deep brain stimulation in the treatment of obsessive-compulsive disorder: Current perspectives. *Neuropsychiatric Disease and Treatment, 15*, 1259–1272. https://doi.org/10.2147/NDT.S178207

Taylor, J. M. (2016, July 25). Mirror neurons after a quarter century: New light, new cracks. *Harvard University: Science in the News.* http://sitn.hms.harvard.edu/flash/2016/mirror-neurons-quarter-century-new-light-new-cracks

TEDx Talks. (2014, January 13). *The science of emotions: Jaak Panksepp at TEDxRainier* [Video]. YouTube. https://www.youtube.com/watch?v=65e2qScV_K8

Thabrew, H., Ruppeldt, P., & Sollers, J. J., III. (2018). Systematic review of biofeedback interventions for addressing anxiety and depression in children and adolescents with long-term physical conditions. *Applied Psychophysiology and Biofeedback, 43*(3), 179–192. https://doi.org/10.1007/s10484-018-9399-z

Thapar, A., Cooper, M., Eyre, O., & Langley, K. (2013). What have we learnt about the causes of ADHD? *The Journal of Child Psychology and Psychiatry, 54*(1), 3–16. https://doi.org/10.1111/j.1469-7610.2012.02611.x

Thayer, J. F. (2007). What the heart says to the brain (and *vice versa*) and why we should listen. *Psychological Topics, 16*(2), 241–250.

Theoharides, T. C. (2015). On the gut microbiome-brain axis and altruism. *Clinical Therapeutics, 37*, 937–940. https://doi.org/10.1016/j.clinthera.2015.04.003

Thienemann, M., Murphy, T., Leckman, J., Shaw, R., Williams, K., Kapphahn, C., Frankovich, J., Geller, D., Bernstein, G., Chang, K., Elia, J., & Swedo, S. (2017). Clinical management of pediatric acute-onset neuropsychiatric syndrome: Part I—Psychiatric and behavioral interventions. *Journal of Child and Adolescent Psychopharmacology, 27*(7). https://doi.org/10.1089/cap.2016.0145

Thompson, P., Vidal, C., Giedd, J. N., Gochman, P., Blumenthal, J., & Nicolson, R., Toga, A. W., & Rapoport, J. L. (2001). Mapping adolescent brain change reveals dynamic wave of accelerated gray matter loss in very early-onset schizophrenia. *Proceedings of the National Academy of Sciences of the United States of America, 98*(20), 11650–11655. https://doi.org/10.1073/pnas.201243998

Tibar, H., El Bayad, K., Bouhouche, A., Ait Ben Haddou, E. H., Benomar, A., Yahyaoui, M., Benazzouz, A., & Regragui, W. (2018). Non-motor symptoms of Parkinson's disease and their impact on quality of life in a cohort of Moroccan patients. *Frontiers in Neurology, 9*, Article 170. https://doi.org/10.3389/fneur.2018.00170

Tickle, E., & Murphy, D. (2014). A journey to client and therapist mutuality in person-centered psychotherapy: A case study. *Person-Centered and Experiential Psychotherapies, 13*(4), 337–351. https://doi.org/10.1080/14779757.2014.927390

Tippmann-Peikert, M., Park, J. G., Boeve, B. F., Shepard, J. W., & Silber, M. H. (2007). Pathologic gambling in patients with restless legs syndrome treated with dopaminergic agonists. *Neurology, 68*(4), 301–303. https://doi.org/10.1212/01.wnl.0000252368.25106.b6

Titchener, E. B. (1909). *Experimental psychology of the thought-processes.* MacMillan.

Tolin, D. F., Davies, C. D., Moskow, D. M., & Hofmann, S. G. (2020). Biofeedback and neurofeedback for anxiety disorders: A quantitative and qualitative systematic review. In Y. K. Kim (Ed.), *Anxiety disorders: Advances in experimental medicine and biology* (Vol. 1191, pp. 265–289). https://doi.org/10.1007/978-981-32-9705-0_16

Tomasik, J., Yolken, R. H., Bahn, S., & Dickerson, F. B. (2015). Immunomodulatory effects of probiotic supplementation in schizophrenia patients: A randomized, placebo-controlled trial. *Biomarker Insights, 10,* 47–54. doi:10.4137/BMI.S22007

Tortosa-Martínez, J., Manchado, C., Cortell-Tormo, J., & Chulvi-Medrano, I. (2018). Exercise, the diurnal cycle of cortisol and cognitive impairment in older adults. *Neurobiology of Stress, 9,* 40–47. https://doi.org/10.1016/j.ynstr.2018.08.004

Trafton, A. (2017, April 6). Neuroscientists identify brain circuit necessary for memory formation. MIT News. http://news.mit.edu/2017/neuroscientists-identify-brain-circuit-necessary-memory-formation-0406

Trahair, L. G., Horowitz, M., & Jones, K. L. (2014). Postprandial hypotension: A systematic review. *Journal of the American Medical Directors Association, 15*(6), 394-409. https://doi.org/10.1016/j.jamda.2014.01.011

Trojsi, F., Christidi, F., Migliaccio, R., Santamaría-García, H., & Santangelo, G. (2018). Behavioural and cognitive changes in neurodegenerative diseases and brain injury. *Behavioural Neurology, 2018,* Article 4935915. https://doi.org/10.1155/2018/4935915

Tulving, E. (2002). Episodic memory: From mind to brain. *Annual Review of Psychology, 53,* 1–25. https://doi.org/10.1146/annurev.psych.53.100901.135114

Tursich, M., Ros, T., Frewen, P. A., Kluetsch, R. C., Calhoun, V. D., & Lanius, R. A. (2015). Distinct intrinsic network connectivity patterns of post-traumatic stress disorder symptom clusters. *Acta Psychiatrica Scandinavica, 132*(1), 29–38. https://doi.org/10.1111/acps.12387

Tusche, A., Bockler, A., Kanske, P., Trautwein, F., & Singer, T. (2016). Decoding the charitable brain: Empathy, perspective taking, and attention shifts differentially predict altruistic giving. *The Journal of Neuroscience, 36*(17), 4719–4732.

Tuskan, G. A., DiFarzio, S., Jansson, S., Bohlmann, J., Grigoriev, I., Hellsten, U., Putnam, N., Ralph, S., Rombauts, S., Salamov, A., Schein, J., Sterck, L., Aerts, A., Bhalerao, R. R., Bhalerao, R. P., Blaudez, D., Boerjan, W., Brun, A., Brunner, A., Busov, V., . . . Rokhsar, D. (2006). The genome of black cottonwood, *Populus trichocarpa* (Torr. & Gray). *Science, 313*(5793), 1596–1604.

Uddin, S., Mamun, A., Kabir, T., Nasrullah, M., Wahid, F., Begum, M., Rahman, S., Islam, T., Amran, S., Abdel-Daim, M. M., & Labu, Z. K. (2018). Neurochemistry of neurochemicals: Messengers of brain functions. *Journal of Intellectual Disability—Diagnosis and Treatment, 5*(4): 137–151. https://doi.org/10.6000/2292-2598.2017.05.04.6

UK Council for Psychotherapy. (n.d.) *What is psychotherapy?* Retrieved December 2020 from https://www.psychotherapy.org.uk/seeking-therapy/what-is-psychotherapy

Ursano, R. J., Bell, C., Eth, S., Friedman, M., Norwood, A., Pfefferbaum, B., Pyonos, J. D. R. S., Zatzick, D. F., Benedek, D. M., McIntyre, J. S., Charles, S. C., Altshuler, K., Cook, I., Cross, C. D., Mellman, L., Moench, L. A., Norquist, G., Twemlow, S. W., Woods, S., Yager, J., . . . Steering Committee on Practice Guidelines. (2004). Practice guideline for the treatment of patients with acute stress disorder and posttraumatic stress disorder. *The American Journal of Psychiatry, 161*(Suppl. 11), 3–31.

Valles-Colomer, M., Falony, G., Darzi, Y., Tigchelaar, E. F., Wang, J., Tito, R. Y., Schiweck, C., Kurilshikov, A., Joossens, M., Wijmenga, C., Claes, S., Van Oudenhove, L., Zhernakova, A., Vieira-Silva, S., & Raes, J. (2019). The neuroactive potential of the human gut microbiota in quality of life and depression. *Nature Microbiology, 4*(4), 623–632. https://doi.org/10.1038/s41564-018-0337-x

van der Hart, O., Nijenhuis, E. R. S., & Steele, K. (2006). *The haunted self: Structural dissociation and the treatment of chronic traumatisation.* W. W. Norton.

van der Kolk, B. (2014). *The body keeps the score: Mind, brain and body in the transformation of trauma.* Alan Lane.

van der Kolk, B. A., Hodgdon, H., Gapen, M., Musicaro, R., Suvak, M. K., Hamlin, E., & Spinazzola, J. (2016). A randomized controlled study of neurofeedback for chronic PTSD. *PLOS ONE, 11*(12), Article e0166752. https://doi.org/10.1371/journal.pone.0166752

van der Kolk, B., Stone, L., West, J., Rhodes, A., Emerson, D., Suvak, M., & Spinazzola, J. (2014). Yoga as an adjunctive treatment for posttraumatic stress disorder: A randomized controlled trial. *The Journal of Clinical Psychiatry, 75*(6), e559–e565. https://doi.org/10.4088/jcp.13m08561

Van Doren, J., Arns, M., Heinrich, H., Vollebregt, M. A., Strehl, U., & Loo, S. K. (2019). Sustained effects of neurofeedback in ADHD: A systematic review and meta-analysis. *European Child & Adolescent Psychiatry, 28*(3), 293–305. https://doi.org/10.1007/s00787-018-1121-4

van Eimeren, T., Ballanger, B., Pellecchia, G., Miyasaki, J. M., Lang, A. E., & Strafella, A. P. (2009). Dopamine agonists diminish value sensitivity of the orbitofrontal cortex: A trigger for pathological gambling in Parkinson's disease? *Neuropsychopharmacology, 34*(13), 2758–2766. https://doi.org/10.1038/npp.2009.124

Van Nuys, D. (2015). Neurofeedback in the treatment of developmental trauma: Interview with Sebern Fisher. *The Neuropsychotherapist, 19,* 14–24.

van Schaik, C. P., & Burkart, J. M. (2011). Social learning and evolution: The cultural intelligence hypothesis. *Philosophical Transactions of the Royal Society of London. Series B, Biological Sciences, 366*(1567), 1008–1016. https://doi.org/10.1098/rstb.2010.0304

Venditti, S., Verdone, L., Reale, A., Vetriani, V., Caserta, M., & Zampieri, M. (2020). Molecules of silence: Effects of meditation on gene expression and epigenetics. *Frontiers in Psychology, 11*, Article 1767. https://doi.org/10.3389/fpsyg.2020.01767

Verkhratsky, A., & Butt, A. (2007). *Glial neurobiology: A textbook.* John Wiley & Sons.

Vickhoff, B., Malmgren, H., Åström, R., Nyberg, G., Engvall, M., Snygg, J., Nilsson, M., & Jörnsten, R. (2013). Music structure determines heart rate variability of singers. *Frontiers in Psychology, 4*, Article 334. https://doi.org/10.3389/fpsyg.2013.00334

Villegas R., Castillo C., & Villegas G. M. (2000). The origin of the neuron: The first neuron in the phylogenetic tree of life. In J. Chela-Flores, G. A. Lemarchand, & J. Oró (Eds.), *Astrobiology* (pp. 195–211). Springer. https://doi.org/10.1007/978-94-011-4313-4_15

Vischer, R. (1994). On the optical sense of form: A contribution to aesthetics (H. F. Mallgrave & E. Ikonomou, Trans.). In *Empathy, form, and space: Problems in German aesthetics, 1873–1893* (pp. 89–123). Getty Center for the History of Art and the Humanities]. (Original work published 1873)

von Bartheld, C. S., Bahney, J., & Herculano-Houzel, S. (2016). The search for true numbers of neurons and glial cells in the human brain: A review of 150 years of cell counting. *The Journal of Comparative Neurology, 524*(18), 3865–3895. https://doi.org/10.1002/cne.24040

Vriend, C. (2018). The neurobiology of impulse control disorders in Parkinson's disease: From neurotransmitters to neural networks. *Cell and Tissue Research, 373*(1), 327–336. https://doi.org/10.1007/s00441-017-2771-0

Waddington, C. H. (1968). The basic ideas of biology. In *Towards a theoretical biology* (Vol. 1, pp. 1–32). Edinburgh University Press.

Waddington, C. H. (2012). The epigenotype. *International Journal of Epidemiology, 41*, 10–13. https://doi.org/10.1093/ije/dyr184 (Reprinted from "The epigenotype," 1942, *Endeavour, 1*, 18–20)

Wampold, B., & Brown, G. S. (2005). Estimating variability in outcomes attributable to therapists: A naturalistic study of outcomes in managed care. *Journal of Consulting and Clinical Psychology, 73*(5), 914–923. https://doi.org/10.1037/0022-006X.73.5.914

Wampold, B. E., Imel, Z. E., Laska, K. M., Benish, S., Miller, S. D., Flückiger, C., Del Re, A. C., Baardseth, T. P., & Budge, S. (2010). Determining what works in the treatment of PTSD. *Clinical Psychology Review, 30*(8), 923–933. https://doi.org/10.1016/j.cpr.2010.06.005

Wampold, B., Flückiger, C., Del Re, A., Yulish, N., Frost, N., Pace, B., Goldberg, S. B., Miller, S. D., Baardseth, T. P., Laska, K. M., & Hilsenroth, M. J. (2017). In pursuit of truth: A critical examination of meta-analyses of cognitive behavior therapy. *Psychotherapy Research, 27*(1), 14–32. https://doi.org/10.1080/10503307.2016.1249433

Wan, L., Li, Y., Zhang, Z., Sun, Z., He, Y., & Li, R. (2018). Methylenetetrahydrofolate reductase and psychiatric diseases. *Translational Psychiatry, 8*, Article 242. https://doi.org/10.1038/s41398-018-0276-6

Watkins, L. E., Sprang, K. R., & Rothbaum, B. O. (2018). Treating PTSD: A review of evidence-based psychotherapy interventions. *Frontiers in Behavioral Neuroscience, 12,* Article 258. https://doi.org/10.3389/fnbeh.2018.00258

Waxenbaum, J. A., Reddy, V., & Varacallo, M. (2020, August 10). Anatomy, autonomic nervous system. *StatPearls* [Internet]. https://www.ncbi.nlm.nih.gov/books/NBK539845

Weaver, I. C., Cervoni, N., Champagne, F. A., D'Alessio, A. C., Sharma, S., Seckl, J. R., Dymov, S., Szyf, M., & Meaney, M. J. (2004). Epigenetic programming by maternal behavior. *Nature Neuroscience, 7*(8), 847–854. https://doi.org/10.1038/nn1276

Weibell, M. A., ten Veldon Hegelstad, W., & Johannessen, J. O. (2016). Substance-induced psychosis: Conceptual and diagnostic challenges in clinical practice. In V. Preedy (Ed.), *Neuropathology of drug addictions and substance misuse* (Vol. 3, Chap. 5). Elsevier.

White, J. F. (2003). Intestinal pathophysiology in autism. *Experimental Biology and Medicine, 228,* 639–649.

Wichers, M., Schreuder, M. J., Goekoop, R., & Groen, R. N. (2019). Can we predict the direction of sudden shifts in symptoms? Transdiagnostic implications from a complex systems perspective on psychopathology. *Psychological Medicine, 49*(3), 380–387. https://doi.org/10.1017/S0033291718002064

Wilkinson, L. A. (2011). Systems theory. In S. Goldstein & J. A. Naglieri (Eds.), *Encyclopaedia of child behavior and development* (p. 147). Springer.

Williams, L. M., Gatt, J. M., Kuan, S. A., Dobson-Stone, C., Palmer, D. M., Paul, R. H., Song, L., Costa, P. T., Schofield, P. R., & Gordon, E. (2009). A polymorphism of the MAOA gene is associated with emotional brain markers and personality traits on an antisocial index. *Neuropsychopharmacology, 34,* 1797–1809. https://doi.org/10.1038/npp.2009.1

Willsey, A. J., Sanders, S. J., Li, M., Dong, S., Tebbenkamp, A. T., Muhle, R. A., Reilly, S. K., Lin, L., Fertuzinhos, S., Miller, J. A., Murtha, M. T., Bichsel, C., Niu, W., Cotney, J., Ercan-Sencicek, A. G., Gockley, J., Gupta, A. R., Han, W., He, X., Hoffman, E. J., . . . State, M. W. (2013). Coexpression networks implicate human midfetal deep cortical projection neurons in the pathogenesis of autism. *Cell, 155*(5), 997–1007. https://doi.org/10.1016/j.cell.2013.10.020

Wilson, R. (n.d.). Getting anxious on purpose: This approach can reduce anxiety symptoms in as little as three weeks. *Psychotherapy Networker.* https://www.psychotherapynetworker.org/blog/details/1389/getting-anxious-on-purpose

Wilson, R. (2016). *Stopping the noise in your head: The new way to overcome anxiety and worry.* Health Communications.

Wingenfeld, K., Rullkoetter, N., Mensebach, C., Beblo, T., Mertens, M., Kreisel, S., Toepper, M., Driessen, M., & Woermann, F. G. (2009). Neural correlates of the individual emotional Stroop in borderline personality disorder. *Psychoneuroendocrinology, 34,* 571–586. https://doi.org/10.1016/j.psyneuen.2008.10.024

Wićniowiecka-Kowalnik, B., & Nowakowska, B. A. (2019). Genetics and epigenetics of autism spectrum disorder: Current evidence in the field. *Journal of Applied Genetics, 60,* 37–47. https://doi.org/10.1007/s13353-018-00480-w

Woodruff, C. C. (2018). Reflections of others and of self: The mirror neuron system's relationship to empathy. In L. Stevens & C. C. Woodruff (Eds.), *The neuroscience of empathy, compassion, and self-compassion* (pp. 157–187). Academic Press.

Wootton, T. (2009). *Bipolar in order: Looking at depression, mania, hallucination, and delusion from the other side.* Bipolar Advantage.

World Health Organization. (2004). *ICD-10: International statistical classification of diseases and related health problems.* World Health Organization

World Health Organization. (2013). *Guidelines for the management of conditions specifically related to stress.* http://apps.who.int/iris/bitstream/handle/10665/85119/9789241505406_eng.pdf;jsessionid$=$A87FC4134F1F50FE3F66C587868D2F32?sequence$=$1

Wu, H., Luo, J., Yu, H., Rattner, A., Mo, A., Wang, Y., Smallwood, P. M., Erlanger, B., Wheelan, S. J., & Nathans, J. (2014). Cellular resolution maps of X chromosome inactivation: Implications for neural development, function, and disease. *Neuron, 81,* 103–119. https://doi.org/10.1016/j.neuron.2013.10.051

Wy, T. J. P., & Saadabadi, A. (2020, November 19). Schizoaffective disorder. *StatPearls* [Internet]. https://www.ncbi.nlm.nih.gov/books/NBK541012

Xu, J., Chmela, V., Green, N. J., Russell, D. A., Janicki, M. J., Góra, R. W., Szabla, R., Bond, A. D., & Sutherland, J. D. (2020). Selective prebiotic formation of RNA pyrimidine and DNA purine nucleosides. *Nature, 582,* 60–66. https://doi.org/10.1038/s41586-020-2330-9

Yalom, V. (2012). *Reid Wilson on strategic treatment of anxiety disorders.* Psychotherapy.net. https://www.psychotherapy.net/interview/Reid-Wilson

Yap, E., & Greenberg, M. (2018). Activity-regulated transcription: Bridging the gap between neural activity and behavior. *Neuron, 100*(2), 330–348. https://doi.org/10.1016/j.neuron.2018.10.013

Young, J. E., Klosko, J. S., & Weishaar, M. E. (2003). *Schema therapy: A practitioner's guide.* Guilford Press.

Young, M. B., Howell, L. L., Hopkins, L., Moshfegh, C., Yu, Z., Clubb, L., Seidenberg, J., Park, J., Swiercz, A. P., & Marvar, P. J. (2018). A peripheral immune response to remembering trauma contributes to the maintenance of fear memory in mice. *Psychoneuroendocrinology, 94,* 143–151. https://doi.org/10.1016/j.psyneuen.2018.05.012

Zanarini, M. C., Frankenburg, F. R., Hennen, J., Reich D. B., & Silk, K. R. (2005). The McLean Study of Adult Development (MSAD): Overview and implications of the first six years of prospective follow-up. *Journal of Personality Disorders, 19*(5), 505–523. https://doi.org/10.1521/pedi.2005.19.5.505

Zhang, J. (2019). *Secrets of the brain: An introduction to the brain anatomical structure and biological function* (IFM Lab Tutorial Series No. 4). Information Fusion and Mining Laboratory. https://arxiv.org/pdf/1906.03314.pdf

Zhang, N. (2015). Epigenetic modulation of DNA methylation by nutrition and its mechanisms in animals. *Animal Nutrition, 1*(3), 144–151. https://doi.org/10.1016/j.aninu.2015.09.002

Zilles, K. (2018). Brodmann: A pioneer of human brain mapping: His impact on concepts of cortical organization. *Brain, 141*(11), 3262–3278. https://doi.org/10.1093/brain/awy273

Zovkic, I. B., Guzman-Karlsson, M. C., & Sweatt, J. D. (2013). Epigenetic regulation of memory formation and maintenance. *Learning & Memory, 20*(2), 61–74. https://doi.org/10.1101/lm.026575.112

Index

Note: Italicized page locators refer to figures; tables are noted with a *t*.

About the Authors

Richard Hill, M.A., M.Ed., MBMSc, presents internationally on the topics of psychotherapy, the brain and the mind, and his specialty: Curiosity & Possibility and the Client-Responsive Approach. He is coauthor with the eminent Ernest Rossi, Ph.D., of *The Practitioner's Guide to Mirroring Hands*; Managing Editor of *The Science of Psychotherapy* monthly magazine; Science Director of CIPPS in Salerno, Italy; Patron of the Australian Society of Clinical Hypnotherapists; and Director of the MindScience Institute. His books include *Choose Hope* and *How the 'Real World' Is Driving Us Crazy!* as well as articles, journal papers and book chapters. Find him at: www.richardhill.com.au

Matthew Dahlitz is both university trained and an autodidactic, whose knowledge spans across the arts, technology, psychology, neuroscience, emergency medicine, and business. He has studied both psychology and music at masters level as well as spending a decade as an advanced care paramedic. He founded *The Neuropsychotherapist Magazine,* now known as *The Science of Psychotherapy,* as well as other initiatives in applied neuroscience. Matthew lives in Brisbane, Australia, and spends the majority of his time managing The Science of Psychotherapy, including producing and directing documentaries about the science of the human condition at thescienceofpsychotherapy.com.